CHRIS ROWTHORN

KYOTO

CITY GUIDE

INTRODUCING KYOTO

Temple visitors can sip the sacred and therapeutic spring water at Kiyomizu-dera (p63)

Kyoto is a city of secrets. Thousands of secrets. Hidden behind ancient walls, down tiny alleyways, under layers of gesture and artifice. Myriad pockets of incredible beauty that reveal themselves to those willing to see and discover.

The joy of travelling in Kyoto is the quest, the pleasure of uncovering that perfect Zen garden, or happening upon a quiet temple at dawn and catching the monks chanting. Of mustering the courage to slide open the door to an unfamiliar restaurant and being rewarded with the perfect bowl of noodles.

It's not hyperbole to claim that Kyoto is the most beautiful city in Asia. Of course, you will not believe this when you step out of Kyoto Station and see the bustling business district around the station. You will think you've been had. And then you'll catch your first hint of Kyoto beauty – maybe the gentle curve of a temple roofline in the distance. And so it begins...

KYOTO LIFE

veryone wants something different from Kyoto. Residents would love to turn the place into a odern city with all the conveniences of Tokyo or Osaka. Japanese and foreign tourists would fer Kyoto remain a kind of living museum for Japan's incredibly rich cultural heritage. Just the city responds to these seemingly contradictory demands is a central issue of Kyoto political life and the topic of many of the conversations you'll hear in restaurants and bars. It's certainly the most pressing problem facing Kyoto today.

Fortunately, many people now realise that these two demands aren't as contradictory as they might first appear. Kyotoites are coming to understand that preserving something of the traditional aspects of the city will benefit everyone, not just those directly involved with tourism. As a result, the city leaders have made some excellent moves recently.

In order to protect the Kyoto cityscape, the city government recently enacted a law that places height restrictions on new buildings. It has also placed restrictions on large and intrusive billboards and neon signs (something you will surely appreciate if you've seen what parts of Tokyo look like).

Better still, the city government has been experimenting with turning parts of the Downtown Kyoto district into a pedestrian-only area in the evenings. One can only hope it pursues this to the obvious conclusion and turns the entire central downtown grid into a pedestrian-only zone both day and night.

The city has also been having a lot of fun with its image as the 'most Japanese' part of Japan. From time to time, the local bus company allows anyone wearing a kimono to ride the buses for free. The result is an increasing number of Japanese couples who explore the city in traditional outfits.

The most welcome trend in the city is the so-called *machiya* boom, in which traditional Kyoto town houses are being converted into extremely atmospheric restaurants, cafés, bars and shops. There is hope that if these *machiya* businesses succeed, it will stem the loss of the lovely traditional structures, a few of which are carted away each day in the back of a truck to be dumped into a landfill on the outskirts of the city.

Perhaps the most exciting trend is this: the world is waking up to the fact Japan is not that expensive! As a result, travellers are streaming into the city and one can hear Italian, French and German in the cafés and restaurants downtown. Similarly, you're just as likely to hear Mandarin as English spoken by the tourist next to you as you wait in line for a sip of holy water at Kiyomizu-dera's famous spring.

All in all, it's a great time to visit Kyoto!

Kyoto's traditional neighbourhoods are at their most atmospheric by night

HIGHLIGHTS

KYOTO STATION AREA

Both the gateway to Kyoto and a thriving shopping district, Kyoto Station also features two awesome temples and one of the world's most impressive train stations.

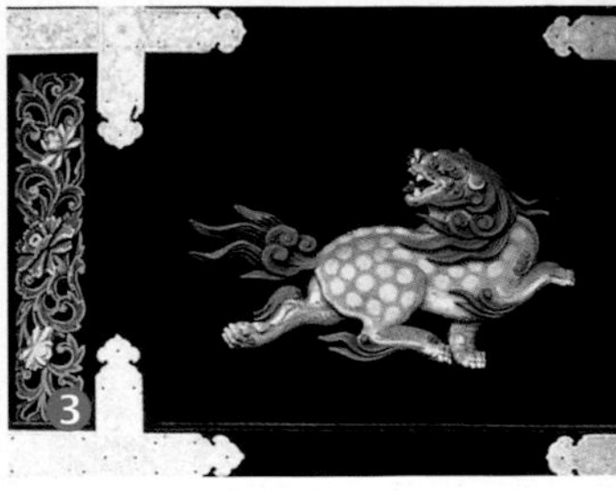

1 Kyoto Station
A soaring glass cathedral for the transport age (p45).

2 Higashi Hongan-ji
One of the largest wooden buildings in the world, with a dazzling golden interior (p45).

3 Nishi Hongan-ji
A temple boasting sumptuous altars and the famed Higurashi-mon (Sunset Gate; p47).

1 Shopping Downtown
Browse through everything from traditional crafts to the latest electronics and fashions in Downtown Kyoto (p107).

2 Nishiki Market
This is Kyoto's finest food market and a gourmet's paradise (p50).

3 Pontochō
One of Asia's most sublime streets runs along the Kamo-gawa (p51).

DOWNTOWN KYOTO

Thick with shops, restaurants, cafés and bars, you could spend a year exploring Downtown Kyoto and only scratch the surface. It also contains Pontochō, one of the loveliest streets in all of Asia.

1

❶ **Kyoto Imperial Palace Park**
A vast green expanse set with wide boulevards (p52).

❷ **Daitoku-ji**
Pay a visit to an enclosed world of temples and Zen gardens (p53).

❸ **Fushimi-Inari-Taisha**
Hypnotic arcades of vermilion shrine gates in the woods (p59).

CENTRAL KYOTO

Home to the traditional heart of the city, the Kyoto Imperial Palace, Central Kyoto is surrounded in all directions by still more incredible sights, such as the Zen world of Daitoku-ji and the fantastic tunnels of shrine gates at Fushimi-Inari-Taisha.

2

3

SOUTHERN HIGASHIYAMA

An area featuring the highest concentration of sights in all of Japan, Southern Higashiyama is a great place to start your exploration of Kyoto. Ancient temples, a holy spring and picturesque alleys – it's all here at the base of the hills.

1 Ishibei-kōji
Perhaps Kyoto's single-most attractive lane (p101).

2 Kiyomizu-dera
Home to a sacred spring and the famous 'Love Shrine' (p63).

3 Chion-in
This vast centre of Pure Land Buddhism is a must-see (p65).

NORTHWEST KYOTO

The famed Golden Pavilion is only the start of what's on offer here in the hilly part of town. You'll also find a mystical rock garden and a shōgun's castle.

❶ Kinkaku-ji
The Golden Pavilion has to be seen to be believed (p77).

❷ Nijō-jō
Squeak across the 'nightingale' floors at this dazzling castle (p73).

❸ Ryōan-ji
Thirteen famous rocks in the world's best-known Zen garden (p77).

1 Tetsugaku-no-Michi
Cherry blossoms line the famed Path of Philosophy, a canalside delight (p70).

2 Nanzen-ji
Stone gardens, brilliant maples and a collection of fine subtemples (p66).

3 Ginkaku-ji
The Silver Pavilion overlooks one of Kyoto's best gardens (p71).

NORTHERN HIGASHIYAMA

You'll be hard pressed to find a neighbourhood any more scenic than this: Northern Higashiyama presents a stunning mountainside row of ancient temples and shrines connected by a Path of Philosophy.

ARASHIYAMA & SAGANO

Welcome to the mystical world of bamboo groves and maple forests at the base of the western hills. Arashiyama and Sagano offer some of the best strolling in Kyoto, along with monkeys and a samurai-movie star's home.

❶ Tenryū-ji
A fine temple boasting some of Kyoto's best scenery (p80).

❷ Arashiyama Bamboo Grove
Take a stroll through Kyoto's enchanted bamboo forest (p79).

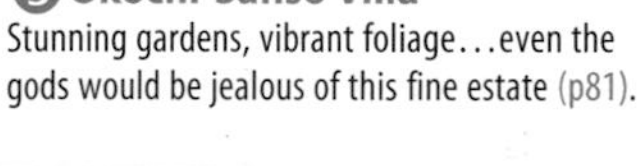

❸ Ōkōchi-Sansō Villa
Stunning gardens, vibrant foliage...even the gods would be jealous of this fine estate (p81).

KITAYAMA AREA & GREATER KYOTO

The deep valleys of the Kitayama Mountains to the north of the city shelter some incredibly quaint villages. It is the perfect place to experience the rural side of Japan and makes an excellent green retreat from city living.

❶ Kurama & Kibune
Beneath the vermilion shrine gate and up the stairs resides Kibune-jinja (p86).

❷ Takao
Mossy stone lanterns populate the gardens of Saimyō-ji (p91).

❸ Ōhara
Take time to admire the lush surroundings at Sanzen-in (p83).

CONTENTS

THE AUTHOR

Chris Rowthorn

Chris is an American who has lived in Kyoto since 1992. Soon after his arrival, he started studying Japanese language and culture. In 1995 he became a regional correspondent for the *Japan Times*, a national English-language newspaper published in Tokyo. Chris joined Lonely Planet in 1996 and has written books about Japan, Malaysia, the Philippines, Victoria (Australia) and, most recently, the island of Borneo. Despite all his work-related travel, he still takes every opportunity to explore the world, in particular the Himalayas and Southeast Asia. When he's not on the road, he spends his time seeking out Kyoto's best restaurants, temples, hiking trails and various other *anaba* (secret places known only to the locals). He also conducts walking tours of Kyoto, Nara and Tokyo. For more on Chris, check out his website at www.chrisrowthorn.com or his blog at www.insidekyoto.com.

CHRIS' TOP KYOTO DAY

The first thing I do in the morning is head to the Tetsugaku-no-Michi (Path of Philosophy) for a contemplative stroll in the early morning light. I might stop in at Hōnen-in, sit on the steps and drink in the silence, or head south to Nanzen-ji if the autumn leaves are working. Then I make my way downtown and grab some eel for lunch at Kane-yo, my favourite *unagi* restaurant in Kyoto. Next, I hit Teramachi-dōri to poke among the shops there, before making my way south for a leisurely pass through Nishiki Market. Following that, I head over to Junkudō bookshop. After browsing, I stop at a nearby coffee shop for a quick pick-me-up and a read. It's then time to visit a good local *sentō* (public bath) for a soak. Clean and refreshed, I head out to meet friends for dinner, perhaps at Aunbo or Ōzawa in Gion. After dinner we stroll along the Kamo-gawa between Shijō-dōri and Sanjō-dōri and then cross the bridge and soak up the evening ambience of Pontochō. Finally, we might head up to Orizzonte at the top of the Kyoto Hotel Ōkura for a drink while gazing over the lights of the city.

GETTING STARTED

Kyoto is one of the easiest destinations in the world to plan for: got a pair of slip-on shoes and a passport? You're most of the way there! Of course, you'll want to give some thought to when you go. Want to see the cherry blossoms? Early April is the time. How about the autumn colours? The month of November is best. If you hope to hit one of Kyoto's excellent flea markets, you'll have to be in town on the 21st or 25th of any month. Naturally, you can't always pick your travel times, but the fact is you can enjoy Kyoto in any month of the year.

If you're considering a trip to Japan, you're probably worried about the cost. Here is the good news: Japan is almost certainly cheaper than you think.

WHEN TO GO

Many travellers plan their trips to coincide with Kyoto's famous cherry-blossom season, which starts in late March or early April. Once those blossoms pop open, they usually last no more than a week. As such, you've got a better chance of catching the autumn colours: if you visit in November, you're almost assured of catching them. The weather in spring and autumn is usually stable, with many clear, warm days.

The problem with both the cherry-blossom season and the foliage season is that *everyone* knows Kyoto is lovely then, so you'll be facing some serious crowds. This is not the problem you might think – you just have to work around it a bit and perhaps visit some less-famous temples, which is a good idea anyway.

Of course, you can visit Kyoto at any time of year. Yes, the winter can be cold, but it's hardly unbearable – temperatures usually climb to the teens during the day and drop into single digits at night. In the summer, particularly August, it gets pretty hot and humid, with temps in the thirties. But, unless you've got a serious aversion to heat or cold, these seasons are perfectly acceptable for touring and each has its own unique beauty. Don't forget, summer is also the season of Kyoto's famed Gion Matsuri festival (see p16).

For information on Japan's public holidays see p194. For more information on Kyoto's climate, see p190.

FESTIVALS

Few cities on earth have as many yearly events and festivals as Kyoto. There's something happening almost every day of the year. Here are the biggies, with a few interesting little ones thrown in for good measure.

January

HATSUMŌDE 1–3 January

This often raucous festival involves the first visit of the New Year to a Shintō shrine, where prayers are said to bring health and good fortune during the ensuing year. Kyoto's two most visited shrines on this occasion are Yasaka-jinja (p64) and Heian-jingū (p72).

TŌSHIYA (ARCHERY CONTEST) 15 January

Held at Sanjūsangen-dō (p60) from 8am to 4pm, this is the largest of Kyoto's three archery events held in January. Tōshiya dates to a 1606 feat by a samurai who is said to have shot 51 arrows in rapid succession along the veranda of the temple. Hundreds of kimono-clad archers gather for a competition of accuracy and strength, standing 118m away from a target 1.5m in diameter into which they try to shoot as many arrows as possible.

February

SETSUBUN 2–4 February

This festival signals the last day of winter according to the lunar calendar. People go to various temples and bless their homes, driving off demons, sickness and misfortune by scattering *mamemaki* (roasted soya beans) in and around the house, while shouting '*Oni-wa-soto, Fuku-wa-uchi*' ('Out with devils, In with luck'). You can enjoy the revelry at and Yasaka-jinja (p64) from 1pm to 3pm.

April

KANNO-CHAKAI (FLOWER-VIEWING FESTIVAL) 1–15 April

Held at Heian-jingū (p72) during the peak of the cherry blossoms. Tea is served and

ADVANCE PLANNING

Several months prior to departure, book your plane ticket (see p181). A month prior to departure (longer if you plan to visit April and May, around July 17, mid-August or November), book your accommodation and make sure your passport and travel insurance are in order. If you intend to do much train travel in Japan outside Kyoto, buy a Japan Rail Pass. You must buy these outside Japan; see p188 for details. Finally, whenever you have a chance, buy a pair of comfortable slip-on walking shoes to make temple and ryokan entry/exit easier.

shrine-goers can stroll among the *shidare-zakura* (weeping cherry trees).

MIBU KYŌGEN 21–29 April

At Mibu-dera (p57) from 5.30pm each night; Buddhist miracle plays are performed to teach doctrine through pantomime. Mibu Kyōgen has been celebrated every spring for the last 700 years.

May

AOI MATSURI (HOLLYHOCK FESTIVAL) 15 May

One of Kyoto's most important and largest festivals, Aoi Matsuri dates to the 6th century and commemorates successful prayers to the gods to stop calamitous weather. Today, the procession involves imperial messengers in ox carts and a retinue of 600 people dressed in traditional costume; hollyhock leaves are carried or used as decoration. The procession leaves around 10am from the Kyoto Imperial Palace (p52) and heads for Shimogamo-jinja (p56) where ceremonies take place. It sets out again at 2pm and arrives at Kamigamo-jinja (p91) at 3.30pm.

June

TAKIGI NŌ 1–2 June

Held at Heian-jingū (p72), this is a festival of nō drama held by flaming torchlight in the outdoor courtyard of the shrine.

TAKEKIRI E-SHIKI 20 June

Held at Kurama-dera (p85), this is a bamboo-cutting festival dating back to an event 1000 years ago, when a priest of Kurama-dera defeated two evil serpents with the aid of Bishamon-tei, the Buddhist guardian enshrined at the temple. Today, eight priests dressed in robes and hoods of *yamabushi* (mountain priests) form two teams and race to hack to pieces four lengths of green bamboo that symbolise the serpents. The festival begins at 2pm.

July

GION MATSURI Peaks 17 July

Perhaps the most renowned of all Japanese festivals, this month-long celebration involves myriad events. Yoi-yama is held on 16 July, when more than 200,000 people throng the Shijō-Karasuma area in Downtown Kyoto (Map p50), and reaches a climax on the 17th, when a Yamaboko-junkō parade of more than 30 floats is held to the accompaniment of flutes, drums and gongs. On the three evenings preceding the 17th, people gather on Shijō-dōri, many dressed in beautiful light summer kimono, to look at the floats and carouse from one street stall to the next. Gion Matsuri was initiated in AD 869, at which time plague had ravished the city. The festival was offered as a prayer of relief to the god Susanō-no-Mikoto (the son of the gods, who, according to Japanese mythology, gave birth to Japan).

August

DAIMON-JI GOZAN OKURIBI 16 August

Mistakenly referred to by many as Daimon-ji-yaki (literally, burning of Daimon-ji), this impressive event is held to bid farewell to the souls of ancestors. Enormous fires are lit in the form of Chinese characters or other shapes on five mountains. The main fire is the character for '*dai*', or 'great', on Daimonji-yama, behind Ginkaku-ji (p71), which is lit at 8pm. The other fires are lit at 10-minute intervals thereafter, working anticlockwise (east to west). It is best to watch this event from the banks of the Kamo-gawa or pay for a rooftop view from a hotel.

SENTŌ KUYŌ 23–24 August

Held at Adashino Nembutsu-ji (p82) in Sagano, this is a dedicatory mass to the souls of the countless *jizō* statues at this temple, which represent the deceased relatives of those attending the colourful ceremony. Reserve in advance by post by 15 June.

September

KARASU ZUMŌ
9 September

Held at Kamigamo-jinja (p91), this festival, which is also called 'crow wrestling', starts at 10am. Young boys compete in bouts of sumō wrestling. The festival is named for a legendary blackbird who came to rest on the arrow of Japan's first emperor, Jimmu.

TSUKIMI
mid-September

During September, moon-viewing festivals take place at several locations, including Daikaku-ji (p82) and Shimogamo-jinja (p56).

October

JIDAI MATSURI (FESTIVAL OF THE AGES)
22 October

One of Kyoto's big three, this festival is of recent origin, dating to 1895. More than 2000 people dressed in costumes ranging from the 8th to the 19th centuries parade from the Kyoto Imperial Palace (p52) to Heian-jingū (p72).

KURAMA HI MATSURI (KURAMA FIRE FESTIVAL)
22 October

This spectacular festival is traced to a rite that uses fires to guide the gods of the nether world on their tours around this world. *Mikoshi* (portable shrines) are carried through the streets and accompanied by young men in loincloths bearing giant flaming torches. The festival climaxes at 10pm at Yuki-jinja in Kurama (p85).

November

SHICHI-GO-SAN
15 November

This is a nationwide event in which proud parents dress kids aged seven, five and three in colourful kimono and visit local shrines to pray for their health and happiness. Yasaka-jinja (p64) and Heian-jingū (p72) are good places to watch the parents and children in their finery.

December

ŌMISOKA (NEW YEAR'S EVE)
31 December

People gather in their homes to ring in the New Year. It's customary to consume *toshikoshi soba* (thin, brown buckwheat noodles) before setting out to the shrine to see off the old year and welcome in the new. The activities continue from about 7pm to 1am, with huge crowds from about 11pm. Yasaka-jinja (p64) and Heian-jingū (p72) are great places to enjoy the action.

KYOTO: CHEAPER THAN YOU THINK

Anyone who has been to Japan recently knows that it can be cheaper to travel here than in parts of Western Europe, the US and Australia.

Still, you can burn through a lot of yen fairly quickly if you're not careful. In order to help stretch those yen, we've put together a list of money-saving tips.

Guesthouses There are plenty of good guesthouses in Kyoto where a night's accommodation costs about ¥3500.

Japan Rail Pass Like the famous Eurail Pass, this is one of the world's great travel bargains. It allows unlimited travel on Japan's brilliant nationwide rail system, including the lightning-fast *shinkansen* bullet trains. See p188.

Shokudō You can get a good, filling meal in these eateries for about ¥700, or US$6, plus the tea is free and there's no tipping. Try that in New York. For more, see p116.

Bentō The ubiquitous Japanese boxed lunch, or *bentō*, costs around ¥500 and is both filling and nutritious.

Use your noodle You can get a steaming bowl of tasty *rāmen* (noodles in a meat-based broth served with meat and vegetable toppings) in Kyoto for as little as ¥500, and ordering is a breeze – you just have to say '*rāmen*' and you're away. *Soba* and *udon* noodles are even cheaper – as low as ¥350 per bowl.

Hyaku-en shops *Hyaku-en* means ¥100, and like the name implies, everything in these shops costs just ¥100, or slightly less than one US dollar. You'll be amazed at what you can find in these places. Some even sell food. There are several in Downtown Kyoto, including one in the Teramachi covered arcade (Map p50).

Flea markets A good new kimono costs an average of ¥200,000 (about US$1700), but you can pick up a fine used one at a flea market for ¥1000, or just under US$10. Whether you're shopping for yourself or for presents for the folks back home, you'll find some incredible bargains in Kyoto's flea markets.

COSTS & MONEY

Japan is generally considered an expensive country in which to travel. Certainly, this is the case if you opt to stay in top-end hotels, take a lot of taxis and eat all your meals in fancy restaurants. But Kyoto does not have to be expensive, indeed it can be *cheaper* than travelling in other parts of the world, if you are careful with your spending. In terms of what you get for your money, Kyoto is good value indeed.

HOW MUCH?

Business hotel accommodation (per person) ¥8000

Midrange meal ¥2500

Local bus ¥220

Temple admission ¥500

Newspaper ¥130

Sentō (public bath) admission ¥390

Can of coffee ¥120

Cross-town taxi ¥2500

Piece of automatic sushi ¥120

Onigiri (rice ball) ¥150

INTERNET RESOURCES

There is no better place to start your explorations than lonelyplanet.com. Here you will find succinct summaries on travelling to most places, as well as the Thorn Tree forum, where you can ask questions before you go, while you are away, or dispense advice when you get back.

Other useful websites include the following:

Japan National Tourist Organization (www.jnto.go.jp) Japan's main national tourist authority.

JR East (www.jreast.co.jp/e/index.html) Information on rail travel in Japan, with details on the Japan Rail Pass.

Kansai Time Out (www.japanfile.com)

Kyoto Temple Admission Fees (www.templefees.com) These change from time to time, so it's best to get the latest info.

Kyoto Visitor's Guide (www.kyotoguide.com) Contains lots of Kyoto-specific information.

SUSTAINABLE KYOTO

Given Japan's location, there aren't many alternatives to flying here, unless you happen to be in South Korea, China or Taiwan, in which case you can take a boat.

Once in Kyoto, however, you can bicycle everywhere; in fact, this one of the best ways to explore the city (see p183). If you don't fancy pedalling, you can get around the city on Kyoto's brilliant public transport system (see p185), or, for that matter, you can simply walk – it's a small city.

There's not much in the way of environmentally friendly accommodation, although most would agree that staying in traditional ryokan or simple guesthouses probably has less of a negative impact on the environment than staying in a modern hotel.

You can do a lot to help the environment by refusing packaging and bags when you purchase things in Kyoto. Here's the key phrase: *'Sono mama de ii desu'* ('It's fine just like that'). Alternatively, *'Fukuro wa irimasen'* ('I don't need a bag').

Finally, think about what you eat: the fish on offer at the sushi restaurant may come from a species that is being depleted, including, unfortunately, *maguro* (tuna).

HISTORY

EARLY HISTORY

Although the origins of the Japanese race remain unclear, anthropologists believe humans first arrived on the islands as early as 100,000 years ago via the land bridges that once connected Japan to Siberia and Korea, and by sea from the islands of the South Pacific. The first recorded evidence of civilisation in Japan is *jōmon* (pottery fragments with cord marks) produced around 10,000 BC. During the Jōmon period (10,000–300 BC), people lived a primitive existence as independent fishers, hunters and food gatherers.

This stone age period was gradually superseded by the Yayoi era, dating roughly from 300 BC to AD 300. The Yayoi people are considered to have had a strong connection with Korea. Their most important developments were the wet cultivation of rice and the use of bronze and iron implements, and they also introduced new practices such as weaving and shamanism. The Yayoi period witnessed the progressive development of communities represented in more than 100 independent family clusters dotting the archipelago.

As more and more of these settlements banded together to defend their land, regional groups became larger and by AD 300 the Yamato kingdom had emerged in the region of present-day Nara. Forces were loosely united around the imperial clan of the Yamato court, whose leaders claimed descent from the sun goddess, Amaterasu, and who introduced the title of *tennō* (emperor). The Yamato kingdom established Japan's first fixed capital in Nara, eventually unifying the regional groups into a single state. By the end of the 4th century, official relations with the Korean peninsula were established and Japan steadily began to introduce arts and industries such as shipbuilding, leather-tanning, weaving and metalwork.

During the Yamato period a highly aristocratic society with militaristic rulers developed. Its cavalry wore armour, carried swords and used advanced military techniques similar to those of northeast Asia. The Yamato government also sent envoys directly to the Chinese court, where they were exposed to philosophy and social structure.

The Yamato period is also referred to as the Kofun period by archaeologists, owing to the discovery of thousands of *kofun* (ancient burial mounds), mainly in western Japan. These massive tombs contained various artefacts including tools, weapons and *haniwa* (clay figurines of people and animals), which had been ceremonially buried with nobles. With the arrival of Buddhism, this labour-intensive custom was abandoned in favour of cremation.

BUDDHISM & CHINESE INFLUENCE

When Buddhism drifted onto the shores of Japan, Kyoto was barely more than a vast, fertile valley. First introduced from China in 538 via the Korean kingdom of Paekche, Buddhism was pivotal in the evolution of the Japanese nation. It eventually brought with it a flood of culture – through literature, the arts and architecture, and kanji, a distinctive system of writing in Chinese characters.

TIMELINE

Early 7th century

The vast, fertile plain of the Kyoto basin, then known as Yamashiro-no-kuni, is first settled by the Hata clan from Korea. Another clan, the Kamo, also settles the area.

622

Kōryū-ji is established in northwest Kyoto to house a statue given to the Hata clan by Prince Shōtoku. The temple becomes the tutelary temple of the clan.

784

Emperor Kammu moves the capital from Nara to Nagaoka (a suburb of Kyoto) to avoid the powerful Buddhist clergy who had previously meddled in the imperial court.

However, initial uptake of Buddhism was slow until Empress Suiko (554–628), the 33rd emperor of Japan, encouraged all Japanese to accept the new faith. Widespread temple construction was authorised and in 588, as recorded in the 8th-century *Nihon Shoki* (Chronicle of Japan), Japan's first great temple complex, Asuka-dera, was completed.

Gradually the wealth and power of the temples began to pose a threat to the governing Yamato court, prompting reforms from Prince Shōtoku (574–622), regent for Empress Suiko. He set up the Constitution of 17 Articles, which combined ideas from Buddhism and Confucianism to outline the acceptable behaviour of the people, and laid the guidelines for a centralised state headed by a single ruler. He also instituted Buddhism as a state religion and ordered the construction of more temples, including Nara's eminent Hōryū-ji (p158), the world's oldest surviving wooden structure. Another significant accomplishment of Prince Shōtoku was the first compilation of Japanese history in 620; however, the book was later burned.

Despite family feuds and coups d'état, subsequent rulers continued to reform the country's administration and laws. Prior to the establishment of the Taiho Code in 701, it had been the custom to avoid the pollution of imperial death by changing the site of the capital for each successive emperor. Reforms and bureaucratisation of government led to the establishment, in 710, of a permanent imperial capital, known as Heijō-kyō, in Nara, where it remained for 74 years.

The prosperous Nara period (710–94) saw further propagation of Buddhism and, by the end of the 8th century, the Buddhist clergy had become so meddlesome that Emperor Kammu decided to sever the ties between Buddhism and government by again moving the capital. He first moved it to Nagaoka (a suburb of Kyoto) in 784, but due to the assassination of the city's principal architect, several ominous natural disasters and superstitious beliefs regarding the location, a decade later he suddenly shifted the capital to Heian-kyō, present-day Kyoto.

ESTABLISHMENT OF HEIAN-KYŌ

The Kyoto basin was first settled in the 7th century when the region was known as Yamashiro-no-kuni. The original inhabitants were immigrants from Korea, the Hata clan, who established Koryū-ji (p78) in 603 as their family temple in what is today the Uzumasa District. A major reason Emperor Kammu proclaimed Heian-kyō the new capital of Japan was his realisation that the city lay within a strategic natural fortress created by the rivers and mountains which surround it on three sides, fulfilling the geomantic requirements derived from proto–feng shui.

As with the previous capital in Nara, the city was laid out in accordance with Chinese geomancy in a grid pattern adopted from the Tang dynasty capital, Chang'an (present-day Xi'an). The rectangle-shaped precincts were established west of where the Kamo-gawa flows. Originally measuring 4.5km east to west and 5.3km north to south, the city was about one-third the size of its Chinese prototype. Running through the centre was Suzaku-ōji, an 85m-wide, willow-lined thoroughfare dividing the eastern (Sakyō-ku) part of the city from the west (Ukyō-ku). The northern tip of the promenade was the site of the ornate Imperial Palace and to the far south stood the 23m-high, two-storey Rajō Gate, over 35m wide and 10m deep. However, to avoid a repeat of the power struggle between the imperial court and Buddhist clergy, only two temples, the West Temple and the East Temple (Tō-ji; p57), were built within the city limits.

Literally, capital of peace *(hei)* and tranquillity *(an),* the ensuing Heian period (794–1185) effectively lived up to its name. Over four centuries the city went beyond its post as a politi-

788

Saichō establishes a monastery atop Hiei-zan (Mt Hiei), north of the city. The temple serves to protect the city from the 'dangerous' northeast direction. Saichō starts a school of Buddhism known as Tendai (or Tenzai).

794

Things go poorly in the new capital at Nagaoka and Emperor Kammu searches to the northeast, in the Kyoto basin, for another site for his capital. Late that year, he finds a suitable spot in present-day Kyoto.

794

A pair of temples, Tō-ji and Sai-ji, are built at the southern edge of the city to protect the city and the imperial court. Sai-ji no longer exists, but Tō-ji can still be visited today.

cal hub to become the country's commercial and cultural centre. Towards the end of the 9th century, contact with China became increasingly sporadic, providing an opportunity for Japan to cultivate an independent heritage. This produced a great flowering in literature, the arts and religious thinking, as the Japanese adapted ideas and institutions imported from China.

The development of hiragana (Japanese characters), whose invention is attributed to the Buddhist priest Kūkai in the 9th century, led to a popular literary trend best recalled by Murasaki Shikibu's legendary saga *Genji Monogatari* (The Tale of Genji). This period in Kyoto's history conjures up romantic visions of riverside moon-gazing parties where literati drew calligraphy and composed poetry while the aristocracy frolicked in their self-imposed seclusion.

Rivalry between Buddhism and Shintō, the traditional religion of Japan, was reduced by presenting Shintō deities as manifestations of Buddha. Religion was separated from politics, and Japanese monks returning from China established two new sects, Tendai (or Tenzai, meaning Heavenly Terrace) and Shingon (True Words), that became the mainstays of Japanese Buddhism. Soon other sects were springing up and temples were being enthusiastically built.

The powerful Fujiwara clan, whose influence stemmed from its matrimonial alliance with the imperial family, dominated Japanese politics during the Heian era. Fujiwara princes served as high ministers of the imperial court and regents for underage monarchs, and were the proverbial 'power behind the throne' for centuries. Despite their supplanting of imperial authority, the Fujiwara clan presided over a period of cultural and artistic prosperity.

The Heian period is considered the apogee of Japanese courtly elegance, but in the provinces a new power was on the rise – the samurai (warrior class), which built up its armed forces to defend its autonomy. Samurai families moved into Kyoto, where they muscled in on the court, and subsequent conflicts between rival military clans led to civil wars. Members of the Fujiwara, Taira and Minamoto families attacked each other, claimed control over conquered tracts of land and set up rival regimes. This was the beginning of a long period of feudal rule by successive Shogunates (samurai families). This feudal system effectively lingered on for seven centuries until imperial power was restored in 1868.

FROM ARISTOCRATIC TO MILITARY RULE

Although Kyoto served as home to the Japanese imperial family from 794 to 1868, it was not always the focus of Japanese political power. During the Kamakura period (1185–1333), Kamakura (near present-day Tokyo) was the national capital, while during the Edo period (1600–1868) the Tokugawa Shōgunate ruled the country from Edo (present-day Tokyo). Still, despite the decline in influence of the imperial court, Kyoto flourished as townspeople continued developing age-old traditions.

By the 12th century the imperial family had become increasingly isolated from the mechanics of political power. In 1185 the corrupt Fujiwara Shōgunate was eclipsed by the Taira clan, who ruled briefly before being ousted by the Minamoto family (also known as the Genji) in the epic battle of Dannoura (Shimonoseki). By this time 'Kyoto' had emerged as the common name of the city.

In 1192, while the emperor remained nominal ruler in Kyoto, Minamoto Yoritomo, the first shōgun of the Kamakura Shōgunate, set up his headquarters in Kamakura. Yoritomo purged members of his own family who stood in his way, but after fatally falling from his horse in

10th century

The centre of the city gradually shifts eastward, closer to the Kamo-gawa and the Higashiyama. During this time, imperial properties in the west are abandoned.

1168

The priest Eisai travels to China and observes Chang Buddhism. He later introduces this as Zen Buddhism in Japan. He also introduces the practice of tea drinking.

1192

Minamoto Yoritomo is appointed shōgun and establishes the political capital in Kamakura. While the imperial court remains in Kyoto, the real power centre of the country leaves the city.

1199, the Hōjō, his wife's family, eliminated all of Yoritomo's potential successors. In 1213 they became true wielders of power behind the shōguns and warrior lords.

During this era the popularity of Buddhism spread to all levels of society. From the late 12th century, Eisei (1145–1215) and other Japanese monks returning from China introduced a new sect, Zen, which encountered resistance from the established sects in Kyoto but appealed to the samurai class. Meanwhile, as the spiritual fervour grew, Japanese merchants prospered in increased trade dealings with China.

Forces beyond the sea undermined the stability of the Kamakura regime. The Mongols, under Kublai Khan, reached Korea in 1259 and sent envoys to Japan seeking Japanese submission. The envoys were expelled and the Mongols sent an invasion fleet which arrived near present-day Fukuoka in 1274. This first attack was only barely repulsed with the aid of a typhoon that destroyed up to 200 Mongol ships. Further envoys sent by Khan were beheaded in Kamakura as a sign that the government of Japan was not interested in paying homage to the Mongols.

In 1281 the Mongols dispatched an army of over 100,000 soldiers to Japan. After an initial success, the Mongol fleet was almost completely destroyed by yet another massive typhoon that assaulted the shores of Kyushu for two days. Ever since, this lucky typhoon has been known to the Japanese as kamikaze (divine wind) – a name later given to the suicide pilots of WWII.

Although the Kamakura government emerged victorious, it was unable to pay its soldiers and lost the support of the warrior class. Emperor Go-Daigo led an unsuccessful rebellion to overthrow the shōgunate and was exiled to the Oki Islands near Matsue. A year later, he escaped from the island, raised an army and toppled the government, ushering in a return of political authority to Kyoto.

COUNTRY AT WAR

After completing his takeover, Emperor Go-Daigo refused to reward his warriors, favouring the aristocracy and priesthood instead. In the early 14th century this led to a revolt by the warrior Ashikaga Takauji, who had previously supported Go-Daigo. When Ashikaga's army entered Kyoto, Go-Daigo fled to Mt Hiei and sent the imperial Sacred Treasures to Ashikaga in conciliation. Ashikaga installed a new emperor and appointed himself shōgun, initiating the Muromachi period (1333–1568). Go-Daigo escaped from Kyoto and, the Sacred Treasures he had sent to Ashikaga being counterfeit, set up a rival court at Yoshino in a mountainous region near Nara. Rivalry between the two courts continued for 60 years until the Ashikaga made an unfulfilled promise that the imperial lines would alternate.

Kyoto gradually recovered its position of political significance and, under the control of the art-loving Ashikaga, enjoyed an epoch of cultural and artistic fruition. Talents now considered typically Japanese flourished, including such arts as landscape painting, classical nō drama, ikebana (flower arranging) and *chanoyu* (tea ceremony). Many of Kyoto's famous gardens date from this period, such as Saihōji's famed Moss Garden (p90) and the garden of Tenryū-ji (p80). Kinkaku-ji (Golden Pavilion; p77) and Ginkaku-ji (Silver Temple; p71) were built by the Ashikaga shōguns to serve as places of rest and solitude. Eventually formal trade relations were reopened with Ming China and Korea, although Japanese piracy remained a bone of contention with both.

The Ashikaga ruled, however, with diminishing effectiveness in a land slipping steadily into civil war and chaos. By the 15th century Kyoto had become increasingly divided as *daimyō*

1202

Eisai establishes Kennin-ji, the Zen temple on the eastern bank of the Kamo-gawa, under sponsorship of the shōgun Minamoto no Yoriie. It remains one of Kyoto's most important Zen temples.

Early 13th century

A priest named Hōnen, troubled by disagreement between Japan's major Buddhist sects, establishes a new populist sect of Buddhism known as Jōdo (Pure Land) Buddhism. He fasts to death in 1212.

Mid-13th century

Shinran, originally a follower of Hōnen, preaches a radical doctrine of Buddhism which becomes known as Jōdo-Shinshū (True Pure Land Buddhism). Followers of this school establish the vast Higashi-Hongan-ji and Nishi-Hongan-ji.

(domain lords) and local barons fought for power in bitter territorial disputes that were to last for a century. In 1467 the matter of succession to the shōgunate between two feudal lords, Yamana and Hosokawa, ignited the most devastating battle in Kyoto's history. With Yamana's army of 90,000 camped in the southwest and Hosokawa's force of 100,000 quartered in the north of the city, Kyoto became a battlefield. The resulting Ōnin-no-ran (Ōnin War; 1467–77) wreaked untold havoc on the city; the Imperial Palace and most of the city were destroyed by fighting and subsequent fires, and the populace was left in ruin.

The war marked the rapid decline of the Ashikaga family and the beginning of the Sengoku-jidai (Warring States period), a long-protracted struggle for domination by individual *daimyō* that spread throughout Japan and lasted until the start of the Azuchi-Momoyama period in 1568.

RETURN TO UNITY

In 1568 Oda Nobunaga, the son of a *daimyō* from Owari province (the western half of present-day Aichi Prefecture), seized power from the imperial court in Kyoto and used his military genius to initiate a process of pacification and unification in central Japan. This manoeuvre marked the start of the short-lived Azuchi-Momoyama period (1568–1600). To support his military and political moves, Nobunaga instituted market reform by invalidating traditional monopolies and promoting free markets. However, Nobunaga is especially remembered for his ruthless destruction of temples and massacres of monks, particularly those of his most tenacious enemy, the members of the Ikkō sect. In 1582, Nobunaga was betrayed by his own general, Akechi Mitsuhide. Under attack from Mitsuhide and seeing all was lost, Nobunaga disembowelled himself in Kyoto's Honnō-ji.

Mitsuhide held Kyoto for 13 days until Toyotomi Hideyoshi sped to Kyoto to attack and ultimately defeat him. Hideyoshi was reputedly the son of a farmer, although his origins are not clear. His diminutive size and pop-eyed features earned him the nickname Saru-san (Mr Monkey). Hideyoshi worked on extending unification so that by 1590 the whole country was under his rule and he developed grandiose schemes to invade China and Korea. The first invasion was repulsed in 1593 and the second was aborted.

By the late 16th century, Kyoto's population had swelled to 500,000 and Hideyoshi was fascinated with redesigning and rebuilding the city, which had been devastated by more than a century of war. Prior to his death in 1598 he transformed Kyoto into a castle town and greatly altered the cityscape by ordering major construction projects including bridges, gates and the Odoi, a phenomenal earthen rampart designed to isolate and fortify the perimeter of the city, and to provide a measure of flood control. He also rebuilt temples burned by Nobunaga, including the stronghold of the Ikkō sect, the great Hongan-ji.

The rebuilding of Kyoto is usually credited to the influence of the city's merchant class, which led a citizens' revival that gradually shifted power back into the hands of the townspeople. Centred in Shimogyō, the commercial and industrial district, these enterprising people founded a *machi-shū* (self-governing body), which contributed greatly to temple reconstruction. Over time, temples of different sects were consolidated in one quarter of the city, creating the miniature Tera-Machi (city of temples), which still exists.

The Azuchi-Momoyama period has been referred to as the 'Japanese Renaissance', during which the arts further prospered. Artisans of the era are noted for their boisterous use of colour

1281

Kublai Khan of Mongolia attempts to conquer Japan for the second time, but the invasion force is destroyed by a massive typhoon (the so-called kamikaze).

1333

The Kamakura Shōgunate is defeated, Emperor Daigo II returns from exile and the political capital is re-established in Kyoto, where it remains until 1868.

1467

The devastating Ōnin War breaks out in Kyoto between two families competing for shogunate succession, leading to a nationwide war known as the Sengoku Jidai (Warring States) period.

and gold-leaf embellishment, which marked a new aesthetic sense in contrast to the more sombre monotones of the Muromachi period. The Zen-influenced tea ceremony was developed to perfection under Master Sen no Rikyū, who also wrote poetry and practised ikebana. The performing arts also matured, along with skill in ceramics, lacquerware and fabric-dyeing. A vogue for building castles and palaces on a flamboyant scale was also nurtured, the most impressive examples being Osaka-jō, which reputedly required three years of labour by up to 100,000 workers, and the extraordinary Ninomaru Palace in Kyoto's Nijō-jō (p73).

PEACE & SECLUSION

The supporters of Hideyoshi's young heir, Toyotomi Hideyori, were defeated in 1600 by his former ally, Tokugawa Ieyasu, at the decisive Battle of Sekigahara in Gifu prefecture. Ieyasu set up his *bakufu* (literally, field headquarters) at Edo, marking the start of the Edo (Tokugawa) period (1600–1868). Meanwhile the emperor and court exercised purely nominal authority in Kyoto.

There emerged a pressing fear of religious intrusion (seen as a siphoning of loyalty to the shōgun) and Tokugawa set out to stabilise society and the national economy. Eager for trade, he was initially tolerant of Christian missionary activities but, fearing the Christians would support Hideyori's efforts to resist the *bakufu* military government, he took steps to prohibit Christianity before destroying the Toyotomi family. Japan entered a period of *sakoku* (national seclusion) during which Japanese were forbidden on pain of death to travel to (or return from) overseas or to trade abroad. As efforts to expel foreign influences spread, only Dutch, Chinese and Koreans were allowed to remain, under strict supervision, and trade was restricted to the artificial island of Dejima at Nagasaki.

The Tokugawa family retained large estates and took control of major cities, ports and mines; the remainder of the country was allocated to autonomous *daimyō*. Foreign affairs and trade were monopolized by the shōgunate, which yielded great financial authority over the *daimyō*. Tokugawa society was strictly hierarchical. In descending order of importance were the nobility, who had nominal power; the *daimyō* and their samurai; farmers; and, at the bottom, artisans and merchants. Mobility from one class to another was blocked; social standing was determined by birth.

To ensure political security, the *daimyō* were required to make ceremonial visits to Edo every alternate year, while their wives and children were kept in permanent residence in Edo as virtual hostages of the government. At the lower end of society, farmers were subject to a severe system of rules that dictated in minutest detail their food, clothing and housing and land surveys which were designed to extract the greatest tax yield possible.

One effect of this strict rule was to create an atmosphere of relative peace and isolation in which the arts excelled. There were great advances in haiku poetry, *bunraku* puppet plays and kabuki theatre. Crafts such as wood-block printing, weaving, pottery, ceramics and lacquerware became famous for their refined quality. Some of Japan's greatest expressions in architecture and painting were produced, including Katsura Rikyū in Kyoto (p71) and the paintings of Tawaraya Sōtatsu, pioneer of the Rimpa school. Furthermore, the rigid emphasis of these times on submitting unquestioningly to rules of obedience and loyalty has lasted in the arts, and society at large, to the present day.

By the turn of the 19th century, the Tokugawa government was characterised by stagnation and corruption. Famines and poverty among the peasants and samurai further weakened the

1591

The ruling shōgun, Toyotomi Hideyoshi, orders the construction of a wall around the city of Kyoto. The wall extends for 23km and is traversable by seven gates.

1600

Tokugawa Ieyasu's forces defeat Toyotomi's army at the Battle of Sekigahara and the Tokugawa Shōgunate government is established in Edo (present-day Tokyo). The capital, however, remains in Kyoto.

1620

Construction starts on Katsura-Rikyū Imperial Villa. The villa was originally built to house an adopted son of Tokugawa Hideyoshi. The imperial family cooperates in the construction.

system. Foreign ships started to probe Japan's isolation with increasing insistence and the Japanese soon realised that their outmoded defences were ineffectual. Russian contacts in the north were followed by British and American visits. In 1853 Commodore Matthew Perry of the US Navy arrived with a squadron of 'black ships' to demand the opening of Japan to trade. Other countries also moved in with similar demands.

Despite being far inland, Kyoto felt the foreign pressure, which helped bring to a head the growing power struggle between the shōgun and emperor, eventually pushing Japan back into a state of internal conflict. A surge of antigovernment feeling among the Japanese followed and Kyoto became a hotbed of controversy. The Tokugawa government was accused of failing to defend Japan against foreigners, and of neglecting the national reconstruction necessary for Japan to meet foreign powers on equal terms. In the autumn of 1867, forces led by Satsuma and Chōshū samurai armed with English weapons attacked the palace demanding an imperial restoration. The ruling shōgun, Keiki, offered his resignation to avoid bloodshed, and Emperor Meiji resumed control of state affairs. This development has since been referred to as the Meiji Restoration.

EMERGENCE FROM ISOLATION

With the Meiji Restoration in 1868, the seat of Japanese national political power was restored to Kyoto, but the following year the capital was transferred to Edo along with the imperial court. Political power now resided in Edo and many great merchants and scholars of the era followed the emperor. After more than a millennium as capital, the sudden changes came as a major blow to Kyoto as the population dropped dramatically and the city entered a state of bitter depression.

Kyoto quickly set its sights on revival, taking steps to secure autonomy and rebuild its infrastructure. It again flourished as a cultural, religious and economic centre, with progressive industrial development. By the late 1800s Kyoto led the country in education reforms by establishing Japan's first kindergarten, elementary and junior high schools, and public library. In 1871 the first Kyoto Exhibition was launched, in which the Maiko and Kamogawa *odori* (dances; p142) originated. In 1880 the nation's first public art school, the Kyoto Prefecture Art School (now the Kyoto City University of Arts) was opened. In the same period the city introduced Japan's first electricity system, water system and fully functioning transport network. In 1885 work began on the monumental Lake Biwa Canal, which, in just five years, made Kyoto the first Japanese city to harness hydroelectric power.

Up until this point, the city of Kyoto was under the jurisdiction of the Kyoto prefectural government. In 1889 a proper city government was finally formed, which helped create an atmosphere in which industry could flourish. As traditional industry pushed on, research developed in the sciences, in particular physics and chemistry. Modern industries such as precision machinery also grew, as did the introduction of foreign technologies such as the automated weaving loom, which bolstered the struggling Nishijin textile industry. To celebrate the 1100th anniversary of the city's founding in 1895, Kyoto hosted the 4th National Industrial Exhibition Fair and established the country's first streetcar system (fuelled by the Keage Hydroelectric Plant). The same year saw the construction of Heian-jingū (actually a five-to-eight scale replica of Daigokuden, the emperor's Great Hall of State; p72), and the birth of the Jidai Matsuri (Festival of the Ages).

1646	1853	1867
Omotesenke tea-ceremony school is founded by Sen Sosa, the great-grandson of Sen no Rikyū, Japan's great tea master. The school remains in Kyoto to this day.	American Commodore Matthew Perry's 'black ships' arrive at Uraga Harbour (part of present-day Yokosuka), leading to a treaty allowing American trade with Japan.	An alliance of the powerful Chōshū and Satsuma *daimyō* and the titular Emperor Meiji overthrows the Tokugawa Shōgunate and restores imperial rule (the so-called 'Meiji Restoration').

Despite the apparent industrial boom, the initial stages of Kyoto's restoration were undermined by a state of virtual civil war. The abolition of the shōgunate was followed by the surrender of the *daimyō*, whose lands were divided into the prefectures that exist today. With the transfer of the capital to Edo, now renamed Tokyo (Eastern Capital), the government was recentralised and European-style ministries were appointed for specific tasks. A series of revolts by the samurai against the erosion of their status culminated in the Saigō Uprising, when they were finally beaten and stripped of their power. The fighting, however, had drained the national treasury, caused serious inflation and driven land values and badly needed taxes down.

Despite nationalist support for the emperor under the slogan of *sonnō-jōi* (revere the emperor, repel the barbarians), the new government soon realised it would have to meet the outside world on its own terms. Promising *fukoku kyōhei* (rich country, strong military), the economy underwent a crash course in westernisation and industrialisation. An influx of foreign experts was encouraged to provide assistance and Japanese students were sent abroad to acquire expertise in modern technologies. Western-style factories were established and mining operations were expanded under the management of *zaibatsu* (wealthy groups), such as Mitsui and Sumitomo. In 1889 Japan created a US-style constitution that gave the appearance of a democracy but preserved the authoritarian rule of the emperor and his select group of advisers.

By the 1890s government leaders were concerned at the spread of liberal ideas and encouraged a swing back to nationalism and traditional values. Japan's growing confidence was demonstrated by the abolition of foreign treaty rights and by the ease with which it trounced China in the Sino–Japanese War (1894–95). The subsequent treaty nominally recognised Korean independence from China's sphere of influence and ceded Taiwan to Japan. Friction with Russia over control of Manchuria and Korea led to the Russo–Japanese War (1904–05), in which the Japanese navy stunned the Russians by inflicting a crushing defeat on their Baltic fleet at the Battle of Tsu-shima. For the first time, the Japanese commanded the respect of the western powers.

THE PURSUIT OF EMPIRE

Upon his death in 1912, Emperor Meiji was succeeded by his son, Yoshihito, whose period of rule was named the Taishō era. When WWI broke out, Japan sided against Germany but did not become deeply involved in the conflict. While the Allies were occupied with war, Japan took the opportunity to expand its economy at top speed.

The Shōwa period commenced when Emperor Hirohito ascended to the throne in 1926. A rising tide of nationalism was quickened by the world economic depression that began in 1929. Popular unrest was marked by political assassinations and plots to overthrow the government. This led to a significant increase in the power of the militarists, who approved the invasion of Manchuria in 1931 and the installation of a Japanese puppet regime, Manchukuo. In 1933 Japan withdrew from the League of Nations and in 1937 entered into full-scale hostilities against China.

As the leader of a new order for Asia, Japan signed a tripartite pact with Germany and Italy in 1940. The Japanese military leaders viewed the US as the main obstacle to their imperial conquest of Asia, and when diplomatic attempts to gain US neutrality failed, the Japanese drew them into WWII with a surprise attack on the US Pacific Fleet in Pearl Harbor on 7 December 1941. The intent of the strike was to neutralise the fleet, which Japan rightly viewed as its main threat in the region.

1869

The 17-year-old Emperor Meiji moves from Kyoto to Edo, renamed Tokyo the year before, where Japan's new political and economic centre capital is established.

1871

Japan's first exposition is held in Kyoto. The Miyako and Kamogawa *odori* (dances performed by geisha and apprentice geisha) are first performed at the Kyoto exhibition the following year.

1915

The first street lamps are installed on Shijō-dōri and the accession of Emperor Taishō is celebrated throughout Japan (although he had officially become emperor three years prior).

At first Japan scored rapid successes, pushing its battle fronts across to India, down to the fringes of Australia and into the mid-Pacific. But eventually the decisive Battle of Midway turned the tide of the war against Japan. Exhausted by submarine blockades and aerial bombing, by 1945 Japan had been driven back on all fronts. In August, the declaration of war by the Soviet Union and the atomic bombs dropped by the USA on Hiroshima and Nagasaki were the final straws: Emperor Hirohito announced unconditional surrender.

Despite being spared from air raids, Kyoto suffered a great drain of people and resources during the war. To prevent the spread of fires, hundreds of magnificent wooden shops and houses were torn down, and some great temple bells and statues were melted down into artillery. Fortunately, however, the majority of its cultural treasures survived.

POSTWAR RECONSTRUCTION & REVIVAL

Japan was occupied by Allied forces until 1952 under the command of General Douglas MacArthur. The chief aim was a thorough reform of Japanese government through demilitarisation, the trial of war criminals and the weeding out of militarists and ultranationalists from the government. A new constitution was introduced which denounced war and banned a Japanese military, and also dismantled the political power of the emperor, who stunned his subjects by publicly renouncing any claim to divine origins.

At the end of the war, the Japanese economy was in ruins and inflation was running rampant. A programme of recovery provided loans, restricted imports and encouraged capital investment and personal saving. In 1945 the Kyoto Revival Plan was drafted and, again, Kyoto was set for rebuilding. In 1949 physicist Hideki Yukawa was the first in a long line of Nobel Prize winners from Kyoto University, and the city went on to become a primary educational centre.

By the late '50s trade was flourishing and the Japanese economy continued to experience rapid growth. From textiles and the manufacture of labour-intensive goods such as cameras, the Japanese 'economic miracle' had branched out into virtually every sector of society and Kyoto increasingly became an international hub of business and culture.

In 1956 Japan's first public orchestra was founded in Kyoto and two years later the city established its first sister-city relationship, with Paris. Japan was now looking seriously towards tourism as a source of income, and foreign visitors were steadily arriving on tours for both business and pleasure. By this time Kyoto had further developed as a major university centre and during the 'Woodstock era' of the late '60s, antiwar movements and Japanese flower power mirrored those of America and brought student activism out into the streets. The year 1966 saw the enactment of a law to preserve historical sites in the city and the opening of the Kyoto International Conference Hall, where the Kyoto Protocol was drafted in 1997.

During the 1970s Japan faced an economic recession, with inflation surfacing in 1974 and again in 1980, mostly as a result of steep price hikes for the imported oil on which Japan is still gravely dependent. By the early '80s, however, Japan had fully emerged as an economic superpower, and Kyoto's high-tech companies, including Kyocera, OMRON and Nintendo, were among those dominating fields such as electronics, robotics and computer technology. The notorious 'bubble economy' that followed marked an unprecedented era of free spending by Japan's nouveau riche. Shortly after the 1989 death of Emperor Shōwa and the start of the Heisei period (with the accession of the current emperor, Akihito) the miracle bubble burst, launching Japan into a critical economic freefall from which it has not yet fully recovered.

1941

The Imperial Japanese Navy attacks the US Pacific Fleet in Pearl Harbor, Hawaii, in a strike designed to prevent American interference in Japan's territorial expansion in Asia.

1966

Kyoto International Conference Hall opens at Takaragaike as the first international conference hall in Japan. Takaragaike later serves as the site for the Kyoto Protocol agreement.

1981

Karasuma subway line starts service between Kyoto and Kitaōji stations. The city's first subway line allows easy north–south travel through the city. The line later extends south to Takeda and north to Takaragaike.

WHAT REALLY SAVED KYOTO?

Kyoto's good fortune in escaping US bombing during WWII is a well-publicised fact. Still, while it may provide patriotic colour for some Americans to hear that the city was consciously spared out of US goodwill and reverence for Kyoto's cultural heritage, not everyone agrees with the prevailing story.

The common belief is that Kyoto was rescued through the efforts of American scholar Langdon Warner (1881–1955). During the latter half of the war Warner sat on a committee that endeavoured to save artistic and historical treasures in war-torn regions. Now, more than a half-century later, Warner is a household name in Japan and is still alluded to in discussions on the future preservation of Kyoto. He is said to have made a desperate plea to top US military authorities to spare the cities of Kyoto, Nara, Kamakura and Kanazawa.

Despite this popular account, other theories have surfaced, along with documentation pointing to an elaborate conspiracy aimed at quelling anti-American sentiment in occupied Japan. The evidence has fuelled a debate as to whether or not it was in fact a well-planned public relations stunt scripted by US intelligence officials to gain the trust of a nation that had been taught to fear and hate the American enemy.

Some historians have suggested that both Kyoto and Nara were on a list of some 180 cities earmarked for air raids. Kyoto, with a population of over one million people, was a prime target (along with Hiroshima and Nagasaki) for atomic annihilation and many avow the choice could easily have been Kyoto. Nara, it has been suggested, escaped merely due to having a population under 60,000, which kept it far enough down the list not to be reached before the unconditional surrender of Japan in September 1945.

Whether the preservation of Kyoto was an act of philanthropy or a simple twist of fate, the efforts of Warner and his intellectual contemporaries are etched into the pages of history and even taught in Japanese schools. Disbelievers avow that the 'rumour' was sealed as fact for good after Warner was posthumously honoured by the Japanese government, which bestowed upon him the esteemed Order of the Sacred Treasure in recognition of his invaluable contribution to the Japanese nation. There is a symbolic tombstone placed as a memorial to Warner in the precinct of Nara's Hōryū-ji.

KYOTO TODAY & TOMORROW

In 1994 Kyoto marked the 1200th anniversary of its founding. While the city celebrated its ancient heritage, however, developers celebrated this milestone by building several structures in excess of the height restrictions that had been put in place to maintain the city's traditional skyline.

Fortunately, in September 2007, the Kyoto city government enacted new ordinances that restrict building heights and ban all rooftop and blinking advertisements. Other recent positive developments include attempts to ban cars from the main Downtown thoroughfare of Shijō-dōri during certain daylight hours, and heightened interest in the city's *machiya* (traditional wooden town houses; see the boxed text, p34).

While the usual tension between old and new plays itself out, Kyoto remains an important cultural and educational centre. Today more than 60 museums and 37 universities and colleges are scattered throughout the city, and more than 200 of Japan's National Treasures and nearly 1700 important Cultural Properties are housed here.

As Kyoto heads into the future, the real challenge is to preserve its ancient history while meeting the desires of its citizens for economic development and modern convenience. Looking back at the many incarnations of Kyoto, one can be hopeful that the city will find its own unique way to meet this challenge.

1994

Kyoto celebrates the 1200th anniversary of its founding and 17 Historic Monuments of Ancient Kyoto are registered as Unesco World Heritage sites, including Kinkaku-ji and Ginkaku-ji.

1997

The futuristic Kyoto Station building, featuring a 60m-high atrium over the main concourse, opens in the same year as the Tōzai (east–west) line, Kyoto's second subway line.

2007

Kyoto city passes a new law limiting building heights and gaudy advertising in an effort to protect the city's skyline and traditional character.

ARTS

Until the 20th century the main influences on Japanese art came from China and Korea, which passed Buddhism on from India in the 6th century. While incorporating these outside influences, the Japanese add something unique to their art. There is a fascination with the ephemeral and the unadorned, and with forms that echo the randomness of nature. A gift for caricature is also obvious, from early Zen ink paintings right up to contemporary manga (Japanese comic books). An interest in the grotesque or the bizarre is also often visible, from Buddhist scrolls depicting the horrors of hell to the highly stylised depictions of body parts in *ukiyo-e* wood-block prints of the Edo period.

When asked to define their aesthetic principles, the Japanese reach for words such as *wabi*, *sabi* and *shibui* (which refer to a kind of spare, natural, rustic and refined beauty). Such ideals are by no means the final say on a long and vibrant artistic tradition that continues to seek new inspirations and produce new forms.

top picks

KYOTO MUSEUMS

- Kyoto National Museum (p60)
- National Museum of Modern Art (p72)
- Kyoto Municipal Museum of Art (p72)
- Kawai Kanjirō Memorial Hall (p61)
- Fureai-kan Kyoto Museum of Traditional Crafts (p72)

PERFORMING ARTS

The two most famous Japanese theatrical traditions are kabuki and nō. Both forms work well as spectacle and some theatres have programmes with an English synopsis or headphones with an English commentary. Other forms of theatre include the comic drama of *kyōgen*; the puppet theatre known as *bunraku*; *rakugo*, which employs comic narrative; and *manzai*, a style of slapstick comedy.

Nō

Nō is a hypnotic dance-drama that reflects the minimalist aesthetics of Zen. The movement is glorious, the chorus and music sonorous, the expression subtle. A sparsely furnished cedar stage directs full attention to the performers, who include a chorus, drummers and a flautist. There are two principal characters: the *shite*, who is sometimes a living person but more often a demon or a ghost whose soul cannot rest; and the *waki*, who leads the main character towards the play's climactic moment. Each nō school has its own repertoire, and the art form continues to evolve and develop. One of the many new plays performed over the last 30 years is *Takahime*, based on William Butler Yeats' *At the Hawk's Well*.

The Takigi nō performance, held annually in the precincts of Heian-jingū (p72) on 1 and 2 June is your best chance to sample nō.

Kabuki

The origins of kabuki lie in the early 17th century when a maiden of a shrine led a troupe of women dancers to raise funds for the shrine. Prostitutes were soon performing the lead roles until the Tokugawa government banned women from the kabuki stage; they were replaced with attractive young men and finally by older men. This had a profound effect on kabuki, as these older male actors required greater artistry to credibly perform their roles. Thus, while remaining a popular art form, kabuki also became a serious art form.

Kabuki employs opulent sets, a boom-crash orchestra and a ramp through the audience to allow important actors to get the most out of their melodramatic entrances and exits. Formalised beauty and stylisation are the central aesthetic principles of kabuki; the acting is a combination of dancing and speaking in conventionalised intonation patterns. Kabuki deals thematically with feudal tragedies of the struggle between duty and inner feelings; the latter has produced a large body of work on the theme of love suicides.

In this style of theatre, the playwright is not the applauded; the play is merely a vehicle for the genius of the actor.

JAPANESE TEA CULTURE *Morgan Pitelka*

Tea came to Japan from China as part of a cultural package that included kanji and Buddhism, but the beverage did not become popular until the medieval period. Buddhist monks drank tea for its medicinal and stimulatory properties, a practice that gradually spread to warrior society and then to commoners. By the 16th century elite urban commoners such as the merchant and tea master Sen no Rikyū (1522–91) had elevated the preparation, serving and consumption of *matcha* (powdered green tea) to an elaborate performance art. In the 17th century tea masters established their own schools of tea, and these institutions codified, spread and protected the practice over subsequent centuries.

Although *chanoyu* (hot water for tea) is often referred to in English as the 'tea ceremony', the practice has always been more focused on collaboration, pleasure and artistic appreciation than on dutiful ritual. Tea gatherings can be short and spontaneous or long and extremely formal. They might be held to mark an anniversary, the changing of the seasons or just as an opportunity to see old friends. Typically a group of guests arrive at the location of the gathering, perhaps a home or a temple with its own tea house, and wait in the outer garden, a peaceful and meditative space. After entering the tea house, they observe while the host arranges the charcoal and serves a special meal known as *kaiseki* cuisine. After the meal, they eat some simple sweets, take a brief intermission, then return for a serving of viscous *koicha* (thick tea) followed in many cases, by a round of *usucha* (thin tea). The movements of the host and guests are carefully choreographed and rehearsed, making the sharing of the beverage a satisfying mutual performance. At certain moments during the gathering, the guests have the chance to admire the hanging scroll, the flower arrangement and the host's careful selection of *chadōgu* (tea utensils).

Tea culture has stimulated and supported the arts and crafts in Japan for centuries, and utensils – including tea bowls, tea caddies, tea scoops and tea whisks – can be purchased in tea shops and galleries or directly from artists. Urban department stores such as Takashimaya and Daimaru (see the boxed text, p109), Seibu and Mitsukoshi, among many others, frequently have whole floors devoted to ceramics, lacquerware and other crafts, as well as galleries in which the finest artists hold solo exhibitions and sales. A trip to a town famous for its crafts, such as Bizen, Hagi or Karatsu, can also present opportunities to buy tea utensils.

Some tea schools, such as Urasenke (p76), Omotesenke, Mushanokojisenke and Dai Nippon Chadō Gakkai, hold tea gatherings that are open to the public, particularly in large cities. Speciality cafés such as the confectionary store Toraya also offer a serving of sweets and tea. Museums that specialise in art associated with tea, such as the Nomura Museum (p67), Raku Museum and Kitamura Museum, display historical tea utensils and on occasion serve tea as well.

Morgan Pitelka, PhD, is the author of Handmade Culture: Raku Potters, Patrons, and Tea Practitioners in Japan

During the Edo period, Kyoto had a total of seven kabuki theatres. The sole remaining theatre is the venerable Minami-za (p142). You can find out what's on while you're in town by asking at the Tourist Information Centre (p199).

Kyōgen

Kyōgen is a comic drama that originally served as a light interlude within a nō play, but that is now more often performed separately between two different nō plays. *Kyōgen* draws on the real world for its subject matter and is acted in colloquial Japanese. The subjects of its satire are often samurai, depraved priests and faithless women – the performers are without masks and a chorus often accompanies.

A famous performance is held annually at Kyoto's Mibu-dera (p57).

IKEBANA

Ikebana, the art of flower arranging, was developed in the 15th century and can be grouped into three main styles: *rikka* (standing flowers), *shōka* (living flowers), and free-style techniques such as *nageire* (throwing-in) and *moribana* (heaped flowers). There are several thousand different schools, the top three being Ikenobō, Ōhara and Sōgetsu, but they share one aim: to arrange flowers to represent heaven, earth and humanity. Ikebana displays were originally used as part of the tea ceremony but can now be found in private homes – in the *tokonoma* (sacred alcove) – and even in large hotels.

Apart from its cultural associations, ikebana is also a lucrative business – its schools have millions of students, including many young women who view proficiency in the art as a means to improve their marriage prospects.

WAK Japan (p191) offers introductory classes in ikebana to foreign tourists in English.

PAINTING

By the end of the Heian period the emphasis on religious themes painted according to Chinese conventions gave way to a purely Japanese style, known as *yamato-e*. *Suiboku-ga* or *sumi-e* (ink paintings) by Chinese Zen artists were introduced during the Muromachi period and copied by Japanese artists, who produced *kakemono* (hanging pictures), *e-maki* (scrolls), and *fusuma-e* (decorated screens and sliding doors). During the Azuchi-Momoyama period, Japan's *daimyō* commissioned artists who painted in flamboyant colours and embellished with copious gold leaf.

European techniques, such as the use of oils, were introduced during the 16th century by the Jesuits, and the ensuing Edo period was marked by the enthusiastic patronage of a wide range of painting styles. The Kanō school was in demand for the depiction of subjects connected with Confucianism, mythical Chinese creatures or scenes from nature, while the Tosa school, whose members followed the *yamato-e* style, were commissioned by the nobility to paint scenes from the classics of Japanese literature.

The Rimpa school not only absorbed the style of these other schools but progressed to produce a strikingly original decorative style. The works produced by Tawaraya Sōtatsu, Honami Kōetsu and Ogata Kōrin rank among the finest of the period.

The best place to sample Japanese painting is at the Kyoto National Museum (p60).

LITERATURE

The first examples of literature in Japanese, the *Kojiki* (Record of Ancient Matters) and *Nihon Shoki* (Chronicle of Japan), were written in the 8th century in emulation of Chinese historical accounts. Later Japanese literature developed its own voice; interestingly, much of the early literature was written by women. One reason for this was that men wrote in imported kanji (Chinese characters), while women were relegated to writing in hiragana (Japanese script). Thus, while the men were busy copying Chinese styles and texts, women were inadvertently producing the first authentic Japanese literature. Among these early female authors is Murasaki Shikibu, who wrote Japan's all-time classic *Genji Monogatari* (The Tale of Genji), documenting the intrigues and romances of early Japanese court life.

The Narrow Road to the Deep North is a travel classic by the revered Japanese poet Bashō Matsuo. *Kokoro*, by Sōseki Natsume, is a 20th-century classic depicting the conflict between old and new Japan in the mind and heart of an aged scholar; while the modern and the traditional also clash in the lives of two couples in *Some Prefer Nettles* by Tanizaki Junichirō. *The Makioka Sisters,* also by Tanizaki, is a family chronicle that has

top picks

KYOTO NOVELS

- The Old Capital (Kawabata Yasunari) A young woman's past is disturbed by the discovery of a twin sister in another family and her future raises a symbolic question for Kyoto: will she follow tradition and stay with her father's kimono business or marry and move forward into the modern age?
- The Temple of the Golden Pavilion (Mishima Yukio) In 1950, a young Buddhist acolyte burned down Kyoto's famous Golden Pavilion, shocking the nation. In this novel (also a film entitled *Conflagration*) Mishima fictionalises the monk's obsession with its beauty and his desire to destroy it.
- Memoirs of a Geisha (Arthur Golden) This hugely popular book details the life of a Kyoto geisha. It was later turned into a successful movie (most of which was not filmed in Kyoto).
- The Lady and the Monk (Pico Iyer) Iyer's account of his relationship with a Japanese woman against the backdrop of Kyoto is a great book to read while you're here.
- Ransom (Jay McInerney) Deals with a young man who winds up in Kyoto after some harrowing travels around Asia. It may not be McInerney's best, but it does capture the feeling of expat Kyoto in the pre-bubble days.

been likened to a modern-day *Monogatari* (below). Meanwhile, Ibuse Masuji's *Black Rain* deals with the aftermath of Japan's defeat in WWII.

Perhaps the most controversial of Japan's modern writers is Mishima Yukio. In *The Temple of the Golden Pavilion,* he reconstructs the life of a novice monk who burned down Kyoto's Kinkaku-ji (p77) in 1950. Many Japanese consider Yukio's work unrepresentative of Japanese culture – his work makes for interesting reading.

top picks

CLASSIC KYOTO FILMS

- **Rashomon** (1950) Kurosawa Akira's classic uses the now non-existent southern gate of Kyoto as the setting for a 12th century rape and murder story told from several conflicting perspectives, raising doubt as to whether the truth can ever be known.
- **Life of Oharu** (1952) Arguably Mizoguchi Kenji's most acclaimed film, the story follows the life of a courtesan who loses her honour in an affair and stumbles from one disaster to the next, ending up as an old prostitute trying to reconcile with her fate.
- **Sisters of Nishijin** (1952) Set in the famous Nishijin textiles district. The father of a silk-weaving family kills himself as the family is caught between the old and the new and cannot adapt to the mechanisation of their trade. Directed by Yoshimura Kozaburō.
- **Peacemaker Kurogane** (2005) This recent *anime* series follows a young man who joins the famous Shinsengumi samurai who defended the shōgunate before the Meiji Restoration. While not exactly classic or even historically accurate, the show is a fun introduction to Kyoto's history.

CINEMA

Japan's film industry is both highly productive and critically acclaimed, with 40% of box-office revenue coming from domestic films and a slew of awards honouring several of Japan's actors and directors, past and present. Japanese genres range from highbrow art to the unique styles of *anime,* to the classic 'monster-stomps-Tokyo' films – Kyoto was where it all started. Inabata Katsutaro, a Kyoto businessman, was studying in Paris when his classmate Auguste Lumière invented the first film projector. Inabata leapt at the chance to purchase a projector and held Japan's first projection in 1897, two years after Lumière's first showing.

At first Japanese films were strongly influenced by kabuki, with kabuki actors taking most leading roles in what was primarily historical subject matter. However, by 1912, two distinct camps had set up: Kyoto's studios, producing *jidaigeki* (period films), and the Tokyo studios, creating *gendaigeki* films (modern themes). However, the great Tokyo earthquake of 1923 caused many Tokyo studios to move to Kyoto's Uzumasa district, establishing it as the 'Hollywood of Japan' and emphasising the period film as the most popular genre. By this time the style had moved away from kabuki and focused more on realistic samurai sword-fighting and special effects. In the years leading up to and during WWII, this same sense of samurai loyalty was heavily promoted in film; of those thousands of films produced, less than 2% still exist.

The golden age of Japanese cinema arrived with the 1950 release of Kurosawa Akira's *Rashōmon,* set against the backdrop of Kyoto's ancient southern gate. The film won the Golden Lion at the 1951 Venice International Film Festival and an Oscar for best foreign film. The increasing realism and high artistic standards of the period are evident in such landmark films as *Tōkyō Monogatari* (Tokyo Story, 1953), by the legendary Ōzu Yasujirō; Mizoguchi Kenji's classics *Ugetsu Monogatari* (Tales of Ugetsu, 1953) and *Saikaku Ichidai Onna* (The Life of Oharu, 1952); and Kurosawa's masterpiece *Shichinin no Samurai* (Seven Samurai, 1954). Annual attendance at the country's cinemas reached 1.1 billion in 1958, and Kyoto – with its large film studios, such as Shōchiku, Daiei and Tōei, and more than 60 cinemas – was at the centre of the boom.

Unfortunately, today Kyoto's studios are all but dead, with the vast majority of production now being done in Tokyo. These days there are two relics of Kyoto's film history: Ōkōchi-Sansō Villa (p81) in Arashiyama, and Eiga Mura. Ōkōchi-sansō Villa was the hilltop villa of one of Kyoto's most successful *jidaigeki* actors, Ōkōchi Denjirō (1898–1962). Playing roles such as scarred and one-armed samurai, Ōkōchi became very wealthy over the course of his long career. His stunning Arashiyama home and garden remain as testament to the popularity of his movies.

Tōei Uzumasa Movie Village (Eiga Mura; p78) is all that remains of Tōei's Kyoto studio. Part studio and part theme park, it is more tourist trap than anything else, but the historical sets are still occasionally used for new *jidaigeki*. Visitors can poke around sets from famous Japanese movies and TV shows, watch actors perform sword fights, and learn more than they thought possible about the multitude of Power Ranger–type characters Tōei has produced for film and TV over the years.

ARCHITECTURE

Kyoto's architecture is a schizophrenic jumble that ranges from some of the world's most sublime traditional wooden structures to one of the world's most modern train stations, with a lot of forgettable concrete buildings in between.

First and foremost, Kyoto is the best city in Japan to feast on the glories of Japanese religious architecture. The temples and shrines of Kyoto are the finest in the country and many are paired with brilliant examples of Japanese garden design.

Kyoto's traditional secular architecture is also stunning, including what some critics have termed the most beautiful wooden structure in the world: Katsura Rikyū, a fine imperial villa. More humble, but equally appealing, are Kyoto's *machiya*, the traditional wooden town houses that are, in some ways, the quintessential Kyoto structures.

TEMPLES

Temples *(tera/dera, ji* or *in)* vary widely in their construction, depending on the type of school and historical era of construction. From the introduction of Buddhism in the 6th century until the Kamakura period, temples were the most important architectural works in Japan and hence exerted a strong stylistic influence on all other types of building.

There were three main styles of early temple architecture: *tenjikuyō* (Indian), *karayō* (Chinese) and *wayō* (Japanese). All three styles were in fact introduced to Japan via China. *Wayō* arrived in the 7th century and gradually acquired local character, becoming the basis of much Japanese wooden architecture. It was named so as to distinguish it from *karayō* (also known as Zen style), which arrived in the 12th century. A mixture of *wayō* and *karayō* known as *setchuyō* eventually came to dominate, and *tenjikuyō* disappeared altogether.

With their origins in Chinese architecture and emphasis on otherworldly perfection, early temples were monumental and symmetrical in layout. A good example of the Chinese influence can be seen in the famous Phoenix Hall, a Tang-style pavilion at Byōdō-in in Uji (p89).

The Japanese affinity for asymmetry eventually affected temple design, leading to the more organic – although equally controlled – planning of later temple complexes. An excellent example in Kyoto is Daitoku-ji (p53), a Rinzai Zen monastery, which is a large complex containing a myriad of subtemples and gardens.

Temples generally have four gates, oriented to the north, south, east and west. The *nandaimon* (south gate), is usually the largest one. The *niō-mon* houses frightful-looking statues of gods such as Rai-jin (the god of lightning) and Fū-jin (the god of wind). There is also a central gate, *chū-mon,* which is sometimes incorporated into the cloister.

SHRINES

Shrines can be called *jinja, jingū, gū* or *taisha*. The original Shintō shrine is Izumo Taisha in Shimane prefecture, which has the largest shrine hall in Japan. It is said to have been modelled on the emperor's residence and its style, known as *taisha-zukuri,* was extremely influential on later shrine design. Shrines tend to use simple, unadorned wood construction, and are built raised above the ground on posts. The roof is gabled, not hipped, while the entrance is generally from the end, not the side; both elements distinguish shrines from temple design. The distinctive roof line of shrine architecture is due to an elaboration of the structural elements of the roof. The crisscross elements are called *chigi* and the horizontal elements are called *katsuogi*.

As Buddhism increased its influence over Shintō it also affected the architecture. The clean lines of the early shrines were replaced with curving eaves and other ornamental details. Worshippers were provided with shelter by extending the roof or even building a separate worship

MACHIYA TOWN HOUSES: LIFE IN THE OLD CITY *Alex Kerr*

A big surprise awaits foreign visitors to Kyoto – the actual look of this fabled cultural capital. Outside temple gates, there stretches a *Bladerunner* landscape of concrete and aluminium apartment buildings, pachinko parlours, pink plastic houses and empty lots filled with parked cars, the whole festooned with a web of electrical wires and out-of-control signage. It's the result of decades of purposeful destruction of the old town, which city fathers saw as 'old fashioned'.

A few blocks, such as the geisha district of Gion, preserve traditional architecture. In the rest of Downtown Kyoto, however, old town houses, called *machiya,* are something you can just occasionally catch a glimpse of: you'll see three or four down one street, just one down another. They're the last remnants of a style of city living that could once be found in all Japanese large towns, but survived as remnants only in Kyoto.

Machiya are long and narrow wooden row houses that functioned as both homes and workplaces. The shop area was located in the front of the house, while the rooms lined up behind it formed the family's living quarters. Nicknamed *unagi no nedoko* (eel bedrooms), the *machiya*'s elongated shape came about because homes were once taxed according to the width of their street frontage.

Inside a *machiya* is a self-contained world, complete with private well, storehouse, Buddhist altar, clay ovens outfitted with iron rice cauldrons, shrines for the hearth god and other deities, and interior minigardens, called *tsuboniwa* (garden in a *tsubo* – two-tatami-mat space). The kitchen area forms a two- or three-storey open atrium, into which smoke rising from the ovens has darkened the dramatic overhead beams.

On the street side, *machiya* present a distinctive 'vocabulary' of elements. Most prominent are the wooden lattices covering walls, doors and windows. Forbidden by law to use painted, gilded or carved decoration (allowed only to samurai and nobility), the merchants of Kyoto played with the right angle. Ingeniously devised lattice frameworks served as a way to let in light and air and maintain privacy at the same time. It's easy to look out but very hard to look in. Along the street they placed curving barriers of bamboo, called *inu-yarai* (dog-avoiders) which functioned as described but also protected against spattered mud. Above street level they carved *mushiko-mado* (narrow slitted windows) out of thick plaster walls. This limited but infinitely varied set of basic features played itself out in a symphonic harmony along the old city streets.

Unfortunately, *machiya* were not conducive to modern life. Dark at all times, they were humid and hot in the summer, damp and cold in the winter, and often encrusted by thick coats of dust and soot. Combine this with ancient electrical wiring and primitive toilet facilities and it was little wonder that modern townspeople rushed to tear them down as soon as they could afford it. At the same time the city was desperate to prove to the world that it had become 'modern' and provided almost no support for historic homes.

Recently *machiya* have made a bit of a comeback. Following a drastic decline in numbers, the remaining town houses acquired an exotic appeal. Developers began converting them into restaurants, clothing boutiques, even hair salons. Others have turned *machiya* into rental homes. Rather than visiting as a guest in a hotel or *ryokan,* you can feel the pulse of the old city by living in a *machiya.*

The turning point arrived in the early 2000s when international techniques of restoration finally came to Japan. People found that they could have both beauty and comfort, which previously seemed impossible. You could restore an old *machiya* by keeping its original structure, but at the same time add good lighting, nice baths and toilets and other conveniences that modern people seek. Meanwhile, spurred by a new interest in developing its tourist industry, Kyoto discovered a new-found pride in its heritage. In 2007 the city government did a dramatic about-face. Kyoto promulgated a Landscape Law, the most sweeping of its type ever established in Japan. It limits heights, encourages new and old buildings to incorporate traditional features, and restricts signage.

The new law is just a beginning and *machiya* are still being torn down and made into car parks. However, Kyoto seems to have turned a corner. The *machiya* will survive and, in some parts of town, even flourish. Unique in all Japan, some echo of that old symphony will still be heard.

If you're keen to experience one of Kyoto's *machiya,* you can have a meal or even stay overnight in one. Here are five of our favourite *machiya* restaurants and accommodations in Kyoto:

Shuhari (p128) This fine old *machiya* has been converted into a casual, hip French restaurant.
Mukade-ya (p123) Sample *kaiseki* cuisine in this fine *machiya* restaurant.
Kailash (p134) On the eastern side of town, this new organic restaurant is located in a simple converted *machiya*.
Café Bibliotec HELLO! (p126) This brilliant café shows the possibilities of Kyoto's traditional town houses.
Iori (p150) Iori has seven beautifully appointed *machiya* that you can spend a night in.

Alex Kerr is author of Lonely Planet's Lost Japan. *In 2004 he founded Iori, a Kyoto-based company dedicated to saving* machiya.

hall. This led to the *nagare* style, the most common type of shrine architecture. Excellent examples in Kyoto can be found at Shimogamo-jinja (p56) and Kamigamo-jinja (p91).

The *gongen* style uses an H-shaped plan, connecting two halls with an intersecting gabled roof and hallway called an *ishi no ma*. This element symbolises the connection between the divine and the ordinary worlds. The best example of this style in Kyoto is at Kitano-Tenman-gū (p76).

At the entrance to the shrine is the *torii* (gateway) marking the boundary of the sacred precinct. The most dominant *torii* in Kyoto is in front of Heian-jingū (p72), a massive concrete structure a considerable distance south of the shrine.

Fushimi-Inari-Taisha (p59), south of Kyoto, has thousands of bright vermilion gates lining paths up the mountain to the shrine itself.

Shimenawa, which are plaited ropes decorated with strips of *gohei* (white paper), are strung across the top of the *torii*. They are also wrapped around sacred rocks or trees, or above the actual shrine entrance. A pair of stone lionlike creatures called *koma-inu* can often be found flanking the main path. One usually has its mouth open in a roar and the other has its mouth closed.

The *kannushi* (chief priest) of the shrine is responsible for religious rites and the administration of the shrine. The priests dress in blue and white; on special occasions they don more ornate clothes and wear an *eboshi* (a black cap with a protruding, folded tip). *Miko* (shrine maidens) dress in vermilion and white.

GARDENS

Garden enthusiasts, look no further. Kyoto is the place to gorge yourself on Japanese gardens in all their splendour. The city is home to a vast collection of Japan's foremost gardens encompassing the entire spectrum of styles.

Broadly speaking, Japanese gardens fall into four basic types: *funa asobi* (pleasure-boat style), *shūyū* (stroll style), *kanshō* (contemplative style) and *kaiyū* (many-pleasure style).

The *funa asobi* garden is centred on a large pond used for pleasure boating, so the best views are from the water. During the Heian period, such gardens were often built around noble mansions, the most outstanding remaining example being the garden that surrounds Byōdō-in in Uji (p89).

The *shūyū* garden is intended to be viewed from a winding path, allowing the garden to unfold and reveal itself in stages and from different vantages. Popular during the Heian, Kamakura and Muromachi periods, *shūyū* gardens can be found around many noble mansions and temples from those eras. A celebrated example is at Ginkaku-ji (p71).

The *kanshō* garden should be viewed from one place. Zen rock gardens, the rock-and-raked-gravel spaces that are also known as *karesansui* (dry mountain stream gardens), are examples of this garden. The *kanshō* garden is designed to facilitate contemplation: such a garden can be viewed over and over without yielding to any one 'interpretation' of its meaning. The most famous *kanshō* garden is at Ryōan-ji (p77).

Lastly, the *kaiyū* features many small gardens surrounding a central pond, often incorporating a teahouse. The structure of this garden, as with the *shūyū* garden, lends itself to being explored on foot and provides the viewer with a variety of changing scenes, many built as miniature landscapes. The most famous *kaiyū* garden is at the Katsura Rikyū Imperial Villa (p71).

Japanese gardens may also use a technique known as *shakkei,* or borrowed scenery, in which features outside the garden – distant hills or even the cone of a volcano – are incorporated into the garden. One example of this is the garden at Shūgaku-in Rikyū Imperial Villa (p58) in the north of the city, which incorporates mountains 10km distant.

For more on gardens, see the boxed text, p75.

ENVIRONMENT

Kyoto is a landlocked city that makes up part of the eastern side of a mountainous region known as the Tamba Highlands, and the northern half of the Kyoto (Yamashiro) Basin. Kyoto City has an area of 827.9 sq km and population of approximately 1.47 million.

The Kyoto Basin is surrounded on three sides by mountains known as Higashiyama (Eastern Mountains), Kitayama (Northern Mountains) and Arashiyama (Stormy Mountains) in the west, all of which rise to less than 1000m above sea level. The city itself is relatively flat, with land highest in the northeast and descending towards the southwest. This interior positioning results in hot, humid summers and cold winters. There are three rivers in the basin: the Kamo-gawa to the east, the Katsura-gawa to the west and the Uji-gawa to the south. The Kamo-gawa originates in the mountains in the north and then flows through the centre of the city. The riverbanks are lined with *sakura* (cherry trees) and paths that are popular walks for residents and tourists, and in summer restaurants open balconies perched alongside the river. In the past, the river was a crucial source of drinking water as well as a means of transportation and irrigation. The purity of the water was highly prized for the production of Fushimi sake and it also played a vital role in *kyō-yūzen* dyeing, a traditional craft of Kyoto.

As well as cherry trees, the flora of Kyoto includes *tsutsuji* (azalea), *tsubaki* (camellia), *momiji* (maple trees), *shidare-yanagi* (weeping willows) and katsura trees. *Kamo* (ducks), *sagi* (herons), and *uiguisu* (bush warblers) can be seen in and around the Kamo-gawa, and *shika* (deer), *inoshishi* (wild boars), *saru* (monkeys) and even *kuma* (bears) are known to roam the surrounding mountains.

GOVERNMENT & POLITICS

The Kyoto city government is made up of 72 council members elected by majority vote with elections being held every four years. In the most recent city council election, in April 2007, the Liberal Democratic Party took 23 seats, followed by the Japan Communist Party with 19, the Democratic Party with 13 and the Kōmei with 12.

Kyoto's present mayor, Kadokawa Daisaku, was elected in February 2008 by a narrow margin. The former head of the city's education department, Kadokawa received the backing of the Liberal Democratic Party. Kadokawa replaced the city's previous mayor, the popular Masumoto Yorikane, who had held power since 1996.

Visitors to the city are most likely to encounter Kyoto's political world if they arrive during the run-up to a local or national election, when speaker trucks ply the city's streets bombarding citizens with entreaties to vote for their candidates.

ECONOMY

Kyoto City has a workforce of about 730,000 people whose combined labour results in a GDP of just over ¥6 billion. The major industries are tourism, which employs roughly 65% of the workforce; electronics; manufacturing; and textile production. With the rest of Japan, the city is slowly recovering from the post-bubble-economy recession of the late 1990s. The city's economy grew by almost a full percentage point in 2006, the third straight year of economic expansion.

While many of Kyoto's traditional industries, such as silk-weaving, fabric-dyeing and cabinet-making, have been in steady decline, several of its high-tech companies are thriving, including international camera giant Kyocera and video game trailblazer Nintendo. Other large corporations include Omron and Nissha.

Kyoto's business and civic leaders today face a dilemma: how to keep tourism and the traditional industries as an integral part of the economy while modernising in order to remain competitive. Some effort is under way to preserve parts of traditional Kyoto (perhaps those most profitable to tourism) and, as part of its plan to boost local infrastructure, the city has invested heavily to create world-class science facilities and in joint private-public ventures, such as Kyoto Research Park, Kyoto Science City and Kansai Science City on the border of Kyoto and Nara Prefectures.

CULTURE

It is often observed that Kyoto is the cultural heart of Japan; that is, the place in which Japanese culture is at its most refined, most intense and most distinctive. Indeed, Kyoto is the place where many Japanese go to learn what it is to be Japanese.

The cultural life of Kyoto was centred around the imperial court for over 1100 years. The court drew to it the finest artisans and craftspeople from all over Japan, resulting in an incredibly rich cultural and artistic atmosphere. Today, Kyoto is still the home of Japan's traditional arts, from textiles, to bamboo craft, to the tea ceremony. The imperial court also left its mark on the language of the city, and true *Kyoto-ben* (Kyoto dialect) has the lilting tones and formality of the now-departed imperial residents.

In addition to playing host to the imperial court, Kyoto has always been the headquarters of Japan's major religious sects, including Zen, Pure Land and Tendai. The astonishing preponderance of temples and shrines in the present-day city is testament to the role that Kyoto has always played in the spiritual life of the Japanese.

Kyoto's cultural life is also deeply informed by the natural world. Due to its geographic location, Kyoto has always enjoyed four very distinct seasons, which are reflected in and celebrated by the yearly procession of Kyoto rituals and festivals. From the hanging scrolls in people's homes, and tableware in *kaiseki* restaurants, to the young lady's *yukata* robe the night before the Gion Matsuri festival (p16), every aspect of Kyoto is a reminder and echo of the season. This rich and complex culture is still apparent to even the most casual visitor and it seems to embody a certain elegance, refinement and style that has few rivals elsewhere in the world.

Of course, it's impossible for a city to develop such a sophisticated culture without arousing the envy and even the ire of outsiders. Ask other Japanese about Kyotoites and they will probably tell you the same thing: that they are cold, arrogant, conservative, haughty, indirect and two-faced. They'll tell you that Kyotoites act as though the city is still the capital and the imperial seat; that your family has to live there for three generations before it will be accepted; and that they never understand what a Kyotoite really means because they never say what they're feeling.

The good news is that as a visitor you'll probably never pick up on a bit of this. In defence of the people of Kyoto, there is a good reason for their famed indirectness: as the seat of Japan's political life for so many centuries, the residents of the city naturally learned to guard their opinions in the presence of shifting political powers. Furthermore, as the seat of Japanese cultural, artistic and spiritual life, it is hardly surprising that Kyotoites feel a certain pride which can easily be mistaken for arrogance. The fact is, they've got a lot of culture to guard, so a little conservatism is only natural.

It's difficult to talk of a Kyoto identity, of course, because it is true that there are two different cultures existing in modern-day Kyoto: that of the old and the young. While most older Kyotoites cling to the traditional ways of the city, the young identify with the national Japanese culture that has its epicentre somewhere in the shopping malls of Tokyo's Shibuya district. The comparison can be jarring when you see a Kyoto *mama-san* (older woman who runs drinking, dining and entertainment venues) sharing the sidewalk with a group of gaudily clad *kogals* (fashionable young things). You might conclude that you're looking at two totally different species.

NEIGHBOURHOODS

top picks

- **Nanzen-ji** (p66)
  A spacious temple with a fine Zen garden.
- **Fushimi-Inari-Taisha** (p59)
  Tunnels of Shintō shrine gates lead you up a mountain.
- **Kurama-dera** (p85)
  A mountaintop temple above a pair of quaint villages.
- **Ginkaku-ji** (p71)
  A wonderful temple that is worth battling the crowds for.
- **Tenryū-ji & bamboo forest** (p80)
  A surreal stroll under a bamboo sky.
- **Ōkōchi-Sansō Villa** (p81)
  The loveliest house in all Kyoto.
- **Kiyomizu-dera** (p63)
  A hillside temple with holy water and a 'love shrine'.
- **Tetsugaku-no-Michi** (p70)
  A flower-lined Path of Philosophy.
- **Nishiki Market** (p50)
  The best market street in Kyoto, hands down.
- **Pontochō** (p51)
  The most atmospheric lane in the city by evening.

What's your recommendation? www.lonelyplanet.com/kyoto

NEIGHBOURHOODS

Kyoto is one of the easiest cities on earth to explore. It's basically a rectangle with mountains on three sides: east, west and north. This rectangle resembles a flat tray with three raised edges. In fact, this is exactly how many Kyotoites describe their city: they call it a *bon-chi* or 'tray land'.

Kyoto Station, where you'll first arrive in the city, is at the south end of the rectangle. There aren't many sights in the Kyoto Station area, but there are plenty of hotels, shops and restaurants. Kyoto Station is the transport hub of the city and many bus lines, a subway line and a private train line operate from here.

> 'Foreign and domestic tourists flock here to see Tenryū-ji, with it's stunning mountain backdrop, and the mysterious bamboo forest'

Downtown Kyoto is smack in the middle of the city and contains the main business, shopping, dining and entertainment districts. There are also several hotels in this part of town for those who like to be in the thick of things.

Surrounding the Downtown area is what we refer to as Central Kyoto, which is not so much a defined neighbourhood as it is a collection of amorphous zones surrounding the more distinct neighbourhoods. Several important sights can be found in Central Kyoto, including the enclosed Zen world of Daitoku-ji and one of Kyoto's oldest temples, Tō-ji, with its stunning pagoda. In addition, you will find a variety of accommodation here as well as some interesting dining and nightlife options.

The mountains that run the length of the east side are called the Higashiyama (literally, East Mountains). The districts at the base of these mountains are known as Southern and Northern Higashiyama and they contain many of Kyoto's most important sights, including the world-famous Kiyomizu-dera, the preserved streets of Ninen and Sannen-zaka, the Tetsugaku-no-Michi (Path of Philosophy) and the mossy paradise of Ginkaku-ji.

The mountains on the west side of the city are called the Arashiyama (Storm Mountains) and the district at their base is known as Arashiyama and Sagano. This is Kyoto's second-most popular sightseeing district. Foreign and domestic tourists flock here to see Tenryū-ji, with its stunning mountain backdrop, and the mysterious bamboo forest, in addition to a collection of small temples and a fine hilltop villa.

Northwest Kyoto is the next major sightseeing district, containing three of Kyoto's most important temples strung out along the base of the mountains that border the city.

Looking north from many parts of Kyoto will reveal a solid wall of mountains. These are the Kitayama (literally, 'North Mountains'). Hidden in the valleys of these mountains are several small villages that make extremely rewarding day trips out of the city.

Finally, the area we refer to as Greater Kyoto in this book includes a number of attractions that lie on the outskirts of the city. To the southwest you'll find Byōdō-in, a fine temple in the town of Uji. To the southwest, you'll find Katsura Rikyū, a sublime imperial villa. To the northwest resides the mountain town of Takao, home to three fine temples, and to the northeast lies the imposing mountain hulk of Hiei-zan, on the shoulder of which sits Enryaku-ji, a mysterious ancient temple.

So, that's a lot of neighbourhoods! Finally, let's give you Kyoto in a nutshell: you'll find the most rewarding sightseeing in Southern and Northern Higashiyama, and in Arashiyama and Sagano (with some interesting outliers in both Central Kyoto and Southeast Kyoto); you will probably eat, sleep, drink and shop in Downtown Kyoto, the Kyoto Station area or the Higashiyama districts; and when you want a break from the city, you'll be wanting to head into the Kitayama.

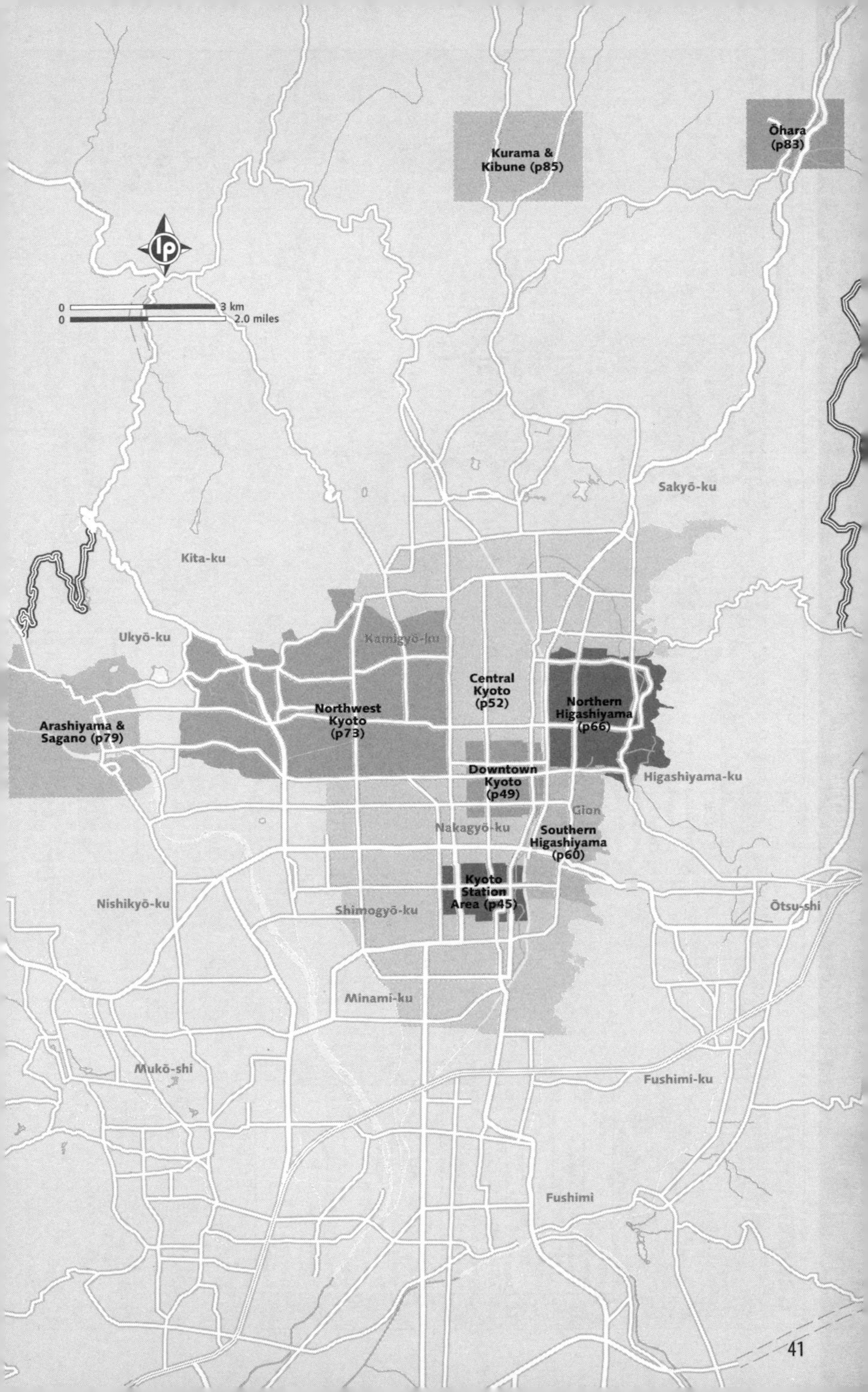

Kurama &
Kibune (p85)
Ōhara
(p83)
0
3 km
0
2.0 miles
Sakyō-ku
Kita-ku
Ukyō-ku
Kamigyō-ku
Central
Kyoto
(p52)
Northern
Higashiyama
(p66)
Northwest
Kyoto
(p73)
Arashiyama &
Sagano (p79)
Downtown
Kyoto
(p49)
Higashiyama-ku
Gion
Nakagyō-ku
Southern
Higashiyama
(p60)
Kyoto
Station
Area (p45)
Nishikyō-ku
Shimogyō-ku
Ōtsu-shi
Minami-ku
Mukō-shi
Fushimi-ku
Fushimi

GREATER KYOTO

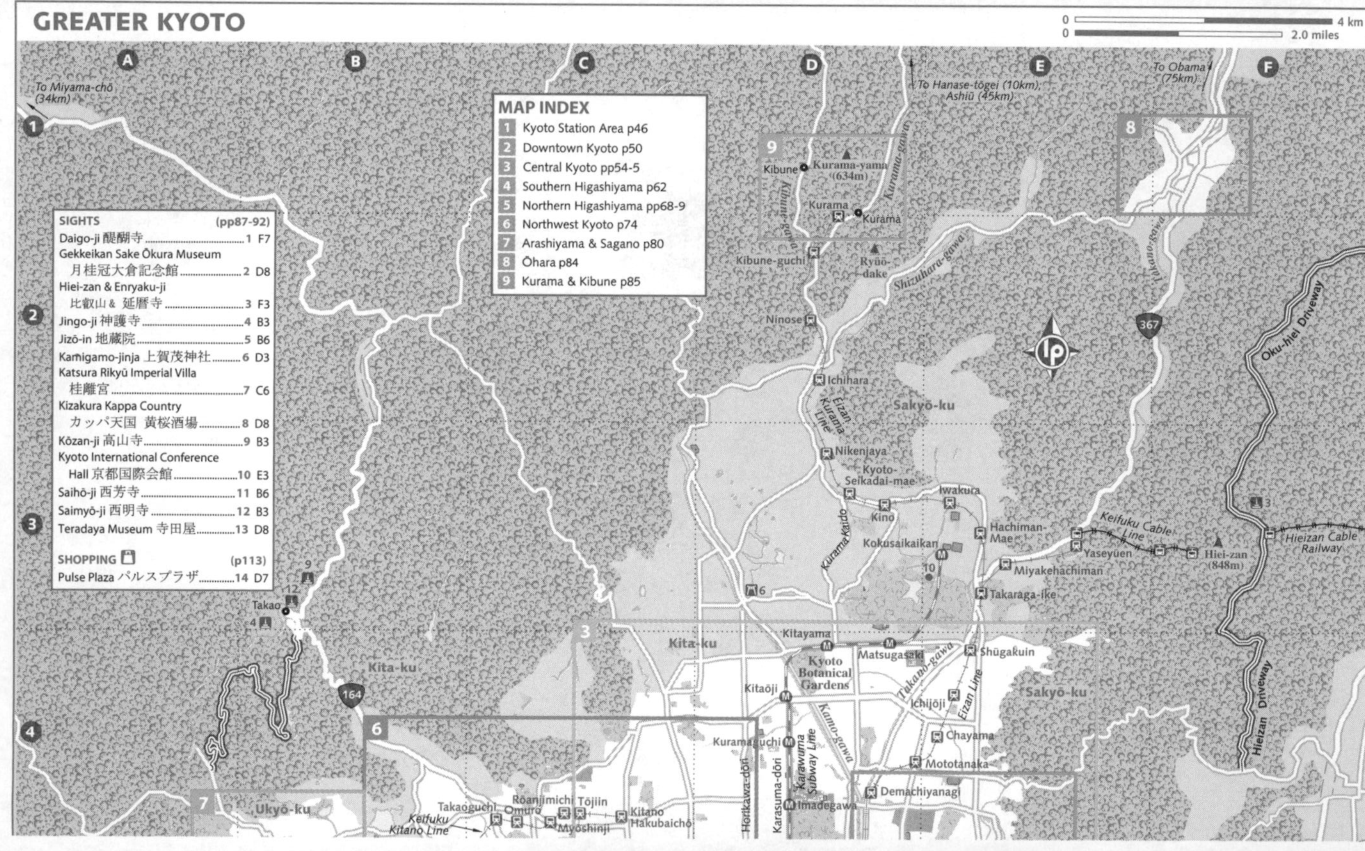

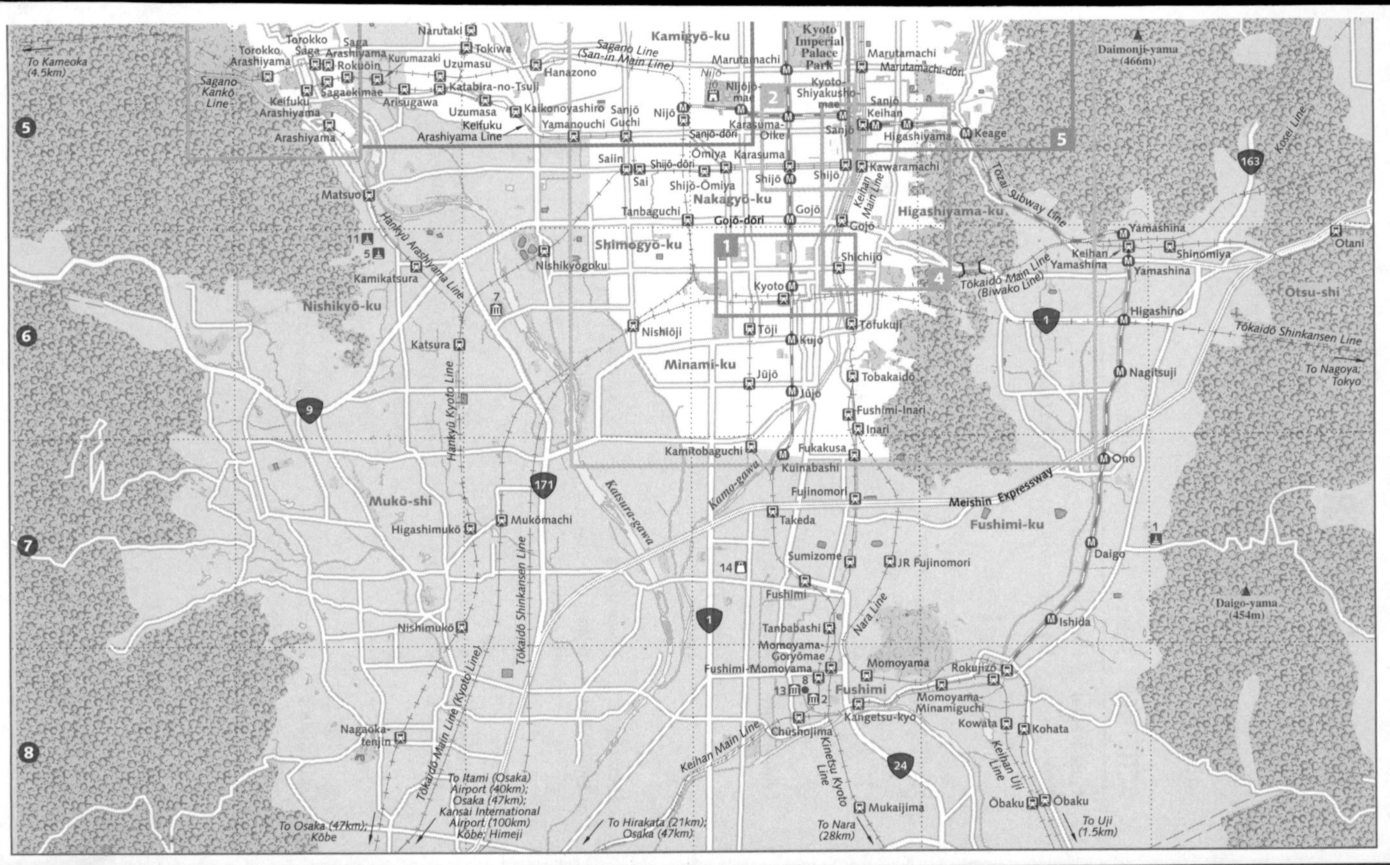
To Kameoka (4.5km)
Torokko Arashiyama
Torokko Saga
Saga Arashiyama
Rokuōin
Kurumazaki
Sagano Kankō Line
Sagaekimae
Keifuku Arashiyama
Arashiyama
Narutaki
Tokiwa
Uzumasu
Hanazono
Katabira-no-Tsuji
Arisugawa
Uzumasa
Kaikonoyashiro
Keifuku Arashiyama Line
Yamanouchi
Sanjō Guchi
Kamigyō-ku
Sagano Line (San-in Main Line)
Nijō
Nijōjō-mae
Marutamachi
Kyoto Imperial Palace Park
Kyoto-Shiyakusho-mae
Marutamachi-dōri
Sanjō
Keihan Sanjō
Higashiyama
Keage
Daimonji-yama (466m)
Kosei Line
Karasuma-Oike
Sanjō-dōri
Saiin
Sai
Shijō-dōri
Ōmiya
Karasuma
Shijō-Ōmiya
Shijō
Kawaramachi
Keihan Main Line
Nakagyō-ku
Tanbaguchi
Gojō-dōri
Gojō
Higashiyama-ku
Tōzai Subway Line
Matsuo
Hankyū Arashiyama Line
Shimogyō-ku
Nishikyōgoku
Shichijō
Kyoto
Kamikatsura
Nishikyō-ku
Nishiōji
Tōji
Kujō
Tōfukuji
Tōkaidō Main Line (Biwako Line)
Yamashina
Keihan Yamashina
Shinomiya
Otani
Ōtsu-shi
Higashino
Tōkaidō Shinkansen Line
To Nagoya; Tokyo
Nagitsuji
Katsura
Minami-ku
Jūjō
Tobakaidō
Fushimi-Inari
Inari
Hankyū Kyoto Line
Kamitobaguchi
Fukakusa
Kuinabashi
Ono
Mukō-shi
Katsura-gawa
Kamo-gawa
Fujinomori
Meishin Expressway
Fushimi-ku
Mukōmachi
Higashimukō
Takeda
Sumizome
JR Fujinomori
Daigo
Daigo-yama (454m)
Fushimi
Nara Line
Ishida
Nishimukō
Tanbabashi
Momoyama-Goryōmae
Fushimi-Momoyama
Momoyama
Rokujizō
Momoyama-Minamiguchi
Kangetsu-kyō
Kowata
Kohata
Nagaoka-tenjin
Chūshojima
Keihan Main Line
Kinetsu Kyoto Line
Keihan Uji Line
Tōkaidō Main Line (Kyoto Line)
To Itami (Osaka) Airport (40km); Osaka (47km); Kansai International Airport (100km) Kōbe; Himeji
To Osaka (47km); Kōbe
To Hirakata (21km); Osaka (47km)
To Nara (28km)
Mukaijima
Ōbaku
To Uji (1.5km)

ITINERARY BUILDER

The table below allows you to plan a day's worth of activities in any area of the city. Simply select which area you wish to explore, and then mix and match from the corresponding listings to build your day. The first item in each cell represents a well-known highlight of the area, while the other items are more off-the-beaten-track gems.

AREA / ACTIVITIES	Sights	Eating	Shopping
Kyoto Station Area	**Kyoto Station** (opposite) **Higashi Hongan-ji** (opposite)	**Eat Paradise** (p122) **The Cube** (p122)	**Bic Camera** (p107) **Isetan Department Store** (p107)
Downtown Kyoto	**Nishiki Market** (p50) **Pontochō** (p51)	**Kane-yo** (p126) **Kerala** (p126) **Yoshikawa** (p122)	**Nishiki Market** (p108) **Downtown Department Stores** (p109) **Morita Washi** (p109)
Central Kyoto	**Kyoto Imperial Palace Park** (p52) **Daitoku-ji** (p53) **Tō-ji** (p57)	**Den Shichi** (p128) **Manzara Honten** (p127) **Prinz** (p128)	
Southern Higashiyama	**Kiyomizu-dera** (p63) **Chion-in** (p65) **Shōren-in** (p65)	**Machapuchare** (p131) **Asuka** (p131) **Ōzawa** (p130)`	
Northern Higashiyama	**Nanzen-ji** (p66) **Hōnen-in** (p71) **Ginkaku-ji** (p71)	**Hinode Udon** (p135) **Omen** (p134) **Ayatori** (p135)	**Kyoto Handicraft Center** (p113)
Arashiyama & Sagano	**Tenryū-ji** (p80) **Bamboo Grove** (p79 **Ōkōchi-Sansō Villa** (p81)	**Kameyama-ya** (p137) **Komichi** (p137) **Yoshida-ya** (p137)	

KYOTO STATION AREA

Eating p121; Shopping p106; Sleeping p148

Dominated by the eponymous Kyoto Station, this area is all about business: the business of funnelling people into and out of Kyoto. Apart from the stunning station building, this area is not particularly attractive, unless your tastes run towards concrete, neon and gaudy billboards. In fact, it looks pretty much like the station area of any other large Japanese city, and tourists arriving here often have a kind of perplexed look – you can see them thinking: 'Is this really Kyoto, the old capital of Japan?' If you're one of those people, we can only assure you that it gets better from here.

Looking north from the station, you'll have no problem picking out Kyoto Tower and the roofs of a pair of giant temples, Higashi Hongan-ji and Nishi Hongan-ji, which are worth exploring. But the real reason to spend any time here is either to lay your head in one of the many convenient hotels and guesthouses in and around the station or to check out the many shops or department stores nearby. In fact, the Kyoto Station area has been pulling Kyoto's centre of gravity southwards for years, stealing a lot of clientele from the traditional Downtown shopping district, a trend that will only increase with the opening of Bic Camera, one of Japan's largest electronics retailers, near the station.

The best way to explore the Kyoto Station area is on foot, and all the major sights are within 15 minutes' walk of the station. Indeed, considering the usual traffic congestion around the station, taking a taxi might actually be slower than walking to some nearby sights. Of course, a bicycle is also a good way to get around the station area.

KYOTO STATION Map p46

☎ 352-5441; Shimogyō-ku, Karasuma-dōri, Shiokōji sagaru, Higashishiokō-ji-chō; Ⓢ Kyoto Station, JR & Kintetsu lines & Karasuma subway line

The Kyoto Station building is a striking steel-and-glass structure – a kind of futuristic cathedral for the transport age. Unveiled in September 1997, the building met with some decidedly mixed reviews. Some critics assail the building as being not keeping with the traditional architecture of Kyoto; others love its wide-open spaces and dramatic lines.

Whatever the case, you are sure to be impressed by the tremendous space that arches above you as you enter the main concourse. Moreover, you will probably enjoy a brief exploration of the many levels of the station, all the way up to the 15th-floor observation level. And be sure to take the escalator from the 7th floor on the east side of the building up to the 11th-floor glass corridor that runs high above the main concourse of the station – not a good spot for those with a fear of heights!

Located in the station building, you will discover several food courts (see the boxed text, p122), as well as the Isetan Department Store (p107), the Kyoto Prefectural International Center (p195), the Kyoto Tourist Information Center (TIC; p199), the Kyoto Tourism Federation (p199), and an outdoor performance space.

KYOTO TOWER Map p46

☎ 361-3215; Shimogyō-ku, Karasuma, Shichijō sagaru; adult ¥770, child ¥150-620; 🕑 9am-8.40pm; Ⓢ 3min walk from central exit, Kyoto Station

If you want to orient yourself as soon as you arrive in town, this is the place to do so. Located right outside the Karasuma (north) gate of the station, this retro tower looks like a rocket perched atop the Kyoto Tower Hotel. The tower provides excellent views in all directions and you can really get a sense for the Kyoto '*bon-chi*'. There are free mounted binoculars to use, and these allow ripping views over to Kiyomizu-dera (p63) and as far south as Osaka.

HIGASHI HONGAN-JI Map p46

☎ 371-9181; Shimogyō-ku, Karasuma-dōri, Shichijō agaru; admission free; 🕑 5.50am-5.30pm, 6.20am-4.30pm winter; Ⓢ 5min walk from central exit, Kyoto Station

A short walk north of Kyoto Station, this temple is the last word in all things grand and gaudy. Considering the proximity to the station, the free admission, the awesome structures and the dazzling interiors, this temple is an obvious spot to visit if you find yourself in the area.

In 1602 when shōgun Tokugawa Ieyasu engineered the rift in the Jōdo Shin-shū (True Pure Land) school of Buddhism, he founded this temple as a competitor to Nishi Hongan-ji (p47). Rebuilt in 1895 after a

KYOTO STATION AREA

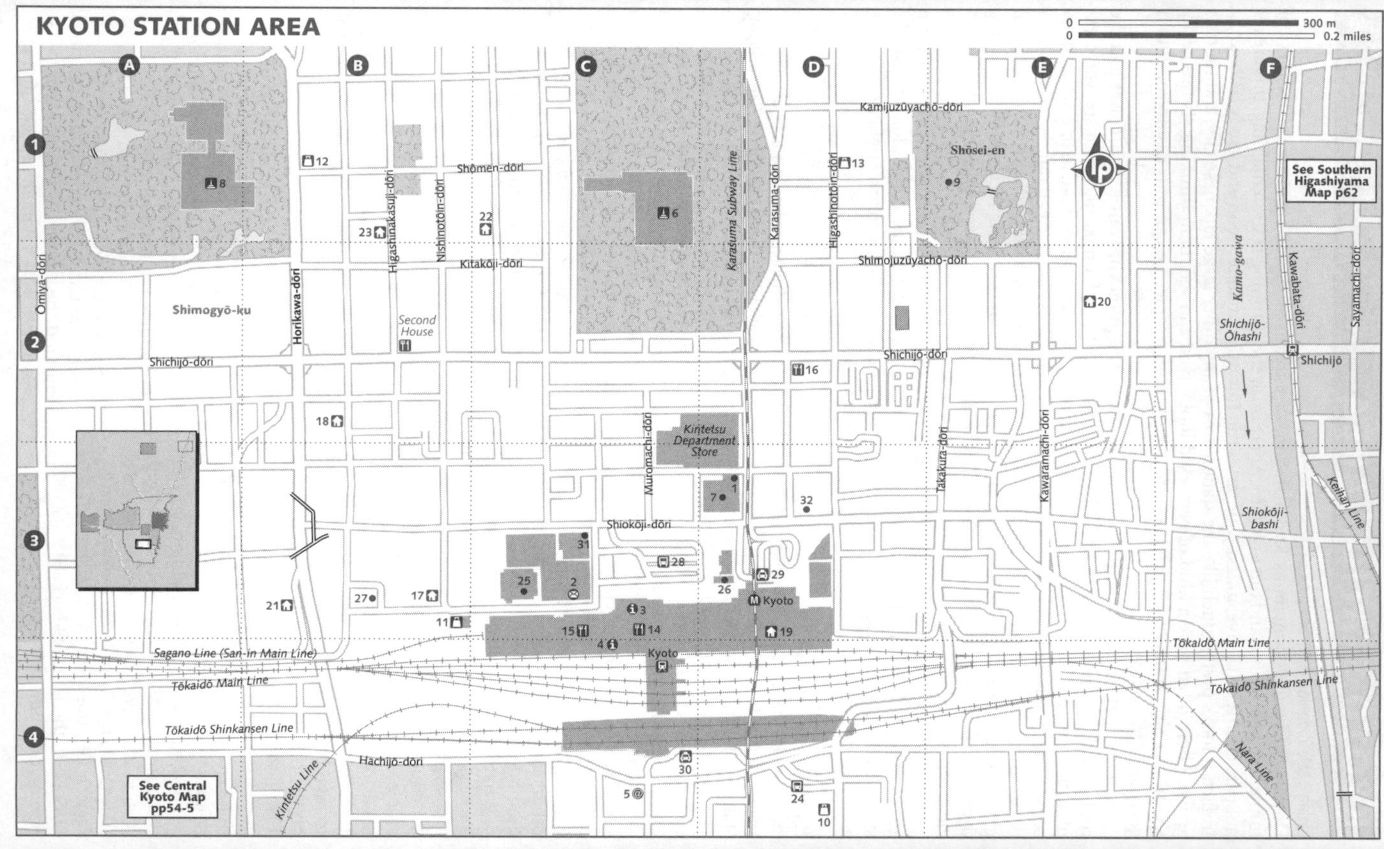

KYOTO STATION AREA

INFORMATION
International ATM 国際ATM 1 D3
Kyōsen-dō 京扇堂 .... (see 13)
Kyoto Central Post Office 京都中央郵便局 2 C3
Kyoto City Tourist Information Center 京都市観光案内所 3 C3
Kyoto Prefectural International Center 京都府国際センター .... (see 4)
Kyoto Tourism Federation 京都府観光センター .... (see 3)
Kyoto Tourist Information Center (TIC) 京都ツーリストインフォメーション 4 C4
Tops Café トップスカフェ 5 C4

SIGHTS (pp45-8)
Higashi Hongan-ji 東本願寺 6 C1
Kyoto Tower 京都タワー 7 D3
Nishi Hongan-ji 西本願寺 8 A1
Shōsei-en 渉成園 9 E1

SHOPPING (pp105-14)
Avanti アバンティ 10 D4
Bic Camera ビックカメラ 11 B3
Isetan Department Store 伊勢丹百貨店 .... (see 4)
Kungyoku-dō 薫玉堂 12 B1
Kyōsen-dō 京扇堂 13 D1

EATING (pp115-38)
Café du Monde カフェデュモンド 14 C3
Cube キューブ 15 C3
Eat Paradise .... (see 14)
Iimura いいむら 16 D2
Rāmen Kōji 京都拉麺小路 .... (see 15)

SLEEPING (pp145-56)
APA Hotel アパ ホテル 17 B3
Budget Inn バジェットイン 18 B2
Hotel Granvia Kyoto ホテルグランヴィア京都 19 D3
K's House Kyoto ケイズハウス京都 20 E2
Rihga Royal Hotel Kyoto リーガロイヤルホテル京都 21 B3
Ryokan Shimizu 旅館しみず 22 C1
Tour Club 旅倶楽部 23 B1

TRANSPORT (pp181-9)
Airport Limousine Bus Stop 京都八条口アバンティ前バス停 24 D4
Bicycle Parking Lot 京都駅前自転車駐車場 25 C3
Bus Information Centre 京都バス案内書 26 D3
Kyoto Cycling Tour Project 京都サイクリングツアープロジェクト 27 B3
Kyoto Station Bus Terminal 京都駅前バスターミナル 28 C3
Kyoto Station Taxi Stand (North) 京都駅前タクシーのりば(北) 29 D3
Kyoto Station Taxi Stand (South) 京都駅前タクシーのりば(南) 30 C4
Nissan Rent-a-Car 日産レンタカー 31 C3
Tōkai Discount Ticket Shop トーカイ格安きっぷ売り場 32 D3

series of fires destroyed all of the original structures, it is certainly monumental but less impressive artistically than its rival. The temple is now the headquarters of the Ōtani branch of Jōdo Shin-shū.

The Taishidō-mon gate stands 27m high and features giant doors made out of a single slab of wood. Wade through the sea of pigeons to the Hondō (Main Hall) – place your shoes in one of the plastic bags and carry them with you so that you can exit from the neighbouring building. This hall enshrines a 13th-century statue of Amida Nyorai (Buddha of the Western Paradise).

In the corridor between the two main buildings, you'll find a curious item encased in glass: a tremendous coil of rope made from human hair. Following the destruction of the temple in the 1880s, an eager group of female temple devotees donated their locks to make the ropes that hauled the massive timbers used for reconstruction.

The enormous Taishi-dō (Founder's Hall) is one of the world's largest wooden structures, standing 38m high, 76m long and 58m wide. The centrepiece is a self-carved likeness of Jōdo Shin-shū founder Shinran. Unfortunately, this building is presently under construction and will be under wraps until December 2008.

It only takes a few minutes to wander through the buildings; ask at the information office just inside the main gate for an English information leaflet.

NISHI HONGAN-JI Map p46

☎ 371-5181; Shimogyō-ku, Horikawa-dōri, Hanaya-chō sagaru; admission free; 5.30am-5.30pm, open later summer; 15min walk from central exit, Kyoto Station

This temple makes for a nice change from the incessant crowds of Higashi Hongan-ji (p45). As with its counterpart, Nishi Hongan-ji is an easy walk from the station and it's free. The interior of the main hall here is both gaudy and sublime.

Nishi Hongan-ji was originally built in 1272 in the Higashiyama Mountains by the priestess Kakushin, daughter of Shinran, who was founder of the Buddhist Jōdo Shin-shū school. The temple complex was relocated to its present site in 1591, on land provided by Toyotomi Hideyoshi (16th-century shōgun). By then, the Jōdo Shin-shū had accumulated immense power and the temple became its headquarters. Tokugawa Ieyasu sought to weaken the power of Jōdo Shin-shū by encouraging a breakaway faction to found Higashi Hongan-ji in 1602. The original Hongan-ji then became known as Nishi Hongan-ji. It is now the headquarters of the Hongan-ji branch of Jōdo Shin-shū, which has over 10,000 temples and 12 million followers worldwide.

top picks

FOR CHILDREN

Japan is an extremely easy place to travel with children: it's safe, clean and easy to get around. The only problem for parents is that you can't expect your kids to enjoy the same things you do. While you might be content to contemplate a rock garden at a Zen temple for hours at a time, your kids will probably have other ideas. Luckily, Kyoto has plenty of attractions to keep them busy, some of which parents are likely to enjoy as well. The following is just a sample of activities and attractions that children will enjoy in Kyoto.

- Arashiyama Monkey Park Iwatayama (p79) Both kids and adults will find the antics of the monkeys here fascinating, and it's easy to combine this with a trip to the sights of Arashiyama.
- Kamo-gawa There's a river running through Kyoto and it's a great place to bring the kids for an afternoon picnic. On hot days they can wade in the river while you relax on the bank. The area around Demachiyanagi (Map pp54–5) is one of the most popular spots for parents and children to play.
- Kyoto Imperial Palace Park (p52) The Central Park of Kyoto, this sprawling expanse of fields, trails, ponds and woods is a great place for a picnic, walk or bicycle ride with the kids.
- Kyoto City Zoo (p72) This small zoo is far from world class but it is quite convenient to the other sights of Northern Higashiyama. You can easily combine it with a trip to the temples, shrines and museums nearby.
- Umekōji Steam Locomotive Museum (p58) With 18 vintage steam locomotives, one of which you can ride, this museum is a must for train-crazy boys and girls.

The temple contains five buildings, featuring some of the finest examples of the architectural and artistic achievements of the Azuchi-Momoyama period (1568–1600). Unfortunately, the Goe-dō hall is presently being restored and won't reopen until 2010. The Daisho-in hall has sumptuous paintings, carvings and metal ornamentation. A small garden and Japan's oldest nō (stylised dance-drama) stages are connected to the Daisho-in hall. The dazzling Chinese-style Kara-mon gate displays intricate ornamental carvings and metalwork. The gate has been dubbed Higurashi-mon (Sunset Gate) by those who purport that its beauty can distract one from noticing the setting sun. Both Daisho-in and Kara-mon were transported here from Fushimi-jō castle in the south of the city.

The Goe-dō dates from 1636 and contains a seated statue of Shinran. The Hondō, last reconstructed in 1760, houses a priceless collection of painted sliding screens with images of the phoenix and peacock.

SHŌSEI-EN Map p46

☎ 371-9181; Karasuma-dōri-Kamijuzuyachō; admission free; 9am-3.30pm; 15min walk from central exit, Kyoto Station

About five minutes' walk east of Higashi Hongan-ji (p45), this garden is a nice green island in a vast expanse of concrete. While it's not on par with many other gardens in Kyoto, it's worth a visit if you find yourself in need of something to do near the station, perhaps paired with a visit to the temple. The lovely grounds, incorporating the Kikoku-tei villa, were completed in 1657. Bring a picnic (and some bread to feed the carp) or just stroll around the beautiful Ingetsu-ike pond.

DOWNTOWN KYOTO

Eating p121; Shopping p107; Sleeping p149

If you didn't give a hoot about temples, shrines and gardens, you might never leave Downtown Kyoto. It's got just about everything else you need: an incredible variety of accommodation, restaurants, nightlife, shopping and entertainment options. And, yes, there are even a few small temples, shrines and museums scattered about.

At the very heart of it all is a tight grid of streets and shopping arcades that is bounded by Kawaramachi-dōri and Karasuma-dōri on the east and west, and Oike-dōri and Shijō-dōri on the north and south. In this crowded grid you'll find a pleasant mix of tradition and modernity, with *machiya* (traditional Japanese town houses) crammed in between modern metal and concrete buildings. Many new businesses are opening in old *machiya,* which pleasantly blurs the borders between old and new.

You can wander endlessly in this area, poking around in the shops and arcades, content in the knowledge that whenever you get hungry or thirsty there'll almost always be a restaurant or café within a few steps. And don't forget Nishiki Market, Kyoto's finest food market, which runs through the southern edge of this district. Not far away, Shijō-dōri is thick with shops, including four of Kyoto's leading department stores.

And when night falls, you can head over to Kiyamachi, the city's bustling nightlife district, which centres on Kiyamachi-dōri. You can dine on any type of Japanese cuisine here and there's a pretty good selection of foreign food on offer as well. Afterwards, you'll be able to choose from an entire constellation of bars, clubs and karaoke joints. If you demand something a little more dignified, you can leave Kiyamachi and stroll over to Pontochō, an elegant and entrancing entertainment district (as long as you go there by night) positively packed with old-Japan atmosphere.

Downtown's Museum of Kyoto provides a reasonable introduction to the history of the city. Those with children will enjoy the Kaleidoscope Museum of Kyoto and those keen on Japanese pop culture will want to check out the Kyoto International Manga Museum.

The best way to get to this neighbourhood from Kyoto Station is by taking the Karasuma subway line to Karasuma-Oike Station. From here you can easily walk to all parts of the area, usually in less than 15 minutes. If you're on the east side of town (say, near the Kamo-gawa), you can take the Keihan line from the north or south to Sanjō or Shijō Stations and start your walk from there.

MUSEUM OF KYOTO Map p50

☎ 222-0888; Nakagyō-ku, Sanjō-dōri, Takakura agaru; adult/child ¥500/free, special exhibits extra; 10am-7.30pm, closed Mon; 5min walk from Karasuma-Oike Station, Karasuma subway line

Housed in and behind the former Bank of Japan, a classic brick Meiji-period building, this museum is worth a visit for those with an interest in Kyoto's long history. The regular exhibits consist of models of ancient Kyoto, audiovisual presentations and a small gallery dedicated to the city's film industry. On the 1st floor, the Roji Tempō is a reconstructed Edo-period merchant area showing 10 types of exterior lattice work. This section can be entered for free; some of the shops sell souvenirs and serve local dishes.

The museum holds special exhibits, most of which have nothing to do with Kyoto (including an exhibit on the treasures of the Ottoman Empire); however, they are often excellent. Check *Kansai Time Out* (p197) or ask at the TIC (p199) for details of upcoming shows.

KYOTO INTERNATIONAL MANGA MUSEUM Map p50

☎ 254-7414; www.kyotomm.com/english/; Karasuma-Oike; adult/child ¥500/100; 10am-8pm, closed Wed; 3min walk from Karasuma-Oike Station, Karasuma subway line

This brand new museum has a collection of some 300,000 manga (Japanese comic books). Set in an atmospheric building that used to house an elementary school, the museum is the perfect introduction to the art of manga. While most of the manga and the displays are, naturally, in Japanese, the collection of translated works is growing.

In addition to the galleries that show both the historical development of manga and original artwork done in manga style, there are beginners' workshops at weekends and opportunities to have your portrait drawn by manga artists. Visitors with children will appreciate the children's library and the humorous traditional Japanese

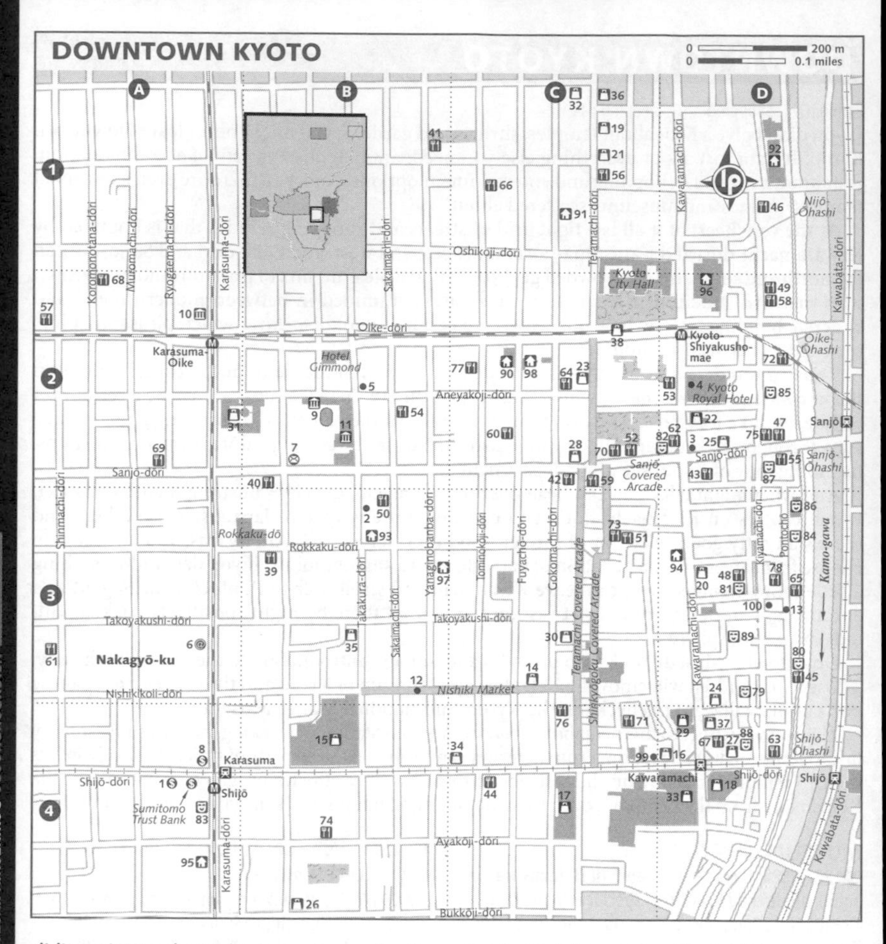

sliding picture shows (in Japanese or silent), not to mention the Astroturf lawn where the kids can run free. The museum hosts six month-long special exhibits yearly; check the website for details. While the collection is large, rest assured that it does not hold any of Japan's infamous *sukebe manga* (dirty comics) – trust us: a friend of ours has looked.

KALEIDOSCOPE MUSEUM OF KYOTO

Map p50

☎ 254-7902; Nakagyō-ku, Aneyakōji, Takakura; adult/child ¥500/free, special exhibits extra; ⏲ 10am-7.30pm, closed Mon; 3min walk from Karasuma-Oike Station, Karasuma subway line

This one-room museum is filled with unexpected wonders. Frankly, we had no idea of the variety and complexity in the field of kaleidoscopes. We don't know who will enjoy this more, children or the adults trying to keep them entertained. It's right behind the Museum of Kyoto (p49).

NISHIKI MARKET Map p50

☎ 211-3882; Nakagyō-ku, Nishiki-kōji-dōri; ⏲ most stores 9am-5pm; 5min walk from Shijō Station, Karasuma subway line

Nishiki Market (Nishiki-kōji Ichiba in Japanese) is one of Kyoto's real highlights, especially if you have an interest in cooking and eating (and we guess that you do). If you want to see all the weird and wonderful foods that go into Kyoto cuisine, this is the place. It's in the centre of town, one block north of Shijō-dōri, running west from Teramachi- dōri. It's a great place to visit on a

DOWNTOWN KYOTO

INFORMATION

Citibank シティバンク 1 A4
Honke Katsura 本家かつら 2 B3
IACE Travel IACEトラベル 3 D2
International ATM 国際ATM 4 D2
Kawara Juku
京都日本研究センター 5 B2
Kinko's キンコーズ 6 A3
Mitsui Sumitomo Bank
(SMBC Bank) 三井住友銀行 .... (see 18)
Nakagyō Post Office 中京郵便局 7 B2
Rakushi-kan 楽紙舘 .... (see 11)
UFJ Bank UFJ銀行 8 A4

SIGHTS (pp49-51)

Kaleidoscope Museum of Kyoto
京都万華鏡ミュージアム 9 B2
Kyoto International Manga Museum
京都国際マンガミュージアム 10 A2
Museum of Kyoto
京都文化博物館 11 B2
Nishiki Market 錦市場 12 B3
Pontochō 先斗町 13 D3

SHOPPING (pp105-14)

Aritsugu 有次 14 C3
Daimaru Department Store
大丸百貨店 15 B4
Erizen ゑり善 16 D4
Fujii Daimaru Department Store
藤井大丸百貨店 17 C4
Hankyū Department Store
阪急百貨店 18 D4
Ippo-dō 一保堂 19 C1
Junkudō ジュンク堂書店 20 D3
Kamiji Kakimoto 紙司柿本 21 C1
Kōjitsu Sansō 好日山荘 22 D2
Kyūkyo-dō 鳩居堂 23 C2
Matsuya 松屋 24 D3
Meidi-ya Store 明治屋 25 D2
Morita Washi 森田和紙 26 B4
Nijūsan-ya 二十三や 27 D4
Nishiharu 西春 28 C2
Nishiki Market 錦市場 .... (see 12)
OPA オーパ 29 D4
Rakushi-kan 楽紙舘 .... (see 11)
Random Walk ランダムウォーク 30 C3
Shin-Puh-Kan 新風館 31 A2
Tadashiya 唯屋 32 C1
Takashimaya Department Store
高島屋百貨店 33 D4
Tanakaya 田中彌 34 C4
Tanakaya 田中屋 35 B3
Teramachi Club 寺町倶楽部 36 C1
Tsujikura 辻倉 37 D4
Zest Underground Shopping
Arcade ゼスト御池 38 C2

EATING (pp115-38)

Anji あんじ 39 B3
Azami あざみ .... (see 11)
Biotei びお亭 40 B2
Café Bibliotec HELLO! カフェ
ビブリオティック ハロー 41 B1
Café Independants
カフェ アンデパンダン 42 C2
Cappriciosa カプリチョーザ 43 D2
Doutor Coffee ドトールコーヒー 44 C4
Fujino-ya 藤の家 45 D3
Ganko Nijō-en がんこ二条苑 46 D1
Ganko Zushi がんこ寿司 47 D2
Hati Hati ハチハチ 48 D3
Ikumatsu 幾松 49 D2
Inoda Coffee イノダコーヒー 50 B3
Kane-yo かねよ 51 C3
Katsu Kura かつくら 52 C2
Kerala ケララ 53 D2
Kōsendō-sumi 光泉洞寿み 54 B2
Kyō-Hayashiya 京はやしや 55 D2
Le Bouchon ル ブション 56 C1
Lugol ルゴール 57 A2
Merry Island Café
メリーアイランド カフェ 58 D2
Mishima-tei 三嶋亭 59 C2
Misoka-an Kawamichi-ya
晦庵河道屋 60 C2
Mukade-ya 百足屋 61 A3
Musashi Sushi むさし寿司 62 D2
Omen Nippon おめん Nippon 63 D4
Park Café パークカフェ 64 C2
Ponto-chō Uan 先斗町卯菴 65 D3
Shin-Shin Tei 新進亭 66 C1
Shirukō 志る幸 67 D4
Shizenha Restaurant Obanzai
自然派レストランおばんざい 68 A2
Somushi Kochaya 素夢子 古茶家 69 A2
Tagoto Honten 田毎本店 70 C2
Tomizushi とみ寿司 71 C4
Tōsuirō 豆水楼 72 D2
Uontana 魚棚 73 C3
Uosue うをすえ 74 B4
Veggie Table ベジテーブル 75 D2
Yak & Yeti ヤック＆イェティ 76 C4
Yoshikawa 吉川 77 C2
Zu Zu 厨厨 78 D3

ENTERTAINMENT (pp139-44)

A-Bar 居酒屋　A（あ） 79 D3
Atlantis アトランティス 80 D3
Ing イング 81 D3
Jumbo Karaoke Hiroba
ジャンボカラオケ広場 82 D2
Kyoto Cinema 京都シネマ 83 A4
Marble Room マーブルルーム 84 D3
McLoughlin's Irish Bar & Restaurant
マクラクランズ アイリッシュ
バー ＆レストラン 85 D2
Orizzonte オリゾンテ .... (see 96)
Ponto-chō Kaburen-jō Theatre
先斗町歌舞練場 86 D3
Rag ラグ .... (see 85)
Rub-a-Dub ラブアダブ 87 D2
Sekisui 積水 .... (see 92)
World ワールド 88 D4
Zappa ザッパ 89 D3

SLEEPING (pp145-56)

Hiiragiya Ryokan 柊屋旅館 90 C2
Hiiragiya Ryokan Annexe
柊屋旅館別館 91 C1
Hotel Fujita Kyoto
ホテルフジタ京都 92 D1
Hotel Matsui ホテル松井 93 B3
Hotel Unizo ホテルユニゾ 94 D3
Karasuma Kyoto Hotel
からすま京都ホテル 95 A4
Kyoto Hotel Ōkura
京都ホテルオークラ 96 D2
Matsui Honkan 松井本館 97 B3
Tawaraya Ryokan 俵屋旅館 98 C2

TRANSPORT (pp181-9)

Discount Ticket Shop
格安きっぷ売り場 99 C4
Pontochō Bicycle Parking Lot
先斗町駐車場 100 D3

rainy day or as a break from temple-hopping. The variety of foods on display is staggering and the frequent cries of *'Irasshaimase'* ('Welcome!') are heart-warming.

PONTOCHŌ Map p50

Nakagyō-ku; 2min walk from Kawaramachi Station, Hankyū line

There are few streets in Asia that rival this narrow pedestrian-only walkway for atmosphere. Not much to look at by day, the street comes alive by night, with wonderful lanterns, traditional wooden exteriors and elegant Kyotoites disappearing into the doorways of elite old restaurants and bars.

Once the city's red-light district, Pontochō is located between the Kamo-gawa and Kiyamachi-dōri. Many of the restaurants and teahouses can be difficult to enter, but a number of reasonably priced, accessible places can be found. Even if you have no intention of patronising one of the businesses here, it makes a nice stroll in the evening, perhaps combined with a walk in nearby Gion.

Pontochō is also a great place to spot geisha and *maiko* (apprentice geisha) making their way between appointments, especially on weekend evenings at the Shijō-dōri end of the street.

CENTRAL KYOTO

Eating p127; Shopping p111; Sleeping p150

Central Kyoto is not really one distinct neighbourhood but a collection of neighbourhoods. The area comprises the entire middle of the city (excepting Downtown Kyoto and the Kyoto Station area), including the traditional heart of Kyoto – the Kyoto Imperial Palace and the lovely park that surrounds it. To the north you'll find Shimogamo-jinja, a fine temple in a forest setting, and to the south the lovely Tō-ji, one of Kyoto's oldest temples. Central Kyoto is also home to Daitoku-ji, a self-contained world of Zen temples, gardens and lanes.

While there are some decent hotels in Central Kyoto and plenty of good restaurants, it's not really an area where one would hang out. You're more likely to visit to see a specific sight or to eat at a specific restaurant.

The best way to reach and explore Central Kyoto is by using the city's extensive bus network. Some of the area's best attractions are located on or near the Karasuma subway line, however, including the Kyoto Imperial Palace and surrounding park, Kyoto Botanical Gardens and Daitoku-ji.

KYOTO IMPERIAL PALACE Map pp54–5

☎ 211-1215; Kamigyō-ku, Kyoto gyōen 3; admission free; 10min walk from Imadegawa Station, Karasuma subway line

The Kyoto Imperial Palace (Kyoto Gosho) is the heart of Kyoto, both spatially and metaphorically. It was built in 794 and has undergone numerous rebirths after destruction by fires. The present building, on a different site and smaller than the original, was constructed in 1855. Ceremonies related to the enthronement of a new emperor and other state functions are still held here.

The Shinsen-den (Ceremonial Hall) is an outstanding, single-storey structure thatched with a cypress-bark roof. Covered walkways connect it to the surrounding buildings. From outside you can see the *takamikura* (throne) where the emperor sat on formal occasions. It is covered with a silk canopy and on each side are stands to hold treasures such as swords, jewels and other imperial regalia. Just in front of the throne are two wooden *koma-inu* (mythological animals guarding Shintō shrines). The palace is full of other treasures, including priceless sliding screens adorned with Tosa school paintings. Though the hall initially was used as living quarters for the emperor, it was later set aside for ceremonial use only.

Twice-yearly, in spring and autumn, the palace grounds are chock-full when the inner sanctum is opened to the public for several days. Otherwise, it is necessary to visit as part of a guided tour (see the boxed text, p57). The tour guide will elaborate in English while you are led for about one hour past the Shishin-den, Ko Gosho (Small Palace), Tsune Gosho (Regular Palace) and Oike-niwa (Pond Garden). Regrettably, it is forbidden to enter any of these buildings.

SENTŌ GOSHO Map pp54–5

☎ 211-1215; Kamigyō-ku, Kyoto gyōen; 10min walk from Imadegawa Station, Karasuma subway line

A few hundred metres southeast of the Imperial Palace is the Sentō Gosho. It was originally constructed in 1630 during the reign of Emperor Go-Mizunō as a residence for retired emperors. The palace was repeatedly destroyed by fire and reconstructed; it continued to serve its purpose until a final blaze in 1854, after which it was never rebuilt. Today only two structures, the Seika-tei and Yūshin-tei teahouses, remain. The magnificent gardens, laid out in 1630 by renowned landscape designer Kobori Enshū, are the main attraction.

Visitors must obtain advance permission from the Imperial Household Agency (see p57) and be more than 20 years old. One-hour tours (in Japanese) start daily at 11am and 1.30pm.

KYOTO IMPERIAL PALACE PARK Map pp54–5

☎ 211-6348; Kamigyō-ku, Kyoto gyōen 3; 8min walk from Imadegawa Station, Karasuma subway line

The Imperial Palace is surrounded by a spacious park with a welcome landscape of trees and open lawn – it's Kyoto's very own Central Park. It's perfect for picnics, strolls and just about any sport that doesn't require retrieving balls over walls. Best of all, it's free. Take some time to visit the pond at the park's southern end, with its gaping carp. The park is most beautiful in the plum- and cherry-blossom seasons (early March and early April, respectively). It is bounded by Teramachi-dōri and Karasuma-dōri on the east and west, and by Imadegawa-dōri and Marutamachi-dōri on the north and south.

DAITOKU-JI Map pp54–5

☎ 491-0019; Kita-ku, Murasakino, Daitokuji-chō 53; admission free; ⏰ dawn to dusk; 🚇 15min walk from exit 2, Kitaōji Station, Karasuma subway line

Daitoku-ji is a separate world within Kyoto – a world of Zen temples, perfectly raked gardens and wandering lanes. It is one of the most rewarding destinations in this part of the city, particularly for those with an interest in Japanese gardens.

Daitoku-ji, the headquarters of the Rinzai Daitoku-ji school, contains an extensive complex of 24 subtemples – including Daisen-in (below), Kōtō-in (right), Obai-in (p56), Ryōgen-in (p56) and Zuihō-in (p56). If you want an intensive look at Zen culture, this is the place to visit.

The eponymous Daitoku-ji is on the eastern side of the grounds. It was founded in 1319, burnt down in the next century and rebuilt in the 16th century. The San-mon gate (1589) has a self-carved statue of its erector, the famous tea-master Sen no Rikyū, on its 2nd storey.

Some sources say that Toyotomi Hideyoshi was so angry when he discovered he'd been demeaning himself by walking under Rikyū's effigy that he forced the master to commit *seppuku* (ritual suicide) in 1591.

If you enter from the main gate, which is on the east side of the complex, you will soon after find Daitoku-ji on your right.

DAISEN-IN Map pp54–5

☎ 491-8346; Kita-ku, Murasakino, Daitokuji-chō 54-1; admission ¥400; ⏰ 9am-5pm Mar-Nov, to 4.30pm Dec-Feb; 🚇 15min walk from exit 2, Kitaōji Station, Karasuma subway line

The two small Zen gardens in this subtemple of Daitoku-ji (above) are elegant examples of 17th-century *karesansui* (dry-landscape rock garden) style. Here the trees, rocks and sand are said to represent and express various spectacles of nature, from waterfalls and valleys to mountain lakes. It's one of the more popular subtemples here, but not as rewarding as Kōtō-in (below) or Obai-in (p56).

top picks

IT'S FREE

A quick glance through the pages of this chapter might convince you that sightseeing in Kyoto is going to require taking out a second mortgage on your home. Luckily, there are plenty of free things you can do. Indeed, you could fill at least a week with activities that cost you absolutely nothing. Here are just a few:

- Temples There is no charge to enter the grounds of many of Kyoto's temples, including Nanzen-ji (p66), Chion-in (p65), Hōnen-in (p71) and Tōfuku-ji (p59).
- Shrines Almost all shrines in Kyoto can be entered free of charge. A few good ones include Fushimi-Inari-Taisha (p59), Heian-jingū (p72), Yasaka-jinja (p64) and Shimogamo-jinja (p56).
- Kyoto Imperial Palace Park (opposite) Kyoto's Central Park is a treasure that many visitors overlook.
- Kamo-gawa (Map pp54–5) Like the Imperial Palace Park, this is a great place to spend a relaxing afternoon strolling and picnicking. In the summer you'll be treated to free fireworks shows as local youths hold impromptu *hanabi-taikai* (fireworks festivals).
- Nishiki Market (p50) It costs nothing to wander through this wonderful market. Of course, you might find something that you just *have* to buy…
- Kyoto Station (p45) Kyoto's station building is pretty impressive, and the view from the rooftop observatory is the best you'll get – short of paying to ascend Kyoto Tower or expending the energy to climb Daimonji-yama.
- Festivals (p15) There's nothing like a colourful Kyoto festival, and they're always free. If you're lucky, you might even be asked to participate.
- Hikes (p144) It doesn't cost anything to enjoy Kyoto's natural beauty. There are myriad hikes in the mountains that surround the city.
- Imperial Properties The Kyoto Imperial Palace (opposite), Shūgaku-in Rikyū Imperial Villa (p58) and Katsura Rikyū Imperial Villa (p89) can all be toured free of charge.

KŌTŌ-IN Map pp54–5

☎ 492-0068; Kita-ku, Murasakino, Daitokuji-chō 73-1; admission ¥400; ⏰ 9am-4.30pm; 🚇 20min walk from exit 2, Kitaōji Station, Karasuma subway line

On the far western edge of the Daitoku-ji (left) complex (you may have to ask directions

CENTRAL KYOTO

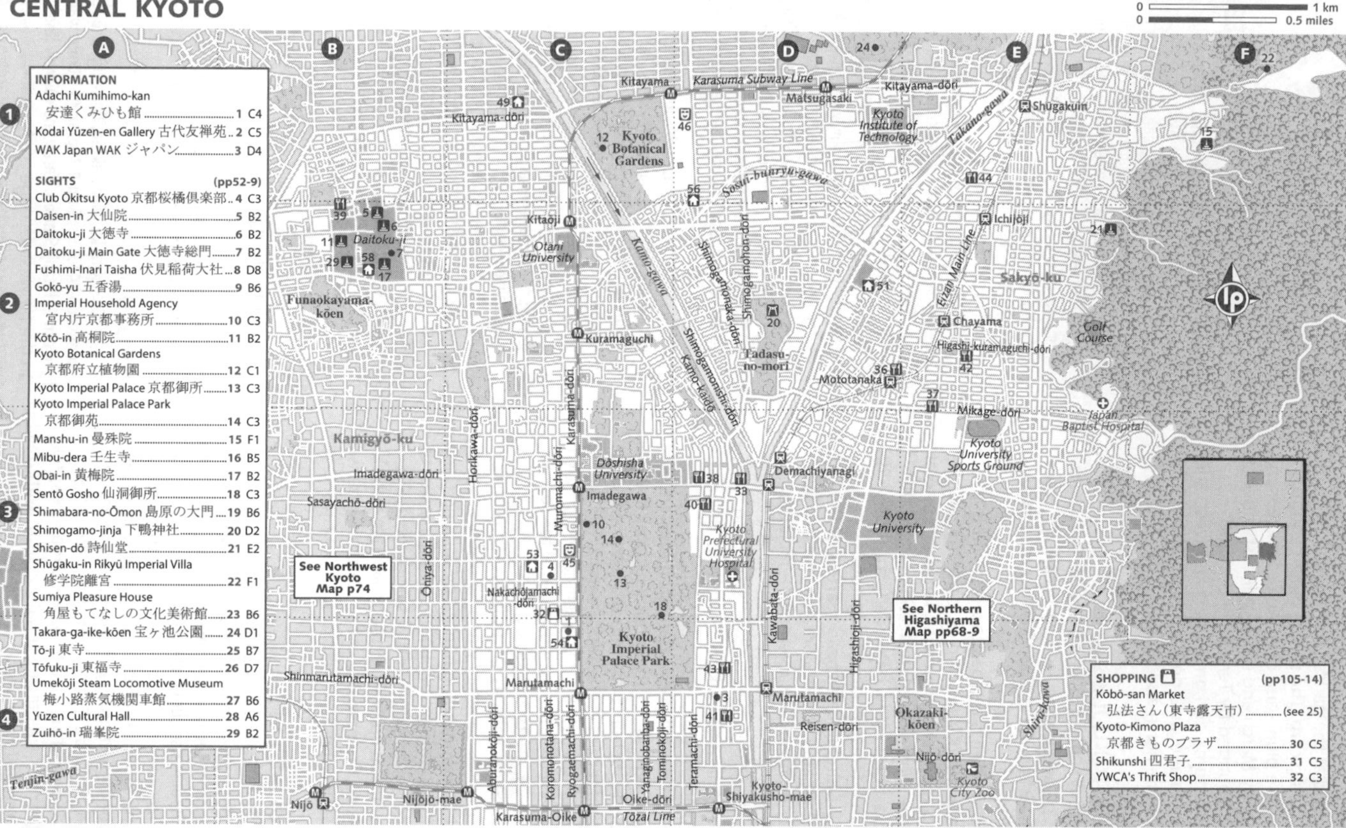

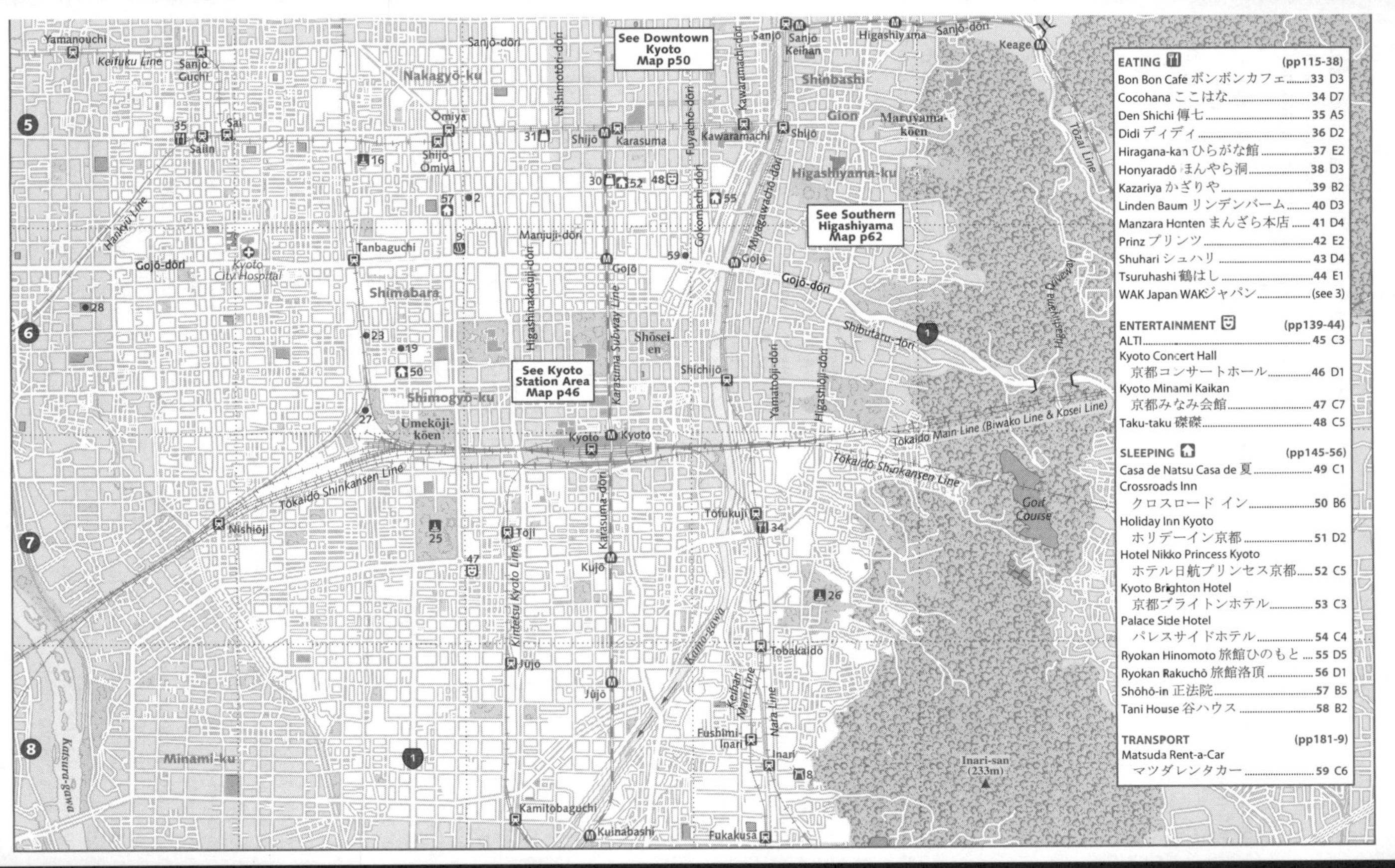
EATING (pp115-38)
Bon Bon Cafe ボンボンカフェ 33 D3
Cocohana ここはな 34 D7
Den Shichi 傳七 35 A5
Didi ディディ 36 D2
Hiragana-kan ひらがな館 37 E2
Honyaradō ほんやら洞 38 D3
Kazariya かざりや 39 B2
Linden Baum リンデンバーム 40 D3
Manzara Honten まんざら本店 41 D4
Prinz プリンツ 42 E2
Shuhari シュハリ 43 D4
Tsuruhashi 鶴はし 44 E1
WAK Japan WAKジャパン (see 3)
ENTERTAINMENT (pp139-44)
ALTI 45 C3
Kyoto Concert Hall
京都コンサートホール 46 D1
Kyoto Minami Kaikan
京都みなみ会館 47 C7
Taku-taku 磔磔 48 C5
SLEEPING (pp145-56)
Casa de Natsu Casa de 夏 49 C1
Crossroads Inn
クロスロード イン 50 B6
Holiday Inn Kyoto
ホリデーイン京都 51 D2
Hotel Nikko Princess Kyoto
ホテル日航プリンセス京都 52 C5
Kyoto Brighton Hotel
京都ブライトンホテル 53 C3
Palace Side Hotel
パレスサイドホテル 54 C4
Ryokan Hinomoto 旅館ひのもと 55 D5
Ryokan Rakuchō 旅館洛頂 56 D1
Shōhō-in 正法院 57 B5
Tani House 谷ハウス 58 B2
TRANSPORT (pp181-9)
Matsuda Rent-a-Car
マツダレンタカー 59 C6
See Downtown Kyoto Map p50
See Southern Higashiyama Map p62
See Kyoto Station Area Map p46
Sanjō-dōri
Nishimotoi-dōri
Nakagyō-ku
Shinbashi
Gion
Maruyama-kōen
Higashiyama-ku
Shimogyō-ku
Minami-ku
Shimabara
Umekōji-kōen
Shōsei-en
Gojō-dōri
Manjuji-dōri
Higashinakasuji-dōri
Karasuma Subway Line
Karasuma-dōri
Fuyachō-dōri
Gokomachi-dōri
Kawaramachi-dōri
Miyagawachō-dōri
Yamatooji-dōri
Higashioji-dōri
Shibutaru-dōri
Higashiyama Driveway
Tōzai Line
Hankyū Line
Keifuku Line
Kintetsu Kyoto Line
Tōkaidō Main Line (Biwako Line & Kosei Line)
Tōkaidō Shinkansen Line
Keihan Main Line
Nara Line
Kamo-gawa
Katsura-gawa
Golf Course
Inari-san (233m)
Kyoto City Hospital
Yamanouchi
Sanjo Guchi
Sai
Saiin
Ōmiya
Shijō-Ōmiya
Tanbaguchi
Shijō
Karasuma
Kawaramachi
Sanjō
Sanjō Keihan
Higashiyama
Keage
Gojō
Kyoto
Shichijō
Nishiōji
Tōji
Kujō
Jūjō
Tōfukuji
Tobakaidō
Fushimi-Inari
Inari
Kamitobaguchi
Kuinabashi
Fukakusa

to find it), this sublime garden is one of the best in all Kyoto and it's worth a special trip. It's located within a fine bamboo grove that you traverse via a moss-lined path. Once inside there is a small stroll garden which leads to the centrepiece: a rectangle of moss and maple trees, backed by bamboo. Take some time on the veranda here to soak it all up.

ZUIHŌ-IN Map pp54–5

☎ 491-1454; Kita-ku, Murasakino, Daitokuji-chō; admission ¥400; 9am-5pm; 20min walk from exit 2, Kitaōji Station, Karasuma subway line

Another subtemple of Daitoku-ji (p53), Zuihō-in enshrines the 16th-century Christian *daimyō* (domain lord) Ōtomo Sōrin. In the early 1960s, a landscape architect named Shigemori Misuzu rearranged the stones in the back rock garden into the shape of a crucifix! More interesting is the main rock garden, which is raked into appealing patterns that remind one of water ripples. It's roughly in the middle of the complex; once again, you may have to ask for directions.

OBAI-IN Map pp54–5

☎ 491-1454; Kita-ku, Murasakino, Daitokuji-chō; admission ¥400; 9am-5pm 6-31 Oct & 13 Nov-9 Dec; 20min walk from exit 2, Kitaōji Station, Karasuma subway line

If you are lucky enough to be in Kyoto during autumn when this subtemple of Daitoku-ji (p53) is opened to the public, then you should make an effort to visit. The subtemple is a world of interlinked gardens, including an incredibly rich moss garden and a starkly simple *karesansui*. Along with nearby Kōtō-in (p53), we rank this as one of the finest gardens in Kyoto. When you enter the Daitoku-ji complex via the east (main) gate, it's on the left.

RYŌGEN-IN Map pp54–5

☎ 491-7635; Kita-ku, Murasakino, Daitokuji-chō; admission ¥400; 9am-5pm; walk from exit 2, Kitaōji Station, Karasuma subway line

Ryōgen-in is yet another fine subtemple in the Daitoku-ji (p53) complex. It's got two pleasing gardens, one moss and one *karesansui*. The *karesansui* has an interesting island in its midst that invites lazy contemplation. When you enter the Daitoku-ji complex via the east (main) gate, it's on the left, just before Obai-in (above).

SHIMOGAMO-JINJA Map pp54–5

☎ 781-0010; Sakyō-ku, Shimogamo Izumigawa-chō 59; admission free; 6am-6pm; 1min walk from Shimogamo-jinja-mae bus stop, bus 205 from Kyoto Station

A long strip of forest sandwiched between the two rivers in the north of the city, Shimogamo-jinja is, like the Kyoto Imperial Palace Park, a good place to go when you need some space and greenery. While it's not worth a special trip, it's a nice place for a stroll if you find yourself in this part of town.

Shimogamo-jinja dates from the 8th century and is a Unesco World Heritage site. The shrine itself is approached along a shady path through the lovely Tadasu-no-mori. This wooded area is said to be a place where lies cannot be concealed and is considered a prime location to sort out disputes.

The shrine is dedicated to the god of harvest. Traditionally, pure water was drawn from the nearby rivers for purification and agricultural ceremonies. The Hondō dates from 1863 and, like the Haiden hall at its sister shrine, Kamigamo-jinja (p91), is an excellent example of *nagare*-style shrine architecture.

KYOTO BOTANICAL GARDENS Map pp54–5

☎ 701-0141; Sakyō-ku, Shimogamohangi-chō; adult ¥200, child ¥80-150; 9am-5pm; 2min walk from Kitayama Station, Karasuma subway line

One of Kyoto's most underappreciated sights, this vast garden, opened in 1914, occupies 240,000 sq metres and features 12,000 plants, flowers and trees. It is pleasant to stroll through the rose, cherry and herb gardens or view the rows of camphor trees and the large tropical greenhouse (adult ¥200). Pack a picnic and bring a Frisbee or a ball to toss and you've got the makings of a very pleasant afternoon on a warm day in Kyoto.

SUMIYA PLEASURE HOUSE Map pp54–5

☎ 351-0024; Shimogyō-ku, Nishishinyashikiageya-chō 32; adult ¥1000, child ¥500-800; 10am-4pm, closed Mon; 7min walk from JR Tanbaguchi Station; 10min walk from Umekōji-kōen-mae bus stop, bus 205 from Kyoto Station

Shimabara, a district northwest of Kyoto Station, was Kyoto's original pleasure quarters. At its peak during the Edo period

RESERVATIONS & ADMISSION TO KYOTO'S IMPERIAL PROPERTIES

Permission to visit the Kyoto Imperial Palace (p52) is granted by the Kunaichō – the Imperial Household Agency (Map pp54–5; ☎ 211-1215; Kunaicho, Kyoto Jimusho; 8.45am-noon & 1-4pm Mon-Fri, closed holidays), which is inside the walled park surrounding the palace, a short walk from Imadegawa Station on the Karasuma line. You have to fill out an application form and show your passport. Children can visit if accompanied by adults more than 20 years of age but are forbidden entry to the other three imperial properties of Katsura Rikyū (p89), Sentō Gosho (p52) and Shūgaku-in Rikyū (p58). Permission to tour the palace is usually granted the same day (try to arrive at the office at least 30 minutes before the start of the tour you'd like to join). Guided tours, sometimes in English, are given at 10am and 2pm from Monday to Friday. The tour lasts about 50 minutes.

The Imperial Household Agency is also the place to make advance reservations to see the Sentō Gosho, Katsura Rikyū and Shūgaku-in Rikyū.

(1600–1867) the area flourished, with more than 20 enormous *ageya* – magnificent banquet halls where artists, writers and statesmen gathered in a 'floating world' ambience of conversation, art and fornication. Geisha were often sent from their *okiya* (living quarters) to entertain patrons at these restaurant-cum-brothels. By the start of the Meiji period, however, such activities had drifted north to the Gion district and Shimabara had lost its prominence.

Though the traditional air of the district has dissipated, a few old structures remain. The tremendous Shimabara-no-Ōmon (Map pp54–5) gate, which marked the passage into the quarter, still stands, as does the Sumiya Pleasure House, the last remaining *ageya,* which is now designated a National Cultural Asset. Built in 1641, this stately two-storey, 20-room structure allows a rare glimpse into Edo-era nirvana. With a delicate latticework exterior, Sumiya has a huge open kitchen and an extensive series of rooms (including one extravagantly decorated with mother-of-pearl inlay).

Special tours in Japanese (requiring advance reservations in Japanese, booked through Sumiya Pleasure House) allow access to the 2nd storey and are conducted daily. An English pamphlet is provided, but you might want to consider arranging a volunteer guide through the TIC (p199).

MIBU-DERA Map pp54–5

☎ 841-3381; Nakagyō-ku, Bōjō, Bukkō-ji Kita iru; admission free; 8.30am-4.30pm; 10min walk from Ōmiya Station, Hankyū line

Mibu-dera was founded in 991 and belongs to the Risshū school. In the late Edo period, it became a training centre for samurai. Mibu-dera houses tombs of pro-shōgunate Shinsen-gumi members, who fought bloody street battles resisting the forces that succeeded in restoring the emperor in 1868. Except for an unusual stupa covered in Jizō statues, visually the temple is of limited interest. It is, however, definitely worth visiting during Mibu *kyōgen* (comic drama) performances in late April, or the Setsubun (p15) celebrations in early February.

TŌ-JI Map pp54–5

☎ 691-3325; Minami-ku, Kujō-chō 1; adult ¥500, child ¥300-400; 8.30am-4.30pm; 15min walk from Kyoto Station

One of the main sights south of Kyoto Station, Tō-ji is an appealing complex of halls and a fantastic pagoda that makes a fine backdrop for the monthly flea market held on the grounds.

This temple was established in 794 by imperial decree to protect the city. In 823 the emperor handed it over to Kūkai (known posthumously as Kōbō Daishi), the founder of the Shingon school of Buddhism. Many of the temple buildings were destroyed by fire or fighting during the 15th century, and most of the remaining buildings were destroyed in the Momoyama period.

The Nandai-mon (Main Gate) was moved here in 1894 from Sanjūsangen-dō (p60) in Southern Higashiyama. The Kōdō (Lecture Hall) dates from the 1600s and contains 21 images representing a Mikkyō (esoteric Buddhist) mandala. The Kondō (Main Hall), rebuilt in 1606, combines Chinese, Indian and Japanese architectural styles and contains statues depicting the Yakushi (Healing Buddha) trinity. In the southern part of the garden stands the gojū-no-tō, a five-storey pagoda which, despite having burnt down five times, was doggedly rebuilt in 1643. Standing at 57m, it is now the highest pagoda in Japan.

The Kōbō-san market fair is held here on the 21st of each month. There is also a regular market that runs on the first Sunday of each month.

UMEKŌJI STEAM LOCOMOTIVE MUSEUM Map pp54–5

☎ 314-2996; Shimogyō-ku, Kannon-ji-chō; museum adult/child ¥400/100, train ride adult/child ¥200/100; 9.30am-5pm, closed Mon; 15min walk from Kyoto Station

A hit with steam-train buffs and kids, this excellent museum features 18 vintage steam locomotives (dating from 1914 to 1948) and related displays. It is in the former JR Nijō Station building, which was recently relocated here and thoughtfully reconstructed. You can take a 10-minute ride on one of the smoke-spewing choo-choos (departures at 11am, 1.30pm and 3.30pm).

SHISEN-DŌ Map pp54–5

☎ 781-2954; Sakyō-ku, Ichijōji, Monguchi-chō 27; adult ¥500, child ¥200-400; 9am-5pm; 5min walk from Ichijōji-kudari-matsu-machi bus stop, bus 5 from Kyoto Station

Most travellers to Kyoto don't venture beyond Ginkaku-ji (p71) when exploring the northern reaches of Higashiyama, but there are several other worthwhile temples in this part of town, including Shisen-dō and Manshu-in (right). These two temples make a nice combination and are usually ignored by the masses who descend on Kyoto's more popular temples. Note that it's too far to walk here from Ginkaku-ji; consider a taxi or the bus.

With a name meaning 'house of poet-hermits', Shisen-dō was built in 1641 by Ishikawa Jōzan, a scholar of Chinese classics and a landscape architect who wanted a place to retire to. Formerly a samurai, Jōzan abandoned his warrior status after a rift with Tokugawa Ieyasu and became a recluse, living here until his death in 1672 at the age of 90.

The hermitage is noted for its display of poems and portraits of 36 ancient Chinese poets, which can be found in the Shisen-no-ma room.

The *karesansui* white-sand garden is lined with azaleas, which are said to represent islands in the sea. The garden also reflects Jōzan's distinct taste for Chinese aesthetics. It's a tranquil place to relax.

In the garden, water flows from a small waterfall to the *shishi-odoshi*, or *sōzu*, a device designed to scare away wild boar and deer. It's made from a bamboo pipe into which water slowly trickles, fills up and swings down to empty. On the upswing to its original position the bamboo strikes a stone with a 'thwack' – just loud enough to interrupt your snooze – before starting to refill.

MANSHU-IN Map pp54–5

☎ 781-5010; Sakyō-ku, Ichijōji, Takenouchi-chō 42; adult ¥500, child ¥300-400; 9am-4.30pm; 20min walk from Shūgakuin Station, Eizan line

About 30 minutes' walk north of Shisen-dō (left) you'll reach the stately gate of Manshu-in, a popular retreat of former emperors and a great escape from the crowds. The temple was originally founded by Saichō on Hiei-zan (p91) but was relocated here at the beginning of the Edo period by Ryōshōhō, the son of Prince Hachijōnomiya Tomohito (who built Katsura Rikyū; p89).

The graceful temple architecture is often compared with Katsura Rikyū for its detailed woodwork and rare works of art, such as *fusuma-e* sliding doors painted by Kanō Eitoku, a famed artist of the Momoyama period. The *karesansui* garden by Kobori Enshū features a sea of gravel intended to symbolise the flow of a waterfall and stone islands representing cranes and turtles.

SHŪGAKU-IN RIKYŪ IMPERIAL VILLA Map pp54–5

☎ 211-1215; Sakyō-ku, Shūgakuin, Yabusoe; admission free; 10min walk from Shūgakuinrikyū-michi bus stop, bus 5 from Kyoto Station

Lying at the foot of Hiei-zan (p91), this superb villa was begun in the 1650s by Emperor Go-Mizunō, following his abdication; work was continued by his daughter Akeno-miya after his death in 1680. It was designed as a lavish summer retreat for the imperial family. The gardens here, with their views down over the city of Kyoto, are worth the trouble it takes to visit.

The villa grounds are divided into three enormous garden areas on a hillside – lower, middle and upper. Each has superb tea-ceremony houses: the upper, Kami-no-chaya, and lower, Shimo-no-chaya, were completed in 1659, and the middle teahouse, Naka-no-chaya, was completed in 1682. The gardens' reputation rests on their ponds, pathways and impressive use of *shakkei* (borrowed scenery) in the form of the surrounding hills. The view from Kami-no-chaya is particularly impressive.

One-hour tours (in Japanese) start at 9am, 10am, 11am, 1.30pm and 3pm; try to arrive early. A basic leaflet in English is provided and more detailed literature is for sale in the tour waiting room.

You must make reservations through the Imperial Household Agency – usually several weeks in advance. See the boxed text, p57, for details.

TAKARA-GA-IKE-KŌEN Map pp54–5

Sakyō-ku, Iwakura, Matsugasaki; 10min walk from exit 5, Kokusaikaikan Station, Karasuma subway line

This expansive park is an excellent place for a stroll or picnic in natural surroundings. Far from the throngs in the city centre, it is a popular place for bird-watching and has spacious gardens. There is a 1.8km loop around the main pond, where rowing boats can be hired for ¥1000 per hour.

In the northeast of the park, the Kyoto International Conference Hall (Map pp42–3) is an unfortunate attempt at replicating Japan's traditional thatched-roof *gasshō-zukuri* style in concrete. Behind the conference hall, the Hosho-an Teahouse (designed by Soshitsu Sen, Grand Tea-Master XV of the Urasenke school) is worth a look.

TŌFUKU-JI Map pp54–5

561-0087; Higashiyama-ku, Honmachi 15-778; admission main temple/subtemples/grounds ¥400/400/free; 9am-4pm Dec-Oct, 8.30am-4.30pm Nov; 1min walk from Tōfuku-ji bus stop, bus 202, 207 or 208 from Kyoto Station; 15min walk from Tōfuku-ji Station (local train only stop), Keihan line

Tōfuku-ji stands at the heart of a world of Zen temples and subtemples. It's one of our favourite temples in Kyoto and it's usually quite peaceful, except in the November autumn-foliage season, when it becomes so crowded that we give it a miss.

Founded in 1236 by the priest Enni, Tōfuku-ji belongs to the Rinzai school. Since this temple was intended to compete with Tōdai-ji (p158) and Kōfuku-ji (p160) in Nara, it was given a name combining characters in each of these.

This impressive temple complex is considered one of the five main Zen temples in Kyoto. The huge San-mon gate is the oldest Zen main gate in Japan. The Hōjō (Garden Hall) was reconstructed in 1890. The gardens, laid out in 1938, are well worth a visit. The northern garden has stones and moss neatly arranged in a chequerboard pattern.

FUSHIMI-INARI-TAISHA Map pp54–5

641-7331; Fushimi-ku, Fukakusa Yabunouchi-chō 68; admission free; dawn to dusk; 1min walk from Inari Station, JR Nara line, or 1min walk from Fushimi-Inari Station, Keihan line

With seemingly endless arcades of vermilion *torii* (shrine gates) spread across a thickly wooded mountain, this vast shrine complex is a world unto its own. It is, quite simply, one of the most impressive and memorable sights in all of Kyoto.

The shrine was dedicated to the gods of rice and sake by the Hata family in the 8th century. As the role of agriculture diminished, deities were enrolled to ensure prosperity in business. Nowadays, the shrine is one of Japan's most popular, and is the head shrine for some 40,000 Inari shrines scattered the length and breadth of the country.

The entire complex, consisting of five shrines, sprawls across the wooded slopes of Inari-san. A pathway wanders 4km up the mountain and is lined with hundreds of red *torii*. There are also dozens of stone foxes. The fox is considered the messenger of Inari, the god of cereals, and the stone foxes, too, are often referred to as Inari. The key often seen in the fox's mouth is for the rice granary. On an incidental note, the Japanese traditionally see the fox as a sacred, somewhat mysterious figure capable of 'possessing' humans – the favoured point of entry is under the fingernails.

The walk around the upper precincts of the shrine is a pleasant day hike. It also makes for a very eerie stroll in the late afternoon and early evening, when the various graveyards and miniature shrines along the path take on a mysterious air. It's best to go with a friend at this time.

On 8 April there's a Sangyō-sai festival with offerings and dances to ensure prosperity for national industry. During the first few days in January, thousands of believers visit this shrine as their *hatsu-mōde* (first shrine visit of the new year) to pray for good fortune.

SOUTHERN HIGASHIYAMA

Eating p129; Shopping p111; Sleeping p152

Southern Higashiyama, the area at the base of the Higashiyama Mountains, is rivalled only by Northern Higashiyama as the richest area in Kyoto for sightseeing. It is thick with temples, shrines, museums, traditional neighbourhoods and shops; the incredible sights range from Sanjūsangen-dō in the south to Shōren-in in the north. Once you ascend above the main artery of the area, Higashiōji-dōri (also known as Higashiyama-dōri), you will find that the area is very pleasant to explore on foot. There are many lovely little streets and pedestrian-only walkways, as well as parks and expansive temple grounds. All in all, you should consider making this the first area you seek out once you get settled in Kyoto. It has ample scope for several days of relaxed exploration.

Southern Higashiyama is also a great place to stay and many of Kyoto's traditional ryokan are located here. It's close enough to Downtown or Kyoto Station so that you certainly won't feel isolated.

With the exception of the rollicking Gion entertainment district, Southern Higashiyama is not particularly rich in restaurants or nightlife. Most of the restaurants here are for the purpose of serving tourists lunch as they make their way along the main tourist track. That isn't to say that they're not good; it's just that Kyoto's best dining and nightlife options are mostly downtown.

We start our coverage of the area at its southern end and work north, but it is possible, of course, to cover this area from north to south, or any direction you please. Note that the more northerly of the Higashiyama attractions, such as Ginkaku-ji and the Tetsugaku-no-Michi (Path of Philosophy) are covered under Northern Higashiyama (p66).

The best way to get to Southern Higashiyama from Kyoto Station is by taking the Karasuma subway line to Karasuma-Oike Station, switching to the Tōzai subway line for either Keage or Higashiyama Stations and walking south into the district. You can also take a variety of city buses to the area, including 206 and 207 from Kyoto Station. If you're near the Kamo-gawa, the Keihan line links to Sanjō and Shijō Stations. Once in the area, the best way to get around is on foot.

SANJŪSANGEN-DŌ Map p62

☎ 525-0033; Higashiyama-ku, Sanjūsangendōmawari-chō 657; adult ¥600, child ¥300-400; 8am-5pm in summer, 9am-4pm in winter; 1min walk from Hakubutsukan/ Sanjūsangendō-mae bus stop, bus 206 or 208 from Kyoto Station; 10min walk from Shichijō Station, Keihan line

The sheer number of Buddhist images at this temple make it among the more interesting and visually arresting sights in Kyoto. It makes a logical starting point to a full-day exploration of Southern Higashiyama.

The original temple, called Rengeō-in, was built in 1164 at the request of the retired emperor Go-shirakawa. After it burnt to the ground in 1249, a faithful copy was constructed in 1266.

The temple's name refers to the 33 *sanjūsan* (bays) between the pillars of this long, narrow building. The building houses 1001 wooden statues of Kannon (the Buddhist goddess of mercy); the chief image, the 1000-armed Senjū-Kannon, was carved by the celebrated sculptor Tankei in 1254. It is flanked by 500 smaller Kannon images, neatly lined in rows.

There are an awful lot of arms, but if you are picky and think the 1000-armed statues don't have the required number, you should remember to calculate according to the nifty Buddhist mathematical formula, which holds that 40 arms are the equivalent of 1000 because each saves 25 worlds.

At the back of the hall are 28 guardian statues in a variety of expressive poses. The gallery at the western side of the hall is famous for the annual Tōshiya (p15) festival, held on 15 January, when archers shoot arrows along the length of the hall. The ceremony dates from the Edo period, when an annual contest was held to see how many arrows could be shot from the southern to northern end in 24 hours. The all-time record was set in 1686, when an archer successfully landed more than 8000 arrows at the northern end.

KYOTO NATIONAL MUSEUM Map p62

☎ 531-7509; Higashiyama-ku, Chaya-chō 527; adult ¥500 (special exhibits extra), child free-¥130;

9.30am-5pm, closed Mon; 1min walk from Hakubutsukan/Sanjūsangendō-mae bus stop, bus 206 or 208 from Kyoto Station; 10min walk from Shichijō Station, Keihan line**

The Kyoto National Museum is the site for some of Kyoto's most important special art exhibitions. It was founded in 1895 as an imperial repository for art and treasures from local temples and shrines. It is housed in two buildings opposite Sanjūsangen-dō (opposite) temple. There are 17 rooms with displays of more than 1000 artworks, historical artefacts and handicrafts. The permanent collection is excellent but somewhat poorly displayed; unless you have a particular interest in Japanese traditional arts, we recommend visiting this museum only when a special exhibition is on.

KAWAI KANJIRŌ MEMORIAL HALL Map p62

561-3585; Higashiyama-ku, Gojō-zaka, Kanei-chō 569; adult/child ¥900/free; 10am-4.30pm, closed Mon; 3min walk from Umamachi bus stop, bus 206 from Kyoto Station

This small memorial hall is one of Kyoto's most commonly overlooked little gems; it's worth a look, though, especially if you have an interest in Japanese crafts such as pottery and furniture. The hall was the home and workshop of one of Japan's most famous potters, Kawai Kanjirō (1890–1966). The 1937 house is built in rural style and contains examples of Kanjirō's work, his collection of folk art and ceramics, and his workshop and a fascinating *nobori-gama* (a stepped kiln). The museum is near the intersection of Gojō-dōri and Higashiōji-dōri.

ROKUHARAMITSU-JI Map p62

561-6980; Higashiyama-ku, Gojō-dōri-Yamatoōji agaru Higashi; treasure house adult ¥500, child ¥300-400; 8am-5pm; 5min walk from Kiyomizu-michi bus stop, bus 206 from Kyoto Station

An important Buddhist pilgrimage stop, this temple was founded in 963 by Kūya Shōnin, who carved an image of an 11-headed Kannon and installed it in the temple in the hope of stopping a plague that was ravaging Kyoto at the time.

The temple itself is unremarkable but the treasure house at the rear contains a rare collection of 15 fantastic statues; the most intriguing is a standing likeness of Kūya, staff in hand and prayer gong draped around his neck, with a string of tiny figurines parading from his gums. Legend holds that while praying one day, these manifestations of the Buddha suddenly ambled out of his mouth.

KENNIN-JI Map p62

561-6363; Higashiyama-ku, Shijō-sagaru; adult ¥500; 10am-4pm; 10min walk from Shijō Station, Keihan line

Founded in 1202 by the monk Eisai, Kennin-ji is the oldest Zen temple in Kyoto. It is an island of peace and calm on the border of the boisterous Gion nightlife district and it makes a fine counterpoint to the worldly pleasures of that area. The highlight at Kennin-ji is the fine and expansive *karesansui* garden. The painting of the twin dragons on the roof of the Hōdō hall is also fantastic; access to this hall is via two gates with rather puzzling English operating instructions (you'll see what we mean).

PRIVATE TOURS OF KYOTO

A private tour is a great way to see the sights and learn about the city without having to worry about transport and logistics. There are a variety of private tours on offer in Kyoto, including the following:

All Japan Private Tours & Speciality Services (www.kyotoguide.com/yjpt) This company offers exclusive unique tours of Kyoto, Nara and Tokyo, as well as business coordination and related services.

Chris Rowthorn's Walks & Tours of Kyoto & Japan (www.chrisrowthorn.com) Lonely Planet *Kyoto* author Chris Rowthorn offers private tours of Kyoto, Nara, Osaka and the rest of Japan.

Johnnie's Kyoto Walking (http://web.kyoto-inet.or.jp/people/h-s-love/) Hirooka Hajime, aka Johnnie Hillwalker, offers an interesting guided walking tour of the area around Kyoto Station and Higashiyama.

Naoki Doi (090-9596-5546; www3.ocn.ne.jp/~doitaxi/) This English-speaking taxi driver offers private taxi tours of Kyoto and Nara.

Windows to Japan (www.windowstojapan.com) Windows to Japan offers custom tours of Kyoto and Japan.

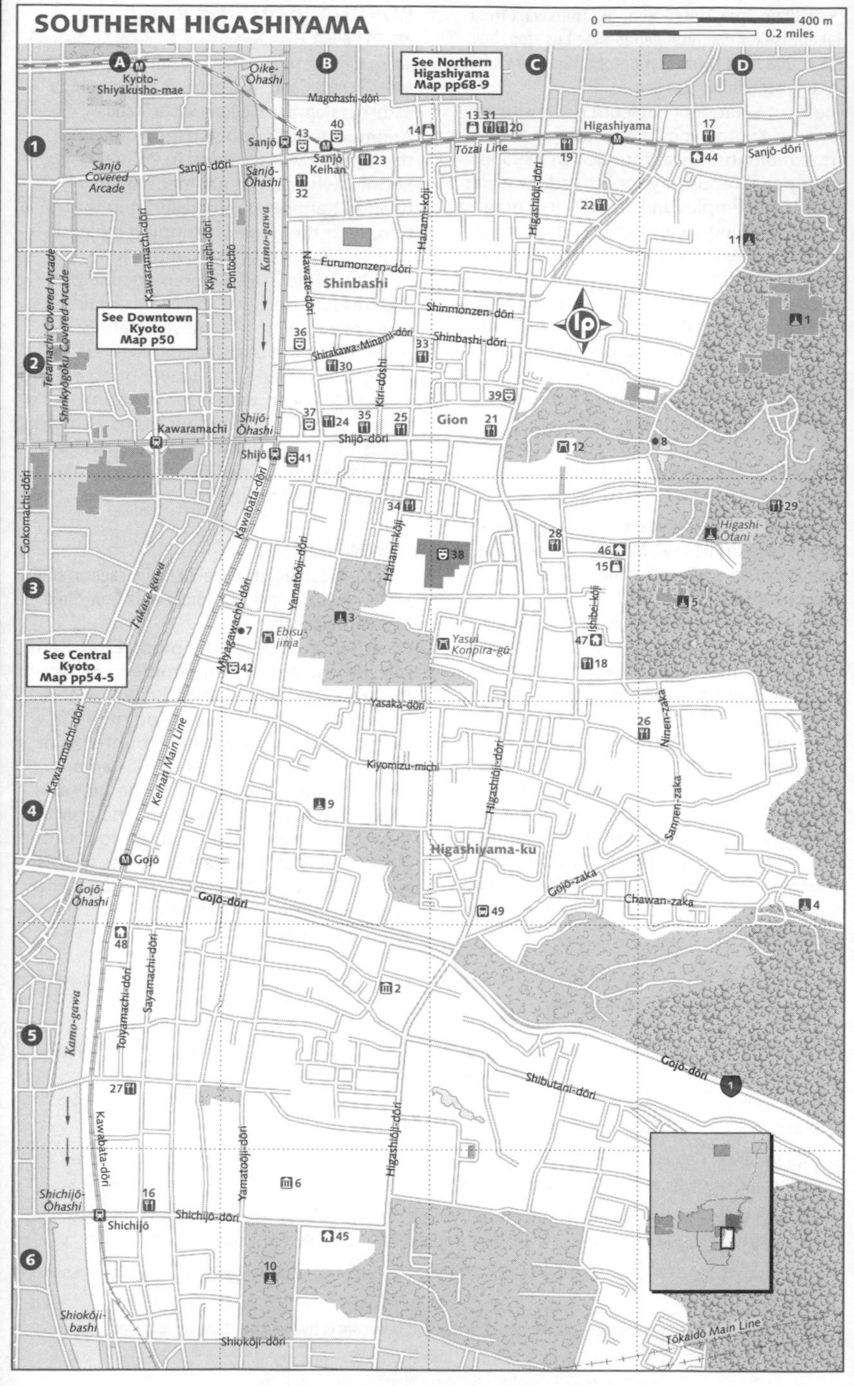
SOUTHERN HIGASHIYAMA
400 m
0.2 miles
See Northern Higashiyama Map pp68-9
See Downtown Kyoto Map p50
See Central Kyoto Map pp54-5
Kyoto-Shiyakusho-mae
Oike-Ohashi
Magohashi-dōri
Sanjō
Sanjō Keihan
Sanjō Covered Arcade
Sanjō-dōri
Sanjō-Ōhashi
Tōzai Line
Higashiyama
Higashiōji-dōri
Hanami-kōji
Furumonzen-dōri
Shinbashi
Shinmonzen-dōri
Shinbashi-dōri
Shirakawa-Minami-dōri
Kiri-dōshi
Nawate-dōri
Kamo-gawa
Pontochō
Kiyamachi-dōri
Kawaramachi-dōri
Teramachi Covered Arcade
Shinkyōgoku Covered Arcade
Kawaramachi
Shijō-Ōhashi
Shijō
Shijō-dōri
Gion
Gokomachi-dōri
Kawabata-dōri
Yamatoōji-dōri
Miyagawachō-dōri
Takase-gawa
Ebisu-jinja
Yasui Konpira-gū
Ishibei-kōji
Higashi-Ōtani
Yasaka-dōri
Ninen-zaka
Kiyomizu-michi
Sannen-zaka
Kawaramachi-dōri
Keihan Main Line
Gojō
Gojō-Ōhashi
Gojō-dōri
Higashiyama-ku
Gojō-zaka
Chawan-zaka
Toiyamachi-dōri
Sayamachi-dōri
Shibutani-dōri
Kamo-gawa
Kawabata-dōri
Yamatoōji-dōri
Higashiōji-dōri
Shichijō-Ōhashi
Shichijō
Shichijō-dōri
Shiokōji-bashi
Shiokōji-dōri
Tōkaidō Main Line

SOUTHERN HIGASHIYAMA

SIGHTS (pp60-5)

Chion-in 知恩院 ... 1 D2
Gion Corner ギオンコーナー ... (see 38)
Gion Kōbu Kaburen-jō Theatre 祇園甲部歌舞練場 ... (see 38)
Kawai Kanjirō Memorial Hall 河井寛治郎記念館 ... 2 B5
Kennin-ji 建仁寺 ... 3 B3
Kiyomizu-dera 清水寺 ... 4 D4
Kōdai-ji 高台寺 ... 5 D3
Kyoto National Museum 京都国立博物館 ... 6 B6
Maika 舞香 ... 7 B3
Maruyama-kōen 円山公園 ... 8 D2
Rokuharamitsu-ji 六波羅蜜寺 ... 9 B4
Sanjūsangen-dō 三十三間堂 ... 10 B6
Shōren-in 青蓮院 ... 11 D1
Tainai-meguri 胎内めぐり ... (see 4)
Yasaka-jinja 八坂神社 ... 12 C2

SHOPPING (pp105-14)

Kagoshin 籠新 ... 13 C1
Onouechikuzaiten 尾上竹材店 ... 14 B1
Tessai-dō てっさい堂 ... 15 C3

EATING (pp115-38)

Amazon アマゾン ... 16 A6
Asuka 明日香 ... 17 D1
Aunbo 阿吽坊 ... 18 C3
Bamboo 晩 boo ... 19 C1
Daikichi 大吉 ... 20 C1
Gion Koishi 祇園小石 ... 21 C2
Gion Morikō ぎをん森幸 ... 22 C1
Ichi-ban 一番 ... 23 B1
Issen Yōshoku 壱銭洋食 ... 24 B2
Kagizen Yoshifusa 鍵善良房 ... 25 B2
Kasagi-ya かさぎ屋 ... 26 D4
Machapuchare マチャプチャレ ... 27 A5
Minokō 美濃幸 ... 28 C3
Momiji-an 紅葉庵 ... 29 D3
Oza-Ōzawa おおざわ ... 30 B2
Ryūmon 龍門 ... 31 C1
Santōka 山頭火 ... 32 B1
Senmonten 泉門天 ... 33 B2
Wabiya Korekidō 侘家古暦堂 ... 34 B3
Yagura やぐ羅 ... 35 B2

ENTERTAINMENT (pp139-44)

Café Bon Appétit カフェ ボナペティ ... 36 B2
Gael Irish Pub ゲールアイリッシュパブ ... 37 B2
Gion Corner ギオンコーナー ... 38 C3
Gion Kaikan Theatre 祇園会館 ... 39 C2
Gion Kōbu Kaburen-jō Theatre 祇園甲部歌舞練場 ... (see 38)
Jumbo Karaoke Hiroba ジャンボカラオケ広場 ... 40 B1
Minami-za 南座 ... 41 B2
Miyagawa-chō Kaburen-jō Theatre 宮川町歌舞練場 ... 42 B3
Pig & Whistle ピッグ&ホイッスル ... 43 B1
Tōzan Bar 登山バー ... (see 45)

SLEEPING (pp145-56)

Higashiyama Youth Hostel 東山ユースホステル ... 44 D1
Hyatt Regency Kyoto ハイアットリージェンシー 京都 ... 45 B6
Ryokan Motonago 旅館元奈古 ... 46 C3
Ryokan Uemura 旅館うえむら ... 47 C3
Seikōrō 晴鴨楼 ... 48 A5

TRANSPORT (pp181-9)

Gojō-zaka Bus Stop 五条坂バス停 ... 49 C4

KIYOMIZU-DERA Map p62

☎ 551-1234; Higashiyama-ku, Kiyomizu 1-294; adult ¥300, child ¥200-300; 6am-6pm; 10min walk from Gojō-zaka bus stop, bus 206 or 100 from Kyoto Station

Along with Nijō-jō (p73), Kinkaku-ji (p77) and Ginkaku-ji (p71), Kiyomizu-dera is one of Kyoto's most popular sights and is almost always swarming with Japanese people and foreign tourists. Fortunately, it's a large complex and it can absorb a lot of visitors. It's worth a visit for the views over the grounds and the city, and the fascinating features scattered around the main hall.

This temple was first built in 798 and devoted to Jūichi-men, an 11-headed Kannon. The present buildings – built under order of Iemitsu, the third Tokugawa shōgun – are reconstructions dating from 1633. As an affiliate of the Hossō school, which originated in Nara, the temple has survived the many intrigues of Kyoto Buddhist schools through the centuries.

The main hall has a huge veranda that juts out over the hillside, supported by 139 15m-high wooden pillars. The terrace commands an excellent view over the city centre.

Just below this hall is Otowa-no-taki spring, where visitors drink the sacred waters believed to have therapeutic properties (and also thought to improve school test results). At Jishu-jinja, the 'Love Shrine' north of the main hall, visitors try to ensure success in love by closing their eyes and walking about 18m between a pair of stones – if you miss, your desire for love won't be fulfilled! (Don't worry, there are instructions in English.)

Before you enter the actual temple precincts, we strongly recommend that you take a few minutes to check out one of the oddest 'sights' that we've come across at a Japanese temple: the Tainai-meguri (Map p62; admission ¥100; 9am-4pm), the entrance to which can be found just to the left (north) of the pagoda that is located in front of the main entrance to the temple (you may have to ask a temple official since there is no English sign). We don't want to tell you too much about this hall as it will take away from the experience. Suffice to say, by entering the hall, you are figuratively entering the womb of Daizuigu Bosatsu, a female Bodhisattva who has the power to grant any human wish. Once you get to the inner sanctum, you are meant to turn the large stone found there in a clockwise direction and make your wish. Be warned, there are several 90-degree turns to navigate in the darkness – walk slowly and keep a hand in front of you.

MAIKO COSTUME

If you ever wondered how *you* might look as a *maiko* (apprentice geisha), Kyoto has many organisations in town that offer the chance. Maika (Map p62; ☎ 551 1661; Higashiyama-ku, Miyagawa suji; 9.30am-4.30pm Mon-Fri, 9am-7pm public holidays; 10min walk from Shijō Station, Keihan line) is in the Gion district. Here you can be dressed up to live out your *maiko* fantasy. Prices begin at ¥6720 for the basic treatment, which includes full make-up and formal kimono (studio photos cost ¥500 per print and you can have stickers made from these). If you don't mind spending some extra yen, it's possible to head out in costume for a stroll through Gion (and be stared at like never before!). The process takes about an hour. Call to reserve at least one day in advance.

NINEN-ZAKA & SANNEN-ZAKA Map p62

Higashiyama-ku, Kiyomizu; 10min walk from Higashiyama-yasui bus stop, bus 206 from Kyoto Station

Just downhill from and slightly to the north of Kiyomizu-dera (p63), you will find one of Kyoto's most lovely restored neighbourhoods. The name refers to the two main streets of the area: Ninen-zaka and Sannen-zaka, literally 'Two-Year Hill' and 'Three-Year Hill'. These two charming streets are lined with old wooden houses, traditional shops and restaurants. If you fancy a break, there are many teahouses and cafés along these lanes.

KŌDAI-JI Map p62

☎ 561-9966; Higashiyama-ku, Kōdai-ji, Shimokawara-chō 526; adult/child ¥600/250; 9am-5pm; 5min walk from Higashiyama-yasui bus stop, bus 206 from Kyoto Station

Kōdai-ji is one of Kyoto's more popular and 'trendy' temples, attracting visitors with a variety of events including seasonal night 'light-ups'. It's a lovely spot but you'll often find yourself jostling with hordes of other visitors who are lured by the temple's unique attractions.

This temple was founded in 1605 by Kita-no-Mandokoro in memory of her late husband, Toyotomi Hideyoshi. The extensive grounds include gardens designed by Kobori Enshū, teahouses designed by the renowned master of tea ceremony Sen no Rikyū, and a lovely little grove of bamboo trees (which are positively otherworldly when illuminated at night).

MARUYAMA-KŌEN Map p62

Higashiyama-ku; 1min walk from Gion bus stop, bus 206 from Kyoto Station

Maruyama-kōen is a favourite of locals and visitors alike. This park is the place to come to escape the bustle of the city centre and amble around gardens, ponds, souvenir shops and restaurants. Peaceful paths meander through the trees and carp glide through the waters of a small pond in the park's centre.

For two weeks in early April, when the park's cherry trees come into bloom, the calm atmosphere is shattered by hordes of drunken revellers having *hanami* (cherry-blossom viewing) parties under the trees. The centrepiece is a massive *shidare-zakura* cherry tree – one of the most beautiful sights in Kyoto, particularly when lit up from below at night. For those who don't mind crowds, this is a good place to observe the Japanese at their most uninhibited. Arrive early and claim a good spot high on the east side of the park, from where you can peer down on the mayhem below.

YASAKA-JINJA Map p62

☎ 561-6155; Higashiyama-ku, Gion-machi; admission free; 24hr; 5min walk from Shijō Station, Keihan line

This colourful and spacious shrine is down the hill from Maruyama-kōen (left). It's considered the guardian shrine of Gion. The present buildings, with the exception of the older, two-storey west gate, date from 1654. The granite *torii* on the south side was erected in 1666 and stands 9.5m high, making it one of the tallest in Japan. The roof of the main shrine is covered with cypress shingles. Among the treasures here are a pair of carved wooden *koma-inu* attributed to the renowned sculptor Unkei.

This shrine is particularly popular as a spot for *hatsu-mōde*. If you don't mind a stampede, come here around midnight on New Year's Eve or on any of the days following. Surviving the crush is proof that you're blessed by the gods!

Yasaka-jinja sponsors Kyoto's biggest festival, Gion Matsuri (p16).

GION DISTRICT Map p62

Higashiyama-ku, Gion-machi; 1min walk from Shijō Station, Keihan line

Gion is the famous entertainment and geisha quarter on the eastern bank of the Kamo-gawa. While Gion's true origins were in teahouses catering to weary visitors to Yasaka-jinja (opposite), by the mid-18th century the area was Kyoto's largest pleasure district. Despite the looming modern architecture, congested traffic and contemporary nightlife establishments that have cut a swath through its historical beauty, there are still some places left in Gion for an enjoyable walk. It looks quite drab by day, but comes alive with people and lights in the evening.

Hanami-kōji runs north to south and bisects Shijō-dōri. The southern section is lined with 17th-century traditional restaurants and teahouses, many of which are exclusive establishments for geisha entertainment. At the south end you reach Gion Corner (p142) and Gion Kōbu Kaburen-jō Theatre (Map p62).

If you walk from Shijō-dōri along the northern section of Hanami-kōji, you will reach Shinbashi-dōri and its traditional restaurants. A bit further north lie Shinmonzen-dōri and Furumonzen-dōri, running east to west. Wander in either direction along these streets, which are packed with old houses, art galleries and shops specialising in antiques – but don't expect flea-market prices here.

For more historic buildings in a beautiful waterside setting, wander down Shirakawa Minami-dōri, which is roughly parallel with, and one block south of, the western section of Shinmonzen-dōri.

CHION-IN Map p62

☎ 531-2111; Higashiyama-ku, Shinbashi-dōri, Yamatoōji Higashi iru 3, Rinka-chō 400; grounds free, inner buildings & garden adult ¥400, child ¥200-400; 9am-4pm Mar-Nov, to 3.40pm Dec-Feb; 10min walk from exit 2, Higashiyama Station, Tōzai subway line

The most impressive single sight in Southern Higashiyama, Chion-in is a must-see for those with a taste for the grand and glorious. It was built by the monk Genchi in 1234 on the site where his mentor, Hōnen, had once taught and eventually fasted to death. Today it is still the headquarters of the Jōdo school, which was founded by Hōnen, and it is a hive of religious activity.

The oldest of the present buildings date from the 17th century. The two-storey San-mon gate at the main entrance is the largest in Japan, and prepares the visitor for the massive scale of the temple. The immense main hall contains an image of Hōnen and is connected with the Dai Hōjō hall by a 'nightingale' floor that squeaks as one walks over it.

After visiting the main hall, with its fantastic gold altar, you can walk around the back of the same building to see the temple's gardens. On the way, you'll pass a darkened hall with a small statue of Amida Buddha on display, glowing eerily in the darkness. It makes a nice contrast to the splendour of the main hall.

The Daishōrō belfry houses a bell that was cast in 1633, measuring 2.7m in diameter and weighing almost 80 tonnes – the largest in Japan. The combined muscle power of 17 monks is required to make the bell budge during the ceremony to ring in the new year.

SHŌREN-IN Map p62

☎ 561-2345; Higashiyama-ku, Awataguchi Sanjōbō-chō; adult/child ¥500/400; 9am-5pm; 3min walk from exit 2, Higashiyama Station, Tōzai subway line

This temple is hard to miss, with its giant camphor trees growing just outside the walls. Fortunately, many tourists manage to do just that, leaving the lovely garden relatively quiet, even when nearby attractions are mobbed.

Shōren-in, commonly called Awata Palace after the road it faces, was originally the residence of the chief abbot of the Tendai school. Founded in 1150, the present building dates from 1895 and the main hall has sliding screens with paintings from the 16th and 17th centuries. Often overlooked by the crowds, who instead descend on other Higashiyama area temples, this is a pleasant place to sit and think while gazing out over one of Kyoto's finest landscape gardens.

NORTHERN HIGASHIYAMA

Eating p132; Shopping p112; Sleeping p152

Strung out along the base of the green Higashiyama, Kyoto's most prominent mountain range, this area is arguably Kyoto's most scenic. It stretches from Nanzen-ji in the south to Ginkaku-ji in the north. The Tetsugaku-no-Michi, Kyoto's famed Path of Philosophy, runs almost the length of the area and is one of the city's best walks. Other main attractions are Hōnen-in, a quiet little temple that is one of our favourites in Kyoto, and the museums around Okazaki-kōen.

If you are the sort of person who prefers a healthy dash of greenery with your sightseeing, then this might well be your favourite neighbourhood in Kyoto. Once you get into the precincts of Nanzen-ji, you can largely avoid cars and concrete until you get to Ginkaku-ji.

It's particularly conducive to those who want to do their exploring by bicycle. You could rent a bike on your first day and never have to get on public transport until you leave the city. It's flat, the roads are fairly wide and calm, and it's got some lovely cycle routes.

While there are enough restaurants here to keep you fuelled for sightseeing, particularly around Kyoto University and the Hyakumamben intersection, this isn't really the place for a night out. Northern Higashiyama has a few ryokan and hotels for those who want to be based here, however, and it's certainly a pleasant area in which to stay.

The best way to get to Southern Higashiyama from Kyoto Station is to take the Karasuma subway line to Karasuma-Oike Station, switch to the Tōzai subway line for Keage Station and walk north into the district. From Kyoto Station you can also take bus 5 to the area. If you're near the Kamo-gawa, take the Keihan line to either Sanjō or Marutamachi Station. Once in the area, the best way to get around is on foot.

NANZEN-JI Map pp68–9

☎ 771-0365; Sakyō-ku, Nanzen-ji, Fukuchi-chō; inner buildings & garden ¥1000; 8.40am-5pm; 10min walk from Keage Station, Tōzai subway line, or 20min walk from Sanjō Station, Keihan line

This temple is one of the most pleasant in Kyoto, with its expansive grounds (that can be entered for free) and numerous subtemples, including Nanzen-in (right), Tenju-an (opposite) and Konchi-in (opposite).

Nanzen-ji began as a retirement villa for Emperor Kameyama but was dedicated as a Zen temple on his death in 1291. Civil war in the 15th century destroyed most of the temple; the present buildings date from the 17th century. It operates now as the headquarters of the Rinzai school.

At the entrance to the temple stands the San-mon gate (1628), its ceiling adorned with Tosa and Kanō school murals of birds and angels. Steps lead up to the 2nd storey (admission costs ¥300), which has a fine view over the city. Beyond the San-mon is the Honden (Main Hall), which contains the main Buddha figures of the temple.

Beyond the Honden, at the base of the mountains, the Hōjō hall has impressive screens painted with a vivid depiction of tigers. While you're in the Hōjō, you can enjoy a cup of tea (¥400) as you sit on tatami mats gazing at a small waterfall; ask at the reception desk. Within the precincts of the same building, the Leaping Tiger Garden is a classic Zen garden well worth a look.

Perhaps the best part of Nanzen-ji is overlooked by most visitors: Nanzen-ji Oku-no-in (Map pp68–9), a small shrine hidden in a forested hollow behind the main precinct. To get here, walk up to the red-brick aqueduct in front of Nanzen-in. Follow the road that runs parallel to the aqueduct up into the hills, past Kōtoku-an (admission free; dawn-dusk) on your left; be sure to stop in at this temple on your way. Continue up the steps into the woods until you reach a waterfall in a beautiful mountain glen. It's here at Nanzen-ji Oku-no-in that pilgrims pray while standing under the falls, sometimes in the dead of winter. Hiking trails lead off in all directions from this point; by going due north for 5km (about two hours' walk) you'll arrive at the top of Daimonji-yama (see p71); go east and you'll get to the town of Yamashina (also about two hours).

NANZEN-IN Map pp68–9

☎ 771-0365; Sakyō-ku, Nanzen-ji, Fukuchi-chō; adult ¥300, child ¥150-250; 8.40am-5pm; 10min walk from Keage Station, Tōzai subway line

This subtemple of Nanzen-ji (left) is up the steps after you pass under the aqueduct. It has an attractive garden designed around a heart-shaped pond. This garden is best seen in the morning or around noon, when sunlight shines directly into the pond and illuminates the colourful carp.

TENJU-AN Map pp68–9

☎ 771-0365; Sakyō-ku, Nanzen-ji, Fukuchi-chō; adult ¥300, child ¥100-200; 8.40am-5pm; 10min walk from Tōzai subway line, Keage Station

Another subtemple of Nanzen-ji (opposite), Tenju-an is located on the south side of San-mon, the main gate of Nanzen-ji. Constructed in 1337, Tenju-an has a splendid garden and a great collection of carp in its pond.

KONCHI-IN Map pp68–9

☎ 771-3511; Sakyō-ku, Nanzen-ji, Fukuchi-chō; adult/child ¥400/200; 8.30am-5pm; 5min walk from Keage Station, Tōzai subway line

Just southwest of the main precincts of Nanzen-ji (opposite), this fine subtemple has a wonderful garden designed by Kobori Enshū. If you seek a good example of the technique of *shakkei,* look no further.

NOMURA MUSEUM Map pp68–9

☎ 751-0374; Sakyō-ku, Nanzen-ji, Shimokawara-chō 61; admission ¥700; 10am-4.30pm, closed Mon; 10min walk from Keage Station, Tōzai subway line

This museum is a 10-minute walk north of Nanzen-ji (opposite). Exhibits include scrolls, paintings, implements used in tea ceremonies and ceramics that were bequeathed by business magnate Nomura Tokushiki. If you have an abiding interest in the tea ceremony or in Japanese decorative techniques such as lacquer and *maki-e* (decorative lacquer technique using silver and gold powders), this museum makes an interesting break from temple hopping.

MURIN-AN VILLA Map pp68–9

☎ 771-3909; Sakyō-ku, Nanzen-ji, Kusakawa-chō; admission ¥350; 9am-4.30pm; 7min walk from Keage Station, Tōzai subway line

Often overlooked by the hordes that descend on the Higashiyama area, this elegant villa was the home of prominent statesman Yamagata Aritomo (1838–1922) and the site of a pivotal 1902 political conference as Japan was heading into the Russo-Japanese War.

Built in 1896, the grounds contain well-preserved wooden buildings, including a fine Japanese tearoom. The Western-style annexe is characteristic of Meiji-period architecture and the serene garden features small streams that draw water from the Biwa-ko Sosui canal. For ¥300 you can savour a bowl of frothy *matcha* (powdered

THE LIVING ART OF THE GEISHA

Behind the closed doors of exclusive teahouses and restaurants that dot the backstreets of Kyoto, women of exquisite grace and refinement entertain gentlemen of considerable means. Patrons may pay more than US$1000 to spend an evening in the company of a *geiko* (the Kyoto term for a fully fledged geisha). A *geiko* or *maiko* (apprentice geisha) is a kimono-clad woman versed in an array of visual and performing arts, including playing the three-stringed *shamisen* (banjo-like instrument), singing old teahouse ballads and dancing.

An evening in a Gion teahouse begins with an exquisite *kaiseki* (Japanese *haute cuisine*) meal that obeys very strict rules of etiquette for every detail, including the setting. While their customers eat, the *geiko* or *maiko* enter the room and introduce themselves in Kyoto dialect.

A *shamisen* performance, followed by a traditional fan dance, is often given, and all the while the *geiko* and *maiko* pour drinks, light cigarettes and engage in charming banter.

It is virtually impossible to enter a Gion teahouse and witness a *geiko* performance without the introduction of an established patron. With the exception of public performances at annual festivals or dance presentations, *geiko* perform only for select customers. Those geisha who decide to open their own teahouses once they retire at 50 or so may receive financial backing from well-to-do clients.

Knowledgeable sources estimate that there are perhaps 80 *maiko* and just over 100 *geiko* in Kyoto. Although their numbers are ever-decreasing, *geiko* and *maiko* can still be seen in some parts of the city, especially after dusk in the backstreets between the Kamo-gawa and Yasaka-jinja and along the narrow Pontochō alley. *Geiko* and *maiko* can also be found in other parts of the country, most notably Tokyo. It is thought, however, that there are fewer than 1000 geisha and *maiko* remaining in all Japan.

Geiko and *maiko* entertainment can be arranged through top-end hotels, ryokan and private tour operators (see the boxed text, p61).

NORTHERN HIGASHIYAMA

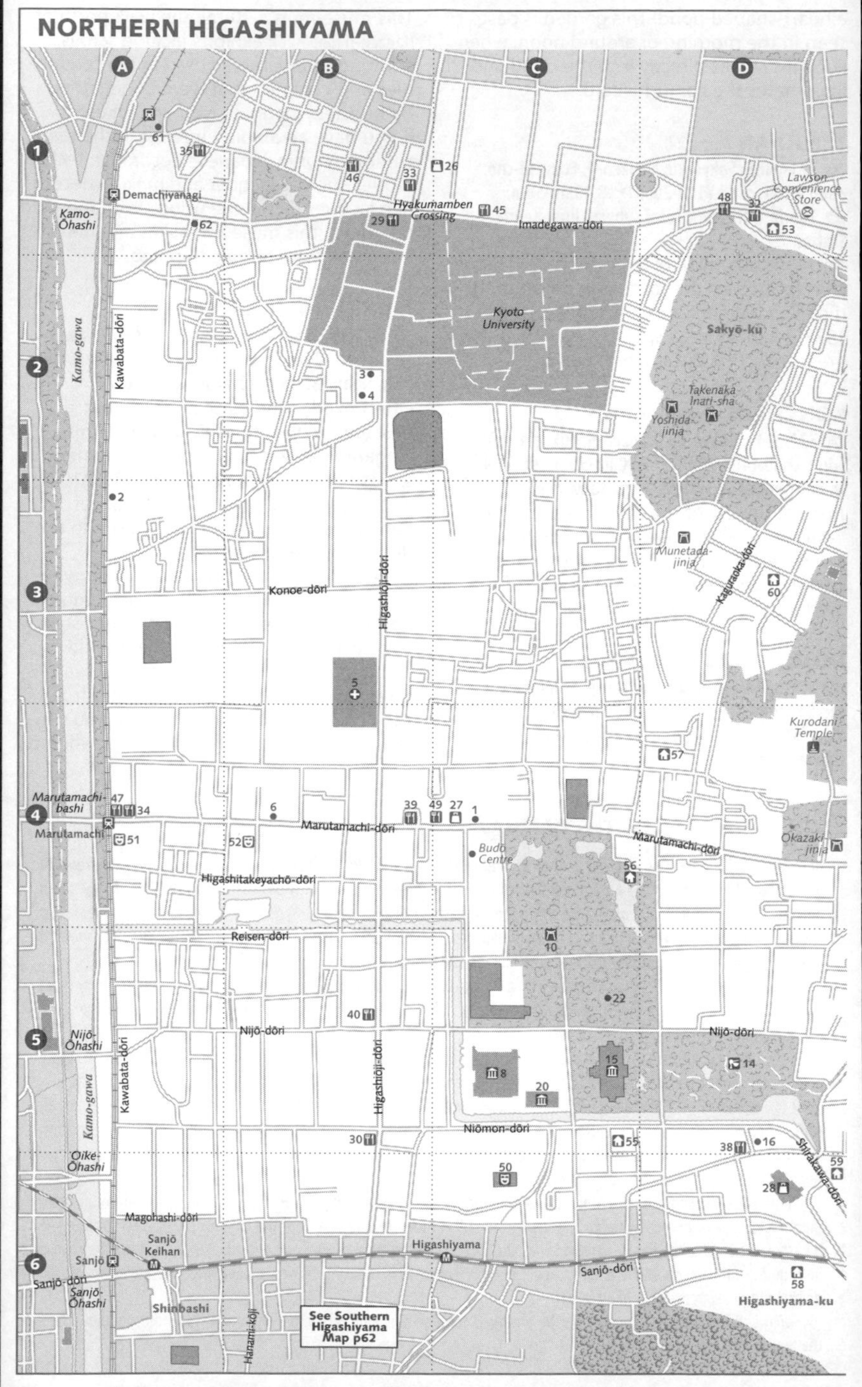

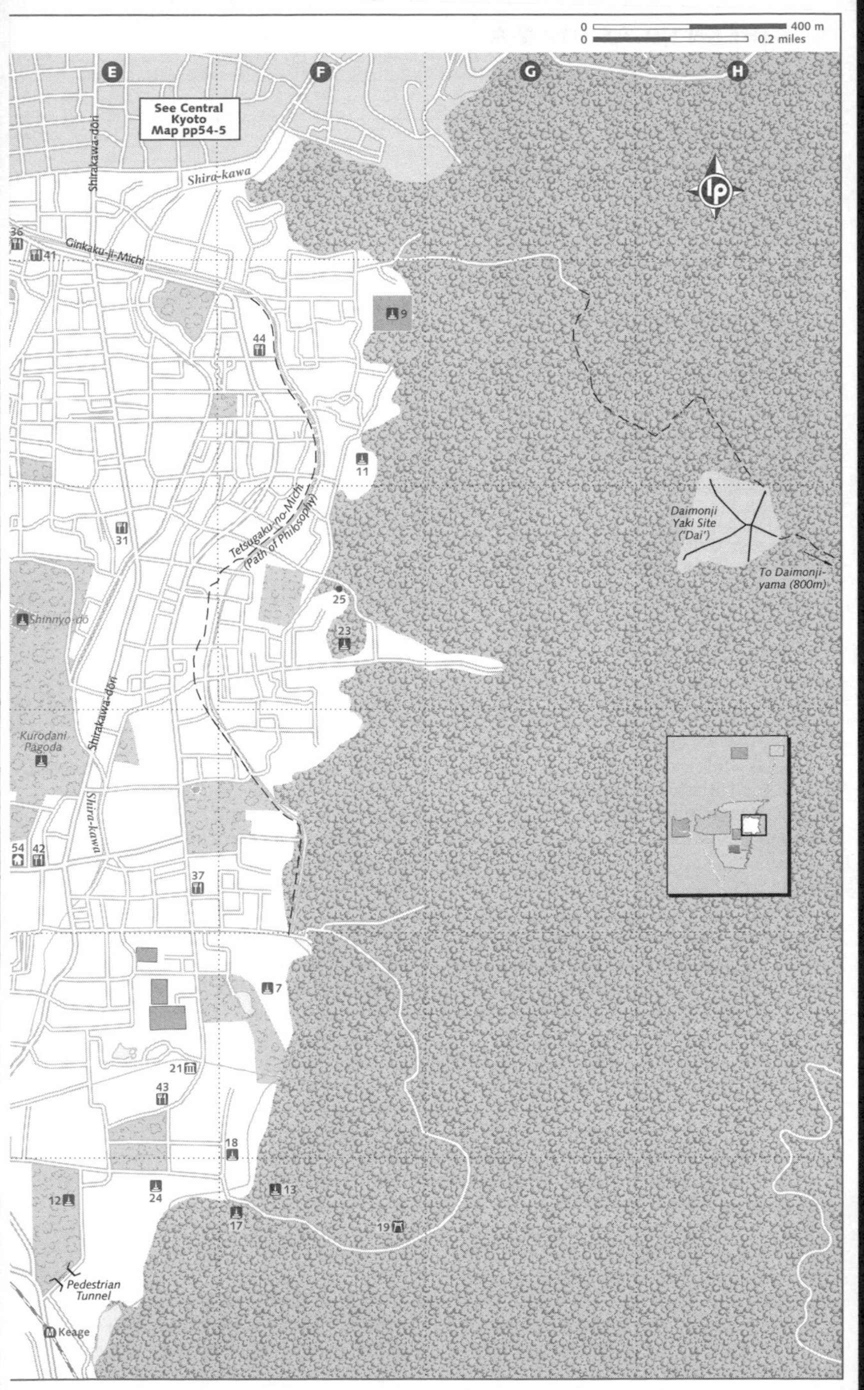

0 400 m
0 0.2 miles
E
F
G
H
See Central Kyoto Map pp54-5
Shirakawa-dōri
Shira-kawa
Ginkaku-ji-Michi
36
41
9
44
11
31
Tetsugaku-no-Michi (Path of Philosophy)
Daimonji Yaki Site ('Dai')
To Daimonji-yama (800m)
25
23
Shinnyo-dō
Shirakawa-dōri
Kurodani Pagoda
Shira-kawa
54
42
37
7
21
43
18
24
13
12
17
19
Pedestrian Tunnel
Keage

NORTHERN HIGASHIYAMA

INFORMATION
Amita-honten アミタ本店 1 C4
Goethe Institute Kyoto 京都ドイツ文化センター 2 A3
Institut Franco-Japonais du Kansai 関西日仏学館京都 3 B2
Instituto Italiano di Cultura di Kansai 関西イタリア文化会館 4 B2
Kyoto International Community House 京都市国際交流会館 ..... (see 28)
Kyoto University Hospital 京都大学医学部附属病院 5 B3
Osaka Immigration Bureau Kyoto Branch 大阪入国管理局京都出張所 6 B4

SIGHTS (pp66-72)
Eikan-dō 永観堂 7 F5
Fureai-kan Kyoto Museum of Traditional Crafts 京都伝統産業ふれあい館 8 C5
Ginkaku-ji 銀閣寺 9 F2
Heian-jingū 平安神宮 10 C5
Hōnen-in 法然院 11 F2
Konchi-in 金地院 12 E6
Kot-Kōtoku-an 高徳庵 13 F6
Kyoto City Zoo 京都市動物園 14 D5
Kyoto Municipal Museum of Art 京都市美術館 15 C5
Murin-an Villa 無鄰菴 16 D5
Nanzen-in 南禅院 17 F6
Nanzen-ji 南禅寺 18 F6
Nanzen-ji Oku-no-in 南禅寺奥の院 19 F6
National Museum of Modern Art 京都国立近代美術館 20 C5
Nomura Museum 野村美術館 21 E5
Okazaki-kōen 岡崎公園 22 C5
Reikan-ji 霊鑑寺 23 F3
Tenju-an 天授庵 24 E6
Tetsugaku-no-Michi 哲学の道 25 F3

SHOPPING (pp105-14)
Chion-ji Tezukuri-ichi 知恩寺手作り市 26 C1
Green e Books グリーン eブックス ..... (see 47)
Kyoto Handicraft Center 京都ハンディクラフトセンター 27 C4
Kyoto International Community House 京都市国際交流会館 28 D6

EATING (pp115-38)
Ayatori あやとり 29 B1
Bouchon Cayenne ブションカイエンヌ 30 B5
Buttercups バターカップス 31 E3
Café Carinho カフェ カリーニョ 32 D1
Café Peace カフェピース 33 B1
Earth Kitchen Company アースキッチンカンパニー 34 A4
Falafel Garden ファラフェルガーデン 35 A1
Grotto ぐろっと 36 E1
Hinode Udon 日の出うどん 37 E4
Hyōtei 瓢亭 38 D5
Kailash カイラス 39 B4
Karako 唐子 40 B5
Kushi Hachi 串八 41 E1
Okariba お狩り場 42 E4
Okutan 奥丹 43 E5
Omen おめん 44 F2
Shinshindō Notre Pain Quotidien 進々堂 45 C1
Sunny Place サニープレイス 46 B1
Torito とりと 47 A4
Yatai 屋台 48 D1
Zac Baran ザックバラン 49 C4

ENTERTAINMENT (pp139-44)
Kanze Kaikan Nō Theatre 観世会館 50 C6
Metro メトロ 51 A4
Tos-Tōsuikai 踏水会 52 B4

SLEEPING (pp145-56)
B&B Juno B&B じゅの 53 D1
Hotel Heian No Mori Kyoto ホテル平安の森京都 54 E4
Kyoto Traveller's Inn 京都トラベラーズイン 55 C5
Three Sisters Inn Annex スリーシスターズイン洛東荘別館 56 C4
Three Sisters Inn Main Building スリーシスターズイン洛東荘本館 57 D4
Westin Miyako Hotel ウエスティン都ホテル 58 D6
Yachiyo Ryokan 八千代旅館 59 D6
Yonbanchi 番地 60 D3

TRANSPORT (pp181-9)
Demachiyanagi Bicycle Parking Lot 出町柳有料自転車置場 61 A1
Eirin 栄輪 62 A1

green tea) while viewing the *shakkei* backdrop of the Higashiyama Mountains. It's particularly beautiful in the maple-leaf season of November.

EIKAN-DŌ Map pp68–9

☎ 761-0007; Sakyō-ku, Eikan-dō-chō 48; adult/child ¥600/400; 9am-5pm; 3min walk from Nanzen-ji Eikandō-michi bus stop, bus 5 from Kyoto Station

Perhaps Kyoto's most famous (and most crowded) autumn-foliage destination, Eikan-dō should probably be avoided in November, but is worth a visit at other times of year.

This temple is made interesting by its varied architecture, its gardens and works of art. A fabulous spot for viewing the autumn colours, the temple was founded as Zenrin-ji in 855 by the priest Shinshō, but the name was changed to Eikan-dō in the 11th century to honour the philanthropic priest Eikan.

In the Amida-dō hall at the southern end of the complex is a famous statue of Mikaeri Amida Buddha glancing backwards.

From Amida-dō, head north to the end of the curving covered *garyūrō* (walkway). Change into the sandals provided, then climb the steep steps up the mountainside to the Tahō-tō pagoda, from where there's a fine view across the city.

TETSUGAKU-NO-MICHI (PATH OF PHILOSOPHY) Map pp68–9

Sakyō-ku, Ginkaku-ji; 7min walk from Ginkaku-ji-Michi bus stop, bus 5 or 17 from Kyoto Station

The Tetsugaku-no-Michi is one of the most pleasant walks in all of Kyoto. Lined with a great variety of flowering plants, bushes and trees, it is a corridor of colour throughout most of the year. The path takes its name from one of its most famous strollers: 20th-century philosopher Nishida Kitarō, who is said to have meandered lost in thought along the path. Follow the traffic-free route along a canal lined with cherry trees that come into spectacular bloom in early April. It only takes 30 minutes to do the walk, which starts at Nyakuōji-bashi, above Eikan-dō (left), and leads to Ginkaku-ji (opposite). During the day you should be prepared for crowds (especially in the cherry-blossom season); a night stroll will definitely be quieter.

REIKAN-JI Map pp68–9

Sakyō-ku, Ginkaku-ji; admission ¥500; early Apr & 22-26 Nov; 7min walk from Ginkaku-ji-Michi bus stop, bus 5 or 17 from Kyoto Station

Only open to the public in spring and autumn, Reikan-ji is one of Kyoto's great lesser-visited attractions. During the spring opening, you will find the grounds positively rioting with camellia. In autumn, the brilliant reds of the maples will dazzle the eye. The small collection of artworks in the main building is almost as good as the colours outside.

HŌNEN-IN Map pp68–9

771-2400; Sakyō-ku, Shishigatani Goshonodan-chō 30; admission free; 6am-4pm; 10min walk from Jyōdo-ji bus stop, bus 5 from Kyoto Station

One of Kyoto's hidden pleasures, this temple was founded in 1680 to honour the priest Hōnen. It's a lovely, secluded temple with carefully raked gardens set back in the woods. The temple buildings include a small gallery where frequent exhibitions featuring local and international artists are held. If you need to escape the crowds that positively plague nearby Ginkaku-ji (right), come to this serene refuge.

Hōnen-in is a 12-minute walk from Ginkaku-ji, on a side street to the east of Tetsugaku-no-Michi (opposite); you may have to ask for directions.

GINKAKU-JI Map pp68–9

771-5725; Sakyō-ku, Ginkaku-ji-chō 2; adult ¥500; 8.30am-5pm Mar-Nov, 9am-4.30pm Dec-Feb; 5min walk from Ginkaku-ji-Michi bus stop, bus 5 from Kyoto Station

With a sublime wooden hall overlooking an impressive stroll garden, Ginkaku-ji is easily one of Kyoto's most beautiful sights. Unfortunately, the beauty of the place guarantees that it is almost always swamped with bus loads of visitors from all over the world. We recommend visiting just after it opens, ideally on a weekday morning. Failing that, try coming just before it closes, as the setting sun casts its golden light over the hills above the temple.

Also known as Jishō-ji, the temple belongs to the Shōkoku-ji sect of the Rinzai school of Zen. In 1482 shōgun Ashikaga Yoshimasa constructed a villa here, which he used as a genteel retreat from the turmoil of civil war. Although 'Ginkaku-ji' translates as Silver Pavilion, this is simply a nickname to distinguish it from Kinkaku-ji (Golden Pavilion). The main hall was originally covered in black lacquer; at present it's simply a nice, weathered woody colour. After Yoshimasa's death it was converted to a temple.

The approach to the main gate runs between tall hedges before turning sharply into the extensive grounds. You will find walkways leading through the gardens, which were laid out by painter and garden designer Sōami. The gardens include meticulously raked cones of white sand known as *kōgetsudai*, designed to reflect

DAIMONJI-YAMA CLIMB

Time Two hours
Distance 5km

Located directly behind Ginkaku-ji (above), Daimonji-yama is the main site of the Daimon-ji Gozan Okuribi (p16) festival. From almost anywhere in town, the Chinese character for 'great' *(dai)* is visible in the middle of a bare patch on the face of this mountain. On 16 August, this character is set ablaze to guide the spirits of the dead on their journey home. The view of Kyoto from the top is unparalleled.

Take bus 5 to the Ginkaku-ji-Michi stop and walk up to Ginkaku-ji. You have the option of visiting the temple first or starting the hike immediately. To find the trail head, turn left in front of the temple and head north for about 50m towards a stone *torii* (shrine gate). Just before the *torii*, turn right up the hill.

The trail proper starts just after a small parking lot on the right. It's a broad avenue through the trees. A few minutes of walking brings you to a red banner (warning of forest fires) hanging over the trail. Soon after this you must cross a bridge to the right then continue up a smaller, switchback trail. When the trail reaches a saddle not far from the top, go to the left. You'll climb a long flight of steps before coming out at the top of the bald patch. The sunset from here is great, but bring a torch. Note that the hike involves several fairly steep sections of steps and should only be attempted by those in reasonably good physical condition.

moonlight and enhance the beauty of the garden at night.

In addition to the Buddha image in the main hall, the Tōgudō (residence of Yoshimasa) houses an effigy of Yoshimasa dressed in monk's garb. The tiny tea room (closed to the public) is said to be the oldest in Japan.

OKAZAKI-KŌEN Map pp68–9

Sakyō-ku, Okazaki; Kyoto Kaikan/Bijyutsukan-mae bus stop, bus 5 from Kyoto Station

Okazaki-kōen is an expanse of parks and canals that lies between Niōmon-dōri and Heian-jingū. Two of Kyoto's significant museums can be found here, as well as two smaller museums and a zoo. If you find yourself in Kyoto on a rainy day and need to do some indoor sightseeing, this area has enough to keep you sheltered for most of the day.

The National Museum of Modern Art (Map pp68–9; ☎ 761-4111; Okazaki, Enshōji-chō; adult ¥420, child free-¥130; 9.30am-5pm, closed Mon) is renowned for its Japanese ceramics and paintings. There is an excellent permanent collection, including many pottery pieces by Kawai Kanjirō. The coffee shop here overlooks a picturesque canal.

The Kyoto Municipal Museum of Art (Map pp68–9; ☎ 771-4107; Okazaki, Enshōji-chō 124; 9am-4.30pm, closed Mon) organises several major exhibitions a year. Adult admission varies by exhibit but children get in for free.

For a break from temple-gazing, pop into the excellent Fureai-kan Kyoto Museum of Traditional Crafts (Map pp68–9; ☎ 762-2670; Okazaki, Seishōji-chō 9-1; admission free; 9am-5pm). Exhibits include wood-block prints, lacquerware, bamboo goods and gold-leaf work. It's in the basement of Miyako Messe (Kyoto International Exhibition Hall).

Those with children might want to stop by the Kyoto City Zoo (Kyoto-shi Dōbutsu-en; Map pp68–9; ☎ 771-0210; Okazaki, Hōshōji-chō; adult/child ¥500/300; 9am-5pm Tue-Sun Mar-Nov, to 4.30pm Dec-Feb). The zoo is home to about 1000 animals and has some decent gardens and groves of cherry trees.

HEIAN-JINGŪ Map pp68–9

☎ 761-0221; Sakyō-ku, Okazaki, Nishitenno-chō; shrine precincts free, garden adult ¥600, child ¥300-600; 6am-6pm, closes earlier winter; 1min walk from Kyoto Kaikan/Bijyutsukan-mae bus stop, bus 5 from Kyoto Station

One of Kyoto's more popular sights, this shrine was built in 1895 to commemorate the 1100th anniversary of the founding of Kyoto. The shrine buildings are gaudy replicas, reduced to a two-thirds scale, of the Imperial Court Palace of the Heian period (794–1185).

About 500m in front of the shrine is a massive steel *torii*. Although it appears to be entirely separate, this is actually considered the main entrance to the shrine itself.

The vast garden here, behind the shrine, is a fine place for a wander and particularly lovely during the cherry-blossom season. With its large pond and Chinese-inspired bridge, the garden is a tribute to the style that was popular in the Heian period. It is well known for its wisteria, irises and weeping cherry trees.

Two major events, Jidai Matsuri (p17) on 22 October and Takigi Nō (p16) on the first two days of June, are held here.

NORTHWEST KYOTO

Eating p136; Shopping p113; Sleeping p153

Northwest Kyoto is a mostly residential district that stretches from Central Kyoto all the way up to the base of the Kitayama and Arashiyama Mountains. Some of Kyoto's most important and impressive sights can be found here, including the ever-popular Nijō-jō with its almost rococo interiors, the dazzling golden hall of Kinkaku-ji, the fabled rock garden of Ryōan-ji and the enclosed world of the Myōshin-ji temple complex. You can walk between Kinkaku-ji, Ryōan-ji and Ninna-ji if you are reasonably fit. Few people stay in this part of town – it's more of a place that you visit for half a day before returning to the fleshpots of Downtown or Central Kyoto. The area lends itself to exploration by bicycle, if you're fit; unlike most of the rest of Kyoto, there are actually a few gentle hills out this way. Otherwise, buses serve the destinations here.

NIJŌ-JŌ Map p74

☎ 841-0096; Nakagyō-ku, Nijō-dōri, Horikawa Nishi iru, Nijōjō-chō 541; adult ¥600, child ¥200-350; 8.45am-4pm (gates close 5pm), closed Tue in Dec, Jan, Jul & Aug; 1min walk from Nijōjō-mae Station, Tōzai subway line

For those with an interest in Japan's feudal past and an eye for magnificent interiors, Nijō-jō is a fascinating destination. Keep in mind, though, that the castle is on the itinerary of every foreign and Japanese tour group and it can be packed. If you're after peace and quiet, try an early-morning or late-afternoon visit.

Nijō-jō was built in 1603 as the official residence of Tokugawa Ieyasu. The ostentatious style was intended as a demonstration of Ieyasu's prestige and to signal the demise of the emperor's power. To safeguard against treachery, Ieyasu had the interior fitted with 'nightingale' floors (intruders were detected by the squeaking boards) and concealed chambers where bodyguards could keep watch and spring out at a moment's notice. Fans of ninja movies will recognise these features immediately.

The Momoyama-era Kara-mon gate, originally part of Hideyoshi's Fushimi-jō in the south of the city, features lavish, masterful woodcarving and metalwork. After passing through the gate, you enter the Ninomaru palace, which is divided into five buildings with numerous chambers. Access to the buildings used to depend on rank – only those of highest rank were permitted into the inner buildings. The Ōhiroma Yon-no-Ma (Fourth Chamber) has spectacular screen paintings.

Don't miss Seiryu-en, designed by Kobori Enshū. This vast garden comprises three separate islets spanned by stone bridges and is meticulously kept. The Ninomaru palace and garden take about an hour to walk through. A detailed fact sheet in English is provided.

The neighbouring Honmaru palace dates from the mid-19th century. After the Meiji Restoration in 1868, the castle became a detached palace of the imperial household and in 1939 it was given to Kyoto City. It's only open for a special autumn viewing.

While you're in the neighbourhood, you might want to take a look at Shinsen-en (admission free), just south of the castle outside the walls. This forlorn garden, with its small shrines and pond, is all that remains of the original 8th-century Imperial Palace, which was abandoned in 1227.

NIJŌ JINYA Map p74

☎ 841-0972; Nakagyō-ku, Sanjō-Ōmiya-chō 37; adult/child ¥1000/800; tours 10am, 11am, 2pm, 3pm, closed Wed; 10min walk from Nijōjō-mae Station, Tōzai subway line

A few minutes' walk south of Nijō-jō (left), Nijō Jinya is an interesting attraction, although it's not really geared to foreign visitors. This former merchant's home was built in the mid-1600s and served as an inn for provincial feudal lords visiting the capital. What appears to be an average Edo-period mansion, however, is no ordinary dwelling.

The house contains fire-resistant earthen walls and a warren of 24 rooms, and was ingeniously designed to protect the *daimyō* against possible surprise attacks. Here you'll find hidden staircases, secret passageways and an array of counterespionage devices. The main room's ceiling skylight is fitted with a trap door from where samurai could pounce on intruders, and sliding doors feature alternate panels of translucent paper to expose the shadows of eavesdroppers.

One-hour tours are conducted several times a day in Japanese and advance

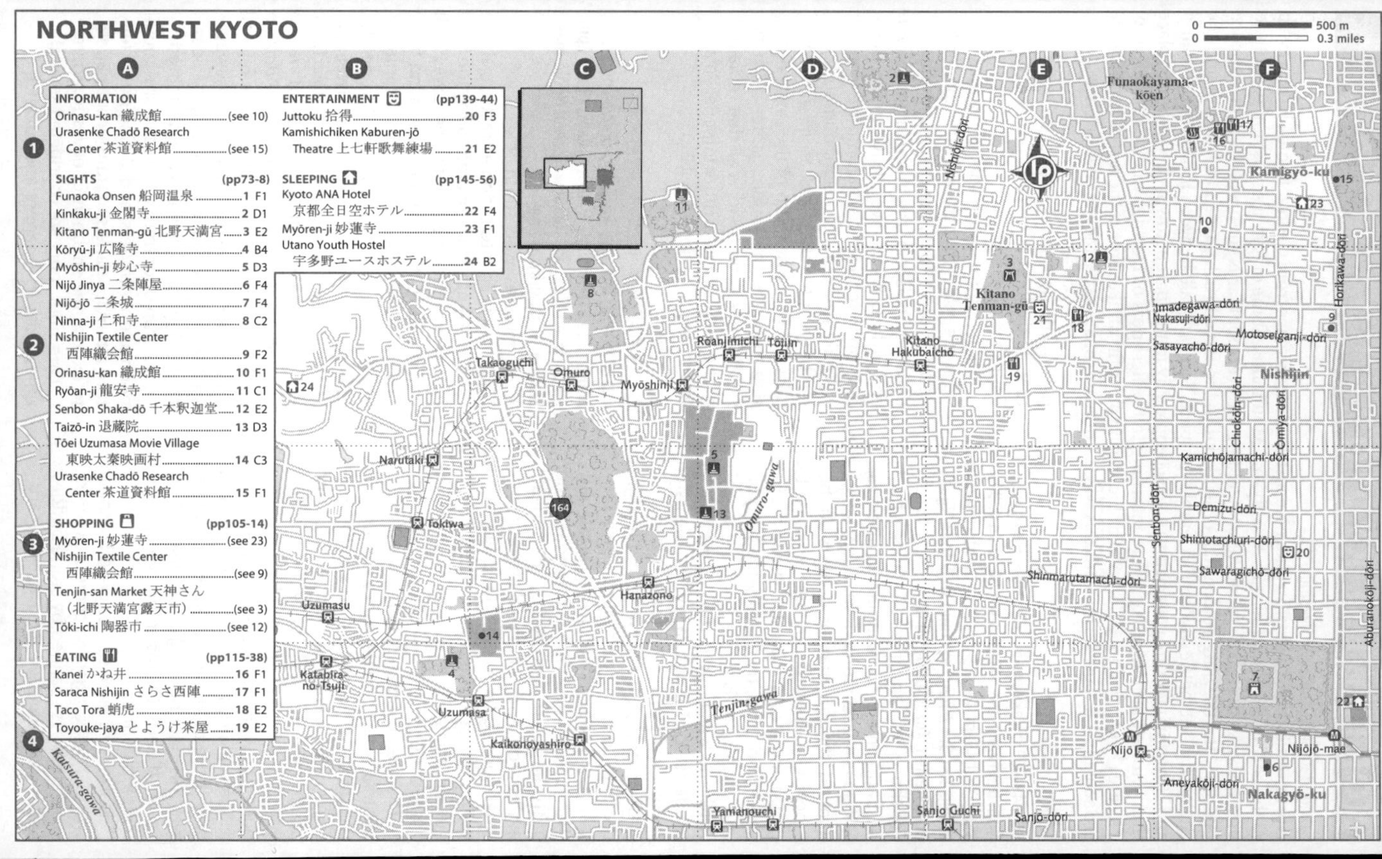
NORTHWEST KYOTO
0 500 m
0 0.3 miles
INFORMATION
Orinasu-kan 織成館 (see 10)
Urasenke Chadō Research Center 茶道資料館 (see 15)
SIGHTS (pp73-8)
Funaoka Onsen 船岡温泉 1 F1
Kinkaku-ji 金閣寺 2 D1
Kitano Tenman-gū 北野天満宮 3 E2
Kōryū-ji 広隆寺 4 B4
Myōshin-ji 妙心寺 5 D3
Nijō Jinya 二条陣屋 6 F4
Nijō-jō 二条城 7 F4
Ninna-ji 仁和寺 8 C2
Nishijin Textile Center 西陣織会館 9 F2
Orinasu-kan 織成館 10 F1
Ryōan-ji 龍安寺 11 C1
Senbon Shaka-dō 千本釈迦堂 12 E2
Taizō-in 退蔵院 13 D3
Tōei Uzumasa Movie Village 東映太秦映画村 14 C3
Urasenke Chadō Research Center 茶道資料館 15 F1
SHOPPING (pp105-14)
Myōren-ji 妙蓮寺 (see 23)
Nishijin Textile Center 西陣織会館 (see 9)
Tenjin-san Market 天神さん (北野天満宮露天市) (see 3)
Tōki-ichi 陶器市 (see 12)
EATING (pp115-38)
Kanei かね井 16 F1
Saraca Nishijin さらさ西陣 17 F1
Taco Tora 蛸虎 18 E2
Toyouke-jaya とようけ茶屋 19 E2
ENTERTAINMENT (pp139-44)
Juttoku 拾得 20 F3
Kamishichiken Kaburen-jō Theatre 上七軒歌舞練場 21 E2
SLEEPING (pp145-56)
Kyoto ANA Hotel 京都全日空ホテル 22 F4
Myōren-ji 妙蓮寺 23 F1
Utano Youth Hostel 宇多野ユースホステル 24 B2
Funaokayama-kōen
Nishiōji-dōri
Kamigyō-ku
Kitano Tenman-gū
Imadegawa-dōri
Nakasuji-dōri
Horikawa-dōri
Motoseiganji-dōri
Sasayachō-dōri
Nishijin
Roanjimichi
Tōjiin
Kitano Hakubaichō
Takaoguchi
Omuro
Myōshinji
Chiekōin-dōri
Ōmiya-dōri
Narutaki
Kamichōjamachi-dōri
Omuro-gawa
Demizu-dōri
Senbon-dōri
Tokiwa
Shimotachiuri-dōri
Sawaragichō-dōri
Shinmarutamachi-dōri
Hanazono
Uzumasa
Aburanokōji-dōri
Katabira-no-Tsuji
Uzumasa
Tenjin-gawa
Kaikonoyashiro
Nijō
Nijōjō-mae
Aneyakōji-dōri
Nakagyō-ku
Katsura-gawa
Yamanouchi
Sanjo Guchi
Sanjō-dōri

reservations must be made. Those who don't speak Japanese are asked to bring a Japanese-speaking guide.

NISHIJIN Map p74

Kamigyō-ku, Horikawa-dōri, Imadegawa; 1min walk from Horikawa-Imadegawa bus stop, bus 9 from Kyoto Station

Nishijin is Kyoto's traditional textile centre, the source of all those dazzling kimono fabrics and obi (kimono sashes) that you see being paraded about town. The area is famous for Nishijin-ori (Nishijin weaving). There are quite a few *machiya* in this district, so it's a good place simply to wander.

NISHIJIN TEXTILE CENTER Map p74

451-9231; Kamigyō-ku, Horikawa-dōri, Imadegawa minami iru; admission free; 9am-5pm; 1min walk from Horikawa-Imadegawa bus stop, bus 9 from Kyoto Station

In the heart of the Nishijin textile district, this centre is a great place to observe the weaving of fabrics used in kimono and their ornamental obi. There are also displays of completed fabrics and kimono. The centre holds occasional kimono fashion shows and has a decent shop upstairs where you can buy goods that are made of Nishijin-ori.

ORINASU-KAN Map p74

431-0020; Kamigyō-ku, Daikoku-chō 693; adult/child ¥500/350; 10am-4pm, closed Mon; 10min walk from Horikawa-Imadegawa bus stop, bus 9 from Kyoto Station

This museum is housed in a Nishijin weaving factory. It has impressive exhibits of Nishijin textiles. The Susamei-sha building

GARDENS BY DESIGN *Marc Peter Keane*

If you ask a Japanese gardener what the most important aspect of garden design is, they will often answer succinctly: *shiki,* the four seasons. All gardens in the world fall into one of two types – those built in harsh environments that attempt to ameliorate that condition (such as water gardens in arid regions) and those built in comfortable environments that revel in the natural world around them. The gardens of Kyoto are the epitome of the latter; incorporating the delights of the ever-changing natural world into their design is fundamental.

When creating a garden, there are some overarching principles that guide its design, beyond incorporating the seasons. Gardens in temples, for instance, often contain allegorical images that symbolise some aspect of the Buddhist worldview. In private homes, geomancy may be applied to ascertain how the garden should be laid out, though this is becoming less common these days. The function of the garden will be considered as well. One must decide if it will either be viewed as a work of art and not physically entered, such as the *karesansui* (dry-landscape) gardens, or if the way you move through the garden will be of great importance, such as with tea gardens and stroll gardens.

Once the overall theme of the garden is determined, the execution of the design will employ certain techniques that give the garden its distinctive quality. The balance of the design, such as that of an ikebana flower arrangement or *bokusuiga* ink painting, is purposefully off-balance. Empty space is punctuated by strong accents; important features are never placed on centre; symmetry is eschewed, as are neatly balanced groupings of even numbers. This gives the design a sense of motion and energy. For this reason, triangles or triads are often used as a basis for design – whether it's the shape of a pruned tree or a grouping of set stones – to give at once a sense of balance and of movement.

Because the Japanese garden is created with primarily natural materials – river boulders, irregularly pruned trees, hand-crafted fences and gates – the design cannot be completely determined on paper beforehand. Rather, it is created on-site from the details up, not from the master plan down. As the various materials are installed, the placement of each affects that of the next, and the overall design is shaped organically during the process of building. In this sense, it is more akin to painting than architecture.

Unlike gardens in Western countries, Japanese gardens are not seen as a place to gather and display a large assortment of plants. On the contrary, the palette of materials used is often very limited, and it is this rarefied palette that is the source of the quietude and subtleness one feels in a Japanese garden. In fact, plants are often less important than stones, the placement of which creates the 'bones' of the garden. The thousand-year-old treatise on garden-making called the Sakuteiki makes this clear in the first line when it refers to gardening as *'ishi wo taten koto'* – the art of setting stones.

Marc Peter Keane is the author of Japanese Garden Design, Sakuteiki *(a translation of Japan's most ancient gardening text) and several other titles on Japanese culture and design. He lived in Kyoto for 20 years and is now based in Ithaca, New York.*

IN HOT WATER

After a day spent marching from temple to temple, nothing feels better than a good hot bath. Kyoto is full of *sentō* (public baths), ranging from small neighbourhood baths with one or two tubs to massive complexes offering saunas, mineral baths and even electric baths. The following baths are worth a visit and could even double as an evening's entertainment. It's best to bring your own bath supplies (soap, shampoo, a towel to dry yourself and another small towel for washing); if you forget, though, you can buy toiletries and rent towels at the front desk. Washing buckets are available for free inside the bathing area.

Funaoka Onsen (Map p74; ☎ 441-3735; Kita-ku, Murasakino, Minami-Funaoka-chō 82-1, Kuramaguchi-dōri; admission ¥390; ⏲ 3pm-1am Mon-Sat, 8am-1am Sun & public holidays; 🚌 5min walk from Senbon-Kuramaguchi bus stop, bus 206 from Kyoto Station) is our favourite *sentō* in Kyoto. This old bath boasts outdoor bathing and a sauna, as well as some museum-quality woodcarvings in the changing room (apparently carved during Japan's invasion of Manchuria). To find it, head west from Horikawa-dōri along Kuramaguchi-dōri. It's on the left, not far past the Lawson convenience store. Look for the large rocks out the front.

Gokō-yu (Map pp54–5; ☎ 841-7321; 590-1 Kakinomoto-chō, Gojō agaru, Kuromon-dōri; admission ¥390; ⏲ 2.30pm-12.30am Tue-Sat, 7am-midnight Sun, closed Mon & 3rd Tue of each month; 🚌 3min walk from Ōmiya-Gojō bus stop, bus 43 or 206 from Kyoto Station), a popular bath, is another great spot to sample the joys of the *sentō*. It's a large two-storey bath with a wide variety of tubs. There's also a giant sauna with two rooms; one is merely hot, the other is incendiary! We also like the TV fish tank in the entrance (you'll see what we mean). Note that Gokō-yu is a little hard to find – turn north off Gojō-dōri at the store that sells charcoal and gas burners.

(recently restored) next door is also open to the public and contains a small café. Across the street, there is another hall with a good collection of Nishijin kimono (entry to this hall is included in the main admission fee). With advance reservations, traditional weaving workshops can be attended.

URASENKE CHADŌ RESEARCH CENTER Map p74

☎ 431-6474; Kamigyō-ku, Horikawa-dōri, Teranouchi agaru; admission ¥500; ⏲ 9.30am-4.30pm; Ⓢ 15min walk from Kuramaguchi Station, Karasuma subway line

Anyone interested in tea ceremony should make their first stop the Urasenke Chadō Research Center. Urasenke is Japan's largest tea school and hosts hundreds of students annually who come from branch schools worldwide to further their studies in 'the way of tea'.

The gallery (admission ¥800; ⏲ 9.30am-4.30pm, closed Mon) located on the 1st and 2nd floors holds quarterly exhibitions on tea-related arts; call to see if there is a show being held during your stay. The entrance fee entitles you to a bowl of *matcha* and a sweet.

The Konnichi-an library (☎ 431-6474; admission free; ⏲ 10am-4pm Mon-Fri, to 3pm Sat, closed Sun & public holidays) has more than 50,000 books (about 100 in English) plus videos on tea, which can be viewed.

If you'd like more information, contact Urasenke's Office of International Affairs (Kokusai Kyoku; ☎ 431-3111).

KITANO TENMAN-GŪ Map p74

☎ 461-0005; Kamigyō-ku, Bakuro-chō; admission free; ⏲ 5am-dusk; 🚌 1min walk from Kitano Tenmangū-mae bus stop, bus 50 or 101 from Kyoto Station

The site of Tenjin-San Market (p113), one of Kyoto's most popular flea markets, this shrine is a nice spot for a lazy stroll and the shrine buildings themselves are beautiful. It's particularly pleasant here in the plum-blossom season of March.

Kitano Tenman-gū was established in 947 to honour Sugawara Michizane (845–903), a noted Heian-era statesman and scholar. It is said that, having been defied by his political adversary Fujiwara Tokihira, Sugawara was exiled to Kyūshū for the rest of his life. Following his death in 903, earthquakes and storms struck Kyoto, and the Imperial Palace was repeatedly struck by lightning. Fearing that Sugawara, re-incarnated as Raijin (god of thunder), had returned from beyond to avenge his rivals, locals erected and dedicated this shrine to him.

The present buildings were built in 1607 by Toyotomi Hideyori; the grounds contain an extensive grove of plum and apricot trees, which are said to have been Sugawara's favourite fruits.

Unless you are trying to avoid crowds, the best time to visit is during the Tenjin-san market fair, held on the 25th of each month – December and January are particularly colourful.

KINKAKU-JI Map p74

☎ 461-0013; Kita-ku, Kinkaku-ji-chō 1; adult ¥400, child ¥300-400; 9am-5pm; 2min walk from Kinkakuji-michi bus stop, bus 205 from Kyoto Station

Second only to Mt Fuji as Japan's most famous sight, this temple is famous for its dazzling gold-covered main hall, which floats like an apparition over its surrounding pond. It's a stunning vision and most people find it to their liking, although some prefer the more subdued appearance of its counterpart, Ginkaku-ji (p71). Needless to say, the temple receives masses of visitors; as usual, we recommend an early-morning or late-afternoon visit.

Also known as Rokuon-ji, Kinkaku-ji belongs to the Shōkokuji school of Buddhism. The original building was constructed in 1397 as a retirement villa for shōgun Ashikaga Yoshi-mitsu. His son, complying with his father's wishes, converted it into a temple.

The three-storey pavilion is covered in bright gold leaf and features a bronze phoenix on top of the roof. The mirrorlike reflection of the temple in the Kyō-ko pond is extremely photogenic, especially when the maples are ablaze in autumn.

In 1950 a young monk consummated his obsession with the temple by burning it to the ground. The monk's story is fictionalised in Mishima Yukio's 1956 novel *The Temple of the Golden Pavilion.*

In 1955 a full reconstruction was completed, which followed the original design exactly, but the gold-foil covering was extended to the lower floors. The temple may not be exactly to everyone's taste but it is nevertheless an impressive feat.

RYŌAN-JI Map p74

☎ 463-2216; Ukyō-ku, Ryōan-ji, Goryōnoshitamachi 13; adult ¥500, child ¥300-500; 8am-5pm Mar-Nov, 8.30am-4.30pm Dec-Feb; 1min walk from Ryōan-ji-mae bus stop, bus 59 from Kawaramachi Station, Hankyū line

You've probably seen a picture of the rock garden here – it's one of the symbols of Kyoto and one of Japan's better-known sights. There is no doubt that it's a mesmerising and attractive sight, but it's hard to enjoy amid the mobs who come to check it off their 'must-see list'. An early-morning visit on a weekday is probably your best hope of seeing the garden under contemplative conditions. If you go when it's crowded, you'll find the less-famous garden around the corner of the stone garden to be a nice escape.

This temple belongs to the Rinzai school and was founded in 1450. The main attraction is the garden, an oblong of sand with an austere collection of 15 carefully placed rocks, apparently adrift in a sea of sand, enclosed by an earthen wall. The designer, who remains unknown, provided no explanation.

Although many historians believe the garden was arranged by Sōami during the Muromachi period (1333–1576), some contend that it is a much later product of the Edo period. It is Japan's most famous *hira-niwa* (a flat garden void of hills or ponds) and reveals the stunning simplicity and harmony of the principles of Zen meditation.

The viewing platform for the garden can become packed solid, but the other parts of the temple grounds are also interesting and less of a target for the crowds. Among these, Kyoyo-chi pond is perhaps the most beautiful, particularly in autumn.

NINNA-JI Map p74

☎ 461-1155; Ukyō-ku, Omuro ōuchi 33; adult/child ¥500/300; 9am-4.30pm; 1min walk from Omuro Ninna-ji bus stop, bus 26 from Kyoto Station

Few travellers make the journey all the way out to this sprawling temple complex, but most who do find it a pleasant spot. It's certainly a good counterpoint to the crowded precincts of Ryōan-ji (left) and Kinkaku-ji (left). If you're after something a bit off the beaten track in Northwest Kyoto, this temple may fit the bill.

Originally containing more than 60 structures, Ninna-ji was built in 888 and is the head temple of the Omuro branch of the Shingon school. The present temple buildings, including a five-storey pagoda, date from the 17th century. On the extensive grounds you'll find a peculiar grove of short-trunked, multi-petal cherry trees called Omuro-no-Sakura, which draw large crowds in April.

Separate admission fees (an additional ¥500 each) are charged for both the Kondō and Reihōkan (Treasure House), which are only open for the first two weeks of October.

MYŌSHIN-JI Map p74

☎ 461-5226; Ukyō-ku, Hanazono 1; adult ¥500, child ¥100-300; 9.10am-3.40pm, closed 1hr at lunch; 10min walk from JR Hanazono Station

As with Daitoku-ji (p53), Myōshin-ji is a separate world within Kyoto, a walled-off complex of temples and subtemples that invites lazy strolling. The subtemple of Taizō-in (below) contains one of the city's more interesting gardens.

Myōshin-ji dates to 1342 and belongs to the Rinzai school. There are 47 subtemples, but only a few are open to the public.

From the north gate, follow the broad stone avenue flanked by rows of temples to the southern part of the complex. The eponymous Myōshin-ji temple here is roughly in the middle of the complex. Your entry fee here entitles you to a tour of several of the buildings of the temple. The ceiling of the *hattō* (lecture hall) here features Tanyū Kanō's unnerving painting *Unryūzu* (meaning 'dragon glaring in eight directions'). Your guide will invite you to stand directly beneath the dragon; doing so makes it appear that it's spiralling up or down.

TAIZŌ-IN Map p74

☎ 463-2855; Ukyō-ku, Hanazono Myōshin-ji 35; adult/child ¥500/300; 9am-5pm; 10min walk from JR Hanazono Station

This subtemple is in the southwestern corner of the grounds of Myōshin-ji (above). The *karesansui* garden depicting a waterfall and islands is well worth a visit.

TŌEI UZUMASA MOVIE VILLAGE Map p74

Tōei Uzumasa Eiga Mura; ☎ 864-7716; Ukyō-ku, Uzumasa Higashi Hachigaoka-chō 10; adult/child 6-18yr/under 6yr ¥2200/1300/1100; 9am-5pm 1 Mar-30 Nov, 9.30am-4pm 1 Dec-28 Feb; 13min walk from Uzumasa Station, Sagano line

In the Uzumasa area, Tōei Uzumasa Movie Village is a notorious tourist trap. It does, however, have some recreations of Edo-period street scenes that give a decent idea of what Kyoto must have looked like before the advent of concrete.

The main conceit of the park is that real movies are actually filmed here. While this may occasionally be the case, more often than not this entails a bunch of bored flunkies being ordered around by an ersatz movie 'director' complete with megaphone and a vintage 1930s-era movie camera. This delights some tourists but left us a little less than convinced.

Aside from this, there are displays relating to various aspects of Japanese movies and regular performances involving Japanese TV and movie characters such as the Power Rangers. This should entertain the kids – adults will probably be a little bored.

KŌRYŪ-JI Map p74

☎ 861-1461; Ukyō-ku, Uzumasa Hachiogaka-chō 32; adult ¥700, child ¥300-350; 9am-5pm Mar-Nov, to 4.30pm Dec-Feb; 2min walk from Uzumasa Station, Keifuku line

A bit out of the way, Kōryū-ji is easily paired with nearby Myōshin-ji (left) to form a half-day tour for those with an interest in Japanese Buddhism. It's notable mostly for its collection of Buddhist statuary and so a visit with a knowledgeable guide is a good way to learn about the different levels of beings in the Buddhist pantheon.

Kōryū-ji, one of the oldest temples in Japan, was founded in 622 to honour Prince Shōtoku, who was an enthusiastic promoter of Buddhism.

The Hattō to the right of the main gate houses a magnificent trio of 9th-century statues: Buddha, flanked by manifestations of Kannon.

The Reihōkan contains numerous fine Buddhist statues, including the Naki Miroku (Crying Miroku) and the renowned Miroku Bosatsu (Bodhisattva of the Future), which is extraordinarily expressive. A national upset occurred in 1960 when an enraptured university student embraced the statue in a fit of passion (at least, that was his excuse) and inadvertently snapped off its little finger.

ARASHIYAMA & SAGANO

Eating p136; Sleeping p154

Separated from the rest of Kyoto by a vast expanse of fairly drab residential district, Arashiyama and Sagano feels like a world apart. Tucked up against a lovely range of mountains and bisected by a scenic river, this area rivals Northern Higashiyama as the most scenic of Kyoto's sightseeing districts. It is a region of bamboo forests, wooded groves and temples surrounded by nature. That is, once you get out of central Arashiyama, which is a bustling tourist area, particularly around the famed Tōgetsu-kyō bridge. The view of the bridge over the Katsura-gawa with its backdrop of mountains has been in nearly as many Kyoto postcards as Kinkaku-ji and is the predominant attraction for local tourists.

The main bamboo grove, just outside the north gate of Tenryū-ji, is one of Kyoto's most famous sites and is a dead ringer for the bamboo forest in the film *Crouching Tiger, Hidden Dragon*. Note that Arashiyama is wildly popular with Japanese tourists and can be packed, particularly in the cherry-blossom and maple-leaf seasons. The further north you go, the more you will escape the masses.

While you can stay here in a range of excellent ryokan and *minshuku*, you will definitely feel isolated from the rest of Kyoto if you do so and it'll be something of a hike to the dining and nightlife options of Downtown. Unless you have a reason for wanting to be based here, we recommend visiting the area as a full-day trip out from Downtown or other parts of Kyoto.

To get here, take bus 28 from Kyoto Station (¥240, 40 minutes) or bus 11 from Keihan line Sanjō Station (¥240, 45 minutes). The best rail connection is the ride from Shijō-Ōmiya Station on the Keifuku Arashiyama line to Arashiyama Station (¥230, 20 minutes).

You can also take the Sagano line (San-in main line) from Kyoto Station (¥230, 20 minutes) or Nijō Station (¥190, 12 minutes) and get off at Saga Arashiyama Station (be careful to take the local train; the express does not stop in Arashiyama).

ARASHIYAMA MONKEY PARK IWATAYAMA Map p80

☎ 861-1616; Nishikyō-ku, Arashiyama, Genrokuzan-chō 8; adult ¥520, child ¥160-420; 9am-5pm 15 Mar-15 Nov, to 4pm 16 Nov-14 Mar; 10min walk from Keifuku Arashiyama Station, Keifuku Arashiyama line

If you want to spend some quality time with our simian cousins or entertain restless children, this park might fit the bill. Just be warned: it's a steep climb up the hill to get to the monkeys. If it's a hot day, you're going to be drenched by the time you get to the spot where they gather.

Though it is common to spot wild monkeys in the nearby mountains, here you can encounter them at a close distance and enjoy watching the playful creatures frolic about. It makes for an excellent photo opportunity, not only of the monkeys but also of the panoramic view over Kyoto. Refreshingly, it is the animals who are free to roam while the humans who feed them are caged in a box!

You enter the park near the south side of Tōgetsu-kyō (right), through the orange *torii* of Ichitani-jinja. Buy your tickets from the machine to the left of the shrine at the top of the steps.

TOGETSU-KYŌ Map p80

Ukyō-ku, Saga Tenryū-ji, Susukinobaba-chō; 5min walk from Keifuku Arashiyama Station, Keifuku Arashiyama line

This bridge is the dominant landmark in Arashiyama and is just a few minutes on foot from either the Keifuku line or Hankyū line Arashiyama Stations. The original crossing, constructed in 1606, was about 100m upriver from the present bridge.

On 13 April *jūsan-mairi*, an important rite of passage for local children aged 13, takes place here. Boys and girls (many in kimono), after paying respects at Hōrin-ji and receiving a blessing for wisdom, cross the bridge under strict parental order not to look back towards the temple until they've reached the northern side of the bridge. Not heeding this instruction is believed to bring bad luck for life!

From July to mid-September, this is a good spot from which to watch *ukai* (cormorant fishing) in the evening. If you want to get close to the action, you can

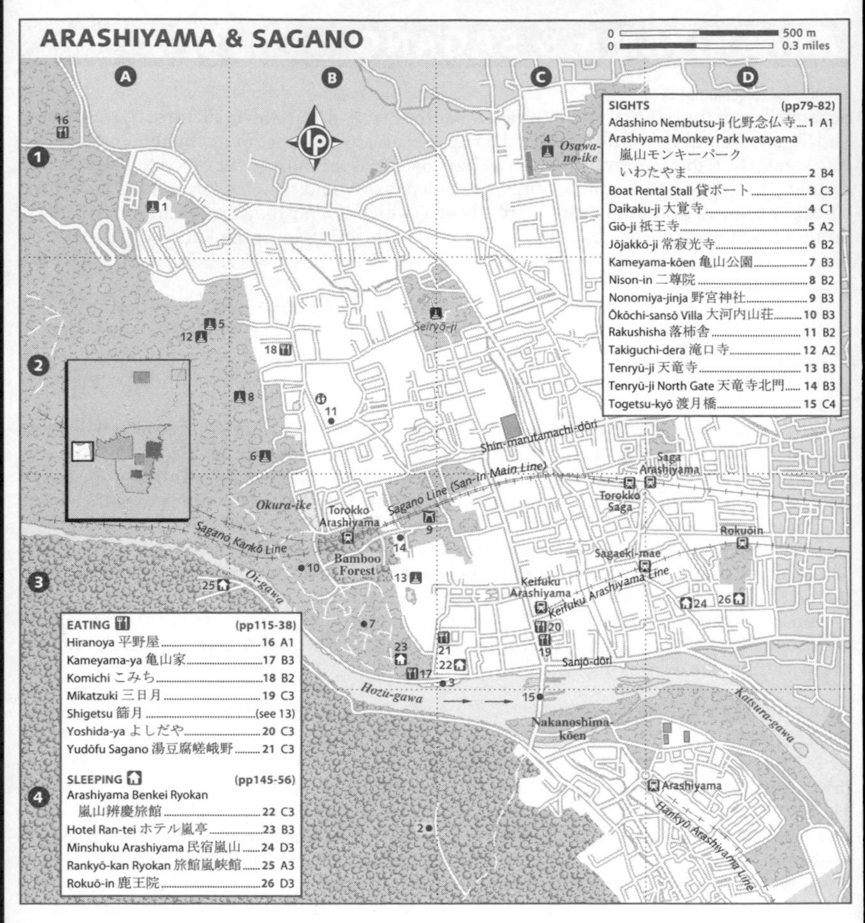

pay ¥1700 to join a passenger boat. The TIC (p199) can provide more details.

You can also rent boats from the boat rental stall (per hr ¥1400; 9am-4.30pm) just upstream from the bridge. It's a nice way to spend some time in Arashiyama and kids love it.

TENRYŪ-JI Map p80

881-1235; Ukyō-ku, Saga Tenryū-ji, Susukinobaba-chō 68; adult/child ¥600/400; 8.30am-5.30pm Mar-Oct, 8.30am-5pm Nov-Feb; 5min walk from Keifuku Arashiyama Station, Keifuku Arashiyama line

This fine temple has one of the most attractive stroll gardens in all of Kyoto, particularly during the spring cherry-blossom and autumn-foliage seasons. The main 14th-century Zen garden, with its backdrop of the Arashiyama Mountains, is a good example of *shakkei*. Unfortunately, it's no secret that the garden here is world class, so it pays to visit early in the morning or on a weekday.

Tenryū-ji is a major temple of the Rinzai school. It was built in 1339 on the old site of Go-Daigo's villa after a priest had a dream of a dragon rising from the nearby river. The dream was seen as a sign that the emperor's spirit was uneasy and so the temple was built as appeasement – hence the name *tenryū* (heavenly dragon). The present buildings date from 1900. You will find Arashiyama's famous bamboo grove situated just outside the north gate of the temple.

HOZU-GAWA RIVER TRIP

The Hozu-gawa river trip (☎ 0771-22-5846; Kameoka-shi, Hozu-chō; adult/child ¥3900/2500; 9am-3.30pm, closed 29 Dec-4 Jan) is a great way to enjoy the beauty of Kyoto's western mountains without any strain on the legs. With long bamboo poles, boatmen steer flat-bottom boats down the Hozu-gawa from Kameoka, 30km west of Kyoto Station, through steep, forested mountain canyons, before arriving at Arashiyama.

Between 10 March and 30 November there are seven trips daily. During winter the number of trips is reduced to four per day and the boats are heated.

The ride lasts two hours and covers 16km through occasional sections of choppy water – a scenic jaunt with minimal danger. The scenery is especially breathtaking during cherry-blossom season in April and maple-foliage season in autumn.

The boats depart from a dock that is eight minutes' walk from Kameoka Station. Kameoka is accessible by rail from Kyoto Station or Nijō Station on the Sagano line (San-in main line). The TIC (p199) provides an English-language leaflet and timetable for rail connections. The fare from Kyoto to Kameoka is ¥400 one way by regular train (don't spend the extra for the express; it makes little difference in travel time).

Tenryū-ji is also a popular place to sample *shōjin ryōri* (Buddhist vegetarian cuisine).

KAMEYAMA-KŌEN Map p80

Just upstream from Tōgetsu-kyō (p79) and behind Tenryū-ji (opposite), this park is a nice place to escape the crowds of Arashiyama. It's laced with trails, the best of which leads up to a lookout over Katsura-gawa and up into the Arashiyama mountains. It's especially attractive during cherry-blossom and autumn-foliage seasons. Keep an eye out for monkeys, which occasionally descend from the nearby hills to pick fruit.

ŌKŌCHI-SANSŌ VILLA Map p80

☎ 872-2233; Ukyō-ku, Saga Ogurayamadabuchi-yama-chō 8; incl tea & cake adult ¥1000, child ¥500-900; 9am-5pm; 15min walk from Keifuku Arashiyama Station, Keifuku Arashiyama line

This is the lavish estate of Ōkōchi Denjirō, an actor famous for his samurai films. The sprawling stroll gardens may well be the most lovely in all of Kyoto, particularly when you consider the brilliant views eastwards across the city. The house and teahouse are also sublime. Be sure to follow all the trails around the gardens (the standard route is clearly marked). Hold onto the tea ticket they give you when you enter – you'll need it to claim the tea and cake that comes with entry.

JŌJAKKŌ-JI Map p80

☎ 861-0435; Ukyō-ku, Saga, Ogura-yama, Ogura-chō 3; adult ¥300, child ¥100-200; 9am-5pm; 20min walk from Keifuku Arashiyama Station, Keifuku Arashiyama line

This temple is perched on top of a mossy knoll and is famed for its brilliant maple trees, which turn a lovely crimson red in November, and its thatched-roof Niō-mon gate. The Hondō was constructed in the 16th century out of wood sourced from Fushimi-jō.

RAKUSHISHA Map p80

☎ 881-1953; Ukyō-ku, Saga, Ogura-yama, Hinomyō-jin-chō 20; admission ¥200; 9am-5pm; 20min walk from Saga Arashiyama Station, Sagano line

This building was the hut of Mukai Kyorai, the best-known disciple of the illustrious haiku poet Bashō. Legend holds that Kyorai dubbed the house Rakushisha (literally 'House of the Fallen Persimmons') after he woke one morning following a fierce storm to find the persimmons he had planned to sell were all fallen from the trees in the garden and scattered on the ground.

NISON-IN Map p80

☎ 861-0687; Ukyō-ku, Saga, Nison-in, Monzenchōjin-chō 27; admission ¥500; 9am-4.30pm; 20min walk from Keifuku Arashiyama Station, Keifuku Arashiyama line

This is a popular spot with maple-watchers. Nison-in was originally built in the 9th century by Emperor Saga. It houses two important Kamakura-era Buddha statues side by side (Shaka on the right and Amida on the left). The temple features lacquered nightingale floors.

TAKIGUCHI-DERA Map p80

☎ 871-3929; Ukyō-ku, Saga, Kameyama-chō 10-4; adult/child ¥300/200; 9am-5pm; 35min walk from Keifuku Arashiyama Station, Keifuku Arashiyama line

The history of this temple reads like the romance of *Romeo and Juliet*. Takiguchi-dera was founded by Heian-era nobleman Takiguchi Nyūdō, who entered the priesthood after being forbidden by his father to marry his peasant consort Yokobue. One day, Yokobue came to the temple with her flute to serenade Takiguchi, but was again refused by him; she wrote a farewell love sonnet on a stone (in her own blood) before throwing herself into the river to perish. The stone remains at the temple.

GIŌ-JI Map p80

☎ 861-3574; Ukyō-ku, Saga, Toriimoto Kozaka-chō 32; admission ¥300; 9am-5pm; 15min walk from Saga Shakadō-mae bus stop, bus 28 or 72 from Kyoto Station

This quiet temple was named for the Heian-era *shirabyōshi* (traditional dancer) Giō, who committed herself here as a nun at age 21 after her romance ended with Taira-no-Kiyomori, the mighty commander of the Heike clan. She was usurped in Kiyomori's affections by a fellow entertainer, Hotoke Gozen (who later deserted Kiyomori to join Giō at the temple). Enshrined in the main hall are five wooden statues: these are Giō, Hotoke Gozen, Kiyomori and Giō's mother and sister (who were also nuns at the temple).

The main attraction here is the lush moss garden outside the thatch-roofed hall of the temple. It's a small spot that is often overlooked by visitors to Arashiyama.

ADASHINO NEMBUTSU-JI Map p80

☎ 861-2221; Ukyō-ku, Saga, Toriimoto, Adashino-chō 17; adult/child ¥500/400; 9am-4.30pm; 4min walk from Toriimoto bus stop, bus 72 from Kyoto Station

This rather unusual temple is where the abandoned bones of paupers without kin were gathered. More than 8000 stone images are crammed into the temple grounds, dedicated to the repose of their spirits. The abandoned souls are remembered with candles each year in the Sentō Kuyō (p16) ceremony held here on the evenings of 23 and 24 August. The temple is not a must-see attraction, but it's certainly interesting and the stone images make unusual photographs.

DAIKAKU-JI Map p80

☎ 871-0071; Ukyō-ku, Saga, Osawa-chō 4; adult/child ¥500/300; 9am-4.30pm; 15min walk from Saga Arashiyama Station, Sagano line

A 25-minute walk northeast of Nison-in (p81) you will find Daikaku-ji, one of Kyoto's less-commonly visited temples. It was built in the 9th century as a palace for Emperor Saga, who then converted it into a temple. The present buildings date from the 16th century and are palatial in style; they also contain some impressive paintings. The large Osawa-no-ike pond was once used by the emperor for boating and is a popular spot for viewing the harvest moon.

KITAYAMA AREA

Eating p137; Sleeping p155

Starting on the north side of Kyoto city and stretching almost all the way to the Sea of Japan, the Kitayama Mountains are a natural escape prized by Kyoto city dwellers and a green retreat for travellers who need a little break from modern life. The steep mountains here are intersected by a series of deep valleys, some of which contain incredibly picturesque villages. Attractions here include the village of Ōhara, with its pastoral beauty, and the fine mountain temple of Kurama. While you can stay in these villages, you'd really need some particular reason to do so, and you'd no doubt find it very inconvenient for sightseeing in the rest of Kyoto. Instead, we recommend choosing one of these worthy destinations and making it a special full-day trip out of central Kyoto.

Ōhara

Since ancient times Ōhara, a quiet farming town about 10km north of Kyoto, has been regarded as a holy site by followers of the Jōdo (Pure Land) school of Buddhism. The region provides a charming glimpse of rural Japan, along with the picturesque Sanzen-in, Jakkō-in and several other fine temples. It's most popular in autumn, when the maple leaves change colour and the mountain views are spectacular. During the peak foliage season (late October to mid-November) avoid this area at weekends as it will be packed.

From Kyoto Station, Kyoto buses 17 and 18 run to Ōhara bus stop. The ride takes about an hour and costs ¥580. From Keihan line's Sanjō Station, take Kyoto bus 16 or 17 (¥470, 45 minutes). Be careful to board a tan-coloured Kyoto bus, not a green Kyoto City bus of the same number.

SANZEN-IN Map p84

☎ 744-2531; Sakyō-ku, Ōhara, Raigōin-chō 540; adult ¥700, child ¥150-400; 8.30am-4.30pm Feb-Dec, 8.30am-4pm Jan; 10min walk from Ōhara bus stop, Kyoto bus 17 or 18 from Kyoto Station

Famed for its autumn foliage, hydrangea garden and stunning Buddha images, this temple is deservedly popular with foreign and domestic tourists alike.

Founded in 784 by the priest Saichō, Sanzen-in belongs to the Tendai school. Saichō, considered one of the great patriarchs of Buddhism in Japan, also founded Enryaku-ji (p91).

The temple's garden, Yūsei-en, is one of the most photographed sights in Japan, and rightly so. Take some time to sit on the steps of the Shin-den hall and admire the garden's beauty. Then head off to see Ōjō-gokuraku-in (Temple of Rebirth in Paradise), the hall in which stands the impressive Amitabha trinity, a large Amida image flanked by attendants Kannon and Seishi (god of wisdom). After this, walk up to the garden at the back of the temple where, in late spring and summer, you can walk among hectares of blooming hydrangeas.

The approach to Sanzen-in is opposite the main bus stop; there is no English sign but you can usually just follow the Japanese tourists. The temple is located about 600m up this walk on your left as you crest the hill.

If you're keen for a short hike after leaving the temple, continue up the hill to see the rather oddly named Soundless Waterfall (Oto-nashi-no-taki). Though in fact it sounds like any other waterfall, its resonance is believed to have inspired Shōmyō Buddhist chanting.

JIKKŌ-IN Map p84

☎ 744-2537; Sakyō-ku, Ōhara, Shōrinin-chō 187; adult/child incl green tea & sweets ¥600/300; 9am-5pm; 10min walk from Ōhara bus stop, Kyoto bus 17 or 18 from Kyoto Station

Only about 50m north of Sanzen-in (left), this small temple is often praised for its lovely garden and *fudan-zakura* cherry tree, which blossoms between October and March. Jikkō-in is worth the visit if you want to escape the crowds that often plague Sanzen-in.

SHŌRIN-IN Map p84

☎ 744-2537; Sakyō-ku, Ōhara, Shōrinin-chō 187; adult ¥300, child ¥200-300; 9am-5pm; 15min walk from Ōhara bus stop, Kyoto bus 17 or 18 from Kyoto Station

This temple is worth a look, even if only through its admission gate, to admire the

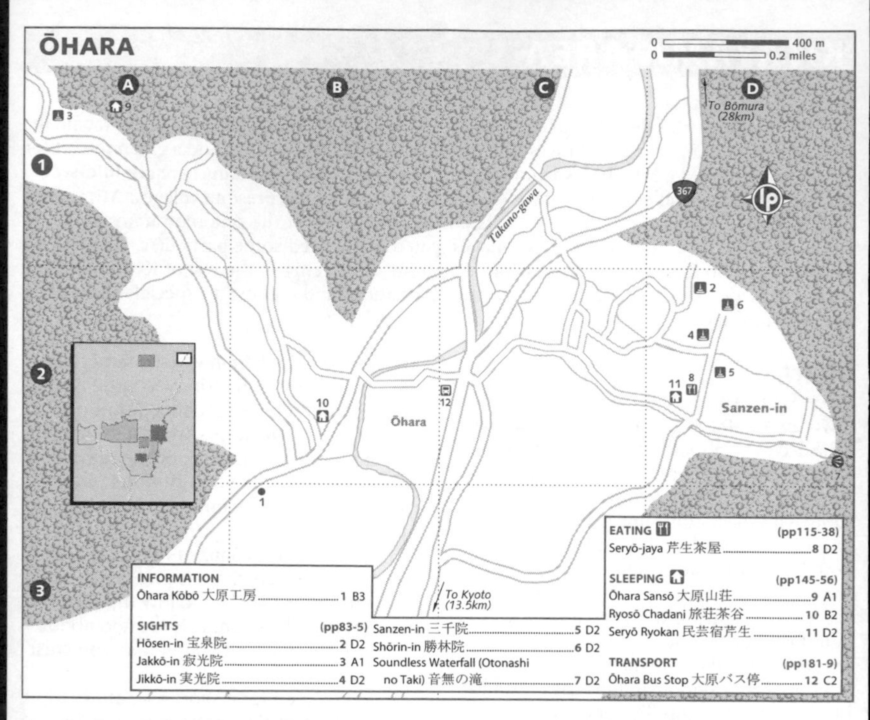

thatched roof of the main hall. It's also a good option if you're trying to avoid crowds.

HŌSEN-IN Map p84

☎ 744-2409; Sakyō-ku, Ōhara, Shōrinin-chō 187; adult ¥800, child ¥600-700; 9am-5pm; 10min walk from Ōhara bus stop, Kyoto bus 17 or 18 from Kyoto Station

A quieter option than Sanzen-in (p83), this temple is just down the path west of the entry gate to Shōrin-in (p83). The main tatami room offers a view of a bamboo garden and the surrounding mountains, framed like a painting by the beams and posts of the building. There is also a fantastic 700-year-old pine tree in the garden. The blood-stained Chi Tenjō ceiling boards came from Fushimi-jō castle.

JAKKŌ-IN Map p84

☎ 744-2545; Sakyō-ku, Ōhara, Kusao-chō 676; adult ¥600, child ¥100-350; 9am-5pm; 10min walk from Ōhara bus stop, Kyoto bus 17 or 18 from Kyoto Station

Jakkō-in sits on the opposite side of Ōhara from the more famous Sanzen-in (p83). It's reached by a very pleasant walk through a quaint 'old Japan' village. It's a relatively small temple that can't compete with the beauty of its popular neighbour, but it does make an interesting end point to a fine walk in the country.

The history of the temple is exceedingly tragic. The actual founding date of the temple is subject to some debate (it's thought to be somewhere between the 6th and 11th centuries), but it acquired fame as the temple that harboured Kenrei Mon-in, a lady of the Taira clan. In 1185 the Taira were soundly defeated in a sea battle against the Minamoto clan at Dan-no-ura. With the entire Taira clan slaughtered or drowned, Kenrei Mon-in threw herself into the waves with her son Antoku, the infant emperor; she was fished out – the only member of the clan to survive.

She was returned to Kyoto, where she became a nun and lived in a bare hut until it collapsed during an earthquake. Kenrei Mon-in was then accepted into Jakkō-in and stayed there, immersed in prayer and sorrowful memories, until her death 27 years later. Her tomb is located high on the hill behind the temple.

The main building of this temple burned down in May 2000 and the newly reconstructed main hall lacks some of the charm of the original. Nonetheless, it is a nice spot.

Jakkō-in is west of Ōhara. Walk out of the bus station up the road to the traffic lights, then follow the small road to the left. Since it's easy to get lost on the way, we recommend familiarising yourself with the kanji for Jakkō-in (see the map key) and following the Japanese signs.

Kurama & Kibune

Located just 30 minutes north of Kyoto, Kurama and Kibune are a pair of tranquil valleys that have been long favoured as places to escape the crowds and stresses of the city. Kurama's main attractions are its mountain temple and *onsen* (mineral hot spring). Kibune, an impossibly charming little hamlet just over the ridge, is a cluster of ryokan overlooking a mountain river. Kibune is best in summer, when the ryokan serve dinner on platforms built over the rushing waters of Kibune-gawa, providing welcome relief from the heat.

The two valleys lend themselves to being explored together. In winter, you can start from Kibune, walk 30 minutes over the ridge, visit Kurama-dera, then soak in the *onsen* before heading back to Kyoto. In summer, the reverse route is best: start from Kurama, walk up to the temple, then down the other side to Kibune to enjoy a meal suspended above the cool river. Either way, a trip to Kurama and Kibune is probably the single best day or half-day trip possible from Kyoto city.

If you happen to be in Kyoto on the night of 22 October, be sure not to miss the Kurama Hi Matsuri (p17) fire festival. It's one of the most exciting festivals in the Kyoto area.

To get to Kurama and Kibune, take the Eizan line from Kyoto's Demachiyanagi Station. For Kibune, get off at the second-to-last stop, Kibune-guchi, take a right out of the station and walk about 20 minutes up the hill. For Kurama, go to the last stop, Kurama, and walk straight out of the station. Both destinations are ¥410 and take about 30 minutes to reach.

KURAMA-DERA Map p85

☎ 741-2003; Sakyō-ku, Kurama, Honmachi 1074; admission ¥200; 9am-4.30pm; 3min walk from Kurama Station, Eizan line

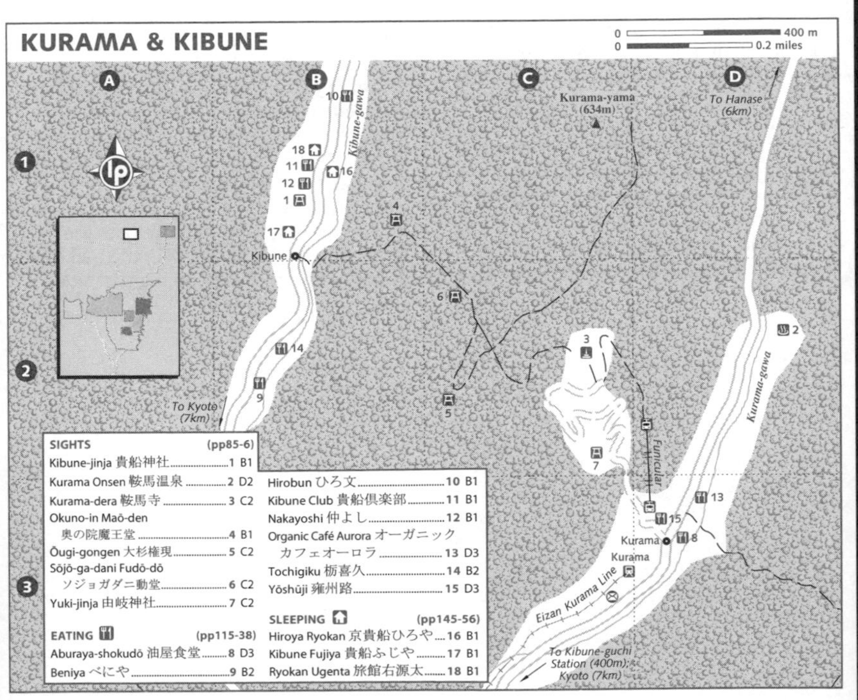

Located high on a thickly wooded mountain, Kurama-dera is one of the few temples in modern Japan that still manage to retain an air of real spirituality. This is a magical place that gains a lot of its power from its brilliant natural setting.

The temple also has a fascinating history: in 770 the monk Gantei left Nara's Toshōdai-ji in search of a wilderness sanctuary in which to meditate. Wandering in the hills north of Kyoto, he came across a white horse that led him to the valley known today as Kurama. After seeing a vision of the deity Bishamon-ten, guardian of the northern quarter of the Buddhist heaven, Gantei established Kurama-dera just below the peak of Kurama-yama. Originally belonging to the Tendai school of Buddhism, Kurama has been independent since 1949, describing its own brand of Buddhism as Kurama-kyō.

The entrance to the temple is just up the hill from Kurama Station. A tram goes to the top for ¥100 or you can hike up in about 30 minutes (follow the main path past the tram station). The trail is worth taking (if it's not too hot), since it winds through a forest of towering old-growth cryptomeria trees, passing Yuki-jinja (Map p85) on the way. Near the peak, there is a courtyard dominated by the Honden; behind this a trail leads off to the mountain's peak.

At the top, you can take a brief detour across the ridge to Ōsugi-gongen (Map p85), a quiet shrine in a grove of trees. Those who want to continue to Kibune can take the trail down the other side. It's a 1.2km, 30-minute hike from the Honden to the valley floor of Kibune. On the way down are two mountain shrines, Sōjō-ga-dani Fudō-dō (Map p85) and Okuno-in Maō-den (Map p85), which make pleasant rest stops.

KURAMA ONSEN Map p85

☎ 741-2131; Sakyō-ku, Kurama, Honmachi 520; adult/child from ¥1100/700; 10am-9pm; 10min walk from Kurama Station, Eizan line

One of the few *onsen* within easy reach of Kyoto, Kurama Onsen is a great place to relax after a hike. The outdoor bath has fine views of Kurama-yama and costs ¥1100/700 per adult/child. For ¥2300/1600 you get to use the indoor bath as well, but even with a sauna and locker thrown in, it's difficult to imagine why you would opt for indoors. For both baths, buy a ticket from the machine outside the door of the main building (instructions are in Japanese and English).

To get to Kurama Onsen, walk straight out of Kurama Station and continue up the main street, passing the entrance to Kurama-dera on your left. The *onsen* is about 10 minutes' walk on the right. There's also a free shuttle bus between the station and the *onsen,* which meets incoming trains.

KIBUNE-JINJA Map p85

Halfway up the village of Kibune on the west side of the street, Kibune-jinja sits at the top of a flight of steps. It's a very charming spot, especially in the November maple-leaf season. The shrine predates the 8th-century founding of Kyoto. It was established to worship the god of water and has been long revered by farmers and sake brewers.

From Kibune you can hike over the mountain to Kurama-dera (p85); the trail starts halfway up the village on the east side.

GREATER KYOTO

Shopping p113

On the fringes of the city you'll find a host of worthwhile sights and districts. To the southeast lies the town of Uji, home to the fine ancient temple of Byōdō-in, and the sake-brewing district of Fushimi. To the southwest you'll find the brilliant Katsura Rikyū Imperial Villa and Saihō-ji (also known as Moss Temple). To the northwest you'll find the mountain town of Takao with its three fine temples and to the northeast you'll find the temple complex of Enryaku-ji atop Hiei-zan.

Buses and trains provide the best means of transport for the Greater Kyoto region. These are described in detail for each sight.

SOUTHEAST KYOTO

Southeast Kyoto contains the town of Uji, home to the lovely temple hall of Byōdō-in, and Fushimi, Kyoto's main sake-brewing district. Over a low mountain range, also to the southeast of the city, you'll find Daigo-ji, a sprawling temple complex with trails that lead up to a mountaintop hall.

DAIGO-JI Map pp42–3

☎ 571-0002; Fushimi-ku, Daigo Higashiōji-chō 22; admission to grounds during cherry-blossom & autumn-foliage seasons ¥600; 9am-5pm; 10min walk from exit 2, Daigo Station, Tōzai subway line

Daigo-ji was founded in 874 by Shobo, who gave it the name Daigo (meaning 'the ultimate essence of milk'). This refers to the five periods of Buddha's teaching, which were compared to the five forms of milk prepared in India – the highest form is called *daigo* in Japanese.

The temple was expanded into a vast complex on two levels, Shimo Daigo (lower) and Kami Daigo (upper). Kami Daigo is atop Daigo-yama, behind the temple. During the 15th century those buildings on the lower level were destroyed, with the sole exception of the five-storey pagoda. Built in 951, this pagoda is treasured as the oldest of its kind in Japan and is the oldest existing building in Kyoto.

In the late 16th century, Hideyoshi took a fancy to Daigo-ji and ordered extensive rebuilding. It is now one of the Shingon school's main temples. To explore Daigo-ji thoroughly and at a leisurely pace, mixing some hiking with your temple-viewing, you will need at least half a day.

The subtemple Sampō-in is a fine example of the amazing opulence of that period. The Kanō paintings and the garden are special features.

From Sampō-in it's a steep and tiring 50-minute climb up to Kami Daigo. To get here, walk up the large avenue of cherry trees, through the Niō-mon gate, out the back gate of the lower temple, up a concrete incline and into the forest, past the pagoda.

To get to Daigo-ji, take the Tōzai line subway east from central Kyoto to the Daigo stop, and walk east (towards the mountains) for about 10 minutes. Make sure that the train you board is bound for Rokujizō, as some head to Hama-Ōtsu instead.

Fushimi

Fushimi, home to 37 sake breweries, is one of Japan's most famous sake-producing regions. Its location on the Uji-gawa made it a perfect location for sake production, as fresh, high-quality rice was readily available from the fields of neighbouring Shiga-ken and the final product could be easily loaded onto boats for export downriver to Osaka.

Despite its fame, Fushimi is one of Kyoto's least-attractive areas. It's also a hard area to navigate due to a lack of English signage. It's probably only worth a visit if you've got a real interest in sake and sake production.

To get to Fushimi, take a local or express (not a limited express) from Sanjō Station on the Keihan line to Chūshojima Station (¥260, 20 minutes). Alternatively, you can take the Kintetsu Kyoto line from Kyoto Station to Momoyama-Goryōmae Station (¥250, 11 minutes). You'll find a useful map on a pillar outside Chūshojima Station that you can use to orient yourself.

GEKKEIKAN SAKE ŌKURA MUSEUM

Map pp42–3

☎ 623-2056; Fushimi-ku, Minamihama-chō 247; adult/child ¥300/100; 9.30am-4.30pm, closed Mon; 10min walk from Chūshojima Station, Keihan line

The largest of Fushimi's sake breweries is Gekkeikan, the world's leading producer of sake. Although most of the sake is now made in a modern facility in Osaka, a limited amount is still handmade in a Meiji-era *sakagura* (sake brewery) here in Fushimi.

The Gekkeikan Sake Ōkura Museum houses a collection of artefacts and memorabilia tracing the 350-year history of Gekkeikan and the sake-brewing process. Giant murals depicting traditional methods of brewing adorn the walls and there is the chance to taste (and of course buy) some of the local brew.

If you are travelling with a tour group that is larger than 20 people and if you call two weeks in advance (☎ 623-2001), you can arrange a guided English tour of the brewery. Otherwise, ask at the TIC (p199) about joining a tour given in Japanese.

The museum is a 10-minute walk northeast of Chūshojima Station on the Keihan line. To get here from the station, go right at the main exit, take a right down an unpaved road, a left at the playground, cross the bridge over the canal and follow the road around to the left; the museum is on the left.

KIZAKURA KAPPA COUNTRY

Map pp42–3

☎ 611-9919; Fushimi-ku, Shioya-chō 228; admission free; 11.30am-2pm & 5-9.30pm Mon-Fri, 11am-10pm Sat & Sun; 6min walk from Chūshojima Station, Keihan line

A short walk from its competitor, Gekkeikan (p87), Kizakura is another sake brewery worth a look while you're in the neighbourhood. The vast complex houses both sake and beer breweries, courtyard gardens and a small gallery dedicated to the mythical (and sneaky) creature Kappa. The restaurant-bar is an appealing option for a bite and a bit of fresh-brewed ale.

TERADAYA MUSEUM Map pp42–3

☎ 611-1223; Fushimi-ku, Minamihama-chō; adult ¥400, child ¥200-300; 10am-3pm; 10min walk from Chūshojima Station, Keihan line

Famed as the inn of choice for rebel samurai Sakamoto Ryōma (1834–67), today Teradaya operates as a museum. Fans of Ryōma faithfully make the pilgrimage here to see the room where he slept.

You might have to ask a passer-by for directions, as the way is poorly marked. There is a sign out the front in English that reads: 'The site of the Teradaya Feud'.

Uji

About 20 minutes south of Kyoto Station by train, the small city of Uji is rich in Heian-period culture. Its main claims to fame are Byōdō-in and Ujigami-jinja (both Unesco World Heritage sites) and tea cultivation. The Uji-bashi Bridge, originally all wood and the oldest of its kind in Japan (it is now constructed of concrete and wood), has been the scene of many bitter clashes in previous centuries, although traffic jams seem to predominate nowadays.

If you've exhausted the sights in the main part of Kyoto and feel like a pleasant half-day trip out of town, Uji is a decent choice.

Uji can be easily reached by rail from Kyoto on the Keihan Uji line (¥460, 30 minutes) from Sanjō Station (change at Chūshojima) or the JR Nara line (¥210, 20 minutes) from Kyoto

UJI TEA

The mountains that surround the town of Uji are perfect for growing tea, and the town has always been one of Japan's main tea-cultivation centres. In fact, tea is usually the first thing most Japanese associate with the name Uji. You won't see any of the plantations unless you rent a car and drive into the mountains to the south, but you will see plenty of shops selling tea in Uji town. As you might expect, this is also a great place to try a simple Japanese tea ceremony.

On the river bank behind Byōdō-in stands the delightful Taihō-an (☎ 0774-23-3334; info@kyoto-uji-kankou.or.jp; Uji-shi Uji Araragi-gawa; admission ¥500; 10am-4pm; 10min walk from Uji Station, Keihan Uji line). The friendly staff conduct a 30-minute tea ceremony (ask for the tatami room, unless you've got knee trouble). Casual dress is fine here and no reservations are necessary. Buy your tickets at the Uji-shi Kanko centre next door.

Another stop for a taste of Uji's famed green tea is Tsūen-jaya (☎ 0774-21-2243; www.tsuentea.com/engindex.htm; Uji-shi Uji Higashiuchi; 9.30am-5.30pm; Uji Station, Keihan Uji line), located just across from the station. Japan's oldest surviving tea shop, Tsūen-jaya has been in the Tsūen family for more than 830 years. The present building, near Uji-bashi, dates from 1672 and is full of interesting antiques. You can try fresh *matcha* (powered green tea), including a sweet, for ¥680.

Station. To get to Byōdō-in from Keihan Uji Station, cross the river on the bridge right outside the station; immediately after crossing the bridge, take a left past a public toilet (don't take the street with the large stone *torii*), and continue straight through the park.

BYŌDŌ-IN off Map pp42–3

平等院

☎ 0774-21-2861; Uji-shi, Uji renge 116; admission ¥600; 🕑 8.30am-5.30pm Mar-Nov, 9am-4pm Dec-Feb; 10min walk from Uji Station, JR Nara line

If you happen to have a ¥10 coin in your pocket, dig it out now and have a look at it. The building depicted on the coin is the main hall of this lovely temple in the centre of Uji. Overlooking a serene pond, the hall is one of the loveliest Buddhist structures in Japan.

This temple was converted from a Fujiwara villa into a Buddhist temple in 1052. The Hōō-dō (Phoenix hall), the main hall of the temple, was built in 1053 and is the only original building remaining. The phoenix used to be a popular mythical bird in China and was revered by the Japanese as a protector of Buddha. The architecture of the building resembles the shape of the bird and there are two bronze phoenixes perched opposite each other on the roof.

The Phoenix hall was originally intended to represent Amida's heavenly palace in the Pure Land. This building is one of the few extant examples of Heian-period architecture, and its graceful lines make you wish that far more had survived the wars and fires that have plagued Kyoto's past. Inside the hall is the famous statue of Amida Buddha and 52 *bosatsu* (Bodhisattvas) dating from the 11th century and attributed to the priest-sculptor Jōchō.

Nearby, the Hōmotsukan Treasure House (admission ¥300; 🕑 9am-4pm 1 Apr-31 May & 15 Sep-23 Nov) contains the original temple bell and door paintings and the original phoenix roof adornments. Allow about an hour to wander through the grounds.

UJIGAMI-JINJA off Map pp42–3

宇治上神社

☎ 0774-21-4634; Uji-shi, Uji Yamada 59; admission free; 🕑 9am-4.30pm; 5min walk from Uji Station, Keihan Uji line

Ujigami-jinja holds the distinction of being Japan's oldest shrine. Despite its historical significance, the shrine is the least interesting of Kyoto's 17 Unesco World Heritage sites.

According to ancient records, Uji-no-waki-Iratsuko, a 5th-century prince, tragically sacrificed his own life to conclude the matter of whether he or his brother would succeed the imperial throne; needless to say his brother, Emperor Nintoku, won the dispute. The main building was dedicated to the twosome and their father, Emperor Ōjin, and enshrines the tombs of the trio.

The shrine is across the river from Byōdō-in and a short walk uphill; take the orange bridge across the river. On the way, you'll pass through Uji-jinja (admission free; 🕑 dawn-dusk), which is actually better looking than its more famous neighbour.

MAMPUKU-JI off Map pp42–3

萬福寺

☎ 0774-32-3900; Uji-shi, Gokashō, Sanbanwari 34; admission ¥500; 🕑 9am-4pm; 5min walk from Ōbaku Station, JR Nara line

For something totally different while in the Uji area, you might consider a side trip to the unusual Mampuku-ji, a seldom visited temple a little bit north of the centre of Uji.

Mampuku-ji was established as a Zen temple in 1661 by the Chinese priest Ingen. It is a rare example in Japan of a Zen temple built in the pure Chinese style of the Ming dynasty. The temple follows the Ōbaku school, which is linked to the mainstream Rinzai school but incorporates a wide range of esoteric Buddhist practices.

SOUTHWEST KYOTO

The southwest area of Kyoto is a sprawling residential and commercial area that few foreign tourists ever visit. Despite the relatively drab surroundings, however, there are three very worthwhile sights here: Katsura Rikyū Imperial Villa; the stunning Saihō-ji, Kyoto's famed Moss Temple; and Jizo-in, a quaint little temple with a tiny moss garden.

For transport to and from this area, see the transport information for the following sights.

KATSURA RIKYŪ IMPERIAL VILLA

Map pp42–3

☎ 211-1215; Nishikyō-ku, Katsura misono; admission free; 7min walk from Katsura Rikyū-mae bus stop, bus 33 from Kyoto Station

Katsura Rikyū, one of Kyoto's imperial properties, is widely considered to be the pinnacle of Japanese traditional architecture and garden design. Set amid an otherwise drab neighbourhood, it is (very literally) an island of incredible beauty and well worth the troublesome application process required to make a visit.

The villa was built in 1624 for the emperor's brother, Prince Toshihito. Every conceivable detail of the villa – the teahouses, the large pond with islets and the surrounding garden – has been given meticulous attention.

Tours (in Japanese) start at 10am, 11am, 2pm and 3pm, and last 40 minutes. Try to be there 20 minutes before the start time. An explanatory video is shown in the waiting room and a leaflet is provided in English.

You must make reservations, usually several weeks in advance, through the Imperial Household Agency – see the boxed text, p57, for details.

SAIHŌ-JI Map pp42-3

☎ 391-3631; Nishikyō-ku, Matsuo Jingatani-chō 56; admission ¥3000; 5min walk from Kokedera bus stop, Kyoto bus 28 from Arashiyama Station, Hankyū line

The main attraction at this temple is the heart-shaped garden, designed in 1339 by Musō Kokushi. The garden is famous for its luxuriant mossy growth – hence the temple's other name, Koke-dera (Moss Temple). It is a truly lovely garden but it costs a fair bit and advance reservations are required (see the boxed text, below).

RESERVATIONS FOR SAIHŌ-JI

To visit Saihō-ji (above), you must make a reservation. Send a postcard at least one week before the date you wish to visit and include your name, number of visitors, address in Japan, occupation, age (you must be over 18) and desired date (choice of alternative dates preferred). The address:

Saihō-ji,
56 Kamigaya-chō,
Matsuo, Nishikyō-ku,
Kyoto-shi 615-8286
JAPAN

Enclose a stamped self-addressed postcard for a reply to your Japanese address. You might find it convenient to buy an Ōfuku-hagaki (send and return postcard set) at a Japanese post office.

JIZŌ-IN Map pp42–3

☎ 381-3417; Nishikyō-ku, Yamadakitano-chō 23; adult/child ¥500/300; 9am-4.30pm; 5min walk from Koke-dera bus stop, Kyoto bus 78 from Arashiyama Station, Hankyū line

This delightful little temple could be called the 'poor man's Saihō-ji'. It's only a few minutes' walk south of Saihō-ji (left) in the same atmospheric bamboo groves. While the temple does not boast any spectacular buildings or treasures, it has a nice moss garden and is almost completely ignored by tourists, making it a great place to sit and contemplate.

From the parking lot near Saihō-ji, there is a small stone staircase that climbs to the road leading to Jizō-in (it helps to ask someone to point the way, as it's not entirely clear).

TAKAO AREA

The Takao area is tucked far away in the northwestern part of Kyoto. It is famed for autumn foliage and a trio of temples: Jingo-ji, Saimyō-ji and Kōzan-ji.

To reach Takao, take bus 8 from Nijō Station to the last stop, Takao (¥500, 40 minutes). From Kyoto Station, take the hourly JR bus to the Yamashiro Takao stop (¥500, 50 minutes). To get to Jingo-ji, walk down to the river and climb the steps on the other side.

JINGO-JI Map pp42–3

☎ 861-1769; Ukyō-ku Takao-chō; adult/child from ¥500/200; 9am-4pm; 20min walk from Yamashiro Takao bus stop, JR bus from Kyoto Station

This mountaintop temple is one of our favourites in all of Kyoto. It sits at the top of a long flight of stairs that stretch from the Kiyotaki-gawa to the temple's main gate. The Kondō (Gold Hall) is the most impressive of the temple's structures, located roughly in the middle of the grounds at the top of another flight of stairs.

After visiting the Kondō, head in the opposite direction along a wooded path to an open area overlooking the valley. Here you'll see people tossing small disks over the railing into the chasm below. These are *kawarakenage,* light clay disks that people throw in order to rid themselves of their bad karma. Be careful, it's addictive and at ¥100 for two it can get expensive (you can buy the disks at a nearby stall). The trick is to flick the disks very gently, convex side up, like a Frisbee. When you get it right, they sail all the way down the valley – taking all that bad karma with them (try not to think about the hikers down below).

SAIMYŌ-JI Map pp42–3

☎ 861-1770; Ukyō-ku, Umegahata Toganoo-chō; admission free; ⌚ 9am-5pm; 🚌 10min walk from Yamashiro Takao bus stop, JR bus from Kyoto Station

About five minutes upstream from the base of the steps that lead to Jingo-ji, this fine little temple is another one of our favourite spots in Kyoto. See if you can find your way around to the small waterfall at the side of the temple. The grotto here is pure magic.

KŌZAN-JI Map pp42–3

☎ 861-4204; Ukyō-ku, Umegahata Toganoo-chō; admission ¥600; ⌚ 8.30am-5pm; 🚌 30min walk from Yamashiro Takao bus stop, JR bus from Kyoto Station

Hidden amid a grove of towering ceder trees, this temple is the least accessible of the three temples in Takao. It's famous for the *chuju giga* scroll in its collection, an ink-brush depiction of frolicking animals that is considered by many to be the precursor of today's ubiquitous manga. The temple is reached by following the main road north from the Yamashiro Takao bus stop or, more conveniently, by getting off the JR bus at the Toga-no-O bus stop, which is right outside the temple.

NORTH & NORTHEAST KYOTO

In the north of Kyoto lies Kamigamo-jinja, a fine Shintō shrine, and the imposing bulk of Hiei-zan with its mountaintop temple complex of Enryaku-ji. Note that attractions further to the north in the Kitayama mountains are covered separately under Kitayama Area (p83).

KAMIGAMO-JINJA Map pp42–3

☎ 781-0011; Kita-ku, Kamigamo, Motoyama 339; admission free; ⌚ 8am-5.30pm; 🚌 5min walk from Kamigamomisonobashi bus stop, bus 9 from Kyoto Station

Kamigamo-jinja is one of Japan's oldest shrines and predates the founding of Kyoto. Established in 679, it is dedicated to Raijin, the god of thunder, and is one of Kyoto's 17 Unesco World Heritage sites. The present buildings (more than 40 in all), including the impressive Haiden hall, are exact reproductions of the originals, dating from the 17th to 19th centuries. The shrine is entered from a long approach through two *torii*. The two large conical white-sand mounds in front of Hosodono hall are said to represent mountains sculpted for gods to descend upon. It's not one of Kyoto's leading sights but it's worth a look if you find yourself in the north.

HIEI-ZAN & ENRYAKU-JI Map pp42–3

☎ 077-578-0001; Shiga-ken, Ōtsu-shi, Sakamoto Honmachi 4220; adult/child ¥550/350; ⌚ 8.30am-4.30pm, closes earlier in winter

A visit to 848m-high Hiei-zan and the vast Enryaku-ji complex is a good way to spend half a day hiking, poking around temples and enjoying the atmosphere of a key site in Japanese history.

Enryaku-ji was founded in 788 by Saichō, also known as Dengyō-daishi, the priest who established the Tenzai school. This school did not receive imperial recognition until 823, after Saichō's death; however, from the 8th century the temple grew in power. At its height, Enryaku-ji possessed some 3000 buildings and an army of thousands of *sōhei* (warrior monks). In 1571 Oda Nobunaga saw the temple's power as a

TRANSPORT: HIEI-ZAN & ENRYAKU-JI

You can reach Hiei-zan and Enryaku-ji by train or bus. The most interesting way is the train/cable-car/ropeway route. If you're in a hurry or would like to save money, the best way is a direct bus from Sanjō Keihan or Kyoto Stations.

Train Take the Keihan line north to the last stop, Demachiyanagi, and change to the Yaseyūen/Hiei-bound Eizan line train (be careful not to board the Kurama-bound train that sometimes leaves from the same platform). Travel to the last stop, Yaseyūen (¥260; about 25 minutes from Demachiyanagi Station), then board the cable car (¥530, nine minutes) followed by the ropeway (¥310, three minutes) to the peak, from which you can walk down to the temples.

Bus Take Kyoto bus (not Kyoto city bus) 17 or 18, both of which run from Kyoto Station to the Yaseyūen stop (¥390, about 50 minutes). From there it's a short walk to the cable-car station from where you can complete the journey (see above).

Alternately, if you want to save money (by avoiding both the cable car and ropeway), there are direct Kyoto buses from Kyoto and Keihan Sanjō Stations to Enryaku-ji, which take about 70 and 50 minutes respectively (both cost ¥800).

threat to his aims to unify the nation and he destroyed most of the buildings, along with the monks inside. Today only three pagodas and 120 minor temples remain.

The complex is divided into three sections: Tōtō, Saitō and Yokawa. The Tōtō (eastern pagoda section) contains the Kompon Chū-dō (Primary Central Hall), which is the most important building in the complex. The flames on the three dharma lamps in front of the altar have been kept lit for more than 1200 years. The Daikō-dō (Great Lecture Hall) displays life-sized wooden statues of the founders of various Buddhist schools. This part of the temple is heavily geared to group access, with large expanses of asphalt for parking.

The Saitō (western pagoda section) contains the Shaka-dō, which dates from 1595 and houses a rare Buddha sculpture of the Shaka Nyorai (Historical Buddha). The Saitō, with its stone paths winding through forests of tall trees, temples shrouded in mist and the sound of distant gongs, is the most atmospheric part of the temple. Hold on to your ticket from the Tōtō section, as you may need to show it here.

The Yokawa is of minimal interest and a 4km bus ride away from the Saitō area. The Chū-dō here was originally built in 848. It was destroyed by fire several times and has undergone repeated reconstruction (most recently in 1971). If you plan to visit this area as well as Tōtō and Saitō, allow a full day for in-depth exploration.

(Continued on page 101)

KYOTO CRAFTS

The sumptuous artistry of a traditional kimono

KYOTO CRAFTS

Wagasa (umbrellas) for all, Kyoto Handicraft Center (p113)

Capital of Japan from 784 to 1868, Kyoto traditionally attracted leading craftspeople from all over the country to service the needs of its imperial court. Kyoto was also home to the headquarters of Japan's main Buddhist sects, the *kizoku* or noble class, the main tea schools, wealthy merchants and cultured samurai. The result was a city of small workshops filled with busy artisans, all competing with each other to tempt the demanding clientele of the city.

It's hardly surprising, then, that the Kyoto 'brand' symbolises elegance, refinement and excellence. Items bearing the prefix *kyō,* such as *kyō-yūzen* (Kyoto dyed fabric), are revered in Japan as the apogee of sophistication.

There are many ways for visitors to experience Kyoto's rich craft heritage. To get a full overview of the range of Kyoto crafts, we recommend a visit to the Fureai-kan Kyoto Museum of Traditional Crafts (p72) and the Kyoto Handicraft Center (p113), just a short walk away. A wander through the heart of Kyoto's downtown area, in the region between Oike-dōri and Shijō-dōri (to the north and south) and Karasuma-dōri and Kawaramachi-dōri (to the east and west) will uncover dozens of shops selling traditional Kyoto crafts interspersed with some of Kyoto's trendiest modern retail outlets.

top picks

CRAFT SHOPS & MARKETS

Morita Washi (p109) The selection of *washi* (Japanese paper) boggles the mind.

Erizen (p110) The place to go for a custom-made kimono.

Kamiji Kakimoto (p109) Great *washi* shop with such things as *washi* printing paper.

Kyōsen-dō (p107) Stop in for a classic *kyō-sensu* (Kyoto fan).

Takashimaya Department Store (see the boxed text, p109) An array of great lacquerware, pottery, wood crafts and so on can be found on the 6th floor.

Kyoto Handicraft Center (p113) High-quality goods at a one-stop handicraft shop; English-speaking salespeople make shopping a breeze.

Kōbō-san (p111) A fabulous flea market for a wide variety of used craft items.

Tenjin-san (p113) Another brilliant flea market for crafts.

POTTERY & CERAMICS

Evidence of the first Kyoto wares (*kyō-yaki;* the *yaki* meaning 'ware') dates to the reign of Emperor Shōmu in the early 8th century. By the mid-1600s there were more than 10 different kilns active in and around the city; of these, only Kiyomizu-yaki remains today. This kiln first gained prominence through the workmanship of potter Nonomura Ninsei (1596–1660), who developed an innovative method of applying enamel glaze to porcelain. This technique was further cultivated by adding decorative features such as *sometsuke* (transparent glaze) and incorporating designs in *aka-e* (red paint) and *seiji* (celadon). Kiyomizu-yaki is still actively produced in Kyoto and remains popular with devotees of tea ceremony.

During the Edo period, many *daimyō* (domain lords) encouraged the founding of kilns and the production of superbly designed ceramic articles. The *noborigama* (climbing kiln) was widely used, and a fine example can be seen at the home of famed Kyoto potter Kawai Kanjirō (see p61). Constructed on a slope, the climbing kiln had as many as 20 chambers and could reach temperatures as high as 1400°C.

During the Meiji period, ceramics waned in popularity but were later part of a general revival in *mingei-hin* (folk arts). This movement was led by Yanagi Sōetsu, who encouraged famous potters such as Kawai, Tomimoto Kenkichi and Hamada Shōji. The English potter Bernard Leach studied in Japan under Hamada and contributed to the folk-art revival. On his return to England, Leach promoted the appreciation of Japanese ceramics in the West.

Those with an interest in Kyoto wares, and Kiyomizu-yaki in particular, should check out the streets below Kiyomizu-dera (p63) in Southern Higashiyama. You'll find all manner of shops here selling Kiyomizu-yaki and other types of Japanese pottery. Nearby, on Gojō-dōri, between Higashiōji-dōri and Kawabata-dōri, the Tōki Matsuri (Ceramics Fair) is held from 7 to 10 August each year; for details, see p112. You can also find a wide variety of ceramics in the shops on Teramachi-dōri, between Marutamachi-dōri and Oike-dōri. Finally, the 6th floor of Takashimaya Department Store (see the boxed text, p109) has a great selection of pottery.

LACQUERWARE

Lacquerware (*shikki* or *nurimono*) is made using the sap from the lacquer tree. Once lacquer hardens, it becomes extraordinarily durable. The most common colour of lacquer is an amber or brown, but additives are used to produce black, violet, blue, yellow and even white. In the better pieces, multiple layers of lacquer are painstakingly applied, left to dry and finally polished to a luxurious shine.

Japanese artisans have devised various ways to further enhance the beauty of lacquer. The most common method is *maki-e,* which involves the sprinkling of silver and gold powders onto liquid lacquer to form a picture. After the lacquer dries, another coat seals the picture. The final effect is often dazzling and some of the better pieces of *maki-e* lacquerware are now National Treasures.

Kyoto pottery, handcrafted with precision

Lacquerware: a perfect combination of luxury and durabilty

There are several places in Kyoto where you can see stunning examples of lacquerware, including *maki-e* lacquerware. The Nomura Museum (p67) has a fine collection of lacquerware utensils used in the tea ceremony. Not far away, the **Hosomi Museum** (☎ 752-5555; Sakyo-ku, Saishoji-cho, Okazaki 6-3; 10am-6pm, closed Mon; 10min walk from Kyoto Kaikan/Bijyutsukan-mae bus stop, bus 5 from Kyoto Station) has another excellent collection of tea utensils, including some brilliant *maki-e* lacquerware pieces. Those looking to take a bit of lacquerware home will find an excellent selection on the 6th floor of Takashimaya Department Store (see the boxed text, p109).

TEXTILES

Kyoto is famous for its *kyō-yūzen* textiles. *Yūzen* is a method of silk-dyeing developed to perfection in the 17th century by fan painter Miyazaki Yūzen. *Kyō-yūzen* designs typically feature simple circular flowers called *maru-tsukushi,* birds and landscapes, and stand out for their use of bright-coloured dyes. The technique demands great dexterity; designs are traced by hand before rice paste is applied to fabric like a stencil to prevent colours from bleeding into other areas of the fabric. By repeatedly changing the pattern of the rice paste, very complex designs can be achieved.

Traditionally, when the dyeing process was complete, the material was rinsed in the Kamo-gawa and Katsura-gawa rivers (believed to be particularly effective in fixing the colours) before being hung out to dry. Every year in mid-August this ritual is re-enacted and the fabrics flap in the wind like rows of vibrant banners.

During the turbulent civil wars of the 15th century, Kyoto's weavers congregated into a textiles quarter called Nishijin (literally, Western Camp) near Kitano-Tenman-gū (p76). The

GEISHA CRAFTS

Kyoto's geisha, properly known in Kyoto as *geiko* or *maiko* (fully fledged and apprentice geisha, respectively), are walking museums of traditional crafts. In fact, if you want to see several of Kyoto's traditional crafts in one quick glance, the best place to look is at a *geiko* or *maiko* shuffling by on her way to an appointment.

Kimono The kimono worn by *geiko* and *maiko* are likely to have been made right here in Kyoto, most probably in the workshops in and around the Nishijin textile district. Kimono represent capital in the geisha world; they are worth thousands or even hundreds of thousands of dollars and are loaned to *maiko* by the *'mama-san'* of her house.

Obi The obi (kimono sash) worn by *geiko* and *maiko* is where the skills of Kyoto's silk weavers are given their freest rein. They are often wild and almost psychedelic explosions of colour.

Flower hairpins Known in Japanese as *hana-kanzashi,* these delicate hairpins are made from silk and light metal, usually decorated with seasonal motifs. *Maiko* wear different *hana-kanzashi* each month.

Boxwood combs Handmade boxwood combs (*kushi* in Japanese) are indispensable for creating the wonderful hairstyles of the *maiko*. One reason for using these combs, apart from their incredibly pleasing appearance, is the fact that they don't produce static electricity.

Umbrellas On a rainy day, *maiko* and *geiko* are sheltered from the rain by *wagasa* (traditional Japanese umbrellas). Made of bamboo frames and either paper or silk, these umbrellas are perfectly suited to the geisha wardrobe.

For more on geisha, see the boxed text, p67.

Geisha adorned with hana-kanzashi (flower hairpins)

Delicately detailed obi (kimono sash), Orinasu-kan (p75)

Craftswoman weaves Nishijin-ori textiles on a hand loom, Nishijin Textile Center (p113)

industry was revamped during the Edo period and the popularity of Nishijin workmanship endured through the Meiji Restoration.

Kyoto is also famed for techniques in *kyō-komon* (stencil-dyeing) and *kyō-kanoko shibori* (tie-dyeing). *Kyō-komon* (*komon* means 'small crest') gained notoriety in the 16th and 17th centuries, particularly among warriors who ordered the adornment of both their armour and kimono, through the stencilling of highly geometric designs onto fine silk with vibrant colours. Typically the patterns incorporate flowers, leaves and other flora.

At the other end of the refined, courtly spectrum, *aizome* (the technique of dyeing fabrics in vats of fermented indigo plants) gave Japan one of its most distinctive colours. Used traditionally in making hardy work clothes for the fields, Japan's beautiful indigo-blue can still be seen in many modern-day textile goods.

Together with Kyoto-dyed fabrics, Nishijin-ori (Nishijin weaving) is internationally renowned and dates to the founding of the city. Nishijin techniques were originally developed to satisfy the demands of the nobility, who favoured the quality of illustrious silk fabrics. Over time new methods were adopted by the Kyoto weavers and they began to experiment with materials such as gauze, brocade, damask, satin and crepe. The best-known Nishijin style is the exquisite *tsuzure,* a tightly woven tapestry cloth produced with a hand loom, on which detailed patterns are preset.

In 1915 the Orinasu-kan textile museum (p75) was established to display Nishijin's fine silk fabrics and embroidery. The museum has two halls that display some stunning examples of Nishijin-ori. Nearby, the Nishijin Textile Center (p75) has decent displays of Nishijin-ori, including a demonstration loom, a shop selling Nishijin items and occasional kimono fashion shows.

If you'd like to purchase a kimono or an obi (kimono sash), you'll find the best prices on used items at either Kōbō-san (p111) or Tenjin-san (p113) flea markets. If you're after a new kimono, try Erizen (p110) or Takashimaya.

DOLLS

Among the finest of Japan's *ningyō* (handcrafted dolls) are Kyoto's *kyō-ningyō*. Elaborate in detail and dressed in fine brocade fabrics, they date from the Heian period and their exquisite costumes reflect the taste and styles of that aristocratic time.

Some other common dolls are daruma dolls, which are based on the figure of Bodhidharma, the religious sage commonly considered to be the founder of Zen Buddhism; *gosho-ningyō,*

Once the privilege of aristocracy, Kyoto's eye-catching fans make stunning souvenirs

chubby plaster dolls sometimes dressed as figures in nō dramas; *kiku-ningyō,* large dolls adorned with real chrysanthemum flowers; and *ishō-ningyō,* which is a general term for elaborately costumed dolls, sometimes based on kabuki characters.

If you'd like to purchase a *kyō-ningyō,* you'll find a good selection at Matsuya (p108), Tanakaya (p108) or the Kyoto Handicraft Center (p113).

FANS

As with many of Japan's traditional crafts, fans were first made in Kyoto and continue to be produced prolifically here. *Kyō-sensu* (Kyoto fans) first found popularity among the early aristocracy, but by the late 12th century had spread to the general populace. Though fans were originally a practical and fashionable tool to keep oneself cool in Japan's sweltering summers, they gradually took on more aesthetic purposes as the country's arts flourished from the 15th century onwards – plain fans were used in tea ceremony and incense smelling; elaborate ones were used in nō drama and traditional dance. Fans are still commonly used as decorative items and for ceremonial purposes.

Originally made from the leaves of the cypress tree, fans are now primarily made with elaborately painted Japanese paper that's fixed onto a delicate skeleton of bamboo ribs. The paper can feature decorations ranging from simple geometric designs to courtly scenes from the Heian period and are often sprinkled with gold or silver leaf powder.

Fans make a lightweight and excellent souvenir and can be purchased at major department stores and at speciality shops such as Kyōsen-dō (p107), which sometimes has demonstrations of fan making.

WASHI

The art of making paper by hand was introduced into Japan from China in the 5th century. It reached its golden age in the Heian era, when it was highly prized by members of the Kyoto court for their poetry and diaries. *Washi* (traditional Japanese paper) is normally made of mulberry but can also be made from mountain shrubs and other plants. One distinctive type of *washi* found in Kyoto is *kyō-chiyogami,* which has traditionally been used by Japanese to wrap special gifts.

Washi was made in large quantities in Japan until the introduction of Western paper in the 1870s. After that time, the number of families involved in the craft plummeted. There are still a number of traditional paper makers active in Kyoto city and in country areas north of the city. Recently, *washi* has enjoyed something of a revival (there's even *washi* for computer printers!). There are several fine *washi* shops in Kyoto, including Morita Washi (p109) and Kamiji Kakimoto (p109).

OTHER CRAFTS

Furniture

Kyoto produces a plethora of wooden furniture and household goods. Particularly admired by collectors of Japanese antiques are chests called *tansu;* the most prized of these is the *kaidan-dansu,* so-named because it doubles as a flight of stairs (*kaidan* means 'stairs'). These are becoming increasingly difficult to find, and increasingly expensive, but determined hunting at flea markets and antique shops may still land the occasional good piece. The best place to look for traditional wooden furniture is on Ebisugawa-dōri, just west of Teramachi-dōri. You can also find some great (but pricey) pieces on offer at the three annual Antiques Grand Fairs held at Pulse Plaza (p113).

Bamboo Crafts

Kyoto is also famous for its superb *chikkōhin* (bamboo crafts), in particular the tools used in tea ceremony such as ladles and whisks (which make interesting souvenirs). Japanese bamboo baskets are among the finest in the world and are remarkable for their complexity and delicacy (as well as their price). There are two shops in Kyoto that specialise in bamboo crafts and, fortunately for the visitor, they are almost next door to one another: Kagoshin (p111) and Onouechikuzaiten (p111).

Prettier than Tupperware: washi (Japanese paper) boxes

The complexity of bamboo baskets revealed, Kagoshin (p111)

Kyoto's kyō-ningyō are among the finest handcrafted dolls in Japan

(*Continued from page 92*)

WALKING TOURS

HILLS, TEMPLES & LANES IN SOUTHERN HIGASHIYAMA

1 Tainai-meguri Just to the left of the ticket window of Kiyomizu-dera, this subterranean walk through the darkness easily qualifies as Kyoto's most unusual attraction. We won't say too much about Tainai-meguri (p63) – just try it.

2 Kiyomizu-dera At the top of Chawan-zaka, this grande dame of Kyoto temples commands an impressive view over the city. While you're visiting Kiyomizu-dera (p63), be sure to check out Jishu-jinga (p63), home of the famous 'Love Shrine', and take a sip of the holy water from the spring below the main hall.

3 Kasagi-ya On the left just after you start down Sannen-zaka, Kasagi-ya (p132) is a charming little teahouse and the ideal place to stop for a cup of hot *matcha* in winter or an *uji kintoki* (shaved ice with sweetened green tea) in summer. Be prepared to ask a local shop owner to point it out.

4 Ishibei-kōji After you descend Sannen-zaka and Ninen-zaka and start along Nene-no-Michi (just past the public toilet), you will find the entrance to this atmospheric pedestrian-only lane on your left. There is no English sign, so be prepared to ask someone, or keep an eye out for the Japanese script (石塀小路). This is Kyoto's single-most attractive street.

5 Kōdai-ji At the top of a flight of steps on the right off Nene-no-Michi, you will find Kōdai-ji (p64), a highly attractive temple famous for interesting evening illuminations of its gardens. The bamboo forest here at night is surreal.

6 Maruyama-kōen This park is wonderful for an alfresco lunch along this route, or just a quick can of coffee or tea (only in Japan). If you are at Maruyama-kōen (p64) during cherry-blossom season, be prepared for a rollicking scene.

7 Yasaka-jinja Below (west) of Maruyama-kōen, you will find this attractive open-plan shrine. Yasaka-jinja (p64) is usually busy with passing worshippers. If you are here on New Year's Eve or the first three days of the new year, be ready for throngs of people.

8 Chion-in A vast Pure Land Buddhist temple, Chion-in (p65) is like the Vatican of Japanese Buddhism – grand in every way. Take off your shoes and enter the main hall and spend some time soaking up the atmosphere. It's free.

9 Shōren-in A nice counterpoint to Chion-in, Shōren-in (p65) is a fine Tendai sect temple with a wonderful garden and a lovely little bamboo forest. You can sip a cup of *matcha* while gazing over the garden. Look for the giant camphor trees out the front.

WALK FACTS

Start Gojō-zaka bus stop on Higashiōji-dōri (bus 18, 100, 206 or 207)
End Jingū-michi bus stop on Sanjō-dōri (bus 5 or 100); Higashiyama-Sanjō Station on the Tōzai subway line
Distance About 5km
Duration Four hours
Fuel stop Kasagi-ya

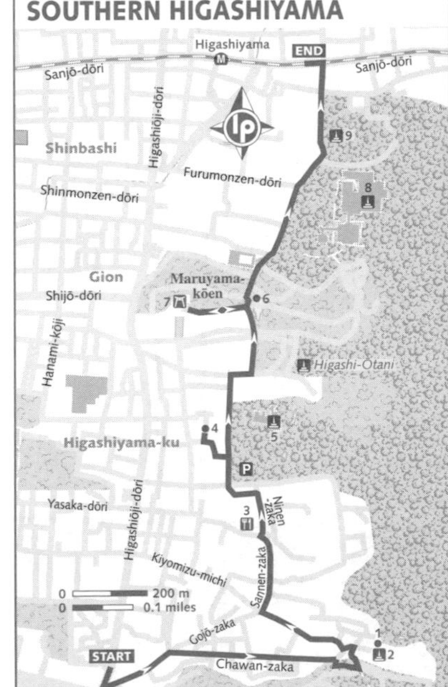

NIGHT WALK THROUGH THE FLOATING WORLD

1 Yasaka-jinja Overlooking Gion, Yasaka-jinja (p64) is a popular shrine, where many in the neighbourhood pray for a successful evening.

2 Tatsumi-bashi bridge After crossing Shijō-dōri and the gaudy hostess club–studded region, you find yourself in an alley of traditional wooden buildings. From here you come out on Tatsumi-bashi bridge, perhaps the most scenic spot in all of Kyoto (at least at night).

3 Tatsumi shrine Just opposite the bridge, you'll find this quaint little shrine on a triangular plot in the middle of Gion's most beautiful district. Note the hostesses and *mama-sans* praying for a good evening.

4 Ōzawa At the western end of Shirakawa-Minami-dōri, over a small footbridge, you will find Ōzawa (p130), a wonderful little tempura restaurant. Time your walk to have dinner here.

5 Issen Yōshoku If you want a snack instead of dinner, head to Issen Yōshoku (p131), this popular, plebeian *okonomiyaki* joint.

6 Minami-za Finding yourself back on Shijō, you will soon see the towering façade of the Minami-za (p142) grand kabuki theatre on your left. Look for the colourful posters advertising forthcoming performances.

7 Pontochō After crossing the Kamo-gawa via Shijō-Ōhashi, you will pass a police box and then immediately find the entrance to this fantastic pedestrian-only lane. Pontochō (p51) is incredibly atmospheric in the evening and the best place to spot geisha or *maiko*. From there you can head down Kiyamachi-dōri for a few drinks or straight to Kawaramachi Station for the trip home if you prefer.

WALK FACTS

Start Yasaka-jinja (at the intersection of Shijō-dōri and Higashiōji-dōri), a 10-minute walk from Keihan line Shijō or Hankyū line Kawaramachi Stations

End Hankyū Kawaramachi Station, at the intersection of Shijō-dōri and Kiyamachi-dōri

Distance About 3km

Duration Two hours

Fuel stop Ōzawa or Issen Yōshoku for food; Pontochō and Kiyamachi-dōri for drinks

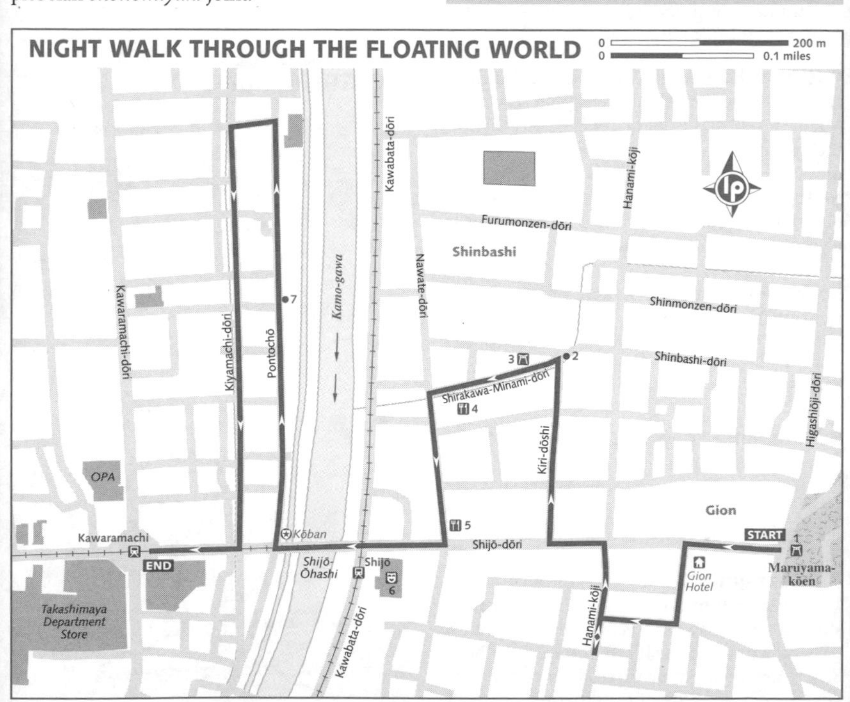

A PHILOSOPHICAL MEANDER

1 Konchi-in Starting from the Westin Miyako Hotel, look up the hill to find the pedestrian tunnel. Walk through the tunnel to get to Konchi-in (p67). This small temple with its fine Zen garden is your first stop. It's on the left about 150m after the tunnel.

2 Nanzen-ji Kyoto's Nanzen-ji (p66) is a vast Zen temple that easily ranks as one of our favourite temples in the city. There is so much to see here and much of it is free.

3 Kōtoku-an From the main hall of Nanzen-ji, walk under the brick aqueduct and turn left up the hill. You will soon come upon the entrance to the fine subtemple of Kōtoku-an, which can be entered for free.

4 Nanzen-ji Oku-no-in Facing the main hall of Kōtoku-an, if you look to your right, you will see a small doorway leading to a dirt path. Take a left up the dirt path and walk uphill into the woods. Follow the steps until you reach the small waterfall of Nanzen-ji Oku-no-In, a fine grotto in the forest.

5 Eikan-dō Return back through Nanzen-ji and work your way north past a school until you reach this fine, sprawling temple. Eikan-dō (p70) is famous for its maples and gets packed with admiring crowds in autumn.

6 Hinode Udon If you leave Eikan-dō and walk straight north for a few minutes, you will find this fine noodle shop on your right (there are usually a few taxis parked nearby). Hinode Udon (p135) is a good choice for a lunch stop.

7 Tetsugaku-no-Michi (Path of Philosophy) Backtrack from Hinode Udon and you will find the sign pointing to the start of the famous Tetsugaku-no-Michi (p70) canalside walkway. It's one of Kyoto's more scenic walks.

8 Hōnen-in Continue along the Tetsugaku-no-michi until you see signs pointing off the path to Hōnen-in (p71). This small temple is one of Kyoto's finest and has free admission. Do not miss it.

9 Ginkaku-ji Leave Hōnen-in and work your way through the narrow streets north to Ginkaku-ji (p71). The route jogs right and left – just try to keep heading basically north. This Unesco World Heritage Site is usually crowded but nonetheless impressive.

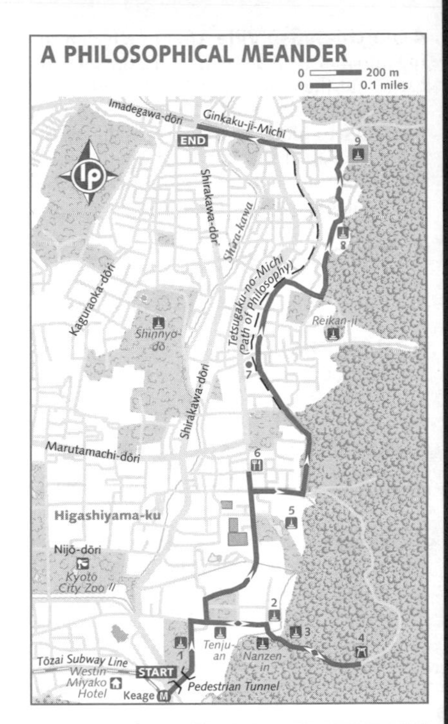

WALK FACTS

Start Keage Station on the Tōzai subway line
End Ginkaku-ji-Michi bus stop, near the intersection of Shirakawa-dōri and Imadegawa-dōri (bus 5, 56, 100, 203 or 204 from Kyoto Station)
Distance About 6km
Duration Four hours
Fuel stop Hinode Udon

AMBLING THROUGH BAMBOO GROVES & TEMPLES

1 Tenryū-ji Start at Tenryū-ji (p80), a popular Zen temple that has one of the loveliest views in all Kyoto – the temple's garden and pond are backed by the mountains of Arashiyama.

2 Bamboo Forest Leave the north gate of Tenryū-ji and, after a brief detour down to Nonomiya-jinja, walk up through the brilliant bamboo forest, one of Kyoto's incredible sights.

3 Kameyama-kōen After reaching the top of the bamboo forest, turn left and walk for 100m into the grounds of scenic Kameyama-kōen (p81), a fine park on a hillside above Arashiyama.

4 Ōkōchi-Sansō Villa After briefly detouring into Kameyama-kōen, return the way you came and then, just opposite the top of the main walkway through the bamboo forest, you will see a slope leading diagonally up the hill past a small shack (which is a ticket office). This is the entrance to the brilliant and unmissable Ōkōchi-Sansō Villa (p81).

5 Jōjakkō-ji Atop a grassy knoll, Jōjakkō-ji (p81) is the first of the main temples after Tenryū-ji and boasts brilliant maples in November.

6 Rakushisha The famed haiku poet Bashō stopped at this quaint little thatched-roof hut called Rakushisha (p81). It's worth a quick look.

7 Nison-in Have a look through the entrance of Nison-in (p81) as you go by. If the maples are working, consider entry.

8 Takiguchi-dera After the main road curves to the left, you'll see four stone waymarks that show the way up to Takiguchi-dera (p82) and Giō-ji.

9 Giō-ji With a fine little moss garden and a thatched-roof main hall, this cute little temple has a peculiar charm. You can sometimes get lucky and have Giō-ji (p82) all to yourself (but not in busy times of spring or autumn).

10 Adashino Nembutsu-ji Thousands of stone statues create a truly unique atmosphere at the unusual temple of Adashino Nembutsu-ji (p82).

11 Atago Torii This large *torii* marks the end of the walk. The thatched-roof houses here are incredibly evocative.

12 Hiranoya For a quick cup of hot *matcha*, try this fine old restaurant. Aya Chaya Hiranoya (p136) is a great way to reward yourself for completing the walk.

WALK FACTS

Start Arashiyama bus stop (bus 11, 28, 61, 62, 71, 72 or 93); Keifuku Arashiyama Station or Torokko Arashiyama Station
End Torii-moto bus stop (bus 62 or 72)
Distance About 4km
Duration Four hours
Fuel stop Ayu Chaya Hiranoya

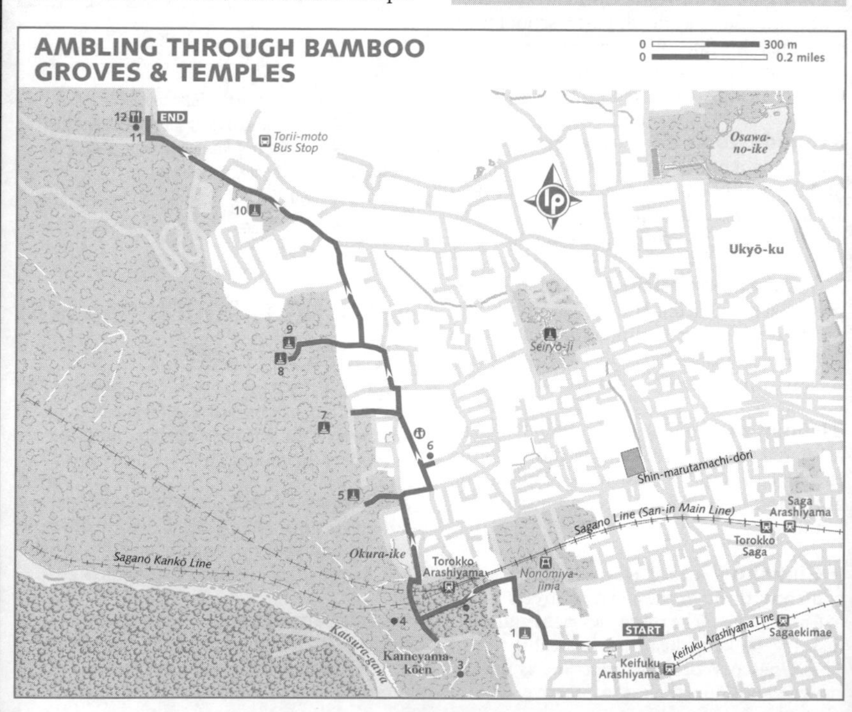

SHOPPING

top picks

- **Ippo-dō** (p109)
  This is *the* place to buy green tea, both *matcha* (powdered) and leaf.
- **Kyoto Handicraft Center** (p113)
  For one-stop souvenir shopping, this place can't be beat.
- **Kyūkyō-dō** (p109)
  A convenient Downtown all-round traditional souvenir shop.
- **Random Walk** (p108)
  This is Kyoto's best bookshop, hands down.
- **Morita Washi** (p109)
  The selection of *washi* (Japanese paper) is just mind-boggling here.
- **Takashimaya Department Store** (p109)
  Our favourite department store in Kyoto – check the 6th floor for traditional souvenirs and the basement for food.

What's your recommendation? www.lonelyplanet.com/kyoto

SHOPPING

Kyoto has a fantastic variety of both traditional and modern shops. Most of these are located in the Downtown area, making the city a very convenient place to shop. Whether you're looking for fans and kimono or the latest electronics and cameras, Kyoto has plenty to choose from.

More than offering simple convenience, however, Kyoto has a long history as Japan's artistic and cultural workshop; it's the place where the country's finest artisans used their skills to produce the goods used in tea ceremonies, calligraphy, flower arrangement and religious ceremonies, as well as in kimono fabrics and other textiles. Indeed, Kyoto is the best place to find traditional arts and crafts in all of Japan.

Of course, Kyoto has far more to offer than just traditional items. You will also find the latest fashions in the Shijō-Kawaramachi shopping district, the latest electronics on Teramachi-dōri and a wondrous assortment of food products in markets such as Nishiki Market. And if you're lucky enough to be in town on the 21st or the 25th of the month, you should make every effort to visit one of the city's excellent flea markets.

SHOPPING AREAS

The heart of Kyoto's shopping district is the intersection of Shijō-dōri and Kawaramachi-dōri in Downtown Kyoto (Map p50). The blocks running north and west of here are packed with all sorts of stores selling both traditional and modern goods. Several of Kyoto's largest department stores are here as well, including Hankyū, Daimaru and Takashimaya (see the boxed text, p109). Nearby is Nishiki Market (p108), which is Kyoto's best food market. It's one of Kyoto's real highlights and should not be missed.

Teramachi-dōri, where it runs south of Shijō-dōri, is Kyoto's electronics district and has the full range of the latest in computers, stereos and home appliances. The same street, north of Oike-dōri, is the place to look for a wide variety of traditional Japanese items. A stroll up this street to the Kyoto Imperial Palace Park (p52) is a great way to spend an afternoon, even if you don't plan on making any purchases.

PLAN TO SHOP?

Many travellers plan their trips around the cherry blossoms or one of Kyoto's great festivals. Few, however, plan their trips around Kyoto's brilliant markets. This is a shame because Kyoto's two monthly markets are among the best flea markets in all of Asia. The two dates to keep in mind are the 21st of each month, for the Kōbō-san Market (p111) at Tō-ji, and the 25th of each month, for the Tenjin-san Market (p113) at Kitano Tenman-gū. You'll note that these are close enough together to hit on one slightly extended stay in Kyoto.

The fashion-conscious should explore Kyoto's department stores or the chic shops on Shijō-dōri. Unfortunately, you'll be hard-pressed to find much of a selection of larger ('*gaijin*-sized') clothes and shoes.

Antiques hunters should head straight for Shinmonzen-dōri in Gion (Map p62), the aforementioned Teramachi-dōri, or one of the city's lively monthly markets – Kōbō-san (p111) or Tenjin-san (p113). To supplement the information in this chapter, pick up a copy of *Old Kyoto: A Guide to Traditional Shops, Restaurants & Inns* by Diane Durston, available at Kyoto's English-language bookshops. *Kyoto Visitors Guide* has a listing of traditional shops and markets in town; it's available from the TIC (p199), which can also help locate unusual or hard-to-find items.

For standard opening hours of shops and department stores, see p190.

BARGAINING

With the exception of antique shops and flea markets, bargaining in Japan is just not done. Possible exceptions are camera and electronics stores (in particular those dealing in used goods). The word 'discount' is usually understood by store clerks. If they are willing to drop the price, their first offer is usually all you'll get – don't haggle further as it will make things very awkward for the clerk.

KYOTO STATION AREA

The Kyoto Station area competes with Downtown Kyoto as the city's retail centre of gravity. The vast new station building itself is bulging with shops, including Isetan Department Store and the giant new Bic Camera shop. North and south of the station, other Japanese camera/electronics chains are about to open huge new shops, which will further lure customers from Kyoto's traditional electronics neighbourhood along Teramachi-dōri in Downtown. For varied shopping and pleasant strolling, the Kyoto Station area can't compete, but for cheap cameras and electronics, it's hard to beat.

BIC CAMERA Map p46 Cameras & Electronics

☎ 353-1111; Shimogyō-ku, Higashishiokōji-chō 927; 10am-9pm; 1min walk from Kyoto Station, Nishinotōin gate

This vast new shop is directly connected to Kyoto Station via the Nishinotōin gate; otherwise, it's accessed by leaving the north (Karasuma) gate and walking west. You will be amazed by the sheer amount of goods this store has on display. Just be sure that an English operating manual is available for your purchases. For computer parts, keep in mind that not all items on offer will work with English operating systems.

AVANTI Map p46 Department Store

☎ 671-8761; Minami-ku, Higashikujō Nishisannō-chō 31; shops 10am-9pm, restaurants 11am-10pm; 1min walk from Kyoto Station, Hachijōguchi exit

This department store has a decent bookshop on its 6th floor, and a food court and supermarket on its B1 floor. It's geared mostly to younger Kyoto shoppers but it's good for browsing if you have time to kill while waiting for a train. Take the underground passage from Kyoto Station.

ISETAN DEPARTMENT STORE
Map p46 Department Store

☎ 352-1111; Shimogyō-ku, Karasuma-dōri, Shiokō-ji sagaru, Higashishiokō-ji-chō; 10am-8pm, closed irregularly; JR Kyoto Station

This large, elegant department store is located inside the Kyoto Station building, making it perfect for a last-minute spot of shopping before hopping on the train to the airport.

KYŌSEN-DŌ Map p46 Fans

☎ 371-4151; Shimogyō-ku, Higashinotōin-dōri, Shōmen agaru, Tsutsugane-chō 46; 9am-5pm Mon-Sat, 10am-6pm Sun & public holidays; 10min walk from Kyoto Station

Kyōsen-dō sells a colourful variety of paper fans; here you can see the process of assembling the fans and even paint your own.

top picks

SHOPPING STRIPS

Shopping neighbourhoods in Kyoto tend to be organised by specialities, which certainly makes things easier if you're after specific items. The following is a list of some of Kyoto's most important shopping streets and what you'll find there.

- **Teramachi-dōri, north of Oike-dōri** (Map p50) Traditional Japanese crafts, tea-ceremony goods, green tea and antiques.
- **Teramachi-dōri, south of Shijō-dōri** (Map p50) Electronics and computers.
- **Shijō-dōri, between Kawaramachi-dōri and Karasuma-dōri** (Map p50) Department stores, fashion boutiques and traditional arts and crafts.
- **Shinmonzen-dōri** (Map p62) Antiques.
- **Gojō-zaka** (Map p62) Pottery.

KUNGYOKU-DŌ Map p46 Incense

☎ 371-0162; Shimogyō-ku, Horikawa-dōri, Nishihonganji-mae; 9am-5.30pm, closed 1st & 3rd Sun of each month; 15min walk from Kyoto Station

A haven for the olfactory sense, this place has sold incense and aromatic woods (for burning, similar to incense) for four centuries. It's opposite the gate of Nishi Hongan-ji.

DOWNTOWN KYOTO

Downtown Kyoto is the best place in the city to shop. The city's main department stores are all located along Shijō-dōri, between Kawaramachi-dōri and Karasuma-dōri. The streets around this prime shopping strip are thick with stores selling everything from traditional crafts to the latest fashions. Heading north from Shijō-dōri, the twin shopping arcades of Shinkyōgoku and Teramachi are the city's main youth shopping areas, and Nishiki Market, the city's best food market, runs west from Teramachi. The stretch of Teramachi that runs south from Shijō-dōri is the city's main electronics district. If you fancy an afternoon of shopping through markets, shops and department stores, look no further than Downtown Kyoto.

JUNKUDŌ Map p50 Bookshop
☎ 253-6460; Nakagyō-ku, Kawaramachi dōri, Sanjō kudaru, Yamazaki-chō 2, Kyoto BAL Bldg; 11am-8pm; 10min walk from Kawaramachi Station, Hankyū line
On the 5th to 8th floors of the BAL building, right downtown, this is one of Kyoto's best bookshops. The 7th floor has a good selection of English books and a smaller selection of books in other European languages. It also stocks English-language manga, magazines, Lonely Planet travel guides, and Japanese-language textbooks and reference books.

RANDOM WALK Map p50 Bookshop
☎ 256-8231; Nakagyō-ku, Teramachi-dōri, Takoyakushi kudaru, Enpukujimae-chō; 10am-8.30pm; 10min walk from Kawaramachi Station, Hankyū line
In the Teramachi shopping arcade, this is the best English-language bookshop in town. There is a good selection of Lonely Planet guidebooks and maps, English manga, books on Japan, art books, novels etc.

CLOTHING SIZES

Women's clothing

Aus/UK	8	10	12	14	16	18
Europe	36	38	40	42	44	46
Japan	5	7	9	11	13	15
USA	6	8	10	12	14	16

Women's shoes

Aus/USA	5	6	7	8	9	10
Europe	35	36	37	38	39	40
France only	35	36	38	39	40	42
Japan	22	23	24	25	26	27
UK	3½	4½	5½	6½	7½	8½

Men's clothing

Aus	92	96	100	104	108	112
Europe	46	48	50	52	54	56
Japan	S		M	M		L
UK/USA	35	36	37	38	39	40

Men's shirts (collar sizes)

Aus/Japan	38	39	40	41	42	43
Europe	38	39	40	41	42	43
UK/USA	15	15½	16	16½	17	17½

Men's shoes

Aus/UK	7	8	9	10	11	12
Europe	41	42	43	44½	46	47
Japan	26	27	27½	28	29	30
USA	7½	8½	9½	10½	11½	12½

Measurements approximate only, try before you buy

NIJŪSAN-YA Map p50 Combs & Hair Clips
☎ 221-2371; Shimogyō-ku, Shijō-dōri, Kawaramachi higashi iru; 10am-8pm, closed 3rd Wed of the month; 1min walk from Kawaramachi Station, Hankyū line
Boxwood combs and hair clips are one of Kyoto's most famous traditional crafts, and they are still used in the elaborate hairstyles of the city's geisha and *maiko* (apprentice geisha). This tiny hole-in-the-wall shop has a fine selection for you to choose from (and if you don't like what's on view, you can ask if it has other choices in stock – it usually does).

MATSUYA Map p50 Dolls
☎ 221-5902; Nakagyō-ku, Kawaramachi-dōri, Shijō agaru, Shimoōsaka-chō; 10.30am-6.30pm, closed Wed; 1min walk from Kawaramachi Station, Hankyū line
Just north of Shijō-dōri, on the eastern side of Kawaramachi-dōri, Matsuya sells an impressive assortment of delicately painted *kyō-ningyō* (Kyoto dolls).

TANAKAYA Map p50 Dolls
☎ 221-1959; Shimogyō-ku, Shijō-dōri, Yanaginobanba higashi iru, Tachiurihigashi-chō 9; 10am-6pm, closed Wed; 5min walk from Shijō Station, Karasuma subway line
Tanakaya is one of the best places in Kyoto to buy *kyō-ningyō*. In addition to the full range of *kyō-ningyō,* the shop sells display stands and screens, Japanese traditional shell game pieces and miniature Gion Matsuri (p16) floats. It occupies a wide stretch of Shijō-dōri and is easy to spot by its dolls in the window.

NISHIKI MARKET Map p50 Food Market
Nakagyō-ku, Nishikikōji-dōri, btwn Teramachi & Karasuma; 9am to 6pm; 10min walk from Karasuma Station, Hankyū line
Known as Nishiki Ichiba in Japanese, Nishiki Market is easily Kyoto's greatest food market and one of the best shopping streets overall. This is the best place to see all the unusual ingredients that go into Kyoto cuisine. There are several spots to eat and drink here, as well as a few souvenir shops.

MEIDI-YA STORE Map p50 Imported Foods

☎ 221-7661; Nakagyō-ku, Sanjō-dōri, Kawaramachi higashi iru, Nakajima-chō 78; 10am-9pm; 5min walk from Sanjō Station, Keihan line

This famous Sanjō-dōri gourmet supermarket has an outstanding selection of imported food and an excellent selection of wine. Prices are high.

KAMIJI KAKIMOTO Map p50 Japanese Paper

☎ 211-3481; Nakagyō-ku, Teramachi-dōri, Nijō agaru, Higashi gawa; 9am-6pm Mon-Fri, 10am-5pm Sun & public holidays, closed irregularly; 5min walk from Kyoto-Shiyakusho-mae Station, Tōzai subway line

A close second to Morita Washi (below) as our favourite *washi* shop in Kyoto. It's got such unusual items as *washi* computer printer paper and *washi* wallpaper. It's very close to Ippo-dō (right) tea shop, with which it makes a very good double bill.

MORITA WASHI Map p50 Japanese Paper

☎ 341-1419; Shimogyō-ku, Higashinotōin-dōri, Bukkōji agaru; 9.30am-5.30pm, closes 4.30pm Sat, closed Sun & public holidays; 3min walk from Shijō Station, Karasuma subway line

A short walk from the Shijō-Karasuma crossing, this place sells a fabulous variety of handmade *washi* (Japanese paper) for reasonable prices. It's one of our favourite shops in Kyoto for souvenirs.

RAKUSHI-KAN Map p50 Japanese Paper

☎ 251-0078; Nakagyō-ku, Sanjō-dōri, Takakura agaru; 10am-7pm Tue-Sun; 5min walk from Karasuma-Oike Station, Karasuma subway line

On the 1st floor of the Museum of Kyoto (p49), this fine little shop sells a variety of *washi* goods and traditional Japanese stationery. There are several interesting items here that make good souvenirs, including fine letter-writing paper and cards. You can also pick up blank *washi* business cards to have printed up when you get back home.

KYŪKYŌ-DŌ Map p50 Japanese Souvenirs

☎ 231-0510; Nakagyō-ku, Shimohonnō-jimae-chō 520; 10am-6pm, closed Sun & 1-3 Jan; 1min walk from Kyoto-Shiyakusho-mae Station, Tōzai subway line

This old shop in the Teramachi covered arcade sells a selection of incense, *shodō* (Japanese calligraphy) goods, tea-ceremony supplies and *washi*. Prices are on the high side but the quality is good.

top picks

DOWNTOWN DEPARTMENT STORES

In addition to Isetan Department Store (p107) and Avanti (p107) in the Kyoto Station area, Kyoto boasts four major department stores, all centrally located in Downtown Kyoto.

- Hankyū Department Store (Map p50; ☎ 223-2288; Shimogyō-ku, Shijō-dōri, Kawaramachi Higashi iru, Shin-chō 68; 11am-8pm Mon-Wed, 11am-9pm Thu-Sun & holidays; above Kawaramachi Station, Hankyū Kyoto line)
- Takashimaya Department Store (Map p50; ☎ 221-8811; Shimogyō-ku, Shijō Tominokōji kado; 10am-8pm, restaurants to 10pm; 1min walk from Kawaramachi Station, Hankyū Kyoto line)
- Daimaru Department Store (Map p50; ☎ 211-8111; Shimogyō-ku, Shijō-dōri, Takakura Nishi iru, Tachiuri Nishi-machi 79; 10am-8pm, restaurants 11am-9pm, closed Jan 1; 1min walk from Shijō Station, Karasuma subway line or Karasuma Station, Hankyū Kyoto line)
- Fujii Daimaru Department Store (Map p50; ☎ 221-8181; Shimogyō-ku, Shijō-dōri Teramachi; 10.30am to 8pm; 2min walk from Kawaramachi Station, Hankyū line

IPPO-DŌ Map p50 Japanese Tea

☎ 211-3421; Nakagyō-ku, Teramachi-dōri, Nijō agaru; shop 9am-7pm Mon-Sat, 9am-6pm Sun & public holidays, café 11am-5pm, closed new year holidays; 8min walk from Kyoto-Shiyakusho-mae Station, Tōzai subway line

This old-style tea shop sells the best Japanese tea in Kyoto. Its *matcha* (powdered green tea used in tea ceremonies) makes an excellent and lightweight souvenir. Try a 40g container of *wa-no-mukashi* (meaning 'old-time Japan') for ¥1600, which makes 25 cups of excellent green tea. Ippo-dō is north of the city hall, on Teramachi-dōri. It has an adjoining tea house.

TADASHIYA Map p50 Kimono & Obi

☎ 212-1167; Nakagyō-ku, Teramachi-dōri, Ebisugawa; 10am-6pm; 10min walk from Kyoto-Shiyakusho-mae Station, Tōzai subway line

This shop has an abundance of high-quality used kimono and obi. The prices are a bit on the high side. It's on the corner with the name of the shop written in English in small letters on the door.

TERAMACHI CLUB Map p50 Kimono & Obi

212-6445; Nakagyō-ku, Teramachi-dōri, Nijō-agaru; 10am-6pm; 10min walk from Kyoto-Shiyakusho-mae Station, Tōzai subway line

Used kimono and obi are only the beginning at this interesting little antique shop. Prices are on the high side but it usually has some interesting items. It's only a little bit further north than the famous Ippo-dō (p109) tea shop.

ARITSUGU Map p50 Knives & Kitchenware

221-1091; Nakagyō-ku, Nishikikōji-dōri, Gokomachi nishi iru, Kajiya-chō 219; 9am-5.30pm; 10min walk from Kawaramachi Station, Hankyū line

While you're in the Nishiki Market, have a look at this store – it's where you can find some of the best kitchen knives in the world. It also carries a selection of excellent and unique Japanese kitchenware.

TANAKAYA Map p50 Noren

221-3076; Nakagyō-ku, Takakura-dōri-Nishikikōji agaru, Kaiya-chō 558-1; 9.30am-7pm, closed 3rd Wed of each month; 10min walk from Shijō Station, Karasuma subway line

This shop sells *noren* (curtains that hang in the entry of Japanese restaurants) and a wide variety of other fabric goods such as placemats, *tenugui* (small hand towels), handkerchiefs and bedding. It's near Daimaru Department Store.

KŌJITSU SANSŌ

Map p50 Outdoor Sporting Goods

257-7050; Nakagyō-ku, Kawaramachi-dōri, Sanjō agaru, Ebisu-chō 427; 10.30am-8pm; 5min walk from Sanjō Station, Keihan line

If you plan to do some hiking or camping while in Japan, you can stock up on equipment at this excellent little shop on Kawaramachi-dōri. You'll find that Japanese outdoor sporting equipment is very high quality (with prices to match).

ZEST UNDERGROUND SHOPPING ARCADE Map p50 Shopping Arcade

253-3100; Nakagyō-ku, Kawaramachi Oike B1; shops 10.30am-8.30pm, restaurants 11am-10pm, closed 1 Jan; 1min walk from Kyoto-Shiyakusho-mae Station, Tōzai subway line

This new mall under Oike-dōri in front of Kyoto City Hall has a variety of boutiques, restaurants and a small branch of Kinokuniya bookshop.

OPA Map p50 Shopping Centre

255-8111; Nakagyō-ku, Kawaramachi-dōri, Shijō agaru; 11am-9pm, closed irregularly; 1min walk from Kawaramachi Station, Hankyū line

This youth-oriented shopping centre is the place to go to see swarms of *ko-gyaru* (brightly clad Japanese girls) and their mates. It's also a decent spot for those who want to check out a wide variety of fashion boutiques and other trendy shops.

SHIN-PUH-KAN Map p50 Shopping Centre

213-6688; Nakagyō-ku, Karasuma dōri, Aneyakōji kudaru, Bano-chō 586-2; shops 11am-8pm Sun-Thu, to 9pm Fri & Sat, restaurants 11am-11pm, closed irregularly; 1min walk from Karasuma-Oike Station, Karasuma subway line

This new Downtown shopping complex has a variety of boutiques and restaurants clustered around a huge open-air atrium. The offerings here run to the trendy and ephemeral, which seems to appeal to all the young folk who congregate here. Occasional art and music performances are held in the atrium.

ERIZEN Map p50 Textiles

221-1618; Shimogyō-ku, Shijō Kawaramachi, Otabi-chō; 10am-6pm, closed Mon; 1min walk from Kawaramachi Station, Hankyū line

Roughly opposite Takashimaya Department Store, Erizen is one of the best places in Kyoto to buy a kimono or kimono fabric. It has a great selection of *kyō-yūzen* (Kyoto dyed fabrics) and other kimono fabrics.

KIDS' STUFF

Kyoto is the prime destination for groups of schoolkids from all over Japan, who are brought here at least once during their schooling to learn about Japan's culture. Of course, as soon as they get a free moment, they ditch the temples to join others of their kind in two of Kyoto's most popular shopping streets, the Teramachi and Shinkyōgoku covered arcades (Map p50). Lined with restaurants, cinemas, a mix of tacky shops and more traditional, upmarket stores, these arcades are a lot of fun and they're the best place to look for kitschy souvenirs such as T-shirts with slogans *Ichi-ban!* (number one) and *Nippon* (Japan).

Prices are not cheap but the service is of a high level. Staff can measure you for a kimono and post it to your home later.

TSUJIKURA Map p50 Umbrellas

☎ 221-4396; Nakagyō-ku, Kawaramachi-dōri, Shijō agaru higashi gawa; 11am-8pm, closed Wed; 2min walk from Kawaramachi Station, Hankyū line

A short walk north of the Shijō-Kawaramachi crossing, Tsujikura has a good selection of waxed-paper umbrellas and paper lanterns with traditional and modern designs.

NISHIHARU Map p50 Wood-Block Prints

☎ 211-2849; Nakagyō-ku, Sanjō-dōri, Teramachi; 2-7pm, closed irregularly; 10min walk from Sanjō Station, Keihan line

This is an attractive shop dealing in wood-block prints. All the prints are accompanied by English explanations and the owner is happy to take the time to find something you really like.

CENTRAL KYOTO

Central Kyoto is really an extension of Downtown Kyoto and it contains many of Kyoto's best shops, with a heavy concentration of traditional craft shops. Teramachi-dōri, between Oike-dōri and Marutamachi-dōri, is Kyoto's single best shopping strip for traditional crafts and tea. Other good shopping options can be found in the streets south of Shijō-dōri.

KŌBŌ-SAN MARKET Map pp54–5 Flea Market

☎ 691-3325; Minami-ku, Kujō-chō 1 (Tō-ji); dawn to dusk, 21st of each month; 10min walk from Kyoto Station

This market is held at Tō-ji (p57) on the 21st of each month to commemorate the death of Kōbō Taishi, who in 823 was appointed abbot of the temple. If you're after used kimono, pottery, bric-a-brac, plants, tools and general Japanalia, this is the place.

YWCA'S THRIFT SHOP
Map pp54–5 Flea Market

☎ 431-0351; Kamigyō-ku, Muromachi-dōri, Demizu agaru, Konoe-chō 44; 11am-2pm, 1st & 3rd Sat of each month; 15min walk from Marutamachi Station, Karasuma subway line

On the first and third Saturday of each month there is a flea market and general get-together of foreigners here.

KYOTO-KIMONO PLAZA
Map pp54–5 Kimono & Obi

☎ 352-2323; Shimogyō-ku, Karasuma Takatsuji agaru; 10am-5pm, closed Tue; 2min walk from Shijō Station, Karasuma subway line

This is one of Kyoto's more approachable kimono shops. As with other shops specialising in new kimono and kimono fabrics, prices are not cheap, but the quality is high. You can be measured for a custom kimono here and the shop will post it to your home.

SHIKUNSHI Map pp54–5 Kimono & Obi

☎ 221-0456; Shimogyō-ku, Shijō-dōri, Nishinotōin higashi iru, Kakukyoyama-chō 12; 10.30am-7pm; 5min walk from Shijō Station, Karasuma subway line

In a wonderful old *machiya* (traditional Japanese town house) on Shijō-dōri, east of Nishinotōin-dōri, this shop sells a variety of kimono. Have a look at the small shop in the restored warehouse at the back.

SOUTHERN HIGASHIYAMA

While Southern Higashiyama is renowned as more of a sightseeing district, you will find plenty of interesting little souvenir shops scattered about, particularly in the streets leading up to Kiyomizu-dera (p63) and down towards Kōdai-ji (p64), such as Ninen-zaka and Sannen-zaka. Shops in this area are particularly good for ceramics and fabric items such as *noren*.

KAGOSHIN Map p62 Bamboo Crafts

☎ 771-0209; Higashiyama-ku, Sanjō-dōri, Ōhashi 4 chōme; 9am-6pm; 3min walk from Sanjō Station, Keihan line

Kagoshin is a small semi-open bamboo craft shop on Sanjō-dōri, only a few minutes' walk east of the Kamo-gawa. It has a good selection of baskets, chopstick holders, bamboo vases, decorations and knick-knacks. The baskets make a good, light souvenir and look great in alcove displays.

ONOUECHIKUZAITEN
Map p62 Bamboo Crafts

☎ 751-2444; Higashiyama-ku, Sanjō-dōri, Ōhashi higashi iru 3-39; 10am-7pm; 3min walk from Sanjō Station, Keihan line

With a name that even residents find hard to pronounce, this fine little specialist

IN THE MARKET FOR...

Ceramics

Kyoto is a great place to pick up some of Japan's famed ceramics. In Southern Higashiyama (Map p62), Ninen-zaka and Sannen-zaka slopes, close to Kiyomizu-dera (p63), are renowned for a distinctive type of pottery known as Kiyomizu-yaki. You'll find more pottery shops along Gojō-dōri between Higashiōji-dōri and Kawabata-dōri. Of course, you'll get far better deals at Kyoto's two great flea markets: Kōbō-san (p111) and Tenjin-san (opposite).

Used Kimono & Obi

If you're in the market for a used kimono or obi (kimono sash), you'll definitely find the widest selection and best prices at Kōbō-san and Tenjin-san. If you're not lucky enough to be in town on the 21st or 25th of the month for these markets, don't give up hope. There are several shops around town where you can buy a used kimono for a lot less than you'd pay for a new one. We suggest Tadashiya (p109) and Teramachi Club (p110) in Downtown Kyoto.

store stocks a selection of bamboo crafts. It's only a few steps away from its main competition, Kagoshin (p111), which allows for easy comparison shopping. Like Kagoshin, it stocks baskets, bamboo vases, decorations and knick-knacks.

TŌKI MATSURI Map p62 Ceramics

Higashiyama-ku, Gojō-dōri, btwn Higashiōji & Kawabata; 10am-8pm, 7-10 Aug; 10min walk from Gojō Station, Keihan line

This is Kyoto's largest ceramics fair and it's a good place to snap up some bargains, especially late on the last day. Even if you don't intend to buy, it's fun to stroll past the stores. The market runs between Kawabata and Higashiōji.

TESSAI-DŌ Map p62 Wood-Block Prints

☎ 531-9566; Higashiyama-ku, Shimokawara-chō 463; 10am-5pm; 7min walk from Higashiyamayasui bus stop, bus 206 from Kyoto Station

While exploring the lovely Nene-no-Michi lane in Higashiyama's main sightseeing district, you might want to step into this fine little wood-block print shop. This shop specialises in original prints, some of which are quite old. Prices average ¥10,000 per print and the owner will be happy to consult with you about what sort of print you are after.

NORTHERN HIGASHIYAMA

Similar to Southern Higashiyama, Northern Higashiyama is more of a sightseeing district than a shopping district. There are a few worthwhile shops scattered about, however, including our favourite one-stop souvenir shop: the Kyoto Handicraft Center. You'll also find a good temple market, the Chion-ji Tezukuri-Ichi, which is held on the 15th of every month.

GREEN E BOOKS Map pp68–9 Bookshop

☎ 751-5033; Sakyō-ku, Kawabata Marutamachi; 1-9pm Mon & Fri, 11am-9pm Sat & Sun; 1min walk from exit 4, Marutamachi Station, Keihan line

This small bookstore has a decent selection of used books. It also organises a variety of interesting events in town.

KYOTO INTERNATIONAL COMMUNITY HOUSE Map pp68–9 Flea Market

☎ 752-3010; Sakyō-ku, Awataguchi, Torii-chō 2-1; 11am-4pm; 5min walk from Keage Station, Tōzai subway line

Twice a year, in spring and autumn, recycled items, clothes and household goods are sold here. Call for dates, as they vary each year.

CHION-JI TEZUKURI-ICHI Map pp68–9 Handmade Crafts

☎ 781-9171; Sakyō-ku, Tanaka Monzen-chō 103; dawn to dusk, 15th of each month; 1min walk from Hyakumamben bus stop, bus 206 from Kyoto Station

The Tezukuri-ichi (handmade market) is held at Chion-ji on the 15th of each month. Wares include food and handmade clothes. This is a good chance to see Kyoto's alternative community out in full force.

KYOTO HANDICRAFT CENTER

Map pp68–9 Japanese Crafts

☎ 761-8001; Sakyō-ku, Shōgo-in Entomi-chō 21; 10am-6pm, closed 1-3 Jan; 10min walk from Marutamachi Station, Keihan line

The Kyoto Handicraft Center is a huge cooperative that exhibits and sells a wide range of Japanese arts and crafts. It also has two in-house wood-block printmakers and a corner where you can try your hand at making some of your own prints.

All in all, this is the best one-stop emporium in the whole of Kyoto. It's located near Heian-jingū (p72).

NORTHWEST KYOTO

Northwest Kyoto is hardly a shopping mecca, but like most Kyoto neighbourhoods it has plenty of stores scattered about. Of most interest to foreign travellers is the famous Tenjin-san Market, held once a month at Kitano Tenman-gū. The area is also home to the Nishijin textile district, which is where you'll find the Nishijin Textile Center.

TŌKI-ICHI Map p74 Ceramics

Kamigyō-ku, Mizomae-chō (Daihōon-ji, Senbon Shaka-dō); 10am-8pm 9-12 Jul; 10min walk Kitano Tenmangū-mae bus stop, bus 50 or 101 from Kyoto Station

This is a large pottery fair held at Senbon Shaka-dō, where around 30 vendors sell various wares.

MYŌREN-JI Map p74 Flea Market

☎ 451-3527; Kamigyō-ku, Teranouchi-dōri, Horikawa nishi iru; 10am-4pm, 12th of each month; 10min walk from Kuramaguchi Station, Karasuma subway line

On the 12th of each month there is a bazaar at Myōren-ji, northwest of Imadegawa-Horikawa. Goods on offer include such items as Japanese textiles and bric-a-brac.

TENJIN-SAN MARKET Map p74 Flea Market

☎ 461-0005; Kamigyō-ku, Bakuro-chō (Kitano Tenman-gū); dawn to dusk, 25th of each month; 1min walk from Kitano Tenmangū-mae bus stop, bus 50 or 101 from Kyoto Station

This market is held once a month at Kitano Tenman-gū (p76) and marks the birthday (and coincidentally the death) of the Heian-era statesman Sugawara Michizane (845–903). Items on offer are similar to those at Kōbō-san (p111). It's pleasant to explore the shrine before or after you do your shopping.

NISHIJIN TEXTILE CENTER

Map p74 Kimono & Obi

☎ 451-9231; Kamigyō-ku, Horikawa-dōri, Imadegawa minami iru; 9am-5pm; 1min walk from Horikawa-Imadegawa bus stop, bus 9 from Kyoto Station

The Nishijin Textile Center (see also p75) is part museum, part event hall and part shop. Downstairs, it occasionally hosts kimono fashion shows, highlighting the area's distinctive Nishijin-ori weaving. Upstairs there are displays where artisans demonstrate the use of traditional looms and dyeing techniques. A variety of goods, including kimono and obi (kimono sashes), are for sale on the 2nd floor.

GREATER KYOTO

Greater Kyoto, which comprises the outskirts of the city, is of little interest to foreign shoppers. Most of the stores exist to serve the needs of the many residential neighbourhoods here. The yearly antique fair held at Pulse Plaza, however, is worth the trip, even if you have no intention of buying anything. The variety of treasures on display will make you wish you were made of money.

PULSE PLAZA Map pp42–3 Antiques

☎ 0771-26-3603; Fushimi-ku, Takeda Tobadono-chō 5; 10am-5pm Fri & Sat, to 4pm Sun; free shuttle bus leaves from northeast exit, Takeda Station, Karasuma subway or Kintetsu line

Several times a year, an Antiques Grand Fair is held here in this hall in the southern part of Kyoto. Check with the TIC (p199) for exact dates.

EATING

top picks

- **Omen** (p134)
- **Den Shichi** (p128)
- **Kane-yo** (p126)
- **Karako** (p135)
- **Grotto** (p133)
- **Aunbo** (p129)
- **Uosue** (p122)
- **Ganko Zushi** (p123)
- **Ōzawa** (p130)
- **Café Bibliotec HELLO!** (p126)

What's your recommendation? www.lonelyplanet.com/kyoto

EATING

Kyoto is one of the world's great food cities. In fact, when you factor in atmosphere, service, quality and price, we reckon that you can eat better here for less money than in some of the more famous food cities, such as Paris and New York.

First off, Kyoto is the place to make a full exploration of Japanese cuisine – you can start with familiar dishes such as tempura and sushi and then head off into unknown territory with all kinds of regional and speciality dishes. Then, if you tire of Japanese food, you can take a break with excellent French, Italian, Chinese and Indian cuisines.

Of course, you might be wondering how you'll order all this good stuff without any Japanese language skills. Are you going to have to invent some new form of culinary sign language or blunder around restaurants pointing to what your fellow diners are eating? On this point, we can put your mind at ease: an increasing number of restaurants in Kyoto have English menus for their foreign guests. Others have picture menus with photos of almost every item they serve. Still others have English-speaking staff. Thus, you can comfortably order whatever you want without any language difficulties whatsoever. You can also use the phrases and sample menus under Food & Drink in the Language chapter (p205) to help you.

EATING IN A JAPANESE RESTAURANT

When you enter a restaurant in Japan, you'll be greeted with a hearty *'Irasshaimase!'* (Welcome!). In all but the most casual places the waiter will next ask you *'Nan-mei sama?'* (How many people?). Answer with your fingers, which is what the Japanese do. You will then be led to a table, a place at the counter or a tatami room.

At this point you will be given an *o-shibori* (hot towel), a cup of tea and a menu. The *o-shibori* is for wiping your hands and face. When you're done with it, just roll it up and leave it next to your place. Now comes the hard part: ordering. If you don't read Japanese, you can use the romanised translations in this book to help you, or direct the waiter's attention to the Japanese script. If this doesn't work there are two phrases that might help: *'O-susume wa nan desu ka?'* (What do you recommend?) and *'O-makase shimasu'* (Please decide for me). If you're still having problems, you can try pointing at other diners' food or, if the restaurant has them, dragging the waiter outside to point at the plastic food models in the window.

When you've finished eating, you can signal for the bill by crossing one index finger over the other to form the sign of an 'x'. This is the standard sign for 'cheque please'. You can also say *'O-kanjō kudasai'*. Remember there is no tipping in Japan and tea is free of charge.

When leaving, it is polite to say to the restaurant staff, *'Gochisō-sama deshita'*, which means 'It was a real feast'. The Language chapter (p205) contains more useful restaurant words and phrases.

RESTAURANT TYPES

Shokudō

A *shokudō* (Japanese-style cafeteria/cheap restaurant) is the most common type of restaurant in Japan, and is found near train stations, tourist spots and just about any other place where people congregate. Easily distinguished by the presence of plastic food displays in the window, these inexpensive places usually serve a variety of *washoku* (Japanese dishes) and *yōshoku* (Western dishes).

At lunch, and sometimes dinner, the easiest meal to order at a *shokudō* is a *teishoku* (set-course meal), which is sometimes also called *ranchi setto* (lunch set) or *kōsu*. This usually includes a main dish of meat or fish, a bowl of rice, miso soup, shredded cabbage and some *tsukemono* (Japanese pickles). In addition, most *shokudō* serve a fairly standard selection of *donburi-mono* (rice dishes) and *menrui* (noodle dishes). When you order noodles, you can choose between *soba* (thin brown buckwheat noodles) and *udon* (thick white wheat noodles), both of which are served with a variety of toppings. If you're at a loss as to what to order, simply say *'kyō-no-ranchi'* (today's lunch) and they'll do the rest. Expect to spend from ¥800 to ¥1000 for a meal at a *shokudō*.

See p206 and p207 for sample menus of the various rice and noodle dishes available at *shokudō*.

Izakaya

An *izakaya* is the Japanese equivalent of a pub. It's a good place to visit when you want a casual meal, a wide selection of food, a hearty atmosphere and, of course, plenty of beer and sake. When you enter an *izakaya,* you are given the choice of sitting around the counter, at a table or on a tatami floor. You usually order a bit at a time, choosing from a selection of typical Japanese foods such as *yakitori* (skewers of grilled chicken and vegetables), sashimi and grilled fish, as well as Japanese interpretations of Western foods such as French fries and beef stew.

Izakaya can be identified by their rustic façades and the red lanterns outside their doors. Since *izakaya* food is casual fare to go with drinking, it is usually fairly inexpensive. Depending on how much you drink, you can expect to get away with spending ¥2500 to ¥5000 per person.

See p206 for a sample menu of *izakaya* fare.

SPECIALITIES

Kyō-ryōri, or Kyoto cuisine, is a style of cooking that evolved out of Kyoto's landlocked location and age-old customs of the imperial court. The preparation of dishes makes ingenious use of fresh seasonal vegetables and emphasises subtle flavours, revealing the natural taste of the ingredients. *Kyō-ryōri* is selected according to the mood and hues of the ever-changing seasons, and the presentation and atmosphere in which it's enjoyed are as important as the flavour.

Kaiseki

Kaiseki (Japanese *haute cuisine*) is the pinnacle of refined dining, where ingredients, preparation, setting and presentation come together to create a dining experience quite unlike any other. Born as an adjunct to the tea ceremony, *kaiseki* is a largely vegetarian affair (though fish is often served). One usually eats *kaiseki* in the private room of a *ryōtei* (traditional, high-class Japanese restaurant) or ryokan. The meal is served in several small courses, giving one the opportunity to admire the plates and bowls, which are carefully chosen to complement the food and seasons. Rice is eaten last (usually with an assortment of pickles) and the drink of choice is sake or beer. The Kyoto version of *kaiseki* is known as *kyō-kaiseki* and it features a variety of *kyō-yasai,* or Kyoto vegetables.

The best way to sample *kaiseki* is by booking a night in a Kyoto ryokan and asking for the breakfast/dinner option. Otherwise, you can enjoy *kaiseki* at restaurants such as Minokō (p129) and Ponto-chō Uan (p122).

A good *kaiseki* (see left) dinner costs upwards of ¥10,000 per person. A cheaper way to sample the delights of *kaiseki* is to visit a *kaiseki* restaurant for lunch. Most places offer a boxed lunch containing a sampling of their dinner fare for around ¥2500.

Unfortunately for foreigners, *kaiseki* restaurants can be intimidating places to enter. If possible, bring a Japanese friend or ask a Japanese-speaker to call ahead and make arrangements.

See p206 for some useful *kaiseki* terms.

Tofu-ryōri

Kyoto is famed for its tofu (soya bean curd); there are numerous *tofu-ya-san* (tofu makers) scattered throughout the city and a legion of exquisite *yudōfu* (bean curd cooked in an iron pot) restaurants – many are concentrated in Northern Higashiyama along the roads around Nanzen-ji (see p132) and in the Arashiyama area (see p136). One typical Kyoto tofu by-product is called *yuba,* sheets of the chewy, thin film that settles on the surface of vats of simmering soy milk. This turns up in many ryokan meals and *kaiseki* restaurants.

COMMON CUISINE TYPES

Yakitori

Yakitori is a popular after-work meal. *Yakitori* is not so much a full meal as an accompaniment for beer and sake. At a *yakitori-ya* (*yakitori* restaurant) you sit around a counter with the other patrons and watch the chef grill your selections over charcoal. The best way to eat here is to order several varieties, then order seconds of the ones you really like. Ordering can be a little confusing since one serving often means two or three skewers (be careful – the price listed on the menu is usually that of a single skewer).

A few drinks and enough skewers to fill you up should cost ¥3000 to ¥4000 per person. *Yakitori* restaurants are usually small places, often near train stations, and are best identified by a red lantern outside and the smell of grilled chicken.

For a *yakitori* sample menu, see p206.

Sushi & Sashimi

Like *yakitori,* sushi is considered an accompaniment for beer and sake. All proper sushi restaurants serve their fish over rice, in which case it's called sushi, or without rice, in which case it's called sashimi or *tsukuri* (or, politely, *o-tsukuri*).

Sushi is not difficult to order. If you sit at the counter of a sushi restaurant you can simply point at what you want, as most of the selections are visible in a refrigerated glass case between you and the sushi chef. You can also order à la carte from the menu. If that's too daunting, you can take care of your whole meal with just one or two words by asking for *mori-awase,* an assortment plate of *nigiri-zushi* (fish served on a small bed of rice). These usually come in three grades: *futsū nigiri* (regular *nigiri*), *jō nigiri* (special *nigiri*) and *toku-jō nigiri* (extra-special *nigiri*). The difference is in the type of fish used. Most *mori-awase* contain six or seven pieces of sushi.

Be warned that meals in a good sushi restaurant can cost upwards of ¥10,000, while an average establishment can run from ¥3000 to ¥5000 per person. One way to sample the joy of sushi on the cheap is to try an automatic sushi place, usually called *kaiten-zushi,* where the sushi is served on a conveyor belt that runs along a counter. You can usually fill yourself up in one of these places for ¥1000 to ¥2000 per person.

Note that most of the items on this sample sushi menu can be ordered as sashimi. Just add the words *'no o-tsukuri'* to get the sashimi version. So, for example, if you want some tuna sashimi, you would order *'maguro no o-tsukuri'*.

See p207 for a sample menu.

Sukiyaki & Shabu-Shabu

Restaurants usually specialise in both these dishes. Popular in the West, sukiyaki is a favourite of most foreign visitors to Japan. Sukiyaki consists of thin slices of beef cooked in a broth of *shōyu* (soy sauce), sugar and sake, and is accompanied by a variety of vegetables and tofu. After cooking, all the ingredients are dipped in raw egg before being eaten. When made with high-quality beef, such as Kōbe beef, it is a sublime experience.

Shabu-shabu consists of thin slices of beef and vegetables cooked by swirling the ingredients in a light broth, then dipping them in a variety of special sesame-seed and citrus-based sauces. Both of these dishes are prepared in a pot over a fire at your private table; don't fret about preparation – the waiter will usually help you get started and keep a close watch as you proceed.

Sukiyaki and *shabu-shabu* restaurants usually have traditional Japanese décor and sometimes a picture of a cow to help you identify them. Ordering is not difficult. Simply say sukiyaki or *shabu-shabu* and indicate how many people are dining. Expect to pay from ¥3000 to ¥10,000 per person.

Tempura

Tempura consists of portions of fish, prawns and vegetables cooked in fluffy, nongreasy batter. When you sit down at a tempura restaurant, you will be given a small bowl of *ten-tsuyu* (a light brown sauce), and a plate of grated *daikon* (white radish) to mix into the sauce. Dip each piece of tempura into this sauce before eating it. Tempura is best when it's hot, so don't wait too long – use the sauce to cool each piece and dig in.

Expect to pay between ¥2000 and ¥10,000 for a full tempura meal. Finding these restaurants is tricky as they have no distinctive façade or décor. If you look through the window, you'll see customers around the counter watching the chefs as they work over large woks filled with oil.

To get you started, see p207 for a sample of tempura menu items.

Rāmen

The Japanese imported this dish from China and put their own spin on it to make what is one of the world's most delicious fast foods. *Rāmen* dishes are big bowls of noodles in a meat broth, served with a variety of toppings, such as sliced pork, bean sprouts and leeks. In some restaurants you may be asked if you'd prefer *kotteri* (thick) or *assari* (thin) soup. Other than this, ordering is simple: just sidle up to the counter and say *'rāmen'*, or ask for any of the other choices on offer. Expect to pay between ¥500 and ¥900 for a bowl. Since *rāmen* is derived from Chinese cuisine, some *rāmen* restaurants also serve *chāhan* or *yaki-meshi* (both dishes are fried rice), *gyōza* (dumplings) and *kara-age* (deep-fried chicken pieces).

Rāmen restaurants are easily distinguished by their long counters lined with customers hunched over steaming bowls of noodles. You can sometimes even hear a *rāmen* shop as you wander by – it is considered polite to slurp the noodles as you eat. In fact, aficionados claim that slurping brings out the full flavour of the broth.

You'll find some useful *rāmen* menu items listed in the food glossary, p207.

Soba & Udon

Soba and *udon* are Japan's answer to Chinese-style *rāmen*. *Soba* are thin, brown buckwheat noodles; *udon* are thick, white wheat noodles. Most Japanese noodle shops serve both *soba* and *udon* in a variety of ways. Noodles are usually served in a bowl containing a light, bonito-flavoured broth, but you can also order them served cold and piled on a bamboo screen with a cold broth for dipping.

By far the most popular type of cold noodles is *zaru soba*, which is served with bits of *nori* (seaweed) on top. If you order these noodles, you'll receive a small plate of *wasabi* (spicy Japanese horseradish) and sliced spring onions – put these into the cup of broth and eat the noodles by dipping them in this mixture. At the end of your meal, the waiter will give you some hot broth to mix with the leftover sauce, which you drink like a kind of tea. As with *rāmen*, you should feel free to slurp as loudly as you please.

Soba and *udon* places are usually quite cheap (about ¥900 a dish), but some fancy places can be significantly more expensive (the décor is a good indication of the price).

See p207 for a glossary of *soba* and *udon* dishes.

Unagi

Unagi (eel) is an expensive and popular delicacy in Japan. Even if you can't stand the creature when served in your home country, you owe it to yourself to try *unagi* at least once while in Japan. It's cooked over hot coals and brushed with a rich sauce of *shōyu* and sake. Full *unagi* dinners can be expensive, but many *unagi* restaurants offer *unagi bentō* (boxed lunches) and lunch sets for around ¥1500. Most *unagi* restaurants display plastic models of their sets in their front windows, and may have barrels of live eels to entice passers-by.

The sample menu, p207, will set you up for ordering *unagi*.

top picks

CUISINE

- Kushiage & kushikatsu Kushi Hachi (p133)
- Shokudō Ayatori (p135)
- Soba & udon Omen (p134); Misoka-an Kawamichi-ya (p123); Tagoto Honten (p125); Hinode Udon (p135)
- Sukiyaki & shabu-shabu Mishima-tei (p122)
- Sushi Den Shichi (p128); Ganko Zushi (p123)
- Tempura Ōzawa (p130); Yoshikawa (p122)
- Yakitori Ichi-ban (p130); Daikichi (p131)

Kushiage & Kushikatsu

This is the fried food to beat all fried foods. *Kushiage* and *kushikatsu* are deep-fried skewers of meat, seafood and vegetables eaten as an accompaniment to beer. *Kushi* means 'skewer' and if something edible can be impaled on one, it's probably on the menu. Cabbage is often eaten with the meal.

You order *kushiage* and *kushikatsu* by the skewer (one skewer is *ippon*, but you can always use your fingers to indicate how many you want). Like *yakitori*, this food is popular with after-work salarymen and students and is therefore fairly inexpensive, though there are upmarket places. Expect to pay ¥2000 to ¥5000 for a full meal and a couple of beers. Not particularly distinctive in appearance, the best *kushiage* and *kushikatsu* places are found by asking a Japanese friend.

You'll find a useful sample menu in the food glossary, p207.

Okonomiyaki

The name means 'cook what you like', and an *okonomiyaki* restaurant provides you with an inexpensive opportunity to do just that. Sometimes described as Japanese pizza or pancake, the resemblance is in form only. At an *okonomiyaki* restaurant you sit around a *teppan* (iron hotplate), armed with a spatula and chopsticks to cook your choice of meat, seafood and vegetables in a cabbage and vegetable batter.

Most *okonomiyaki* places also serve *yakisoba* (fried noodles) and *yasai-itame* (stir-fried vegetables). All of this is washed down with mugs of draught beer.

The food glossary, p208, will help you place your order.

DRINKS

Alcoholic Drinks

Drinking plays a big role in Japanese society and there are few social occasions where beer or sake is not served. We list some common drinks in the food glossary, p208. If you don't drink alcohol, however, it's no big deal. Simply order *oolong cha* (oolong tea) in place of beer or sake. While some folks might put pressure on you to drink alcohol, you can diffuse this pressure by saying '*sake o nomimasen*' (I don't drink alcohol).

Izakaya and *yakitori-ya* are cheap places for beer, sake and food. They offer a casual atmosphere resembling that of a pub. Otherwise, if that's not your thing, see p140 for some likely drinking holes.

Nonalcoholic Drinks

Kōhii (coffee) served in a *kisaten* (coffee shop) tends to be expensive in Japan, costing between ¥350 and ¥500 a cup, with some places charging up to ¥1000. A cheap alternative is one of the newer coffee-restaurant chains such as Doutor or Pronto, or doughnut shops such as Mr Donut (which offers free refills). An even cheaper alternative is a can of coffee, hot or cold, from a vending machine. Although unpleasantly sweet, at ¥120 the price is hard to beat.

When ordering coffee at a coffee shop in Japan, you'll be asked whether you prefer it *hotto* (hot) or *aisu* (cold). Black tea also comes hot or cold, with *miruku* (milk) or *remon* (lemon). An excellent way to kick off your day of sightseeing in Kyoto is with a *mōningu setto* (morning set) of tea or coffee, toast and eggs. All up it will cost you around ¥400.

JAPANESE TEA

Unlike black tea, which Westerners are familiar with, most Japanese tea is green and contains a lot of vitamin C and caffeine. The powdered form used in the tea ceremony is called *matcha* and is drunk after being whipped into a frothy consistency. The more common form, a leafy green tea, is simply called *o-cha,* and is drunk after being steeped in a pot. In addition to green tea, you'll probably drink a lot of a brownish tea called *bancha,* which restaurants serve for free. In summer, a cold beverage called *mugicha* (roasted barley tea) is served in private homes.

See p208 for some sample menu items.

COOKING COURSES

If you enjoy the food you eat in Kyoto, why not deepen your appreciation of the cuisine by taking a cooking class at WAK Japan (Map pp54–5; ☎ 212-9993; www.wakjapan.com; Kamigyō-ku, Iseya-chō 412-506). WAK offers cooking courses and can create one to suit your special interests.

PRACTICALITIES

How Much?

You may be surprised at how cheap it is to eat in Kyoto, especially if you're used to paying the inflated prices charged by Japanese restaurants abroad. And don't forget that there's no tipping in Japan and tea is free, so eating is actually very reasonable indeed.

You can eat simple meals in Japanese restaurants at lunch and dinner for less than ¥1000 per head (not including alcohol) if you stick to noodle/rice shops and *shokudō*. If you want something a bit nicer and in slightly more elegant surroundings, you can count

SAKE

Sake (pronounced sah-kay, not sah-key) is Japan's traditional rice wine. While much of what is available overseas is pretty foul, the good stuff consumed on its home turf is bound to be a revelation.

There are several major types of sake, including *nigori* (cloudy), *nama* (unrefined) and regular, clear sake. Of these, clear sake is by far the most common. Clear sake is usually divided into three grades: *tokkyū* (premium), *ikkyū* (first grade) and *nikyū* (second grade). *Nikyū* is the routine choice. Sake can be further divided into *karakuchi* (dry) and *amakuchi* (sweet). As well as the national brewing giants, there are thousands of provincial brewers producing local brews called *jizake*.

Sake is served *atsukan* (warm) and *reishu* (cold), with warm sake, not surprisingly, being more popular in winter. When you order sake, it will usually be served in a small flask called *tokkuri*. These come in two sizes, so you should specify whether you want *ichigō* (small) or *nigō* (large). From these flasks you pour the sake into small ceramic cups called *o-choko* or *sakazuki*. Another way to sample sake is to drink it from a small wooden box called *masu,* with a bit of salt on the rim.

PRICE GUIDE

The following is a guide to the pricing system in this chapter. Price indicators are per person per meal.

¥¥¥	over ¥5000
¥¥	¥1000-5000
¥	under ¥1000

on around ¥1500 to ¥2500 at lunch and ¥2500 to ¥4000 for dinner (not including alcohol). Of course, you can pay much more at some top-end places, especially for dinner.

Finally, keep in mind that even very fancy restaurants often serve reasonably priced lunch sets, allowing you to sample the good stuff without breaking the bank.

Self-Catering

If you get tired of eating out all the time, you will have no problem buying food and preparing your own simple meals in Kyoto. First off, there are good shopping and food market streets all over town, including the famous Nishiki Market (p50). You'll also find Western-style supermarkets in most residential neighbourhoods and food floors in most of Kyoto's department stores, such as Takashimaya and Daimaru (see the boxed text, p109). You will be utterly amazed by the variety of both Western and Japanese food on offer at these places. If you are after speciality imported foods, try Meidi-ya (p109). Finally, Kyoto's ubiquitous convenience stores sell a surprising variety of meal-worthy items such as rice balls, fruit, milk, juice and – needless to say – the full range of salty/crunchy/chewy/sweet junk food.

Getting a Reservation

You won't need a reservation at most of the restaurants listed in this chapter. And, unlike in some Western cities, you don't need connections to get into most places – as long as you're carrying yen, you're welcome (there are a few notable exceptions, none of which appear in this book). During busy seasons or at traditional upper-budget restaurants, however, a reservation is a good idea. If you don't speak Japanese, the easiest thing to do is simply ask someone at the place you're staying to call and make the reservation for you. When they call, it's often a good idea to have them order your meal (usually a course). This makes things easier for everyone involved – you don't have to worry about ordering and the folks at the restaurant don't have to worry about communication.

KYOTO STATION AREA

Unlike train stations elsewhere in the world, Kyoto Station is loaded with good places to eat. In the streets surrounding the station, you'll also find a few decent choices. The food courts in the station building itself (see the boxed text, p122) usually operate from 11am to 10pm daily, with some shops and cafés opening significantly earlier to serve commuters. Restaurants around the station keep normal business hours.

IIMURA Map p46 Japanese ¥

☎ 351-8023; Shimogyō-ku, Shichijō-dōri, Higashinotōin Nishi iru, Maoya-chō 216; 11.30am-2pm; lunch sets ¥650; 5min walk from Kyoto Station

Try this classic little restaurant for its ever-changing set lunch – usually simple Japanese home-style cooking. Dishes might include a bit of fish or meat and the usual accompaniments of rice, miso soup and pickles. It's in a traditional Japanese house set back a bit from the street, alongside a new five-storey building (look for the black-and-white sign).

DOWNTOWN KYOTO

The area between Oike-dōri and Shijō-dōri (north and south) and Kiyamachi-dōri and Karasuma-dōri (east and west) has the highest concentration of restaurants in the city. There's a wide range of both international and Japanese eateries in all price ranges. This is definitely the best place for a meal out in Kyoto. And if you're up for an after-dinner drink, there are plenty of bars and clubs here, too.

IKUMATSU Map p50 Kaiseki ¥¥¥

☎ 231-1234; Nakagyō-ku, Kiyamachi-dōri, Oike agaru; 11.30am-3pm & 5.30-10pm; lunch from ¥5500, kaiseki dinner from ¥14,000; 2min walk from exit B2, Kyoto-Shiyakusho-mae Station, Tōzai subway line

Ikumatsu is one of Kyoto's classical old *ryōri ryokan* (cuisine ryokan). In front of the ryokan is a more modern brick building in which the brilliant food is served to nonstaying guests. The ¥1030 *katsura kogoro* (lunch set) here is phenomenal value. Dinner sets start at ¥1900. The dining room décor is neither here nor there, but the food is top shelf.

TRAIN STATION GOURMET

For a quick cuppa while waiting for a train at Kyoto Station, try Café du Monde (Map p46) on the 2nd floor overlooking the central atrium. For more substantial meals there are several food courts scattered about. The best of these can be found on the 11th floor on the west side of the building: the Cube (Map p46) food court and Isetan Department Store's Eat Paradise (Map p46) food court. In the Cube, we like Katsu Kura, a popular *tonkatsu* (deep-fried, breaded pork cutlet) specialist that usually has a tasty lunch special. In Eat Paradise, we highly recommend Tenichi for sublime tempura, and Wakuden for approachable *kaiseki* (Japanese *haute cuisine*) fare. To get to these food courts, take the west escalators from the main concourse all the way up to the 11th floor and look for the Cube on your left and Eat Paradise straight in front of you.

Other options in the station include Rāmen Koji (Map p46), a collection of seven *rāmen* (noodles in meat broth with meat and vegetables) restaurants on the 10th floor (underneath the Cube). Buy tickets for *rāmen* from the machines, which don't have English but have pictures on the buttons. In addition to *rāmen,* you can get green-tea ice cream and other Japanese desserts at Chasen and *tako yaki* (fried, battered octopus balls) at Miyako.

If you're departing by train or bus from Kyoto Station and want to pick up some nibblies for the ride, head downstairs to the B1 floor Porta underground shopping arcade. Here, you can purchase excellent sushi *bentō* (lunch boxes) at Kyōtaru and good bread and pastries at Shinshindō. Both are near the *kita* (north) exit of the Karasuma subway line.

Problem is, with only a few tables, the place is often full. Look for the brick façade.

YOSHIKAWA Map p50 Tempura ¥¥¥

☎ 221-5544; Nakagyō-ku, Tominokōji-dōri, Oike kudaru; 🕑 11am-2pm & 5-8pm, closed Sun; lunch ¥2000-6000, dinner ¥6000-12,000; 5min walk from Kyoto-Shiyakusho-mae Station, Tōzai subway line

For superb tempura, head for Yoshikawa. It offers fancy table seating, but it's much more interesting (and cheaper) to sit and eat around the small counter and observe the chefs at work. Look for the English sign reading 'Yoshikawa Inn'; the restaurant entrance is next door.

PONTO-CHŌ UAN Map p50 Kaiseki ¥¥¥

☎ 221-2358/2269; Nakagyō-ku, Pontochō Sanjō sagaru; 🕑 5-10pm, closed Wed; dinner from ¥5000; 8min walk from Kawaramachi Station, Hankyū line

Ponto-chō Uan (formerly Uzuki) is an elegant *kaiseki* restaurant with a great platform for riverside dining in the summer. We recommend that you have a Japanese speaker call to reserve and choose your meal. Look for the rabbit on the sign.

MISHIMA-TEI Map p50 Sukiyaki ¥¥¥

☎ 221-0003; Nakagyō-ku, Teramachi-dōri Sanjō kudaru, Sakurano-chō 405; 🕑 11.30am-10pm, closed Wed; sukiyaki sets from ¥4400; 5min walk from Sanjō Station, Keihan line

This is an inexpensive place to sample sukiyaki. The quality of the meat here is very high – hardly surprising when you consider there is a butcher right downstairs. There is an English menu and a discount for foreign travellers! It's in the intersection of the Sanjō and Teramachi covered arcades.

TŌSUIRŌ Map p50 Tofu ¥¥

☎ 251-1600; Nakagyō-ku, Kiyamachi-dōri, Sanjō agaru, Kamiōsaka-chō 517-3; 🕑 11.30am-2pm & 5-9.30pm Mon-Sat, noon-8.30pm Sun, closed irregularly; lunch/dinner ¥2000/5000; 5min walk from Kyoto-Shiyakusho-mae Station, Tōzai subway line

We really like this tofu specialist. It's got great traditional Japanese décor and in summer you can sit on the *yuka* (dining platform) outside with a view of the Kamo-gawa. You will most probably be amazed by the incredible variety of dishes that can be created with tofu. At lunch, the *machiya-zen* (tofu set; ¥2100) is highly recommended. At dinner, we suggest the Higashiyama tofu set (¥3675). Tōsuirō is at the end of an alley on the north (left) side.

UOSUE Map p50 Japanese ¥¥

☎ 351-1437; Shimogyō-ku, Ayakōji-dōri, Higashinotōin Higashi iru, Shinmei-chō 724; 🕑 11am-2pm & 5-10pm, closed Sun; lunch/bentō ¥1050, dinner from ¥3990; 1min walk from Karasuma Station, Hankyū line

Uosue is one of the best value Japanese places in town. It's a traditional Kyoto-style restaurant with a clean interior and friendly proprietors. For lunch, try the wonderful *nijū bentō* for ¥1000. At dinner, the *omakase ryōri kōsu* is a great way to sample *kaiseki ryōri* without breaking the bank: it costs just ¥3800. It's next to a tiny shrine – keep an eye out for the sake barrels out the front.

MISOKA-AN KAWAMICHI-YA

Map p50 Soba ¥¥

☎ 221-2525; Nakagyō-ku, Fuyachō, Sanjō agaru; 11am-8pm, closed Thu; dishes ¥700-3800; 3min walk from Kyoto-Shiyakusho-mae Station, Tōzai subway line

For a taste of some of Kyoto's best *soba* in traditional surroundings, head to this place, where noodles have been made by hand for 300 years. Try a simple bowl of *nishin* (fish-topped) *soba*, or the more elaborate *nabe* dishes (cooked in a special cast-iron pot). There is a small English sign.

UONTANA Map p50 Izakaya ¥¥

☎ 221-2579; Nakagyō-ku, Rokkaku-dōri, Shinkyōgoku-dōri, Higashi iru; noon-3pm & 5-10pm, closed Wed; dinner from ¥3000; 7min walk from Sanjō Station, Keihan line

This upscale *izakaya* is a good spot to try a range of sake and elegantly presented Japanese fare (sashimi, fried dishes, salads). The design is sleek, modern and more Tokyo than Kyoto. There is an English menu and a tiny lantern out the front.

TOMIZUSHI Map p50 Sushi ¥¥

☎ 231-3628; Nakagyō-ku, Shinkyōgoku-dōri, Shijō agaru, Higashi iru; 5pm-midnight, closed Thu; dinner ¥3000; 5min walk from Kawaramachi Station, Hankyū line

For good sushi in lively surroundings, try Tomizushi, where you can rub elbows with your neighbours at a long marble counter and watch as some of the fastest sushi chefs in the land do their thing. Go early or be prepared to wait in a queue. It's near the Shijō-Kawaramachi crossing; look for the lantern and the black-and-white signs.

ZU ZU Map p50 Izakaya ¥¥

☎ 231-0736; Nakagyō-ku, Pontochō, Takoyakushi agaru, Nishi gawa; 6pm-2am; dinner from ¥3000; 5min walk from Kawaramachi Station, Hankyū line

This Pontochō *izakaya* is a fun place to eat. The best bet when ordering is to ask the waiter for a recommendation. The fare is sort of nouveau-Japanese, with menu items such as shrimp with tofu and chicken with plum sauce. Look for the white stucco exterior and black bars on the windows.

GANKO ZUSHI Map p50 Japanese ¥¥

☎ 255-1128; Nakagyō-ku, Sanjō-dōri, Kawaramachi Higashi iru; 11.30am-10.30pm; lunch/dinner ¥1000/3000; 3min walk from Sanjō Station, Keihan line

This giant four-storey dining hall is part of Kansai's biggest sushi chain. The ground floor is the sushi area (you can order non-sushi dishes here as well); it has a long sushi counter and plenty of tables. Despite the fact that it's a giant plebeian dining hall, it's actually one of the most convenient spots in Downtown Kyoto for travellers to dine in, and the extensive English/picture menu makes ordering a breeze. The set meals are good value. Downstairs is an *izakaya* and upstairs has rooms for parties. This place may have the most plastic-looking food models out of any restaurant window in Kyoto. It's near the Sanjō-Ōhashi bridge.

MUKADE-YA Map p50 Japanese ¥¥

☎ 256-7039; Nakagyō-ku, Shinmachi-dōri-Nishikikōji; 11am-2pm & 5-9pm, closed Wed; meals from ¥3000; 5min walk from Shijō Station, Karasuma subway line

Mukade-ya is an atmospheric restaurant located in an exquisite *machiya* west of Karasuma-dōri. For lunch try the special *bentō:* two rounds (five small dishes each) of delectable *obanzai* (Kyoto-style home cooking) fare. *Kaiseki* courses start at ¥5000.

MERRY ISLAND CAFÉ

Map p50 International ¥¥

☎ 213-0214; Nakagyō-ku, Kiyamachi-dōri, Oike kudaru; 11.30am-11pm, closed Mon; lunch/dinner ¥800/3000; 2min walk from Kyoto-Shiyakusho-mae Station, Tōzai subway line

This popular restaurant strives to create the atmosphere of a tropical resort. The menu is *mukokuseki* (without nationality) and most of what is on offer is pretty tasty. It does a good risotto and occasionally offers a nice piece of Japanese steak. In warm weather the front doors are opened and the place takes on the air of a sidewalk café (it doesn't hurt that it's located on one of the prettiest streets in Kyoto). There are English menus and an English sign.

SHIRUKŌ Map p50 Obanzai ¥¥

☎ 221-3250; Shimogyō-ku, Nishikiyamachi, Shijō agaru; 11.30am-9pm, closed Wed; lunch & dinner from ¥2600; 2min walk from Kawaramachi Station, Hankyū line

For a light meal, Shirukō has been serving simple Kyoto *obanzai-ryōri* since 1932. The restaurant features more than 10 varieties of miso soup, and the *rikyū bentō* (mixed lunch box; ¥2600) is a bona fide work of art. Shirukō is down a somewhat seedy pedestrian alley near Shijō-Kawaramachi crossing; look for the bamboo out the front.

FUJINO-YA Map p50 Japanese ¥¥

☎ 221-2446; Nakagyō-ku, Pontochō-dōri, Shijō agaru; 5-8pm, closed Wed; tempura sets ¥2500; 3min walk from Kawaramachi Station, Hankyū line

This is one of the easiest places for non-Japanese to enter on Pontochō, a street where many of the other restaurants turn down even unfamiliar Japanese diners. Here you can feast on tempura, *okonomiyaki*, *yaki-soba* and *kushikatsu* in tatami rooms overlooking the Kamo-gawa.

LE BOUCHON Map p50 French ¥¥

☎ 211-5220; Nakagyō-ku, Teramachi-dōri-Nijō; 11.30am-2.30pm, 5.30-9.30pm, closed Thu; dinner sets ¥2500; 3min walk from Kyoto-Shiyakusho-mae Station, Tōzai subway line

This reliable French place serves tasty lunch and dinner sets and has a pleasant, casual atmosphere. The kitchen does great work with fish, salads and desserts, and the *pommes frites* (French fries) are excellent. The owner speaks English, French and Japanese and will make you feel right at home. The set dinner (appetiser, main and dessert) is great value. Lunch sets cost less than ¥1000. It's near the corner; look for the blackboard displaying the day's specials.

GANKO NIJŌ-EN Map p50 Japanese ¥¥

☎ 223-3456; Nakagyō-ku, Kiyamachi-dōri, Nijō kudaru; 11.30am-10pm; lunch/dinner from ¥1500/2500; 3min walk from Kyoto-Shiyakusho-mae Station, Tōzai subway line

This is an upscale branch of the Ganko Zushi chain that serves sushi and simple *kaiseki* sets. There's a picture menu and you can stroll in the stunning garden before or after your meal. It's near the Nijō-Kiyamachi crossing; you can't miss the grand entrance or the food models in the glass window.

SHIZENHA RESTAURANT OBANZAI Map p50 Obanzai ¥¥

☎ 223-6623; Nakagyō-ku, Koromonotana-dōri-Oike; 11am-9pm, closed dinner Wed; lunch/dinner ¥840/2100; 5min walk from Karasuma-Oike Station, Karasuma subway line

A little out of the way, but nevertheless good value, this place serves a decent buffet-style lunch and dinner of mostly organic Japanese vegetarian food. It's northwest of the Karasuma-Oike crossing, set back a bit from the street.

VEGGIE TABLE Map p50 Hot Salad ¥¥

☎ 241-0359; Nakagyō-ku, Sanjō, Kawaramachi Higashi iru, Sanjō Kiyamachi Bldg 1st & 2nd fl; 11.30am-3.30pm & 6-10pm Mon-Fri, 11.30am-4.30pm & 5-10pm Sat & Sun, closed irregularly; lunch/dinner ¥1000/2000; 5min walk from Sanjō Station, Keihan line

Right near one of the busiest corners in the Kiyamachi-Sanjō entertainment-dining district, this clean, well-lit new restaurant specialises in 'hot salad' sets (steamed vegetables and a variety of side dishes, including brown rice). It's a healthy addition to a neighbourhood that has, up until now, focused more on *rāmen* and booze. It has an English sign on the street; otherwise, look for the glass front.

CAPRICCIOSA Map p50 Italian ¥¥

☎ 221-7496; Nakagyō-ku, Kawaramachi-dōri-Sanjō kudaru; 11.30am-11pm; dinner from ¥1500; 5min walk from Sanjō Station, Keihan line

For heaped portions of pasta at rock-bottom prices you won't do much better than this longtime student favourite. Pasta dishes start at around ¥800 and you can choose from pizzas, salads, and various meat and fish dishes. It will definitely not be the best Italian you've ever had, but you'll probably leave full and happy. It's near the Sanjō-Kawaramachi crossing; look for the red-brick steps and the green awning. There's an English menu and an English sign.

OMEN NIPPON Map p50 Japanese/Udon ¥¥

☎ 253-0377; Nakagyō-ku, Shijō-dōri, Pontochō Nishi iru; 11.30am-3pm & 5-10pm, closed Thu; Omen ¥1050; 2min walk from exit 1, Kawaramachi Station, Hankyū line

This is one of two Downtown branches of the famous Ginkaku-ji noodle restaurant. It serves a variety of healthy set meals, including a good ¥1900 lunch set that includes noodles and a few sides. It's a small, calm place that's a nice oasis amid the

Downtown mayhem, good for a light lunch while out shopping, and it has an English menu to boot. Look for the word 'Nippon' on the sign.

AZAMI Map p50 Japanese/Chicken ¥¥

☎ 252-1860; Nakagyō-ku, Sanjō-dōri, Takakura agaru, Museum of Kyoto 1st fl; 🕑 11am-10pm, closed Mon; meals from ¥1000; 🚇 3min walk from Karasuma-Oike Station, Karasuma subway line

Located on the ground floor of the Museum of Kyoto, on the northeast side of the building, this chicken specialist serves a wide variety of excellent dishes in a fairly traditional Japanese atmosphere. Choices range from *yakitori* to *tsukune* (chicken meatballs) to a healthy chicken salad. If you don't mind sitting on tatami, downstairs rooms are highly recommended.

ANJI Map p50 Izakaya ¥¥

☎ 231-5375; Nakagyō-ku, Rokkaku-dōri, Karasuma Higashi iru, Hoshinoko Rokkaku Bldg. 2nd fl; 🕑 5pm-2am, closed Sun; meals ¥1000; 🚇 5min walk from Karasuma-Oike Station, Karasuma subway line

This smoky *izakaya*-style fish specialist is a great place to sample a wide variety of sashimi, cooked fish and standard *izakaya* dishes. You can sit on the tatami mats in the *zashiki* (communal room), but you'll have to have a high tolerance for cigarette smoke. If you don't smoke, and don't want to be smoked, we recommend the counter. There is no English menu, so you'll have to bring a Japanese-speaking friend or point at what your neighbours are eating. Anji is up a flight of steps festooned with signs (in Japanese) advertising the menu; you'll know the place when you see it.

BIOTEI Map p50 Japanese Vegetarian ¥

☎ 255-0086; Nakagyō-ku, Sanjō-dōri, Higashinotōin Nishi Minami kado 2F; 🕑 11.30am-2pm & 5-8.30pm, closed dinner Sun, Mon & Thu, lunch Sat & public holidays; lunch/dinner ¥840/1050; 🚇 5min walk from Karasuma-Oike Station, Karasuma subway line

Located diagonally across from the Nakagyō post office, this is a favourite of Kyoto vegetarians and has an English menu. It serves daily sets of Japanese vegetarian food (the occasional bit of meat is offered as an option, but you'll be asked your preference). The seating is rather cramped but the food is very good and carefully made from quality ingredients. It's up the metal spiral steps.

SOMUSHI KOCHAYA

Map p50 Korean Teahouse ¥

☎ 253-1456; Nakagyō-ku, Karasuma, Sanjō Nishi iru; 🕑 10am-9pm, closed Wed; tea from ¥500, meals from ¥1000; 🚇 3min walk from Karasuma-Oike Station, Karasuma subway line

This is the only Korean teahouse we've ever seen in Japan. It's a good place to go when you need a change from the creeping monoculture of coffee chain stores. It's a dark, woodsy and atmospheric spot with a variety of herbal teas (the menu details what they're good for). The teahouse also serves a few light meals, including some unusual Korean favourites (just don't expect Korean barbecue).

TAGOTO HONTEN Map p50 Soba ¥

☎ 221-3030; Nakagyō-ku, Sanjō-dōri, Teramachi Higashi iru; 🕑 11am-9pm; noodles from ¥997; 🚇 10min walk from Shijō Station, Karasuma subway line

This casual restaurant in the Sanjō covered arcade serves a variety of *soba* and *udon* dishes. It can get crowded at lunchtime and the service can be rather brusque, but the noodles are very good and the English/picture menu helps with ordering. The tempura *teishoku* makes a great lunch.

PARK CAFÉ Map p50 Café ¥

☎ 211-8954; Nakagyō-ku, Gokomachi-dōri, Aneyakōji kado; 🕑 noon-midnight; lunch sets ¥940; 🚇 3min walk from Kyoto-Shiyakusho-mae Station, Tōzai subway line

This cool little café always reminds us of a Melbourne coffee shop. It's on the edge of the Downtown Kyoto shopping district and is a convenient place to take a break. The comfy seats invite a nice long linger over a cuppa and the owner has an interesting music collection.

LUGOL Map p50 Café ¥

☎ 213-2888; Nakagyō-ku, Shinmachi-dōri, Oike agaru, Nakano-chō 50-1; 🕑 11.30am-11pm; lunch sets ¥920; 🚇 5min walk from Karasuma-Oike Station, Karasuma subway line

For a quick cuppa or a snack in groovy surroundings, this cosy coffee shop on the west side of Downtown Kyoto is a very nice choice. We go there for decorating ideas as much as for the drinks.

KYŌ-HAYASHIYA Map p50 Café ¥

☎ 231-3198; Nakagyō-ku, Sanjō-dōri, Kawaramachi Higashi iru, Takase Bldg 6F; 11.30am-9.30pm, closed irregularly; matcha sweets ¥900; 3min walk from exit 6, Sanjō Station, Keihan line

If you need a change from large American coffee chains and want to try some good Japanese green tea – and enjoy a nice view over the mountains while you're at it – this is the place for it. Kyō-hayashiya also has a handy picture menu.

KANE-YO Map p50 Unagi ¥

☎ 221-0669; Nakagyō-ku, Shinkyōgoku, Rokkaku Higashi iru; 11.30am-9pm; unagi over rice ¥890; 10min walk from Sanjō Station, Keihan line

This is a good place to try *unagi*, that most sublime of Japanese dishes. You can choose to either sit downstairs with a nice view of the waterfall, or upstairs on the tatami. The *kane-yo donburi* (eel over rice; ¥890) set is excellent value. Look for the barrels of live eels outside and the wooden façade.

KŌSENDŌ-SUMI Map p50 Japanese ¥

☎ 241-7377; Nakagyō-ku, Aneyakōji-dōri, Sakaimachi Higashi iru; 11am-4pm, closed Sun & public holidays; lunch from ¥870; 5min walk from Karasuma-Oike Station, Karasuma subway line

For a pleasant lunch downtown, try this unpretentious little restaurant located in an old Japanese house. The daily lunch special, which is usually simple and healthy Japanese fare, is always displayed out the front for your inspection. It's near the Museum of Kyoto, next to a small parking lot.

KERALA Map p50 Indian ¥

☎ 251-0141; Nakagyō-ku, Kawaramachi-dōri, Sanjō agaru Nishi gawa; 11.30am-2pm & 5-9pm; lunch from ¥850; 3min walk from Kyoto-Shiyakusho-mae Station, Tōzai subway line

This narrow restaurant upstairs on Kawaramachi-dōri is Kyoto's best Indian restaurant. The ¥850 lunch set menu is an excellent deal, as is the vegetarian lunch, and the English menu is a bonus. Dinners run closer to ¥2500 per head and are of very high quality. Finish off the meal with the incredibly rich and creamy coconut ice cream. Kerala is located on the 2nd floor; look for the display of food down on street level.

KATSU KURA Map p50 Tonkatsu ¥

☎ 212-3581; Nakagyō-ku, Teramachi-dōri, Sanjō Higashi iru; 11am-9.30pm; tonkatsu from ¥819; 10min walk from Sanjō Station, Keihan line

This restaurant in the Sanjō covered arcade is a good place to sample *tonkatsu* (deep-fried breaded pork cutlets). Most of the cutlets come with a set that includes rice, miso soup and cabbage (extra helpings of these are free). It's not the best in Kyoto but it's relatively cheap and casual, and it has an English menu.

CAFÉ BIBLIOTEC HELLO! Map p50 Café ¥

☎ 231-8625; Nakagyō-ku, Nijō-dōri-Yanaginobanba higashi iru; noon-11pm, closed irregularly; dishes from ¥700; 10min walk from Karasuma-Oike Station, Karasuma subway line

As the name suggests, books line the walls of this cool café located in a converted *machiya*. You can get the usual range of coffee and tea drinks here, as well as light café lunches. It's popular with young ladies who work nearby and it's a great place to relax with a book or magazine. Look for the plants out the front.

YAK & YETI Map p50 Nepalese ¥

☎ 213-7919; Nakagyō-ku, Gokomachi-dōri, Nishikikōji kudaru; 11.30am-4.30pm & 5-9.30pm, closed Mon; curry lunch sets from ¥600; 5min walk from Shijō Station, Karasuma subway line

This tiny joint serves more than just the *dal bhaat* (rice and lentil curry) that most people associate with Nepalese cuisine. In fact, the fare (good curries and tasty nan bread) is probably closer to Indian. There is counter seating, but we like to sit on the comfortable cushions here. English menus are available. The staff is pretty chuffed about being listed in our guides and has posted a picture of an old edition out the front – should be no trouble finding it.

HATI HATI Map p50 Indonesian ¥

☎ 212-2228; Nishikiyamachi-dōri-Takoyakushi; 6pm-2am Sun-Thu, to 3am Fri & Sat; dishes from ¥600; 5min walk from Kawaramachi Station, Hankyū line

Hati Hati offers some of the best Indonesian food in Kyoto, including all the standard favourites, such as *nasi goreng* (fried rice) and *mee goreng* (fried noodles). It's on the basement floor of the Kankō building; look for the green stairwell. It also doubles as a bar-club – stop by and see what's up if you're in the area.

SHIN-SHIN-TEI Map p50 Rāmen ¥

☎ 221-6202; Nakagyō-ku, Nijō-dōri-Fuyachō; 10.30am-4pm, closed Sun, Mon & public holidays; rāmen from ¥600; 4min walk from Kyoto-Shiyakusho-mae Station, Tōzai subway line

This place is famous for its *shiro* (white) miso *rāmen,* which has a distinctive thick soup and good chewy noodles. The restaurant scores minimal points for ambience, which is typical for *rāmen* joints. The claim to fame here is that Keanu Reeves once ate here. Look for the yellow-and-black sign.

INODA COFFEE Map p50 Café ¥

☎ 221-0507; Nakagyō-ku, Sakaimachi-dōri, Sanjō kudaru; 7am-8pm; coffee from ¥500; 5min walk from Karasuma-Oike Station, Karasuma subway line

This chain is a Kyoto institution and has branches throughout the city. Though slightly overrated for the price, the old-Japan atmosphere at this, Inoda's main shop, is worth a try, especially if you want something Japanese rather than international.

CAFÉ INDEPENDANTS Map p50 Café ¥

☎ 255-4312; Nakagyō-ku, Sanjō-dōri, Gokomachi; 11.45am-midnight; coffee from ¥300, salads & sandwiches from ¥400; 10min walk from Sanjō Station, Keihan line

Located beneath a gallery, this cool subterranean café offers a range of light meals and café drinks in a bohemian atmosphere (after you eat, you can check out the gallery space upstairs). A lot of the food offerings are laid out on display for you to choose from. The emphasis is on healthy sandwiches and salads. Take the stairs on your left before the gallery.

DOUTOR COFFEE Map p50 Café ¥

☎ 213-4041; Shimogyō-ku, Shijō-dōri-Fuyachō nishi iru; 7.30am-10pm Mon-Sat, 8am-10pm Sun & public holidays; coffee ¥180; 10min walk from Kawaramachi Station, Hankyū line

A lot of Western travellers have discovered the joys of Doutor Coffee, which has branches all over Kyoto. The coffee itself is dirt cheap but the real draw here are the surprisingly tasty sandwiches – just the thing when you need a break from the usual insipid things they call sandwiches in Japan. The picture menu makes ordering easy.

MUSASHI SUSHI Map p50 Sushi ¥

☎ 222-0634; Nakagyō-ku, Kawaramachi-dōri, Sanjō agaru; 11am-10pm; dishes ¥100; 5min walk from Sanjō Station, Keihan line

If you've never tried *kaiten-zushi,* don't miss this place – all the dishes are a mere ¥130. It's not the best sushi in the world, but it's a heckuva lot better than most 'sushi trains' outside Japan. Needless to say, it's easy to eat here: you just grab what you want off the conveyor belt. If you can't find what you want on the belt, there's also an English menu. Musashi is just outside the entrance to the Sanjō covered arcade; look for the miniature sushi conveyor belt in the window.

CENTRAL KYOTO

Central Kyoto has a wide variety of restaurants, both Japanese and international, in all budget ranges. Many of the lunch places serve cheap specials for the folks who work nearby. Several of the restaurants in this section are worth making a special trip for and most are close to public transport.

LINDEN BAUM Map pp54–5 European ¥¥

☎ 213-3979; Kamigyō-ku, Teramachi-dōri, Imadegawa kudaru, Higashi gawa, Ōgi-chō 273-2; 11.30am-2.30pm & 5.30-10.30pm, closed Mon & 2nd Tue of each month; lunch sets from ¥1000, dinner ¥4200; 8min walk from Imadegawa Station, Karasuma subway line

This pleasant hideaway near the Kyoto Imperial Palace serves what it describes as 'European cooking', which often involves pasta and fish. It's usually quiet and relaxing, and has lovely long wooden tables. The set lunch is generally a very good deal. Linden Baum is down a narrow alley; look for the English sign.

MANZARA HONTEN
Map pp54–5 Modern Japanese ¥¥

☎ 253-1558; Nakagyō-ku, Kawaramachi-dōri, Ebisugawa agaru; 5pm-midnight; dinner sets from ¥4000; 10min walk from Marutamachi Station, Karasuma subway line

Located in a converted *machiya* (traditional Japanese town house), Manzara represents a pleasing fusion of traditional and modern Japanese culture. The fare here is creative modern Japanese and the surroundings are decidedly stylish. The *omakase* (chef's recommendation) course is good value, with eight dishes for ¥4000, and à la carte dishes are available from ¥500. Last orders are at 11.30pm.

DEN SHICHI Map pp54–5 Sushi ¥¥

☎ 323-0700; Ukyō-ku, Shijō-dōri-Sai; 🕑 11.30am-2pm & 5-10.30pm, closed Mon; lunch/dinner from ¥480/3000; 🚇 3min walk from Saiin Station, Hankyū line

This is our favourite sushi restaurant in Kyoto. It's a classic – long counter, bellowing sushi chefs and great fresh fish. The lunch sets are unbelievable value and the glass sushi cases make ordering a little easier than at some other places. It's almost always hopping and doesn't take reservations, so you may have to give your name and wait – but it will definitely be worth it. Look for the black-and-white sign about 100m west of Saiin Station on Shijō-dōri.

SHUHARI Map pp54–5 French ¥¥

☎ 222-6815; Kamigyō-ku, Kawaramachi-dōri, Marutamachi agaru; 🕑 noon-11pm Mon-Thu, noon-2am Fri-Sun; lunch/dinner ¥850/2500; 🚇 10min walk from Marutamachi Station, Karasuma subway line

Shuhari is a great example of Kyoto's newest dining trend – fine restaurants in renovated *machiya*. In this case, the food is casual French, with an emphasis on light fish dishes and healthy salads. Look for the red stove pipe with the name of the restaurant written on it out the front.

PRINZ Map pp54–5 Café ¥

☎ 712-3900; Sakyō-ku, Higashi-kuramaguchi-dōri-Shirakawa; 🕑 8am-2am; lunch sets from ¥1200; 🚇 2min walk from Chayama Station, Eizan line

Behind the blank white façade of Prinz, you'll find a café-restaurant, gallery, bookshop, garden and library – a chic island of coolness in an otherwise bland residential neighbourhood. You can sit at the counter and request music from the CDs that line the walls. The lunch set usually includes a light assortment of Western and Japanese dishes, generally on the healthy side of things. Coffee starts at ¥300. All in all, this is a very interesting stop while you're in the northeast part of town. Note that last orders are at 11.30pm.

top picks

CAFÉS

Kyoto is known the world over for its elegant traditional restaurants. What few travellers realise, however, is that the city is also home to a great number of groovy cafés, which are easy to enter, fun to hang out in and surprisingly inexpensive. Some of these cafés have art galleries or small libraries on the premises; others hold art events and live music shows; and most serve light meals throughout the day and drinks in the evening. So, if you need a cuppa and a break from temple-hopping, pop into one of the cafés listed here.

- Café Bibliotec HELLO! (p126) A literary café a short walk from the centre of town.
- Café Independants (p127) A subterranean slice of bohemian life in the centre of town.
- Prinz (below) An intriguing shop-library-gallery-restaurant way up north in Kyoto.
- Lugol (p125) A mod retreat in Downtown Kyoto.
- Bon Bon Café (opposite) An open-air café with riverside seating, near Demachiyanagi Station.
- Café Carinho (p134) A casual Western-style lunch spot in the Ginkaku-ji area.

DIDI Map pp54–5 Indian ¥

☎ 791-8226; Sakyō-ku, Tanaka-Ōkubo-chō 22; 🕑 11am-9.30pm, closed Wed; lunch/dinner from ¥750/900; 🚇 1min walk from Mototanaka Station, Eizan line

A cosy little spot in the north of town past Hyakumamben and Kyoto University, this friendly smoke-free restaurant serves passable Indian lunch and dinner sets. There are plenty of vegetarian choices on the menu, which is available in English. Didi is easy to spot from the street.

HIRAGANA-KAN Map pp54–5 Shokudō ¥

☎ 701-4164; Sakyō-ku, Tanakahinokuchi-chō 44; 🕑 11.30am-4pm & 6-10pm, closed Tue; lunch & dinner from ¥800; 🚇 8min walk from Mototanaka Station, Eizan line

This place, popular with Kyoto University students, dishes up creative variations on chicken, fish and meat. Most mains come with rice, salad and miso soup. The menu is in Japanese only, but if you're at a loss for what to order try the tasty 'roll chicken *katsu*', a delectable and filling creation of chicken and vegetables. Look for the words 'Casual Restaurant' on the white awning.

HONYARADŌ Map pp54–5 Japanese ¥
☎ 222-1574; Kamigyō-ku, Imadegawa, Teramachi Nishi iru; 10am-10pm; lunch ¥700; 1min walk from Kawaramachi Imadegawa bus stop, bus 205 from Kyoto Station
This woodsy place overlooking the Kyoto Imperial Palace Park is an institution. It was something of a gathering spot for Kyoto's countercultural elite during the hippy days. It has the lived-in feeling of an eccentric friend's house, with stacks of books and magazines and interesting decorations. The lunch deal (a daily stew set) is good value. Surprisingly, considering the ambience, there aren't many veggie options. It's a good place to relax over coffee.

COCOHANA Map pp54–5 Korean ¥
☎ 525 5587; Higashiyama-ku, Honmachi 13-243-1; 11am-11pm Thu-Mon, to 5.30pm Tue, closed Wed; lunch from ¥680; 2min walk from Tōfukuji Station, Keihan line
This place is one of a kind: a Korean café in a converted old Japanese house. Dishes here include *bibimbap* (a Korean rice dish) and *kimchi* (Korean pickles). A full range of coffee and tea is also available. It's a woody, rustic place with both table and tatami seating. There is no English menu but the friendly young staff will help with ordering. This makes a great stop while exploring southeastern Kyoto.

TSURUHASHI Map pp54–5 Rāmen ¥
☎ 722-3434; Sakyō-ku, Ichijōji nishi Suginomiya-chō; 11am-2pm & 5-11pm, closed Thu; rāmen from ¥600; 5min walk from Ichijōji Station, Eizan line
Kyoto *rāmen* fans make the trek to this unprepossessing little joint for its unique duck-flavoured soup, a serious rarity in Japan. For lunch, big eaters will enjoy the B set, which includes duck-soup *rāmen,* rice and *karaage* (pieces of deep-fried chicken). Look for the yellow awning and the red-and-yellow sign.

KAZARIYA Map pp54–5 Sweets ¥
☎ 491-9402; Kita-ku, Murasakino Imamiya-chō; 10am-5pm, closed Wed; sweets ¥500; 1min walk from Imamiya-jinja bus stop, bus 46 from Kyoto Station
For more than 300 years, Kazariya has been specialising in *aburi-mochi* (grilled rice cakes coated with soya-bean flour) and served with *miso-dare* (sweet-bean paste). It's a nice place to go for some tea and a sweet after exploring the grounds of Daitoku-ji (p53).

BON BON CAFÉ Map pp54–5 Café ¥
☎ 213-8686; Sakyō-ku, Kawaramachi, Imadegawa, Higashi iru-Kita gawa; 10am-midnight; coffee/sandwiches from ¥300/500; 3min walk from Demachiyanagi Station, Keihan line
If you find yourself in need of a light meal or drink while you're in the Demachiyanagi area, this casual open-air café is an excellent choice. There is a variety of cakes and light meals on offer. While there is no English menu, much of the ordering can be done by pointing, and the young staff can help you figure out what's not on display. It's on the west bank of the Kamo-gawa and outdoor seats here are very pleasant on warm evenings.

SOUTHERN HIGASHIYAMA

Southeast Kyoto is second only to Downtown in terms of variety and number of restaurants. You'll find the largest concentration of eateries in Gion, with others scattered around the main sightseeing spots at the base of the Higashiyama Mountains. This area contains many of Kyoto's fanciest and most elite restaurants but there are, of course, more humble places to enjoy as well.

MINOKŌ Map p62 Kaiseki ¥¥¥
☎ 561-0328; Higashiyama-ku, Gion, Shimokawara; 11.30am-2.30pm & 5-8pm; lunch ¥4500-10,000, dinner from ¥13,000; 12min walk from Shijō Station, Keihan line
This classic Gion restaurant serves a lunch *bentō* for ¥4500 and *kaiseki* dinners starting at ¥13,000. The décor is classic old Kyoto, the service is excellent and the food is of high quality. There is no English sign; it's across from a parking lot – look for the metal lantern out the front.

AUNBO Map p62 Japanese ¥¥¥
☎ 525-2900; Higashiyama-ku, Yasaka Torii mae kudaru, Shimokawara-machi; noon-2pm, 5.30-10pm, closed Wed; lunch ¥2500, dinner ¥6000-10,000; 10min walk from Shijō Station, Keihan line
Aunbo serves elegant, creative Japanese cooking in traditional Gion surroundings. The last time we were here we started with

VEGETARIAN KYOTO

If you eat fish, you should have almost no trouble dining in Kyoto: almost all *shokudō* (Japanese-style cafeteria–cheap restaurant), *izakaya* (Japanese pub-eatery) and other common restaurants offer a set meal with fish as the main dish. If you don't eat fish or fish products, you will have to get your protein from tofu and other bean products. Note that most *miso-shiru* (miso soup) is made with *dashi* (stock) that contains fish.

For ways in which to express your dietary preferences to restaurant staff, see p206.

The following is a list of specifically vegetarian or vegan restaurants as well as restaurants that have plenty of vegetarian dishes on the menu:

Machapuchare (opposite) The *obanzai* (Kyoto-style home cooking) set here is the best veggie meal in Kyoto.

Sunny Place (p134) Cheap and friendly organic spot near Kyoto University.

Café Peace (p135) Another great organic spot near Kyoto University.

Buttercups (p135) Not strictly veggie, but there are several good choices here.

Kailash (p134) This is a true organic spot in a nice traditional town house.

Shizenha Restaurant Obanzai (p124) For all-you-can-eat organic veggie, this is the spot.

Biotei (p125) High-quality veggie right downtown.

Veggie Table (p124) A new 'hot salad' place downtown.

Kerala (p126) The best Indian restaurant in Kyoto – try the veggie lunch set.

Didi (p128) Plenty of good veggie choices at this Indian eatery.

sublime sashimi, moved on to fried *yuba* pockets and went from there. We recommend asking for the set and leaving the difficult decisions to the master. Aunbo takes reservations in the evening. There is an English menu but no English sign; look for the traditional Japanese façade.

WABIYA KOREKIDŌ Map p62 Yakitori ¥¥

☎ 532-3355; Higashiyama-ku, Shijō Hanami-kōji kudaru, Gion-machi, Minami gawa; 🕒 11.30am-2pm & 5-11pm, closed Tue; lunch/dinner ¥1050/6000; Ⓢ 10min walk from Shijō Station, Keihan line

This slick restaurant on Gion's atmospheric Hanami-kōji serves what, for lack of a better term, we will call *'haute yakitori'*. It's the nicest *yakitori* we've had, and the setting is a lot more elegant than your typical *yakitori* joint. At dinner, the *shunsaiwabiya kōsu* (full chicken course; ¥3675) is excellent. At lunch, choose from one of the meals on the picture menu outside. The name of the place is written in English in tiny letters on the black-and-white sign.

ŌZAWA Map p62 Tempura ¥¥

☎ 561-2052; Higashiyama-ku, Gion, Shirakawa Nawate Higashi iru Sth; 🕒 11.30am-10pm, closed Thu; lunch/dinner ¥2500/3800; Ⓢ 5min walk from Shijō Station, Keihan line

Located on one of the most beautiful streets in Gion – Shirakawa-minami-dōri (also known as Shimbashi) – this charming little restaurant offers excellent tempura in refined Japanese surroundings. Unless you choose a private tatami room, you'll sit at the counter and watch as the chef prepares each piece of tempura individually right before your eyes. Considering the location and the quality of the food, this place is great value. Ōzawa also has an English menu. The restaurant is across a bridge; look for the sign on the street.

GION MORIKŌ Map p62 Cantonese ¥¥

☎ 531-8000; Higashiyama-ku, Shirakawa-suji Chion-in-bashi agaru Nishi gawa 556; 🕒 11.30am-2pm & 5-9.30pm, closed Wed; lunch/dinner sets from ¥800/3000; Ⓢ 3min walk from Higashiyama Station, Tōzai subway line

All the usual Cantonese favourites in a fairly casual Japanese setting are the draw at this friendly little place. Á la carte dishes start from ¥900. Gion Morikō is located along the picturesque Shira-kawa canal on the northern edge of Gion. The master speaks some English and can help with ordering.

ICHI-BAN Map p62 Yakitori ¥¥

☎ 751-1459; Higashiyama-ku, Sanjō Ōhashi Higashi iru; 🕒 5.30pm-midnight, closed Sun & public holidays; dinner from ¥3000; Ⓢ 3min walk from Sanjō Station, Keihan line

This popular *yakitori* joint has an English menu and a friendly owner to help with ordering. Best of all, it has that classic old *yakitori-ya* ambience – smoking charcoal grills, old beer posters on the walls and *oden* (winter stew) bubbling away on the counter. Look for the yellow-and-red sign and the big lantern.

DAIKICHI Map p62 Yakitori ¥¥

☎ 771-3126; Higashiyama-ku, Sanjō-dōri Ōhashi higashi; 5pm-1am; dishes ¥3000; 3min walk from Higashiyama Station, Tōzai subway line

This is a good *yakitori* restaurant with a friendly owner. The place is a little brightly lit for our taste, but it's easy to enter and the *yakitori* is tasty. Daikichi is on Sanjō-dōri; look for the red lanterns outside.

BAMBOO Map p62 Izakaya ¥¥

☎ 771-5559; Higashiyama-ku, Higashiyama Sanjō Higashi iru, Minami gawa 1st fl; 5.30pm-midnight, closed Thu; dishes ¥1000; 5min walk from Higashiyama Station, Tōzai subway line

Bamboo is one of Kyoto's more approachable *izakaya*. It's on Sanjō-dōri, near the mouth of a traditional, old shopping arcade. You can sit at the counter here and order a variety of typical *izakaya* dishes, watching as the chefs do their thing.

YAGURA Map p62 Soba ¥

☎ 561-1035; Higashiyama-ku, Shijō-dōri, Yamatoōji Nishi iru; 11am-9.30pm, closed Thu; soba ¥1000; 1min walk from Shijō Station, Keihan line

Across from Minami-za (p142) kabuki theatre, this noodle specialist somehow reminds us of an American diner, with a row of wooden booths and mamas running the show. We recommend the *nishin soba* (¥1000). Yagura is located between a *rāmen* joint and a Japanese gift shop – look for the bowls of noodles in the window.

ASUKA Map p62 Shokudō ¥

☎ 751-9809; Higashiyama-ku, Sanjō-dōri, Jinbūmichi Nishi iru; 11am-11pm; meals ¥1000; 3min walk from Higashiyama Station, Tōzai subway line

With an English menu, and a staff of friendly Kyoto *mama-sans* who are at home with foreign customers, this is a great place for a cheap lunch or dinner while sightseeing in the Higashiyama area. The tempura *mori-awase* (assorted tempura set) is a big pile of tempura for only ¥1000. Look for the red lantern and pictures of the set meals.

RYŪMON Map p62 Chinese ¥

☎ 752-8181; Higashiyama-ku, Sanjō-dōri, Higashiōji Nishi iru, Kita gawa; 5pm-5am; dishes ¥1000; 3min walk from Higashiyama Station, Tōzai subway line

This place may look like a total dive but the food is reliable and authentic, as the crowds of Kyoto's Chinese residents will attest. There's no English menu but there is a picture menu and some of the waitresses can speak English. Décor is strictly Chinese kitsch, with the exception of the deer head over the cash register – still trying to figure that one out. Look for the food pictures out the front.

MACHAPUCHARE Map p62 Obanzai/Nepalese ¥

☎ 525-1330; Higashiyama-ku, Sayamachi-dōri, Shōmen kudaru, Kamihoritsume-chō 290; 11.30am-8pm, closed Tue; lunch from ¥800; 5min walk from Shichijō Station, Keihan line

This organic vegetarian restaurant serves a sublime vegetarian *obanzai* set. The post and beam construction of the place and the friendly owner are added attractions. The problem is that the restaurant keeps somewhat irregular hours and the *obanzai* is not always available. Get a Japanese speaker to call and check before trekking here. It's opposite Shōmen-yu *sento* (public bath).

SANTŌKA Map p62 Rāmen ¥

☎ 532-1335; Higashiyama-ku, Sanjō kudaru Higashi gawa; 11am-2am; rāmen from ¥750; 1min walk from Sanjō Station, Keihan line

The young chefs at this sleek restaurant dish out some seriously good Hokkaidō-style *rāmen*. You will be given a choice of three kinds of soup when you order: *shio* (salt), *shōyu* or miso – we highly recommend you go for the miso soup. For something totally decadent, try the *tokusen toroniku rāmen,* which is made from pork cheeks, of which only 200g can be obtained from one animal. The pork will come on a separate plate from the *rāmen* – just shovel it all into your bowl. The restaurant is located on the east side and ground floor of the new Kyōen restaurant and shopping complex.

ISSEN YŌSHOKU Map p62 Okonomiyaki ¥

☎ 533-0001; Higashiyama-ku, Gion, Shijō Nawate kado; 11am-3am Mon-Sat, 10.30am-10pm Sun & public holidays; okonomiyaki ¥630; 5min walk from Shijō Station, Keihan line

Heaped with red ginger and green scallions, the *okonomiyaki* at this Gion institution is a garish snack – which somehow seems fitting considering the surrounding neighbourhood. It's open to the elements and you can't miss the griddles out the front.

MOMIJI-AN Map p62 Tea Shop ¥

☎ 561-2933; Higashiyama-ku, Maruyama-chō; 🕑 9am-5pm, closed Thu; tea & sweet beans ¥600; 15min walk from Shijō Station, Keihan line
Located in a rustic old-Kyoto house overlooking Maruyama-kōen, this is a great spot for a rest while touring the Higashiyama area. Ask for the *usucha* (thin green tea; ¥600) and the staff will do the rest. It's just to the right of a traffic mirror, up a flight of steps.

KASAGI-YA Map p62 Sweets ¥

☎ 561-9562; Higashiyama-ku, Kōdaiji, Masuya chō; 🕑 11am-6pm, closed Tue; sweets from ¥600; 7min walk from Kiyomizumichi bus stop, bus 206 from Kyoto Station
At Kasagi-ya, on Sannen-zaka near Kiyomizu-dera (p63), you can enjoy a nice cup of *matcha* and a variety of sweets. This funky old wooden shop has atmosphere to boot and a friendly staff – which makes it worth the wait if there's a queue. Highly recommended. It's hard to spot – you may have to ask one of the local shop owners.

GION KOISHI Map p62 Tea Shop ¥

☎ 531-0331; Higashiyama-ku, Gion-chō, kita; 🕑 10.30am-7.30pm, closed 2nd & 4th Wed of each month; tea from ¥500; 10min walk from Shijō Station, Keihan line
If it's a hot summer's day and you need a cooling break, try this tea shop for some typical Japanese summer treats. The speciality here is *uji kintoki* (¥700), a mountain of shaved ice flavoured with green tea, sweetened milk and sweet beans (it tastes a lot better than it sounds, trust us). It's the fifth shop in from the corner, between two souvenir-craft shops.

SENMONTEN Map p62 Chinese ¥

☎ 531-2733; Higashiyama-ku, Hanami-kōji-dōri, Shinbashi kudaru Higashi gawa; 🕑 6pm-2am, closed Sun & public holidays; per 10 dumplings ¥460; 5min walk from Shijō Station, Keihan line
This place serves one thing only: crisp fried *gyōza*, which come in lots of 10 and are washed down with beer or Chinese *raoshu* (rice wine). If you can break the record for the most *gyōza* eaten in one sitting, your meal will be free and you'll receive – guess what? – more *gyōza* to take home. The last time we were here, the men's record was around 150 *gyōza*. Look for the red-and-white sign and the glass door.

KAGIZEN YOSHIFUSA Map p62 Sweets & Tea ¥

☎ 525-0011; Higashiyama-ku, Shijō-dōri; 🕑 9.30am-6pm, closed Mon; tea from ¥400; 5min walk from Shijō Station, Keihan line
This Gion institution is one of Kyoto's oldest and best-known *okashi-ya* (sweet shops). It sells a variety of traditional sweets and has a lovely tea room out the back where you can sample cold *kuzukiri* (transparent arrowroot noodles) served with a *kuromitsu* (sweet black sugar) dipping sauce, or just a nice cup of *matcha* and a sweet. All in all, it's one of the best spots in Gion for a rest. Look for the sweets in the window, the wide front and the *noren* (curtains in the window of a Japanese restaurant).

AMAZON Map p62 Café ¥

☎ 561-8875; Higashiyama-ku, Keihan Shichijō Higashi iru, Shimohoritsume-chō 235; 🕑 7.30am-6pm, closed Wed; coffee from ¥400; 2min walk from Shichijō Station, Keihan line
This typical Japanese coffee shop, near Sanjūsangen-dō (p60), turns out some surprisingly good sandwiches and coffee; it's one of the few decent options in this area.

NORTHERN HIGASHIYAMA

Northeast Kyoto has an excellent variety of restaurants and cafés, both Japanese and international. For those on a tight budget, the Hyakumamben intersection near Kyoto University is crammed with cheap student eateries. Due to the number of foreign students and teachers at the university, most places here are totally unfazed when a *'gaijin'* blunders in off the street.

HYŌTEI Map pp68–9 Kaiseki ¥¥¥

☎ 771-4116; Sakyō-ku, Nanzen-ji Kusagawa-chō 35; 🕑 11am-7.30pm; meals from ¥4555; 10min walk from Keage Station, Tōzai subway line
The Hyōtei is considered to be one of Kyoto's oldest and most picturesque traditional restaurants. In the main building you can sample exquisite *kaiseki* courses in private

JAPANESE SWEETS

The range of Japanese confections is so vast that were you to try one sweet a day, it would take a lifetime to try them all. Sweets in Japan (generically known as *wagashi*) are commonly made from some combination of sugar, beans and rice. The more exotic ingredients include cherry leaves, burdock root and seaweed.

Wagashi can be as delicious as they are beautiful; however, some visitors find the sweet, red adzuki-bean paste called *anko* rather off-putting. Used in many Japanese sweets, it can turn up in even the most innocuous-looking pastries.

Sweets are usually enjoyed outside mealtimes – traditional Japanese restaurants have no dessert menu – and the most exquisite were created for the tea ceremony, their sweetness the perfect counterpoint to the bitterness of *matcha* (powdered green tea).

As the tea ceremony originated in Kyoto, it stands to reason that the city has the greatest concentration of speciality sweet shops. Sampling a sweet is as easy as pie: step into a shop, gesture at an intriguing sweet in the display case and the accommodating staff will smartly wrap your delectable treat.

Kyoto's most ubiquitous sweet is a real crowd-pleaser – it's a bite-sized wafer of cinnamon-spiced *mochi* (pounded rice cake) called *yatsuhashi*. These come in soft or crunchy varieties and the newest flavours are sesame, green tea and even strawberry. Beware: the triangular ones often hide a dab of that dreaded *anko!*

On the approach to Kiyomizu-dera (p63), you can watch the crunchy version being made by hand.

One of the best places to try Japanese sweets in refined surroundings is Kagizan Yoshifusa (opposite).

tea rooms. Set meals are available from ¥4500. It's very close to the Kyoto International Community House (p112) and Nanzen-ji (p66). You can't miss the traditional building.

OKUTAN Map pp68–9 Tofu ¥¥

☎ 771-8709; Sakyō-ku, Nanzen-ji, Fukuchi-chō 86-30; 10.30am-5pm, closed Thu; set meals ¥3000; 10min walk from Keage Station, Tōzai subway line

Just outside the precincts of Nanzen-ji (p66), you'll find Okutan, a restaurant inside the luxurious garden of Chōshō-in. This is a popular place that has specialised in vegetarian temple food for hundreds of years. Try a course of *yudōfu* together with vegetable side dishes (¥3000). It can get crowded here in the cherry-blossom and autumn-foliage seasons.

GROTTO Map pp68–9 Japanese ¥¥

☎ 771-0606; Sakyō-ku, Jōdoji Nishida-chō 114; 6pm-midnight, closed Sun; meals ¥4500; 3min walk from Ginkakuji-michi bus stop, bus 5 from Kyoto Station

This stylish little place on Imadegawa-dōri serves a killer dinner set menu that will take you through the major tastes in the Japanese gastronomy. It's a great way to spend two or three hours with someone special. Reservations are highly recommended and last orders are at 10pm.

OKARIBA Map pp68–9 Wild Game ¥¥

☎ 751-7790; Sakyō-ku, Okazaki, Higashitenno-chō 43-4; 5-10.30pm, closed Mon; dinner ¥4000; 1min walk from Higashitenno-chō bus stop, bus 203 from Kyoto Station

For an experience you won't soon forget, try Okariba, near Hotel Heian no Mori Kyoto (p153). If it crawls, walks or swims, it's probably on the menu. The *inoshishi* (wild boar) barbecue is a good start. Those who don't eat meat can try the fresh *ayu* (Japanese trout). Look for the sign of the hunting pig out the front.

TORITO Map pp68–9 Yakitori ¥¥

☎ 752-4144; Sakyō-ku, Higashi Marutamachi 9-5; 5.30pm-1am, closed Sun; dinner ¥2000-4000; 2min walk from Marutamachi Station, Keihan line

This is part of the new wave of *yakitori* restaurants in Kyoto that are updating the old standards in interesting and tasty ways. It's a crowded spot, with a counter and a few small tables. The food is very good and will likely appeal to non-Japanese palates. Dishes include *kamo rōsu* (duck roast; ¥1050), *negima* (long onions and chicken; ¥294 for two sticks) and *tsukune* (chicken meatballs; ¥482). It's near the corner of Marutamachi and Kawabata-dōri; you can see inside to the counter.

KUSHI HACHI Map pp68–9 Kushikatsu ¥¥

☎ 751-6789; Sakyō-ku, Imadegawa, Kitashirakawa Nishi iru, Minami gawa; 5-11.30pm, closed Mon; dinner from ¥2000; 5min walk from Ginkaku-ji-Michi bus stop, bus 5 from Kyoto Station

Kushi Hachi, part of a popular Kyoto chain, is a fun spot to sample *kushikatsu*, a fried dish that is well suited to Western tastes. We enjoy sitting at the counter and watching as the frenetic chefs work the grills and deep-fryers. With a picture/English menu, ordering is a snap. Look for the garish lantern out the front.

BOUCHON CAYENNE Map pp68–9 French ¥¥

☎ 771-3340; Sakyō-ku, Higashiōji-dōri, Niōmon-dōri kudaru, Kita Monzen-chō 499; ⌚ noon-2pm & 6-9.30pm, closed Mon & 2nd Sun of each month; lunch sets ¥1600, dinner from ¥1500; Ⓢ 7min walk from Higashiyama Station, Tōzai subway line

We always feel a little guilty eating at this intimate French place, especially at lunch. It just doesn't seem right to be getting this kind of food for these prices. The chef does a brilliant egg tart and is a good hand with lamb dishes. The menu is in French and Japanese. It's near the corner; look for the grey front and the English sign.

SUNNY PLACE

Map pp68–9 Japanese Vegetarian ¥¥

☎ 722-1738; Kita-ku, Kamigamo Iwagakakiuchi-chō; ⌚ 11.30am-9pm, closed Mon; set meals from ¥1200; Ⓢ 5min walk from Kitayama Station, Karasuma subway line

Sunny Place is a fine little organic vegetarian eatery not far from the Hyakumamben intersection (within walking distance of Ginkaku-ji (p71)). It has a long wooden counter at which everyone tends to chat with both their neighbour and the friendly owner. The standard set includes a nonmeat protein dish (such as tempeh), three vegetable sides, rice and miso soup. Sunny Place is a bit tricky to find. Starting from the Hyakumamben crossing, walk west on Imadegawa-dōri to the first set of traffic lights; turn right and walk about 200m (you'll cross one fairly large street). It will be on the right; there's usually an English sign out the front.

OMEN Map pp68–9 Udon ¥¥

☎ 771-8994; Sakyō-ku, Jōdo-ji, Ishibashi-chō 74; ⌚ 11am-10pm, closed Thu; noodle dishes ¥1000; 🚌 1min walk from Ginkaku-ji-mae bus stop, bus 5 from Kyoto Station

This elegant noodle shop is named after the thick white noodles that are served in a hot broth with a selection of seven fresh vegetables. Just say *'omen'* and you'll be given your choice of hot or cold noodles, a bowl of soup to dip them in and a plate of vegetables (you put these into the soup along with some sesame seeds). It's a great bowl of noodles but that's not the end of the story: everything on the frequently changing menu is delicious. You can get a fine salad here, brilliant *tori sansho yaki* (chicken cooked with Japanese mountain spice), good tempura and occasionally a nice plate of sashimi. Best of all, there's a menu in English. It's about five minutes' walk from Ginkaku-ji (p71) in a traditional Japanese house with a lantern outside. Highly recommended.

KAILASH Map pp68–9 Organic Café ¥

☎ 752-3127; Sakyō-ku, Shōgoin Sannō-chō 19-2; ⌚ restaurant 11.30am-2.30pm & 5.30-8pm, café 11.30am-8pm, closed Wed & 2nd & 4th Thu of each month; lunch sets ¥850; Ⓢ 2min walk from Marutamachi Station, Keihan line

In an atmospheric old Japanese town house, this new organic restaurant is a very welcome addition to the Kyoto restaurant scene. The set lunch here usually includes a salad, rice, *tsukemono*, soup and a main dish. It has an English menu. We like to relax at the low tables upstairs. Look for the plants.

CAFÉ CARINHO Map pp68–9 Café ¥

☎ 752-3636; Sakyō-ku, Imadegawa-dōri-Shirakawa; ⌚ 11am-10pm Tue-Thu, to 11pm Fri-Sun; lunch from ¥750; 🚌 5min walk from Ginkaku-ji-Michi bus stop, bus 5 from Kyoto Station

This excellent little café near Ginkaku-ji (p71) is one of the only places in town where you can find proper bagel sandwiches. It also serves daily specials, light meals and excellent tea and coffee (from ¥400). There is wi-fi for those with laptops. The owner speaks English and Portuguese, which makes ordering a breeze. All told, this is one of the best spots in the neighbourhood for a drink or meal.

EARTH KITCHEN COMPANY

Map pp68–9 Bentō ¥

☎ 771-1897; Sakyō-ku, Kawabata, Marutamachi-dōri, Higashi Marutamachi; ⌚ 10.30am-6.30pm Mon-Fri, to 3.30pm Sat, closed Sun & public holidays; lunch ¥700; Ⓢ 1min walk from Marutamachi Station, Keihan line

Located on Marutamachi-dōri near the Kamo-gawa, this tiny spot seats just two people but does a bustling business serving tasty takeaway lunch *bentō*. If you fancy a picnic lunch for your temple-hopping, and the ease of an English menu, this is the place.

AYATORI Map pp68–9 Shokudō ¥

☎ 752-2468; Sakyō-ku, Yoshida Izumiden-chō 1-86; 🕑 1.30-2pm & 5.30-9.30pm Mon-Fri, 5.30-9.30pm Sat; katsudon ¥680; 10min walk from Demachiyanagi Station, Keihan line

Very close to the Hyakumamben intersection, this place is your classic *shokudō*. It's a friendly spot that is popular with local workers, resident foreigners and university students. A variety of standard fish and meat set dishes are served, which average around ¥800. In winter, the *kaki furai teishoku* (fried oyster set meal; ¥1100) is lovely. Strangely, considering this is a Japanese restaurant, Ayatori also serves a wonderful potato salad. English menus are available. To find this place, look for the big red-and-black sign.

KARAKO Map pp68–9 Rāmen ¥

☎ 752 8234; Sakyō-ku, Okazaki Tokusei-chō 12-3; 🕑 11.30am-3pm & 6pm-midnight, closed Tue; rāmen from ¥650; 15min walk from Sanjō Station, Keihan line

Karako is our favourite *rāmen* restaurant in Kyoto. While it's not much on atmosphere, the *rāmen* here is excellent – the soup is thick and rich and the *chashū* (pork slices) melt in your mouth. We recommend that you ask for the *kotteri* (thick soup) *rāmen*. Look for the lantern outside.

CAFÉ PEACE Map pp68–9 Vegetarian ¥

☎ 707-6856; Sakyō-ku, Higashiōji-dōri-Imadegawa, Hyakumamben; 🕑 11.30am-10.30pm Mon-Sat, 11.30am-9.30pm Sun & public holidays; drinks from ¥550, dishes from ¥600; 10min walk from Demachiyanagi Station, Keihan line

This is a pleasant spot for a cuppa or a light organic vegetarian meal. It's a little cramped but the soothing décor makes up for this. Lunch sets include green curry, sandwiches and Japanese fare. The English menu will help with ordering. Café Peace is on the 3rd floor but there's a small sign at street level.

BUTTERCUPS Map pp68–9 Café ¥

☎ 751-7837; Sakyō-ku, Jōdo-ji, Shimobanba-chō 103; 🕑 noon-11pm, closed Tue; coffee from ¥300, meals from ¥580; 5min walk from Kinrinshako-mae bus stop, bus 5 from Kyoto Station

Buttercups is a favourite of the local expat community and a great place for lunch, dinner or a cup of coffee. The menu (available in English) is international and the vibe is chilled and arty. There are usually pictures, paintings or photos on display. Dishes include Mexican rice, fish and chips, salads and tacos. Look for the plants and whiteboard menu outside.

FALAFEL GARDEN Map pp68–9 Israeli ¥

☎ 712-1856; Sakyō-ku, Tanaka Shimoyanagi-chō 3-16; 🕑 11am-9.30pm, closed Wed; sandwiches from ¥500; 2min walk from exit 7, Demachiyanagi Station, Keihan line

Close to the Keihan and Eizan lines' Demachiyanagi Station, this funky Israeli-run place has excellent falafel and a range of other dishes, as well as offering a set menu (¥1200). We like the style of the open-plan converted Japanese house and the minigarden out the back, but the main draw is those tasty falafels! It's easy to spot, across the street from a post office. Last orders are at 9pm.

ZAC BARAN Map pp68–9 International ¥

☎ 751-9748; Sakyō-ku, Shōgo-in, Sannō-chō 18; 🕑 6pm-4am; dishes from ¥500; 5min walk from Kumanojinja-mae bus stop, bus 206 from Kyoto Station

Near the Kyoto Handicraft Centre (p113), this is a good spot for a light meal or a drink. It serves a variety of spaghetti dishes as well as a good lunch special. Look for the picture of the Freak Brothers near the downstairs entrance. If you fancy dessert, step upstairs to the Second House Cake Works.

HINODE UDON Map pp68–9 Udon & Soba ¥

☎ 751-9251; Sakyō-ku, Nanzenji, Kitanobō-chō 36; 🕑 11am-6pm, closed Sun; noodles from ¥400; 5min walk from Higashitennō-chō bus stop, bus 5 from Kyoto Station

Filling noodle and rice dishes are served at this pleasant little shop with an English menu. Plain *udon* is only ¥400 but we recommend you spring for the *nabeyaki udon* (pot-baked *udon* in broth) for ¥800. This is a good spot for lunch when temple-hopping near Ginkaku-ji (p71) or Nanzen-ji (p66).

SHINSHINDŌ NOTRE PAIN QUOTIDIEN Map pp68–9 Café ¥

☎ 701-4121; Sakyō-ku, Kitashirakawa, Oiwake-chō 88; 🕑 8am-6pm, closed Tue; coffee from ¥340; 2min walk from Hyakumamben bus stop, bus 206 from Kyoto Station

This atmospheric old Kyoto coffee shop is a favourite of Kyoto University students for its curry and bread lunch set (¥780), which is kind of an acquired taste. It's located near the university. Look for the glazed tile bricks and the big window out the front.

There's a small English sign and English menus are available.

YATAI Map pp68–9 Yatai ¥

Sakyō-ku, Imadegawa-dōri; dusk to midnight; dishes from ¥300; 10min walk from Demachiyanagi Station, Keihan line

This *yatai* (tent) pops up along Imadegawa-dōri every evening and serves a variety of food to accompany beer and sake, such as *yakitori, oden* and meatballs. It's fun but don't expect English to be spoken (pointing at what you want is the easiest way to go).

NORTHWEST KYOTO

There are many good restaurants scattered across this largely residential area. As they are so spread out, plan ahead and find one located near sights that you want to see. Of course, if you don't feel like doing any special planning, you will find the usual standard-issue *shokudō* near the main sights in the neighbourhood.

SARACA NISHIJIN Map p74 Café ¥

432-5075; Kita-ku, Murasakino Higashifujinomori-chō 11-1; noon-10pm, closed Wed; lunch from ¥900; 7min walk from Daitoku-ji-mae bus stop, bus 206 from Kyoto Station

This is one of Kyoto's most interesting cafés – it's built inside an old *sentō* (public bathhouse) and the original tiles have been preserved. Light meals and coffee (¥400) are the staples here. The *honjitsu Nishijin* (daily Nishijin lunch; ¥890) plate is decent value. Service can be slow and scattered but the interesting ambience makes it worth a look. It's near Funaoka Onsen (p76) and is easy to spot.

KANEI Map p74 udon & soba ¥

441-8283; Kita-ku, Murasakino Higashifujinomori-chō 11-1; 11.30am-2.30pm & 5-7pm, closed Mon; noodles from ¥850; 7min walk from Daitoku-ji-mae bus stop, bus 206 from Kyoto Station

A small traditional place not far from Funaoka Onsen (see the boxed text, p76), Kanei is the place to go if you're a *soba* connoisseur – the noodles are made by hand here and are delicious. The owners don't speak much English, so here's what to order: *zaru soba* (¥850) or *kake soba* (*soba* in a broth; ¥900). Note that handmade *soba* quickly loses its taste and texture, so we recommend that you eat it quickly. The servings are small and the dishes are only likely to please real *soba* fans. Kanei is on the corner, a few metres west of Saraca Nishijin (above).

TOYOUKE-JAYA Map p74 Tofu ¥

462-3662; Kamigyō-ku, Imadegawa-dōri-Onmae Nishi iru; 11am-3pm, closed Thu; set meals from ¥650; 1min walk from Kitanotenmangū-mae bus stop, bus 101 from Kyoto Station

Locals line up for the tofu lunch sets at this famous restaurant across from Kitano Tenman-gū (p76). Set meals start at ¥650 and usually include tofu, rice and miso soup. Problem is, it gets very crowded, especially when a market is on at the shrine. If you can get here when there's no queue, pop in for a healthy meal.

TACO TORA Map p74 Tako Yaki ¥

461-9292; Kamigyō-ku, Imadegawa-dōri-Nanahonmatsu Nishi iru; 5pm-2am, closed Tue; per 9 octopus balls ¥600; 5min walk from Kitanotenmangū-mae bus stop, bus 101 from Kyoto Station

Try this spot for Kyoto's best *tako yaki* (fried, battered octopus balls – no, not those balls). The place doesn't have much in the way of ambience, but, then, what *tako yaki* place does? Be careful: the balls are served piping hot and you can easily burn your mouth if you're not patient. It's near Kitano Tenman-gū (p76).

ARASHIYAMA & SAGANO

The area to the far west of Kyoto is a hugely popular destination with both foreign and Japanese travellers and it's packed with eateries, many of which serve the speciality of the area: *yudōfu*. Simpler meals can be had in the *shokudō* that line the street outside Arashiyama Station.

HIRANOYA Map p80 Tea & Kaiseki ¥¥¥

861-0359; Ukyō-ku, Saga Toriimoto Sennō-chō 16; 11.30am-9pm; tea ¥840, dinner from ¥15,000; 5min walk from Otaginenbutsu-ji-mae bus stop, bus 72 from Kyoto Station

Located next to the Atago Torii (Shintō shrine gate), this thatched-roof restaurant is about as atmospheric as they get. While you can sample full-course *kaiseki* meals here from ¥15,000 (by telephone reservation in Japanese only), we prefer to soak up the atmosphere over a simple cup of *matcha* for a relatively modest ¥840 (it comes with a traditional sweet). It's the perfect way to cool off after a long slog around the temples of Arashiyama and Sagano. Just ask for '*o-cha*' and you're away.

YUDŌFU SAGANO Map p80 Tofu ¥¥

☎ 871-6946; Ukyō-ku, Saga, Tenryū-ji, Susuki-nobaba-chō 45; 🕑 11am-7pm; lunch & dinner from ¥3800; 🚉 15min walk from Saga Arashiyama Station, Sagano line

This is a popular place to sample *yudōfu*. It's fairly casual, with a spacious dining room. You can usually eat here without having to wait and there's both indoor and outdoor seating. Look for the old cartwheels outside.

SHIGETSU Map p80 Buddhist Vegetarian ¥¥

☎ 882-9725; Ukyō-ku, Saga, Tenryū-ji, Susukinobaba-chō 68; 🕑 11am-2pm; lunch from ¥3000; 🚉 5min walk from Keifuku Arashiyama Station, Keifuku Arashiyama line

To sample *shōjin ryōri* (Buddhist vegetarian cuisine), try Shigetsu in the precinct of Tenryū-ji (p80). This healthy fare has been sustaining monks for more than a thousand years in Japan, so it will probably get you through an afternoon of sightseeing, although carnivores may be left craving something. Shigetsu has beautiful garden views.

MIKATZUKI Map p80 japanese ¥

☎ 861-0445; Ukyō-ku, Saga, Tenryū-ji, Tsukurimichi-chō 35-2; 🕑 11am-5pm, closed Tue; meals ¥600-1800; 🚉 10min walk from Saga Arashiyama Station, Sagano line

There are several *shokudō* on the main drag in Arashiyama and this is one of them. The thing that distinguishes this place is its English menu and the fact that it is a little more spacious than the others. Dishes include the typical *shokudō* noodle and rice classics. The tempura *teishoku* (¥1600) gives value for money and should power you through a few hours of Arashiyama sightseeing. The sign is in Japanese; it's black-and-white and one of the Japanese characters looks like a bullseye.

KAMEYAMA-YA Map p80 Japanese ¥

☎ 861-0759; Ukyō-ku, Saga, Kamenoo-chō; 🕑 10am-5pm (roughly), closed irregularly; meals ¥550-1500; 🚉 15min walk from Saga Arashiyama Station, Sagano line

We love this semi-outdoor restaurant on the banks of the Hozu-gawa. The service can be gruff, the food is only pretty good, but the location is impossible to beat. Dishes include tempura over rice and noodles. There is no English sign but there are a couple of vending machines near the entrance.

YOSHIDA-YA Map p80 Noodles ¥

☎ 861-0213; Ukyō-ku, Saga, Tenryū-ji, Tsukurimichi-chō 20-24; 🕑 10am-6pm, closed Tue; lunch from ¥800; 🚉 2min walk from Keifuku Arashiyama Station, Keifuku Arashiyama line

This quaint and friendly little *teishoku-ya* (set-meal restaurant) is the perfect place to grab a simple lunch while in Arashiyama. All the standard *teishoku* favourites are on offer, including things such as *oyakodon* (egg and chicken over a bowl of rice) for ¥1000. You can also cool off here with a refreshing *uji kintoki* for ¥600. There is no English sign; the restaurant is the first place south of the station and it has a rustic front.

KOMICHI Map p80 Café ¥

☎ 872-5313; Ukyō-ku, Saga, Nison-in Monzen Ōjōin-chō 23; 🕑 10am-5pm, closed Wed; matcha ¥600; 🚉 20min walk from Keifuku Arashiyama Station, Keifuku Arashiyama line

This friendly little teahouse is perfectly located along the Arashiyama tourist trail. In addition to hot and cold tea and coffee, it serves *uji kintoki* in summer and a variety of light noodle dishes year-round. The picture menu helps with ordering. The sign is green and black on a white background.

KITAYAMA AREA

If you're heading up to any of the three villages in the Kitayama area – Kurama, Kibune or Ōhara – you don't need to worry about packing a lunch: there are several restaurants in each. Ōhara and Kurama restaurants tend towards standard *shokudō*, while Kibune is a bit more of a fine-dining destination.

ŌHARA

There are several restaurants around the main gate of Sanzen-in and on the path to Jakkō-in. Seryō-jaya (below) is of particular note.

SERYŌ-JAYA Map p84 Japanese ¥¥

☎ 744-2301; Sakyō-ku, Ōhara, Shōrinin-chō 24; 🕑 11am-5pm; lunch sets from ¥2756; 🚌 10min walk from Ōhara bus stop, Kyoto bus 17 or 18 from Kyoto Station

Just by the entry gate to Sanzen-in (p83), Seryō-jaya serves wholesome *sansai ryōri* (mountain-vegetable cooking), fresh river fish and *soba* noodles topped with grated yam. There is outdoor seating in warmer months. To find this place, look for the food models.

KURAMA & KIBUNE

Most of the restaurants in Kurama are clustered on the main road outside Kurama-dera's main gate.

Visitors to Kibune from June to September should not miss the chance to dine at one of the picturesque restaurants beside the Kibune-gawa. Known as *kawa-doko*, meals are served on platforms suspended over the river as cool water flows underneath. Most of the restaurants offer a lunch special for around ¥3000. For a *kaiseki* spread (¥5000 to ¥10,000), have a Japanese speaker call to reserve it in advance. In the cold months you can dine indoors overlooking the river.

NAKAYOSHI Map p85 — Kaiseki ¥¥

☎ 741-2000; Sakyō-ku, Kurama, Kibune-chō 71; 11am-7pm; lunch from ¥3500, kaiseki dinner from ¥8500; 5min taxi ride from Kibune-guchi Station, Eizan line

One of the more reasonably priced restaurants in the area, Nakayoshi serves a lunch *bentō* for ¥3500. It has dining platforms over the river and the food is well prepared.

TOCHIGIKU Map p85 — Kaiseki ¥¥

☎ 741-5555; Sakyō-ku, Kurama, Kibune-chō 17; 11.30am-9pm, closed irregularly; sukiyaki from ¥8000; 5min taxi ride from Kibune-guchi Station, Eizan line

Try this lovely riverside restaurant for chicken and beef sukiyaki, wild boar stew and *kaiseki* sets. There is a small English sign. Last orders are at 7.30pm.

HIROBUN Map p85 — Japanese ¥¥

☎ 741-2147; Sakyō-ku, Kurama, Kibune-chō; 11am-10pm; noodles ¥1200, kaiseki from ¥7000; 5min taxi ride from Kibune-guchi Station, Eizan line

Here you can try *nagashi-somen* (¥1200), which are thin noodles that flow to you in globs down a split-bamboo gutter; just pluck them out and slurp away. This dish is served until 5pm. To find Hirobun, look for the black-and-white sign and the lantern. It's at the top of the village.

BENIYA Map p85 — Kaiseki ¥¥

☎ 741-2041; Sakyō-ku, Kurama, Kibune-chō 17; 11.30am-7.30pm; meals from ¥3000; 5min taxi ride from Kibune-guchi Station, Eizan line

This elegant riverside restaurant serves *kaiseki* sets for ¥6000, ¥8000 or ¥10,000, depending on size. There is a wooden sign with white lettering out the front.

YŌSHŪJI Map p85 — Japanese ¥¥

☎ 741-2848; Sakyō-ku, Kurama, Honmachi 1074; 10am-6pm, closed Tue; meals from ¥1050; 5min walk from Kurama Station, Eizan line

Yōshūji serves superb *shōjin ryōri* in a delightful old Japanese farmhouse with an *irori* (open hearth). The house special, a sumptuous selection of vegetarian dishes served in red lacquered bowls, is called *kurama-yama shōjin zen* (¥2500). If you're just wanting a quick bite, try the *uzu-soba* (*soba* topped with mountain vegetables; ¥1050). It's halfway up the steps leading to the main gate of Kurama-dera (p85); look for the orange lanterns out the front.

ORGANIC CAFÉ AURORA Map p85 — Café ¥

☎ 741-5178; Sakyō-ku, Kuramahonmachi 308; 10.30am-6pm, closed irregularly; lunch ¥1000; 3min walk from Kurama Station, Eizan line

This fine little café in a traditional Japanese house is a good spot for a cuppa before or after visiting the temple. You can choose from 25 varieties of tea. Simple meals are also served. The small garden is nice to gaze out on as you sip your tea. It's a few minutes' walk up the road from the station, on the right. There is an English sign.

ABURAYA-SHOKUDŌ Map p85 — Shokudō ¥

☎ 741-2009; Sakyō-ku, Kuramahonmachi 252; 9.30am-5.30pm, closed last 3 days of each month; meals from ¥800; 5min walk from Kurama Station, Eizan line

Just down the steps from the main gate of Kurama-dera (p85), this classic old-style *shokudō* reminds us of what Japan was like before it got rich. The *sansai teishoku* (¥1700) is a delightful selection of vegetables, rice and *soba* topped with grated yam. Simpler noodle and rice dishes can be had for around ¥800. It's on the corner.

KIBUNE CLUB Map p85 — Café ¥

☎ 741-2146; Sakyō-ku, Kurama, Kibune-chō 76; 11.30am-6pm; coffee from ¥450; 5min taxi ride from Kibune-guchi Station, Eizan line

The exposed wooden beams and open, airy feel of this rustic café make it a great spot for a cuppa while exploring Kibune. In the winter, the staff sometimes crank up the wood stove, which makes the place rather cosy. It's easy to spot.

ENTERTAINMENT

top picks

- **Minami-za** (p142)
- **Kyoto Cinema** (p143)
- **Orizzonte** (p140)
- **Metro** (p141)
- **Jumbo Karaoke Hiroba** (p141)
- **A-Bar** (p140)

ENTERTAINMENT

Kyoto is far more than temples, museums and shops. By day, you can choose from sports such as swimming and hiking, not to mention movies and game centres. By night, you can party down in one of Kyoto's three main nightlife districts: Gion, which is generally fairly upscale; Pontochō, which is both upscale and traditional; and Kiyamachi, which is plebeian, raucous and a whole lot of fun. You can choose from *izakaya* (Japanese pub-eateries), bars, clubs and karaoke boxes, many of which stay open almost until dawn. The fact is, Kyoto knows how to party – it's just a matter of whether you can keep up.

As for traditional Japanese culture, you will have to work a little harder. Most of Kyoto's cultural entertainment is of an occasional nature, and you'll need to check with the Kyoto Tourist Information Center (TIC; p199) to find out what's on while you're in town. Alternatively, check the *Kansai Time Out* (p197) or the *Kyoto Visitor's Guide* (p197).

DRINKING

Kyoto has an astounding variety of bars, from exclusive Gion clubs, where it's possible to spend ¥100,000 in a single evening, to grungy *gaijin* (foreigner) bars. Most bars are concentrated in Downtown Kyoto (Map p50), around Kawaramachi-dōri and Kiyamachi-dōri. For something a little more upscale than the bars and pubs listed in this section, try one of the bars in any of Kyoto's upmarket hotels (see the boxed text, below).

It would be crazy to come all the way to Japan and not sing karaoke! If you shy away from karaoke back home, where singing on stage is the norm, you'll feel much more comfortable in Kyoto, where the 'karaoke box' is king. Here, you and your friends get a small room and karaoke system to yourselves.

Yes, you can also dance the night away in the cultural heart of Japan and give the temples and shrines a miss the next day while you sleep off your hangover. Most clubs charge an admission fee of ¥2000, which usually includes a drink or two.

top picks

HOTEL BARS

Some of the best bars in Kyoto are inside hotels. These are usually very easy to enter and you will have no communication problems. Here are our favourites:

- **Orizzonte** (Map p50) In the **Kyoto Hotel Ōkura** (p149); this is a restaurant by day, lounge by night, usually from 8.30pm to 11pm). The view over Kyoto is stunning.
- **Sekisui** (Map p50) Open from 5pm until 1am, this bar on the basement floor of the **Hotel Fujita Kyoto** (p149) looks out over water falling onto stones (hence the name, which means 'stone and water').
- **Tōzan Bar** (Map p62) We love this cosy and cool underground retreat below the **Hyatt Regency Kyoto** (p152), one of Kyoto's best hotels. It's worth a visit just to marvel at the design.

A-BAR Map p50 Bar

☎ 213-2129; Nishikiyamachi-dōri; drinks from ¥350; 5pm-midnight; 10min walk from Sanjō Station, Keihan line

This is a raucous student *izakaya* with a log-cabin interior located in the Kiyamachi area. There's a big menu to choose from and everything's cheap. The best part comes when they add up the bill – you'll swear they've undercharged you by half. It's a little tough to find – look for the small black-and-white sign at the top of a flight of concrete steps above a place called Reims.

ATLANTIS Map p50 Bar

☎ 241-1621; Shijō-Pontochō agaru; drinks around ¥1000; 6pm-2am; 5min walk from Shijō Station, Keihan line

This is one of the few bars on Pontochō that foreigners can walk into without a Japanese friend. It's a slick, trendy place that draws a fair smattering of Kyoto's beautiful people, and wannabe beautiful people. In summer you can sit outside on a platform looking over the Kamo-gawa. It's often crowded here so you may have to wait a bit to get in, especially if you want to sit outside.

CAFÉ BON APPÉTIT Map p62 Bar, Café

☎ 525-0585; Shirakawa Nawate; drinks from ¥500; 11am-11pm; 5min walk from Shijō Station, Keihan line

Not exactly a bar, not exactly a café, this is a fine spot to sip a drink and watch the characters of Gion stroll by. It's near the Shira-kawa canal and right alongside some of Kyoto's best cherry trees.

ING Map p50 Bar, Izakaya

☎ 255-5087; Nishikiyamachi-dōri-Takoyakushi; drinks from ¥580; 6pm-2am Mon-Thu, to 5am Fri & Sat; 8min walk from Sanjō Station, Keihan line

This bar/*izakaya* on Kiyamachi is one of our favourite spots for a drink in Kyoto. It offers cheap bar snacks and drinks, good music, and friendly staff. It's in the Royal building on the 2nd floor; you'll know you're getting close when you see all the hostesses out trawling for customers on the streets nearby.

MARBLE ROOM Map p50 Bar

☎ 213-0753; Pontochō Sanjō kudaru; drinks from ¥700; 5.30pm-3am Sun-Thu, 3pm-3am Fri & Sat; 5min walk from Sanjō Station, Keihan line

The Marble Room is what a lot of people in the 1950s imagined the year 2000 would look like. It's a mod space that draws Kyoto's fashionable young set for decent drinks and snacks. If you're over 30 here, you'll probably feel like an antique. It's on the 4th floor of the Pontochō Building, which has a white front.

MCLOUGHLIN'S IRISH BAR & RESTAURANT Map p50 Bar

☎ 212-6339; Empire Bldg, Kiyamachi Sanjō-agaru; drinks from ¥500; 6pm-late; 5min walk from Sanjō Station, Keihan line

This is our favourite expat bar in town. It has ripping views over the Higashiyama mountains, great beer on tap, good food and a nice, open feeling. It also hosts some excellent music events and is an ideal spot to meet some local folks, both expat and Japanese. There is wi-fi internet access in case you want to do some surfing while drinking your beer.

RUB-A-DUB Map p50 Bar

☎ 256-3122; Kiyamachi-dōri-Sanjō; drinks from ¥600; 7pm-2am Sun-Thu, to 4am Fri & Sat; 5min walk from Sanjō Station, Keihan line

At the northern end of Kiyamachi-dōri, Rub-a-Dub is a funky little reggae bar with a shabby tropical look. It's a good place for a quiet drink on weekdays, but on Friday and Saturday nights you'll have no choice but to bop along with the crowd. Look for the stairs heading down to the basement beside the popular (and delightfully 'fragrant') Nagahama Rāmen shop.

ZAPPA Map p50 Bar, Restaurant

☎ 255-4437; Takoyakushi-dōri-Kawaramachi; drinks from ¥500; 6pm-midnight; 10min walk from Sanjō Station, Keihan line

Unbeatable if you're looking for a more intimate venue. It's a cosy little place that once played host to David Bowie (he's said to have discovered the place by chance and decided to drop in for a drink). Zappa serves savoury Southeast Asian fare and a few Japanese titbits for good measure. It's down a narrow alley; turn south at the wooden *torii* (shrine gate).

METRO Map pp68–9 Club

☎ 752-4765; Kawabata-dōri-Marutamachi kudaru; admission around ¥1000-2000; 10pm-3am Sun-Thu, to 5am Fri & Sat; Marutamachi Station, Keihan line

Metro is part disco, part 'live house' (small concert hall) and it even hosts the occasional art exhibition. It attracts an eclectic mix of creative types and has a different theme every night, so check ahead in *Kansai Time Out* (p197) to see what's going on. Some of the best gigs are Latin night and the popular Non-Hetero-at-the-Metro night, which draws gay and lesbian clubbers and everyone in-between. Metro is inside exit 2 of the Marutamachi Station. Admission varies by event.

WORLD Map p50 Club

☎ 213-4119; Nishikiyamachi-dōri-Shijō agaru; admission from ¥1500, drinks from ¥500; 10pm-5am; 1min walk from Kawaramachi Station, Hankyū line

World is Kyoto's largest club and it naturally hosts some of the biggest events. It has two floors, a dance floor and lockers where you can leave your stuff while you dance the night away. Events include everything from deep soul to reggae and techno to salsa.

JUMBO KARAOKE HIROBA Map p62 Karaoke

☎ 761-3939; Kawabata-dōri-Sanjō, Sanjō-Ōhashi East; per person per hr before 7pm/after 7pm

¥280/640; 🕑 11am-6am; 🚇 1min walk from Sanjō Station, Keihan line

Expats love this place as it's in the same building as the Pig & Whistle (below) – and more than one drunken evening has started at the Pig and moved on to this place! There's a decent selection of English songs and the price includes all drinks. There's also a Sanjō Kawaramachi branch (Map p50; ☎ 231 6777; Kawaramachi-dōri-Sanjō, northwest; 🚇 3min walk from Sanjō Station, Keihan line) in Downtown Kyoto.

PIG & WHISTLE Map p62 Pub

☎ 761-6022; Kawabata-dōri-Sanjō; drinks from ¥500; 🕑 5pm-midnight Sun-Thu, to 1am Fri & Sat; 🚇 1min walk from Sanjō Station, Keihan line

The Pig is a British-style pub with darts, pint glasses, and fish and chips. While many of its patrons have moved on to other venues, we still like this place for its relaxed layout and homey interior. The two main drawcards are Guinness on tap and friendly bilingual staff. The Pig's on the 2nd floor of the Shobi building near the Sanjō-Kawabata crossing.

GAEL IRISH PUB Map p62 Pub

☎ 525-0680; Yamatoōji-dōri-Shijō agaru; drinks from ¥600; 🕑 5pm-1am, later on Thu & Fri; 🚇 5min walk from Keihan Shijō Station

The Gael is a welcoming and convivial Irish pub on the edge of Gion. It's got table and counter seats, a good menu with a variety of pub food, and excellent beer on tap. It's a good place to go if you're travelling solo – you'll soon find yourself involved in a conversation. It's on the 2nd floor of the Kamo Higashi building; take the steps on your right just after you enter.

ARTS

As the cultural capital of Japan, it's no surprise that Kyoto is the best place to sample some of the country's traditional performing arts. You can choose from kabuki, geisha dances, nō and traditional music concerts. Of course, you can also enjoy the full range of modern entertainment; Kyoto has several excellent cinemas and an active music scene.

THEATRE

Kyoto is the best city in Japan in which to see traditional forms of Japanese theatre. The easiest way to find out what's on while you're in town is to check *Kansai Time Out* (see p197) or to ask at the TIC (p199).

For nō performances, the main theatre is Kanze Kaikan Nō Theatre (Map pp68–9; ☎ 771-6114; Sakyō-ku-Okazaki; admission free-¥8000; 🕑 9am-5pm, closed Mon; 🚇 10min walk from Higashiyama Station, Tōzai subway line). Alternatively, Takigi Nō is a picturesque form of nō performed in the light of blazing fires on the evenings of 1 and 2 June at Heian-jingū (p72). Tickets cost ¥2000 if you pay in advance at local ticket agencies or ¥3300 at the entrance gate.

GION CORNER Map p62

☎ 561-1119; Gion-Hanami-kōji-dōri; admission ¥2800; 🕑 performances 7pm & 8pm 1 Mar-30 Nov, closed 16 Aug; 🚇 5min walk from Shijō Station, Keihan line

Gion Corner presents regularly scheduled shows that include a bit of tea ceremony, koto (Japanese zither) music, ikebana (flower arrangement), *gagaku* (court music), *kyōgen* (ancient comic plays), *kyōmai* (Kyoto-style dance) and *bunraku* (classical puppet theatre). It's geared to a tourist market and is fairly pricey for what you get.

MINAMI-ZA Map p62

☎ 561-0160; Shijō-Ōhashi; admission ¥4200-12,600; 🕑 irregular; 🚇 1min walk from Shijō Station, Keihan line

The oldest kabuki theatre in Japan is the Minami-za theatre in Gion. The major event of the year is the Kaomise festival (1 to 26 December), which features Japan's finest kabuki actors. Other performances take place on an irregular basis. Those interested should check with the TIC (p199). The most likely months for performances are May, June and September.

GEISHA DANCES

Annually in spring and autumn, geisha and their *maiko* (apprentice geisha) from Kyoto's five schools dress elaborately to perform traditional dances in praise of the seasons. The cheapest tickets cost about ¥1650 (unreserved seating on tatami mats); better seats cost ¥3000 to ¥3800, and spending an extra ¥500 includes participation in a quick tea ceremony. The dances are similar from place to place and are repeated several times a day. Dates and times vary, so check with the TIC (p199).

Gion Odori (☎ 561-0224; Higashiyama-ku-Gion; ¥3500, incl tea ¥4000; 🕑 1pm & 3.30pm) From 1 to 10

November at the Gion Kaikan Theatre (Map p62), near Yasaka-jinja.

Kamogawa Odori (☎ 221-2025; Pontochō-Sanjō kudaru; regular/special/special incl tea ¥2000/3800/4300; 12.30pm, 2.20pm & 4.10pm) From 1 to 24 May at Pontochō Kaburen-jō Theatre (Map p50), Pontochō.

Kitano Odori (☎ 461-0148; Imadegawa-dōri-Nishihon-matsu nishi iru; ¥3800, incl tea ¥4300; 1pm & 3pm) From 15 to 25 April at Kamishichiken Kaburen-jō Theatre (Map p74), east of Kitano-Tenman-gū.

Kyō Odori (☎ 561-1151; Kawabata-dōri-Shijō kudaru; ¥3800, incl tea ¥4300; 12.30pm, 2.30pm & 4.30pm) From the first to the third Sunday in April at the Miya-gawa-chō Kaburen-jō Theatre (Map p62), east of the Kamo-gawa between Shijō-dōri and Gojō-dōri.

Miyako Odori (☎ 561-1115; Higashiyama-ku-Gion-chō South; nonreserved/reserved/reserved incl tea ¥1900/3800/4300; 12.30pm, 2pm, 3.30pm & 4.50pm) Held throughout April at the Gion Kōbu Kaburen-jō Theatre (Map p62), on Hanami-kōji, just south of Shijō-dōri.

CINEMA

You'll find a large number of movie theatres in Kyoto's Downtown area around Kawara-machi-dōri and Kiyamachi-dōri. These theatres are dominated by Hollywood films, which arrive in Japan up to six months after their original release. Foreign films are screened in their original language, with Japanese subtitles. Tickets average around ¥1800. The exception to this is the first Tuesday of each month (Eiga-no-Hi, or 'Movie Day'), when tickets cost ¥1000.

KYOTO CINEMA Map p50

☎ 353-4723; Shimogyō-ku, Karasuma dōri Shijō sagaru, Suiginya-chō 620, Cocoon Karasuma 3F; generally 10am-9pm (varies by movie); Shijō Station, Karasuma subway line

This new art-house theatre right downtown is a tremendously welcome addition to the Kyoto cultural scene. It rivals Kyoto Minami Kaikan (below) as Kyoto's best place for arty films. It's directly connected to Shijō Station; take exit 2.

KYOTO MINAMI KAIKAN Map pp54–5

☎ 661-3993; Minami-ku, Nishi-Kujō, Higashihieijo-chō; admission ¥1800; varies; 2min walk from Tōji Station, Kintetsu Kyoto line

Try this theatre for lesser-known imports and eclectic Japanese films, including Japanese *anime* (animation). It's on Kujō-dōri.

MUSIC

Rock, Folk & Acoustic

There are several options for live music. Most venues vary the type of music they feature from night to night. Check *Kansai Time Out* (see p197) to see what's happening at the following 'live houses'.

JUTTOKU Map p74

☎ 841-1691; Ōmiya-dōri-Shimotachiuri; admission ¥1000; 5.30pm-midnight, live music 7-9pm; 10min walk from Nijōjō-mae Station, Tōzai subway line

Juttoku is located in an atmospheric old *sakagura* (sake warehouse). It plays host to a variety of shows – check *Kansai Time Out* to see what's on.

TAKU-TAKU Map pp54-5

☎ 351-1321; Tominokōji-dōri-Bukkōji; admission ¥1500-3500; 7-9pm, closed irregularly; 10min walk from Shijō Station, Hankyū Kyoto line

This is one of Kyoto's most atmospheric clubs, located in another old *sakagura*. It's central and tends to present major acts (the Neville Brothers, Los Lobos and Dr John have all performed here).

Jazz

Live jazz takes place irregularly at several clubs in Kyoto. The best is Rag (Map p50; ☎ 241-0446; 5th fl, Empire Bldg, Kiyamachi-dōri-Sanjō; admission ¥1500-4000; varies; 5min walk from Sanjō Station, Keihan line).

Classical

The Kyoto Concert Hall (Map pp54–5; ☎ 361-6629; Sakyō-ku, Kitayama-dōri; admission varies; performances vary, office 10am-5pm, closed 1st & 3rd Mon of each month; 3min walk from Kitayama Station, Karasuma subway line) and ALTI (Kyoto Fumin Hall; Map pp54–5; ☎ 441-1414; Karasuma-dōri-Ichijō kudaru; admission varies; 9am-9.30pm, office to 6pm, closed 1st & 3rd Mon of each month; 5min walk from Imadegawa Station, Karasuma subway line) both hold regular performances of classical music and dance (traditional and contemporary). Ticket prices average between ¥3000 and ¥5000. Check with the TIC (p199) for current schedules.

Traditional Performances

Performances featuring the koto, *shamisen* (three-stringed Japanese instrument) and *shakuhachi* (traditional Japanese bamboo flute) are held irregularly in Kyoto. Performances of *bugaku* (court music and dance) are held at shrines during festivals and occasionally you might catch a contemporary *butō* dance. Check with the TIC (p199) to see if any performances are scheduled while you are in town.

SPORTS & ACTIVITIES

Kyoto offers much more than just high culture, temples and shopping. You'll find there are plenty of ways to burn off the calories from last night's tempura feast. The park-like banks of the Kamo-gawa, which flows through the middle of the city, are a great place for walking, cycling or other sports, as is the Kyoto Imperial Palace Park (p52). There is also great hiking in the hills around the city, and you can swim in pools and even in the Kamo-gawa during summer months (unless you happen to be a drunk Kyoto University student, in which case it seems to be a year-round activity).

GAME CENTRES

Japanese kids are wild about video games and the city is full of game centres, ranging from the ultra-high-tech to simpler spots with only a few machines. If you or your kids love these sorts of games, you've come to the right place!

HIKING

Kyoto has great hiking in the hills surrounding the city. The best hikes are in the Higashiyama above Ginkaku-ji (p71) and Nanzen-ji (p66). A great hike within easy reach of the city is the climb up Daimonji-yama (see the boxed text, p71). It's a relatively easy two-hour return trip if taken at a moderate pace. For more on hiking in and around Kyoto, pick up a copy of Lonely Planet's *Hiking in Japan,* which is available at Kyoto's English-language bookshops.

SWIMMING

You can swim in the Kamo-gawa in the summer. The best spot is about 1km north of Kamigamo-jinja (p91); just look for all the people. Keep in mind that swimming here is not without hazard and people have drowned swimming in this river. Parents should keep a close eye on their kids. Otherwise, try **Tōsuikai** (Map pp68–9; ☎ 761-1275; Marutamachi-dōri; per visit ¥1200; 10am-3pm Mon-Sat, noon-5pm Sun; 10min walk from Shijō Station, Hankyū Kyoto line). This place has Kyoto's only 50m outdoor pool. It's pretty shallow and is sometimes taken over by local swim teams for summer training, but it's your best option for lap swimming in Kyoto.

SLEEPING

top picks

- **Tour Club** (p148)
- **Budget Inn** (p148)
- **Utano Youth Hostel** (p154)
- **Ryokan Uemura** (p152)
- **Ryokan Shimizu** (p148)
- **Ryokan Motonago** (p152)
- **Hotel Unizo** (p150)
- **Palace Side Hotel** (p151)
- **Karasuma Kyoto Hotel** (p149)
- **Hyatt Regency Kyoto** (p152)

SLEEPING

When it comes to accommodation, you're spoiled for choice in Kyoto. Want to try a night in a traditional ryokan (Japanese-style inn)? This is the place to do so and you'll find ryokan in all budget ranges. How about a night in a world-class hotel? Again, you've got plenty to choose from in Kyoto, and the service at a good Japanese hotel is unrivalled. If you're on a tight budget, you'll still find lots of comfortable options in Kyoto – the city accommodates backpackers from all over the world and there are plenty of guesthouses, youth hostels and cheap ryokan at ease with foreign guests.

Bear in mind that much of Kyoto's accommodation can be booked out during Kyoto's two tourist high seasons: the early-April cherry-blossom season and the November autumn-foliage season. It can also be hard to find rooms during Golden Week (29 April to 5 May) and O-bon (mid-August). Whatever you do, try to reserve as early as possible if you plan to be in town during these times.

Credit cards are accepted at most hotels but don't expect to pay with plastic at any of the budget places. As for ryokan, the higher the price, the better your chances of being able to use a credit card.

ACCOMMODATION STYLES

The following are the most common accommodation types you will encounter in this book and on your travels.

Business Hotels

A very common form of midrange accommodation is the so-called 'business hotel'. Generally these are economical and functional places geared to the lone traveller on business, although most in Kyoto also take couples. In Kyoto, a room in a business hotel will have a pay TV and tiny bathroom, and cost between ¥6000 and ¥12,000. As is the case with various ryokan, some business hotels accept credit cards, but you should always ask when you check in. There is no room service and you will usually be required to check out at 10am or 11am and check in after 3pm or 4pm. At some of the nicer business hotels, there are large shared baths and saunas in addition to the private ones in the guest rooms.

Business hotels are identifiable by their small size (usually three to five floors), their simple (often concrete) exteriors, and a sign (usually in both English and Japanese) out the front. Although you can't expect much English from the front desk clerk, if you smile and speak slowly you should be okay.

Standard or Luxury Hotels

In addition to business hotels, you will find a variety of standard/luxury hotels in Kyoto. These will be similar to standard/luxury hotels anywhere else in the developed world, although, this being Japan, you can expect the service to be on a superior level. English is spoken at these hotels, and the rooms are usually very well maintained and larger than business-hotel rooms. In addition, most standard/luxury hotels in Kyoto have several good restaurants and bars on their premises, some of which offer outstanding views over the city.

Ryokan

Although some ryokan will allow you to pay by credit card, you should always ask when you make reservations.

Youth Hostels

Kyoto's youth hostels are much like youth hostels that you'll find elsewhere: not much atmosphere and a mixture of dorms and private rooms. They can also be noisy. On the plus side, they are used to foreigners and are cleaner than many of their overseas counterparts. A room in a typical youth hostel costs

PRICE GUIDE

The following is a guide to the pricing system in this chapter. Prices are per room per night, including bathroom and air-con (unless otherwise stated).

¥¥¥	over ¥15,000
¥¥	¥6000-15,000
¥	under ¥6000

STAYING IN A RYOKAN

Let's face it: a hotel is a hotel wherever you go. Just as you want to try local food when you're on the road, you probably also want to try a night in traditional local accommodation. If so, then you'll definitely want to spend at least one night in a ryokan.

Ryokan (written with the Japanese characters for 'travel' and 'hall') are usually fine old wooden Japanese buildings, with tatami mats, futons, gardens, deep Japanese bathtubs, traditional Japanese service and kitchens that turn out classic Japanese cuisine.

Due to language difficulties and unfamiliarity, staying in a ryokan is not as straightforward as staying in a Western-style hotel. It's not exactly rocket science, however, and with a little education it can be a breeze, even if you don't speak a word of Japanese. Here's the basic drill:

When you arrive, leave your shoes in the *genkan* (the entrance/foyer) and step up into the reception area. Here, you'll be asked to sign in and perhaps show your passport (you pay when you check out). You'll then be shown around the place and then to your room, where you will be served a cup of tea, or shown a hot-water flask and some tea cups so you can make your own. You'll note that there is no bedding to be seen in your room – your futon are in the closets and will be laid out later. You can leave your luggage anywhere except the *tokonoma* (sacred alcove), which will usually contain some flowers or a hanging scroll. If it's early enough, you can then go out to do some sightseeing.

When you return, you can change into your *yukata* (lightweight Japanese robe) and be served dinner in your room or in a dining room. In a ryokan, dinner is often a multicourse feast of the finest local delicacies. After dinner, you can take a bath. If it's a big place, you can generally bathe anytime in the evening until around 11pm. If it's a small place, you'll be given a time slot. While you're in the bath, some mysterious elves will go into your room and lay out your futon so that it will be waiting for you when you return all toasty from the bath.

In the morning, you'll be served a Japanese-style breakfast (some places these days serve a simple Western-style breakfast for those who can't stomach rice and fish in the morning). You pay on check-out, which is usually around 11am. The only problem with staying in a good ryokan is that it might put you off hotels for the rest of your days! Enjoy.

about ¥3200, cash only. Membership might not be necessary.

Guesthouses

Guesthouses are similar to youth hostels, without the regimented atmosphere and without any need for membership. With a long history of hosting foreign travellers, Kyoto has far more guesthouses than most Japanese cities, including Tokyo. There are still a few notorious flea pits left over from the days when Japan was a stop on the hippy trail, but these days clean, modern, well-maintained guesthouses are the norm. Guesthouses usually have both dorms, which average ¥2500 per person, and a variety of private rooms, which average ¥3500 per person.

Shukubō

Staying in a *shukubō* (temple lodging) is one way to experience another facet of traditional Japan. Sometimes you are allocated a simple room in the temple precincts and left to your own devices. At other times, you may be asked to participate in prayers, services or *zazen* (seated meditation). Nightly rates hover at around ¥4000 per person (most with breakfast included), and guests usually use public baths near the temples.

A number of *shukubō* in Kyoto are hesitant to take foreigners who cannot speak Japanese, although those listed in this chapter have English speakers on hand and are used to having non-Japanese guests. At the TIC (p199) you can also pick up a copy of *Shukubōs in Kyoto,* which has a list of local temple lodgings.

RESERVATIONS & INFORMATION

Making phone reservations in English is usually possible; providing you speak clearly and simply, there will usually be someone around who can get the gist of what you want.

The International Tourism Center of Japan (www.itcj.jp/), formerly the Welcome Inn Reservation Center, is a free reservation service that represents hundreds of *minshuku* (Japanese-style B&Bs), ryokan, inns and *pensions* in Japan. In Kyoto it operates a counter at the TIC (p199) and at the main tourist information counters in Narita and Kansai airports. You can also make reservations online through its website (which is also an excellent source of information on member hotels and inns).

KYOTO STATION AREA

The area around Kyoto Station is thick with hotels, ryokan and guesthouses, including one hotel right above the station itself. There is no question that this is a convenient place to be based in terms of transport and shopping, and there are a fair number of dining options in and around the station. It's a bit of a hike from the main sightseeing districts, but since the station is the transport hub of Kyoto, it should take less than 30 minutes to reach them by bus, subway or taxi.

HOTEL GRANVIA KYOTO

Map p46 Hotel ¥¥¥

☎ 344-8888; www.granvia-kyoto.co.jp/e/; Shimogyō-ku, Karasuma-dōri, Shiokōji Sagaru; d/tw ¥23,100/25,410; Kyoto Station;

Imagine being able to step out of bed and straight into the *shinkansen* (bullet train). This is almost possible when you stay at the Hotel Granvia, a fine establishment located directly above Kyoto Station. The rooms are clean, spacious and elegant, with deep bathtubs. This is a very professional operation with some decent on-site restaurants, some of which have good views over the city.

RIHGA ROYAL HOTEL KYOTO

Map p46 Hotel ¥¥¥

☎ 341-1121; www.rihga.com/kyoto/; Shimogyō-ku, Horikawa-dōri-Shiokōji; d/tw ¥23,100/25,410; 10min walk from Kyoto Station;

Though a little dated, and too busy and large for some people's taste, this long-running hotel has all the facilities that you'd expect from a first-class hotel, including a revolving rooftop restaurant. The location is convenient to Kyoto Station, but a little distant from the Higashiyama sightseeing district.

APA HOTEL Map p46 Business Hotel ¥¥

☎ 365-4111; ahkyoto@apa.co.jp; Shimogyō-ku, Nishinotōin-dōri, Shiokōji sagaru, Minami Fudōdō-chō 806; s/tw from ¥10,500/20,000; 5min walk from Kyoto Station;

Only five minutes on foot from Kyoto Station, this excellent business hotel is a good midpriced hotel choice. Rooms are on the large size, with firm, clean beds and unit bathrooms. The staff are professional and seem at ease dealing with foreign guests.

BUDGET INN Map p46 Guesthouse ¥

☎ 344-1510; www.budgetinnjp.com; Shimogyō-ku, Shichijō sagaru, Aburanokōji, Aburanokōji-chō 295; dm/tr/q ¥2500/10,980/12,980; 7min walk from Kyoto Station;

This well-run guesthouse is excellent. It has two dorm rooms and six Japanese-style private rooms, all of which are clean and well maintained. All rooms have their own bath and toilet, and there is a spacious quad room that's good for families. The staff here is very helpful and friendly, and internet access, laundry and bicycle rental are available. All in all, this is a great choice in this price range. It's a seven-minute walk from Kyoto Station; walk west on Shiokōji-dōri and turn north one street before Horikawa and look for the English-language sign out front.

TOUR CLUB Map p46 Guesthouse ¥

☎ 353-6968; www.kyotojp.com; Shimogyō-ku, Shōmen-sagaru, Higashinakasuji, Momiji-chō 362; dm ¥2450, d ¥6980-7770, tr ¥8880-9720; 10min walk from Kyoto Station;

Run by a charming and informative young couple, this clean, well-maintained guesthouse is a favourite of many foreign visitors. Facilities include internet access, bicycle rentals, laundry, wireless LAN, and free tea and coffee. Most private rooms have a private bath and toilet, and there is a spacious quad room for families. This is probably the best choice in this price bracket. It's a 10-minute walk from Kyoto Station; turn north off Shichijō-dōri at the Second House coffee shop (looks like a bank) and keep an eye out for the English sign.

RYOKAN SHIMIZU Map p46 Ryokan ¥

☎ 371-5538; www.kyoto-shimizu.net; Wakamiya Shichijō agaru; r per person from ¥5250; Kyoto Station;

A short walk north of Kyoto Station's Karasuma central gate, this fine new ryokan is quickly building a loyal following of foreign and Japanese guests, and for good reason: it's clean, well run and friendly. Rooms are standard ryokan style with one difference: all have attached bathrooms and toilets. Bicycle rental is available.

K'S HOUSE KYOTO Map p46 Guesthouse ¥

☎ 342-2444; kshouse.jp/index.html; Shimogyō-ku, Dotemachi-dōri Shichijō agaru, Naya-chō 418; dm/s/d per person from ¥2500/3500/2900; 10min walk from Kyoto Station;

K's House is a large 'New Zealand–style' guesthouse with both private and dorm rooms. The rooms are simple but adequate and there are spacious common areas. It's a sociable place that is currently in the process of building a large, new building next door.

DOWNTOWN KYOTO

If you want easy access to an incredible variety of dining, entertainment and shopping options, staying in Downtown Kyoto is a good idea. Although there are relatively few ryokan and no guesthouses, there are plenty of hotels in this area. Kyoto's two subway lines converge here and plenty of buses run through, so it's convenient in terms of transport as well. You can get to the main sightseeing districts from Downtown Kyoto in less than half an hour. On the downside, it can be a little busy and not particularly scenic. If you're after soothing Kyoto cityscapes, you might prefer to try the Higashiyama districts.

HIIRAGIYA RYOKAN Map p50 Ryokan ¥¥¥

☎ 221-1136; www.hiiragiya.co.jp/en/; Nakagyō-ku, Fuyachō, Aneyakōji-agaru; r per person incl meals ¥30,000-90,000; 10min walk from Shijō Station, Karasuma subway line;

This elegant ryokan has long been favoured by celebrities from around the world. Facilities and services are excellent and the location is hard to beat. Ask for one of the newly redone rooms.

HIIRAGIYA RYOKAN ANNEXE

Map p50 Ryokan ¥¥¥

☎ 231-0151; fax 231-0153; Nakagyō-ku, Nijō kudaru, Gokomachi-dōri; r per person incl meals from ¥15,000; 10min walk from Karasuma-Oike Station, Karasuma subway line;

Not far from the Hiiragiya Ryokan (above) main building, the Hiiragiya Ryokan Annexe offers the traditional ryokan experience at slightly more affordable rates. The *kaiseki* (Japanese *haute cuisine*) served here is delicious, the gardens are lovely and the bathtubs are wonderful. Service is professional, if a little cool.

TAWARAYA RYOKAN Map p50 Ryokan ¥¥¥

☎ 211-5566; fax 221-2204; Nakagyō-ku, Fuyachō-Oike kudaru; r per person incl meals ¥35,000-75,000; 10min walk from Karasuma-Oike Station, Karasuma subway line;

Tawaraya has been operating for more than three centuries and is one of the finest places to stay in the world. From the decorations to the service to the food, everything at the Tawaraya is simply the best available. It's a very intimate, warm and personal place that has many loyal guests. It's centrally located within easy walk of two subway stations and many good restaurants.

KYOTO HOTEL ŌKURA Map p50 Hotel ¥¥¥

☎ 211-5111; www.kyotohotel.co.jp/khokura/english/index.html; Nakagyō-ku, Kawaramachi-dōri-Oike; s/tw/d from ¥20,212/28,875/37,537; 1min walk from Kyoto-Shiyakusho-mae Station, Tōzai subway line;

This towering hotel in the centre of town commands an impressive view of the Higashiyama Mountains. Rooms here are clean and spacious and many have great views, especially the excellent corner suites – we just wish we could open a window to enjoy the breeze. You can access the Kyoto subway system directly from the hotel, which is convenient on rainy days or if you've got luggage.

HOTEL FUJITA KYOTO Map p50 Hotel ¥¥

☎ 222-1511; information@fujita-kyoto.com; Nakagyō-ku, Kamogawa Nijō-Ōhashi Hotori; s/tw/d from ¥10,395/16,170/26,565; 10min walk from Kyoto-Shiyakusho-mae Station, Tōzai subway line;

Located on the banks of the Kamo-gawa, this hotel has rooms of an acceptable to decent standard and a great on-site bar. The hotel is usually rather quiet and has a restful feeling. It's a short walk to the Downtown Kyoto entertainment district. Japanese-style rooms are available.

KARASUMA KYOTO HOTEL

Map p50 Hotel ¥¥

☎ 371-0111; www.kyotohotel.co.jp/karasuma/index_e.html; Nakagyō-ku, Karasuma-dōri-Shijō kudaru; s/tw/d ¥10,164/18,480/23,100; 5min walk from Shijō Station, Karasuma subway line;

This busy place occupies the middle ground between a business hotel and a standard hotel, with clean, well-maintained rooms. It's very popular with business people and travellers, many of whom enjoy the convenience of a Starbucks right in the lobby.

STAY IN A MACHIYA

Machiya, Kyoto's traditional town houses, are the wooden heart of the city. Built entirely of traditional materials, they are naturally soothing and incredibly pleasing to the eyes. Now, thanks to Alex Kerr's Iori (www.kyoto-machiya.com/www_english/index.html; per person per night ¥5700-65,000), it is possible to spend the night in a *machiya*.

Iori has purchased and completely renovated seven beautiful *machiya* in various parts of Kyoto and turned them into elegant accommodation. Each is available for exclusive rental to groups or individuals – kind of like having your own private *machiya* for a night or longer.

The *machiya* have been updated for comfort and include showers, Western-style toilets and beds. The decorations are beautiful and the buildings themselves are stunning. This is a great chance to experience a night in a bit of living Kyoto history. For more information on *machiya*, see the boxed text, p34.

HOTEL UNIZO Map p50 Hotel ¥¥

☎ 241-3351; www.hotelunizo.com/eng/kyoto/index.html; Nakagyō-ku, Kawaramachi-dōri-Sanjō kudaru; s/d ¥8505/12,810; 5min walk from Sanjō Station, Keihan line;

They don't get more convenient than this business hotel: it's smack in the middle of Kyoto's nightlife, shopping and dining district – you can walk to hundreds of restaurants and shops within five minutes. It's a standard-issue business hotel, with tiny but adequate rooms and unit baths. Nothing special here, but it's clean, well run and used to foreign guests. Front rooms can be noisy, so see if you can get something on an upper floor or at the back.

MATSUI HONKAN Map p50 Ryokan ¥¥

☎ 221-3535; www.matsui-inn.com/index_english.php; Nakagyō-ku, Yanaginobanba Rokkaku kudaru; r per person incl breakfast from ¥11,000; 8min walk from Shijō Station, Karasuma subway line;

This is the main branch of the Hotel Matsui (below). It's slightly more elegant and Japanese in style but essentially offers the same experience. Rates per person rise to ¥16,000 if you'd prefer to be served both breakfast and dinner.

HOTEL MATSUI Map p50 Ryokan ¥¥

☎ 221-6688; www.matsui-inn.com/index_english.php; Nakagyō-ku, Rokkaku Takakura Higashi iru; r per person incl breakfast from ¥8000; 5min walk from Karasuma-Oike Station, Karasuma subway line;

This centrally located ryokan-style hotel has spacious Japanese-style rooms and a friendly staff, some of whom speak English. It's getting more popular with foreign guests, who appreciate the reasonable rates. For ¥14,000 per person you can have dinner as well as breakfast at the hotel.

CENTRAL KYOTO

The area we refer to as Central Kyoto in this guide covers a huge section of the city. The neighbourhoods contained here vary tremendously from relatively quiet residential areas to busy Downtown commercial districts. We try to give some idea of the location in the following reviews.

KYOTO BRIGHTON HOTEL

Map pp54–5 Hotel ¥¥¥

☎ 441-4411; www.kyotobrighton.com; Kamigyō-ku, Shinmachi-dōri, Nakatachiuri; tw/d/tr from ¥38,115/34,650/49,665; 8min walk from Imadegawa Station, Karasuma subway line;

The Brighton is a large hotel located on the west side of the Kyoto Imperial Palace, something of an out-of-the-way location. The lobby here is vast, with a couple of restaurants. The rooms are similarly large and well appointed, and service is good. We reckon the rooms here are bit overpriced, but if you can get a good rate, you might consider it. Take exit 6 from the station.

HOTEL NIKKO PRINCESS KYOTO

Map pp54–5 Hotel ¥¥¥

☎ 342-2111; www.princess-kyoto.co.jp/en/index.html; Shimogyō-ku, Karasuma Takatsuji Higashi iru; s/d from ¥20,790/34,650; 3min walk from Shijō Station, Karasuma subway line;

Nikko's entry into the Kyoto market is a welcome addition and maintains the chain's high standards. Centrally located only a short walk from most Downtown attractions, this smart, understated hotel has excellent service and good on-site restaurants. The standard rooms here are on the small side, as is common in Japan, but they are clean and well outfitted. All in all, this is a great choice if you want to be downtown. Take exit 5 as you leave Shijō Station.

HOLIDAY INN KYOTO Map pp54–5 Hotel ¥¥

☎ 721-3131; onetoone@hi-kyoto.co.jp; Sakyō-ku, Takano, Nishihiraki-chō 36; tw/d¥9000/12,000; 🚌 5min walk from Takanobashi-Higashizume bus stop, Kyoto bus 17 from Kyoto Station; 💻

Up in the north end of town, near Takano, this hotel has good facilities but is a bit of a hike to the major attractions. The rooms are pretty standard, with nice bathtubs and windows that open to let in the north Kyoto breezes. A short walk away you'll find a large American-style shopping mall with loads of restaurants. There's a shuttle bus to and from Kyoto Station.

RYOKAN HINOMOTO

Map pp54–5 Ryokan ¥¥

☎ 351-4563; fax 351-3932; Shimogyō-ku, Kawaramachi-dōri, Matsubara agaru; d/tr from ¥8000/12,000; 🚌 1min walk from Kawaramachi-Matsubara bus stop, bus 17 or 205 from Kyoto Station

This cute little ryokan is very conveniently located for shopping and dining in Downtown Kyoto, as well as sightseeing on the east side of town. It has a nice wooden bathtub and simple rooms. It's not the most private place in town, but it's decent value.

RYOKAN RAKUCHŌ Map pp54–5 Ryokan ¥

☎ 721-2174; www003.upp.so-net.ne.jp/rakucho-ryokan/indx.html; Sakyō-ku, Shimogamo, Higashi hangi chō 67; s/tw/tr from ¥5300/8400/12,600; Ⓢ 7min walk from Kitaōji Station, Karasuma subway line; 💻

There is a lot to appreciate about this fine little foreigner-friendly ryokan in the northern part of town: it's entirely nonsmoking; there is a nice little garden; and the rooms are clean and simple. Meals aren't served, but staff can provide you with a good map of local eateries. The downside is the somewhat out-of-the-way location.

PALACE SIDE HOTEL Map pp54–5 Hotel ¥

☎ 415-8887; www.palacesidehotel.co.jp/english/fr-top-en.html; Kamigyō-ku, Karasuma-dōri, Shimotachiuri agaru; s/tw/d from ¥5040/7350/6825; Ⓢ 3min walk from Marutamachi Station, Karasuma subway line; 💻

Overlooking the Kyoto Imperial Palace Park, this excellent-value budget hotel has a lot going for it, starting with a friendly English-speaking staff, great service, washing machines, an on-site restaurant, well-maintained rooms and free internet terminals. The rooms are small but serviceable.

SHŌHŌ-IN Map pp54–5 Shukubō ¥

☎ /fax 811-7768; Shimogyō-ku, Matsubara-dōri, Ōmiya Nishi iru, Bōmon-chō 845; r per person incl breakfast ¥4725; 🚌 5min walk from Ōmiya-Matsubara bus stop, bus 6 or 206 from Kyoto Station

If you want a break from the usual hotel/ryokan experience, try this *shukubō,* which offers clean rooms and a decent location. The temple also offers lessons in Japanese calligraphy. You must have at least two people in your party to stay here. To inquire in English, call Ms Katō (☎ 090-3947 4520).

TANI HOUSE Map pp54–5 Guesthouse ¥

☎ 492-5489; Kita-ku, Murasakino, Daitokuji-chō 8; dm ¥1800, d ¥4200-4600; 🚌 5min walk from Kenkunjinja-mae bus stop, bus 206 from Kyoto Station; 💻

This place is an old favourite for both short-term and long-term visitors on a tight budget. There is a certain charm to this fine old house with its warren of rooms and quiet location next to Daitoku-ji (p53). You might have to ask at the police box near the temple for directions once you get into the area.

CASA DE NATSU Map pp54–5 Guesthouse ¥

☎ 491-2549; natu@sa3.so-net.ne.jp; Koyamamotomachi Kita-ku; r per person incl breakfast ¥4500; Ⓢ Kitayama Station, Karasuma subway line, exit 4; 💻 ⊠

Up in the north of town, this cosy little Japanese-style guesthouse is a good spot for those who want to escape the hubbub of Downtown. There are two rooms, each decorated in the traditional style, and a fine little garden.

CROSSROADS INN Map pp54–5 Guesthouse ¥

www.rose.sannet.ne.jp/c-inn/; Shimogyō-ku, Banba-chō, Ebisu 45-14; r per person from ¥4000; Ⓢ 20min walk from Kyoto Station; ⊠

Crossroads Inn is a charming little guesthouse with clean, well-maintained rooms and a friendly owner. The entire inn is nonsmoking. It's good value but a little hard to find: turn north off Shichijō-dōri just west of the Umekōji-kōen-mae bus stop across from the Daily Yamazaki convenience store. Reservations are by email only.

SOUTHERN HIGASHIYAMA

Southern Higashiyama, in the southeast of Kyoto, is an excellent place to be based if you're keen to have easy access to the city's most important sightseeing areas. The other bonus is that it's also quieter and more attractive than Downtown or the Kyoto Station area.

HYATT REGENCY KYOTO

Map p62 Hotel ¥¥¥

☎ 541-1234; www.hyattregencykyoto.com/english/index.php; Higashiyama-ku, Sanjūsangendō-mawari 644-2; r ¥22,000-43,000, deluxe ¥26,000-49,000; 5min walk from Shichijō Station, Keihan line;

The new Hyatt Regency is an excellent, stylish foreigner-friendly hotel at the southern end of Kyoto's Southern Higashiyama sightseeing district. Many travellers consider this to be the best hotel in Kyoto, and almost all mention the great restaurants and its fabulous Tōzan bar (see the boxed text, p140). The rooms and bathrooms have lots of neat touches. The concierges are helpful and they'll even lend you a laptop to check your email if you don't have your own (the hotel has wi-fi). The only downside we can see is the location – it's a bit of a hike to the main sightseeing district. However, there are plenty of transport options nearby, including the Keihan train line down the hill and buses that ply Higashiōji-dōri.

SEIKŌRŌ Map p62 Ryokan ¥¥¥

☎ 561-0771; www.seikoro.com/top-e.htm; Higashiyama-ku, Toiyamachi-dōri, Gojō kudaru, Nishi Tachibana-chō 3 chō-me 467; r per person incl meals from ¥31,500; Kawaramachi-Gojō bus stop, bus 17 or 205 from Kyoto Station;

The Seikōrō is a classic ryokan that welcomes foreign guests. It's a fairly spacious place, with excellent, comfortable rooms and attentive service. The location is a bit odd – next to the river a little south of Gojō-dōri, but it's only a short walk to Keihan line Gōjo Station and Gion.

RYOKAN MOTONAGO Map p62 Ryokan ¥¥¥

☎ 561-2087; www.motonago.com; Higashiyama-ku, Kōdaiji-michi, Washio-chō 511; r per person incl meals from ¥21,000; Gion bus stop, bus 206 from Kyoto Station;

This ryokan may have the best location of any in the city, and it hits all the right notes for one in this class: classic Japanese décor, friendly service, nice bathtubs and a few small Japanese gardens.

RYOKAN UEMURA Map p62 Ryokan ¥¥

☎ /fax 561-0377; Higashiyama-ku, Shimogawara, Ishibe-kōji; r per person incl breakfast ¥9000; 5min walk from Higashiyama-Yasui bus stop, bus 206 from Kyoto Station

This beautiful little ryokan is at ease with foreign guests. It's on a quaint cobblestone alley, just down the hill from Kōdai-ji (p64). Book well in advance, as there are only three rooms. Note that the manager prefers bookings by fax and asks that cancellations also be made by fax – with so few rooms, it can be costly when bookings are broken without notice. There's a 10pm curfew.

HIGASHIYAMA YOUTH HOSTEL

Map p62 Youth Hostel ¥

☎ 761-8135; fax 761-8138; Higashiyama-ku, Sanjō-dōri Shirakawabashi, Goken-chō 112; dm from ¥3360; 3min walk from Higashiyama-Sanjō bus stop, bus 5 from Kyoto Station;

This spiffy hostel is an excellent base for the sights in eastern Kyoto. Unfortunately, it's also rather regimented and certainly not a good spot to stay if you want some nightlife (there is a 10.30pm curfew). You can walk here from the Sanjō Keihan area. Bicycle rental is available.

NORTHERN HIGASHIYAMA

The northeast of Kyoto is another excellent area in which to be based. Northern Higashiyama is much quieter than bustling Downtown Kyoto, and you will benefit from the convenience of being near the main sightseeing spots of the Higashiyama district, such as Ginkaku-ji and Nanzen-ji.

WESTIN MIYAKO KYOTO

Map pp68–9 Hotel ¥¥¥

☎ 771-7111; www.westinmiyako-kyoto.com/english/index.html; Higashiyama-ku, Sanjō-dōri, Keage; s/tw/deluxe from ¥26,600/32,400/52,000; 1min walk from Keage Station, Tōzai subway line;

This sprawling complex is perched atop the Higashiyama area, making it one of the best locations for sightseeing in Kyoto. The hotel is at home with foreign guests. Rooms are clean and well maintained, but some visitors complain that the standard rooms are getting a little scruffy. The deluxe rooms are a major step up and Japanese-style rooms are available, starting at ¥52,000. On the downside, the main breakfast restaurant is dimly lit and some complain about the level of service, which isn't helped by the usually busy scene at the front desk.

YACHIYO RYOKAN Map pp68–9 Ryokan ¥¥¥

☎ 771-4148; www.biwa.ne.jp/~yachiyo/oideyasu-e.html; Sakyō-ku, Nanzen-ji, Fukuchi-machi 34; r incl meals from ¥18,000; 5min walk from Keage Station, Tōzai subway line

Located just down the street from Nanzen-ji (p66), this large ryokan is at home with foreign guests. Rooms are spacious and clean, and some look out over private gardens. English-speaking staff are available.

HOTEL HEIAN NO MORI KYOTO

Map pp68–9 Hotel ¥¥¥

☎ 761-9111; fax 761-1333; Sakyō-ku, Okazaki, Higashitenno-chō 51; d/tw from ¥15,750/16,800; 2min walk from Higashi-Tennō-chō bus stop, bus 5 from Kyoto Station

This large, pleasant hotel is located close to Ginkaku-ji, Nanzen-ji and the Tetsugaku-no-michi (Path of Philosophy). The hotel is getting a little long in the tooth, but the location is excellent. The rooftop beer garden has a great view of the city in summer.

THREE SISTERS INN MAIN BUILDING

Map pp68–9 Ryokan ¥¥

Rakutō-sō; ☎ 761-6336; fax 761-6338; Sakyō-ku, Okazaki, Higashi-Fukunokawa-chō 18; s/d/tr from ¥8900/13,000/19,500; 5min walk from Kumanojinja-mae bus stop, bus 206 from Kyoto Station

Perfectly situated for exploration of eastern Kyoto, this long-time favourite of foreign travellers is a good choice for those who want to try a ryokan without any language difficulties. It's very close to the interesting Yoshida-Yama area and not far from Heian-jingū (p72) and Okazaki-kōen (p72).

THREE SISTERS INN ANNEX

Map pp68–9 Ryokan ¥¥

Rakutō-sō Bekkan; ☎ 761-6333; fax 761-6335; Sakyō-ku, Okazaki, Irie-chō 89; s/d/tr ¥10,810/18,170/23,805; 5min walk from Dōbutsu-en-mae bus stop, bus 5 from Kyoto Station

An annexe of the Three Sisters Inn (left), this ryokan is well run, comfortable and used to foreigners. It has a pleasant breakfast nook that overlooks a wonderful Japanese garden. The bamboo-lined walkway is another highlight. It's right behind Heian-jingū (p72) and relatively close to the sights of Northern Higashiyama.

KYOTO TRAVELLER'S INN

Map pp68–9 Business Hotel ¥¥

☎ 771-0225; traveler@mbox.kyoto-inet.or.jp; Sakyō-ku, Okazaki, Enshō-ji-chō; s/tw ¥5775/10,500; 2min walk from Kyotokaikan/Bijyutsukan-mae bus stop, bus 5 from Kyoto Station;

This small business hotel is very close to Heian-jingū (p72) and offers Western- and Japanese-style rooms (the latter getting better reviews by readers). The restaurant on the 1st floor is open till 10pm. It's good value for the price and the location is dynamite for exploring the Higashiyama area.

YONBANCHI Map pp68–9 B&B ¥

www.thedivyam.com; Sakyō-ku, Shinnyō-chō 4; per person ¥5000; Kinrinshako-mae bus stop, bus 5 or 57 from Kyoto Station;

Yonbanchi is a charming B&B ideally located for sightseeing in the Ginkaku-ji (p71) and Yoshida-Yama area. One of the two guest rooms looks out over a small Japanese garden. The house is a late-Edo-period samurai house located just outside the main gate of Shinnyo-dō, a temple famed for its maple leaves and cherry blossoms. There is a private entrance, wi-fi and no curfew. Reservation by email only.

B&B JUNO Map pp68–9 B&B ¥

www.gotokandk.com; Sakyō-ku, Jōdo-ji, Nishida-chō; r per person ¥5000; Shirakawa-mae bus stop, bus 17 from Kyoto Station

Located close to Ginkaku-ji (p71), just east of Kyoto University, facing a green hill park in a quiet traditional neighbourhood, this large B&B, in an old private compound, has three bright Japanese-style rooms. It is run by a charming international couple with a wealth of inside information on Kyoto. B&B Juno also has wi-fi.

NORTHWEST KYOTO

Northwest Kyoto is no rival for Downtown or the Higashiyama areas in terms of convenience to nightlife and sightseeing. Kyoto's excellent public transport system, however, means the accommodation in this section is all reasonably handy to other parts of the city. There are two good hotels near Nijō-jō and a few other choices scattered across the area.

KYOTO ANA HOTEL Map p74 Hotel ¥¥¥

☎ 231-1155; www.ana-hkyoto.com/; Nakagyō-ku, Horikawa-dōri, Nijōjō-mae; s/tw/d from ¥15,015/26,565/24,255; 3min walk from Nijōjō-mae Station, Tōzai subway line;

Directly opposite Nijō-jō on the west side of Downtown Kyoto, this large hotel gets plenty of foreign guests. Rooms are typical for a hotel of this class, and there are all the usual on-site facilities (pool, restaurants and bars). There's also something you won't find at most other hotels: an on-site fortune-teller. The free shuttle to Kyoto Station is a welcome service for those doing a bit of exploring.

MYŌREN-JI Map p74 Shukubō ¥

☎ 451-3527; fax 451-3597; Kamigyō-ku, Teranouchi-dōri, Horikawa Nishi-iru; r per person ¥3800; 5min walk from Horikawa-Teranouchi bus stop, bus 9 from Kyoto Station

This pleasant temple is used to dealing with foreign guests. It's right in the heart of the Nishijin area, for those with an interest in Kyoto textiles and *machiya*. The garden here is lovely. There is no air-con.

UTANO YOUTH HOSTEL

Map p74 Youth Hostel ¥

☎ 462-2288; web.kyoto-inet.or.jp/org/utano-yh/; Ukyō-ku, Uzumasa, Nakayama-chō 29; dm ¥2800; 1min walk from Yūsu-Hosuteru-mae bus stop, bus 26 from Kyoto Station

The best hostel in Kyoto, Utano is friendly and well organised and makes a convenient base for the sights of northwestern Kyoto. If you want to skip the hostel food, turn left along the main road to find several coffee shops offering cheap *teishoku* (set-course meals). There is a 10pm curfew.

ARASHIYAMA & SAGANO

Nestled at the base of the western mountains, the Arashiyama and Sagano area is one of Kyoto's most important sightseeing areas. It's quite scenic, with lots of bamboo groves and temples. It's something of a hike to the rest of town, though, so we only recommend staying here if you either want to concentrate your sightseeing in the west of town, or if you don't mind spending a fair bit of time on trains or buses.

HOTEL RAN-TEI Map p80 Hotel ¥¥¥

☎ 371-1119; hotelrantei@kyoto-centuryhotel.co.jp; Ukyō-ku, Saga Tenryū-ji, Susukinobaba-chō 12; r per person ¥16,000-34,000; 10min walk from Keifuku Arashiyama Station, Keifuku Arashiyama line;

The excellent Ran-tei has spacious gardens and both Japanese- and Western-style accommodation. The rooms are spacious and quiet here and there is a great view from the bath. The Japanese-style breakfast may not suit all palates but it is filling.

ARASHIYAMA BENKEI RYOKAN

Map p80 Ryokan ¥¥¥

☎ 872-3355; www.benkei.biz/; Ukyō-ku, Saga Tenryū-ji, Susukinobaba-chō 34; r per person incl meals from ¥21,000; 15min walk from Keifuku Arashiyama Station, Keifuku Arashiyama line

This elegant ryokan has a pleasant riverside location and serves wonderful *kaiseki* cuisine. The service is kind and friendly and the river view from all rooms is great. The rooms are spacious and the whole place is scented with Japanese incense.

RANKYŌ-KAN RYOKAN

Map p80 Ryokan ¥¥¥

☎ 871-0001; yoyaku@rankyokan.com; Nishikyō-ku, Arashiyama Ganrokuzan-chō 11-2; r per person incl meals from ¥18,000; 7min walk from Keifuku Arashiyama Station, Keifuku Arashiyama line

Sitting in a secluded area on the south bank of the Oi-gawa in Arashiyama, this is a classic Japanese-style inn that boasts manicured gardens, hot-spring baths and river views from most rooms. Walk five minutes up the riverside path or, better still, call ahead and be chauffeured by private boat from Togetsu-kyō (p79)!

MINSHUKU ARASHIYAMA

Map p80 Minshuku ¥

☎/fax 861-4398; info@arasiyama.net; Ukyō-ku, Saga Kitahori-chō 38; r per person ¥4725; 5min walk from Sagaekimae Station, Keifuku Arashiyama line

This little *minshuku* is great for its convenient location and pleasant rooms. It's full of homey atmosphere with home-cooked meals (rooms per person including breakfast and dinner cost ¥7350). Suitable for long stays.

ROKUŌ-IN Map p80 Women-Only Shukubō ¥

☎/fax 861-1645; Ukyō-ku, Saga Kitahori-chō 24; r per person incl breakfast ¥4500; 3min walk from Rokuōin Station, Keifuku Arashiyama line

Close to Arashiyama, this is one of the few women-only *shukubō* in town. It's quiet enough but the rooms are divided only by *fusuma* (sliding doors). You can see the Zen garden from each room, which is lovely. The curfew is 7.30pm.

KITAYAMA AREA

If you decide you'd like to stay outside Kyoto City proper, there are several choices in the Kitayama Mountains north of town. The two villages of Ōhara and Kibune have a variety of nice places to choose from. It's cooler here in the summer than down in Kyoto, as well as being quieter and more peaceful. You really need to have a reason for staying this far out of town, however, since you'll be facing at least an hour each way to/from the city for sightseeing.

ŌHARA

The quaint little village of Ōhara would be a charming spot to spend a quiet night or two outside Kyoto City.

SERYŌ RYOKAN Map p84 Ryokan ¥¥¥

☎ 744-2301; www.seryo.co.jp/english.htm; Sakyō-ku, Ōhara Sanzen-in hotori; r per person incl meals from ¥19,250; 10min walk from Ōhara bus stop, Kyoto bus 17 or 18 from Kyoto Station

A stone's throw from Sanzen-in (p83), this would be a good spot to stay for those who really want to linger over the temples of Ōhara. There is a lovely garden and a small, cosy outdoor bathtub. The friendly owner speaks some English.

ŌHARA SANSŌ Map p84 Ryokan ¥¥

☎ 744-2227; www.ohara-sansou.com/english/index.htm; Sakyō-ku, Ōhara, Kusao-chō 17; r per person incl meals from ¥9000; 13min walk from Ōhara bus stop, Kyoto bus 17 or 18 from Kyoto Station

A pleasant inn, Ōhara Sansō has a soothing outdoor bath. Unfortunately, the rooms are on the small side and the walls are thin. It's just before Jakkō-in (p84); look for the large *tanuki* (racoon dog) figure out the front.

RYOSŌ CHADANI Map p84 Ryokan ¥¥

☎ 744-2952; info@r-chatani.com; Sakyō-ku, Ōhara, Kusao-chō 160; r per person incl meals ¥6825; 5min walk from Ōhara bus stop, Kyoto bus 17 or 18 from Kyoto Station;

Not far from the Ōhara bus stop, Ryosō Chadani is part of the Welcome Inn Group of hotels. The atmosphere is homey and the service is friendly. Free bicycle rental is available. Look for the large stones out the front.

KURAMA & KIBUNE

Like Ōhara, Kibune is something of a getaway from Kyoto proper. There are several ryokan located along the banks of the Kibune-gawa, most of which offer dining on platforms suspended above the river in summer. Again, as with Ōhara, you'd need a specific reason for staying this far out of town.

AIRPORT HOTELS

If you find yourself in need of a bed close to your flight from Itami or Kansai airports, there are a couple of decent options.

Hotel Crevette (☎ 06-6843-7201; fax 6843-0043; Osaka-fu, Ikeda-shi, Kūkō 1-9-6; s/d from ¥7500/13,860;) Right across from the airport (within walking distance – 10 minutes from the south terminal – if you had to), this friendly little hotel is the best deal near Itami. Prices are discounted if you reserve through the main tourist information counter at the airport. Rooms are small but sufficient for a night before an early departure. The helpful folks at the information counter can also arrange for the hotel's shuttle bus to come and pick you up.

Hotel Nikkō Kansai Airport (☎ 0724-55-1111; www.nikkokix.com/e/top.html; Osaka-fu, Izumisano-shi, Senshū Kūkō Kita 1; s/tw/d from ¥21,945/32,340/30,030;) The only hotel at the airport is the excellent Hotel Nikkō Kansai Airport, just a five-minute walk from the international arrivals hall. The rooms here are in good condition, are fairly spacious and are comfortable enough for brief stays. It's somewhat overpriced, but you can't beat the convenience. Try to book online or ask for a promo rate.

RYOKAN UGENTA Map p85 Ryokan ¥¥¥

☎ 741-2146; Sakyō-ku, Kurama, Kibune-chō 76; r per person incl meals from ¥39,900; Kibune-guchi Station, Eizan line;

The Ugenta is an attractive old inn with a wonderful stone bathtub. There are only two rooms here, one Japanese-style and one Western-style. Both have private cypress-wood outdoor bathtubs. The Ugenta offers a free shuttle bus to and from the station.

HIROYA RYOKAN Map p85 Ryokan ¥¥¥

☎ 741-2401; hiroya-goroh@kyoto.zaq.ne; Sakyō-ku, Kurama, Kibune-chō 56; r per person from ¥33,000; Kibune-guchi Station, Eizan line

This is a pleasant ryokan famous for its food. In winter it serves either a *kaiseki* or *botan-nabe* (wild boar cooked in an iron pot) dinner, while in summer the fare is *kawa-doko-ryōri* (rivertop dining). The rooms are very comfortable and the service is good here. There's a free shuttle-bus service to and from the station.

KIBUNE FUJIYA Map p85 Ryokan ¥¥¥

☎ 741-2501; fujiya@kibune.or.jp; Sakyō-ku, Kurama, Kibune-chō 40; r per person incl meals from ¥24,675; Kibune-guchi Station, Eizan line

This is another nice ryokan with a lovely riverside location and a free shuttle-bus service from the station. The food is tasty and the rooms are cosy at this long-running spot. It's right in front of the *torii* (shrine gate) of Kibune-jinja (p86).

EXCURSIONS

Kyoto is located in the centre of Japan's Kansai region, which is the cultural heartland of Japan. The Japanese nation was literally born in Kansai and much of its history played out here. Thus, it's hardly surprising that Kyoto is surrounded by some of Japan's most important and interesting sights.

Less than an hour away by train lies Nara, Japan's first permanent capital. Here you'll find a wonderful collection of sights packed into the green expanse of Nara-kōen, a park where hundreds of deer roam free. It's easily the most rewarding day trip out of Kyoto.

Also less than an hour from Kyoto by train, Osaka is a great place to sample the Japanese urban experience – if you're not going to Tokyo, you'll want to spend a day and evening here soaking up the *Blade Runner* ambience.

Another half an hour down the same train line, the cosmopolitan seaside city of Kōbe offers pleasant strolling and excellent international food.

Continuing west past Kōbe for an hour or so brings you to Himeji, home to Japan's most magnificent castle; it's an absolute must for fans of samurai epics and those with kids in tow.

Finally, if you crave a bit of country Japan, the rural vistas and thatch-roofed houses of Miyama-chō are a great way to take a break from the city.

NARA

☎ 0742

If it weren't for the incredible riches of Kyoto so close by, Nara might be considered Japan's top destination. The first permanent capital of Japan, Nara is the stage on which the opening act of Japan's imperial drama was played out. It is much smaller than Kyoto and most of the sights are located in Nara-kōen, which can easily be explored on foot. Leading the list, which includes no fewer than eight Unesco World Heritage sites, are Tōdai-ji, with its awesome *daibutsu* (Great Buddha), and Kasuga Taisha, a sprawling shrine hidden amid deep forest.

Nara's two main train stations, JR Nara Station and Kintetsu Nara Station, are roughly in the middle of the city. Nara-kōen is on the east side against the bare flank of a mountain called Wakakusa-yama. Most of the other sights are southwest of the city and are best reached by buses that leave from both train stations (or by train in the case of Hōryū-ji). It's easy to cover the city centre and the major attractions in nearby Nara-kōen on foot, though some visitors may prefer to rent a bicycle (see p160).

Nara-kōen Area

Nara's most important sights are located in Nara-kōen, a sprawling park that covers much of the east side of the city. Created from wasteland in 1880, the park covers a large area at the foot of Wakakusa-yama. The Japan National Tourist Organization (JNTO) leaflet *Walking Tour Courses in Nara* (also available at the Kyoto TIC; see p199) includes a map for this area. Although walking time is estimated at two hours, you'll need at least half a day to see a selection of the sights and a full day to see the lot.

The park is home to about 1200 deer, which in old times were considered to be messengers of the gods and today enjoy the status of national treasures. They roam the park and surrounding areas in search of hand-outs from tourists. You can buy special biscuits called *shika-sembei* (¥150) from vendors to feed the deer (don't eat them yourself, as we saw one misguided foreign tourist doing).

Nara's main attraction – and a must-see for any visitor to the city – is Tōdai-ji (☎ 22-5511; Zōshi-chō 406-1; 🕑 8am-4.30pm Nov-Feb, to 5pm Mar, 7.30am-5.30pm Apr-Sep, 7.30am-5pm Oct), a huge temple complex on the north side of Nara-kōen. On your way to the temple you'll pass through the Nandai-mon, which contains two fierce-looking Niō guardians. The gate's recently restored wooden images, carved in the 13th century by the sculptor Unkei, are some of the finest wooden statues in all of Japan, if not the world. These truly dramatic works of art seem ready to spring to life at any moment.

Tōdai-ji's Daibutsu-den (Hall of the Great Buddha; admission ¥500) is the largest wooden building in the world. Unbelievably, the present structure, rebuilt in 1709, is a mere two-thirds the size of the original! The *daibutsu* (Great Buddha) contained within is one of the largest

FUKUI-KEN
Fukui (31km)
Expressway
Nagahama
Biwa-ko
Maibara
Hikone
Takashima
Chimiguchi
Kitamura
Dea
Ashiū
Fukuchiyama
Ayabe
Miyama-chō (p178)
Agake
Sasari-tōgei Pass
0 10 km
0 6 miles
Wachi
27
9
KYOTO-FU
8
Shūzan
Hanase-tōgei Pass
Ōmihachiman
HYŌGO-KEN
Kurama
Ōhara
9
Moriyama
Meishin Expressway
Kusatsu
Nishiwaki
Kameoka
Ōtsu
KYOTO
Minakuchi
SHIGA-KEN
Sanda
Chūgoku Expressway
OSAKA-FU
Uji
Himeji (p176)
Kawanishi
To Okayama (65km); Hiroshima (190km)
Kansai
Jōyō
Takarazuka
Ono
Itami
24
Ueno
Nishinomiya
MIE-KEN
Kōbe (p173)
Osaka (p165)
2
Nara (p158)
Akashi
NARA-KEN
Osaka-wan
Nabari
26
Awaji-shima
To Kansai International Airport (32km)
To Wakayama (52km)

TRANSPORT: NARA

Getting There

Distance from Kyoto 37km

Direction South

Train Unless you have a Japan Rail Pass (see p188), the best option is the Kintetsu line (sometimes written in English as the Kinki Nippon railway), which links Kyoto (Kintetsu Kyoto Station) and Nara (Kintetsu Nara Station). Take either a *tokkyū* (direct limited express train; ¥1110, 33 minutes) or *kyūkō* (ordinary express train; ¥610, 40 minutes). The latter may require a change at Saidai-ji. Kintetsu Kyoto Station is on the southwest corner of the main Kyoto Station building; go to the south side of the station – the *shinkansen* (bullet train) side – and follow the signs. The JR Nara line also connects Kyoto Station with JR Nara Station. Your best bet is a *kaisoku* (rapid train; ¥690, 53 minutes), but departures are often few and far between.

Getting Around

Bus Most of the area around Nara-kōen is covered by two circular bus routes. Bus 1 runs counter-clockwise and bus 2 runs clockwise. There's a ¥170 flat fare. You can easily see the main sights in the park on foot and use the bus as an option if you are pressed for time or tired.

Cycle Nara is a convenient size for getting around on a bicycle. Eki Renta Car (☎ 26-3929; Honmachi 1-1, Sanjo; ⌚ 8am-8pm) is very close to JR Nara Station and rents regular bicycles for ¥300 per day – unbelievable value. If you can't be bothered to pedal along Nara's mostly flat streets, you can opt for an electric bicycle (¥1500 per day).

bronze figures in the world and was originally cast in 746. The present statue, recast in the Edo period, stands just over 16m high and consists of 437 tonnes of bronze and 130kg of gold.

As you circle the statue, towards the back of the Buddha you'll see a wooden column with a hole through its base. Popular belief maintains that those who can squeeze through the hole, which is exactly the same size as one of the Great Buddha's nostrils, are ensured of enlightenment. It's fun to watch the kids wiggle through nimbly and the adults get wedged in like champagne corks. A hint for determined adults: it's a lot easier to go through with both arms held above your head.

From the entrance to Daibutsu-den, walk east and climb a flight of stone steps, and continue to your left to reach the following two halls. Nigatsu-dō (admission free) is famed for its Omizutori festival (p164) and a splendid view across Nara that makes the climb worthwhile – particularly at dusk. A short walk south of Nigatsu-dō is Sangatsu-dō (admission ¥500) which is the oldest building in the Tōdai-ji complex. This hall contains a small collection of fine statues from the Nara period.

About 15 minutes' walk roughly south of Sangatsu-dō is Kasuga Taisha (☎ 22-7788; Kasugano-chō 160; admission free; ⌚ 6am-6pm), Nara's most important shrine. It was founded in the 8th century by the Fujiwara family and was completely rebuilt every 20 years according to Shintō tradition, until the end of the 19th century. It lies at the foot of the hill in a pleasant wooded setting with herds of sacred deer awaiting hand-outs.

The approaches to the shrine are lined with hundreds of lanterns and there are many more hundreds in the shrine itself. The lantern festivals held twice a year at the shrine are a major attraction (see p164), as are other festivals held at the nearby Wakamiya-jinja (Map p162).

Nara's most splendid garden, Isui-en (☎ 22-2173; Suimon-chō 74; admission incl Neiraku Art Museum ¥650; ⌚ 9.30am-4pm, closed Tue), is a short walk north of Tōdai-ji. The garden dates from the Meiji era and is beautifully laid out with abundant greenery and a pond filled with ornamental carp. It's without a doubt the best garden in the city and is well worth a visit. Next to Isui-en is the Neiraku Art Museum (admission incl entry to Isui-en ¥650; ⌚ 9.30am-4pm, closed Tue), which displays Chinese and Korean ceramics and bronzes.

Walking to or from Nara-kōen, you can't miss the soaring main pagoda of Kōfuku-ji (☎ 22-7755; Noborioji-chō 48; grounds free; ⌚ dawn-dusk), which was transferred here from Kyoto in 710 as the main temple for the Fujiwara family. Although the original temple complex had 175 buildings, fires and destruction through power struggles have left only a dozen still standing. There are actually two pagodas, a three-storey one dating from 1143 and a five-storey pagoda dating from 1426. The taller of the two pagodas is the second tallest in Japan, outclassed by the one at Kyoto's Tō-ji by only a few centimetres. In the grounds of the temple, Kōfuku-ji National Treasure Hall (Kokuhō-kan; admission ¥500; 9am-4.30pm) contains a variety of statues and art objects salvaged from previous structures.

Just east of Kōfuku-ji, you'll find the Nara National Museum (☎ 22-7771; Noborioji-chō 50; general admission ¥500; 9am-4.30pm), which is divided into two main galleries linked by an underground passage. The western gallery exhibits archaeological finds and the eastern gallery has displays of sculptures, paintings and calligraphy. A special exhibition is held in May and the contents of the Shōsō-in hall, which holds the treasures of Tōdai-ji, are displayed here from around 21 October to 8 November (call the tourist centre to check as these dates vary slightly each year). The exhibits include priceless items from the cultures along the Silk Road. Note that entry to special exhibits costs an additional fee, usually around ¥800.

Naramachi Area

South of Sanjō-dōri and Sarusawa-ike pond, you will find the pleasant neighbourhood of Naramachi with its many well-preserved *machiya* (traditional Japanese town houses). It's a nice place for a stroll before or after hitting the big sights of Nara-kōen and there are several good restaurants in the area to entice hungry travellers (see p164).

Highlights of Naramachi include the Naramachi Shiryō-kan Museum (☎ 22-5509; Nishi-shinya-chō 14; admission free; 10am-4pm, closed Mon), which has a decent collection of bric-a-brac from the area, including a display of old Japanese coins and bills. A good place to check out a *machiya* is the Naramachi Koushi-no-Ie (☎ 22-4820; Gangōji-chō 44; admission free; 9am-5pm, closed Mon). Also in Naramachi is the interesting Naramachi Monogatari-kan (☎ 26-3476; Nakanoshima-chō 2-1; admission free; 9am-5pm Tue-Sun), a small art gallery with changing displays built inside a fine old *machiya*.

Temples Southwest of Nara City

Three of Nara's most important temples, Hōryū-ji, Yakushi-ji and Tōshōdai-ji, are located southwest of Nara, well outside the city centre. All three can be visited in one afternoon. To get to Hōryū-ji, take the JR Kansai line from JR Nara Station to Hōryūji Station (¥210, 10 minutes). From there, bus 73 shuttles the short distance between the station and Hōryū-ji (¥170, five minutes) or you can walk there in 20 minutes. Alternatively, take bus 52, 60, 97 or 98 from either JR Nara Station or Kintetsu Nara Station and get off at the Hōryūji-mae stop (¥760, 50 minutes). From Hōryū-ji you continue by bus 52, 97 or 98 (¥560, 30 minutes) up to Yakushi-ji and Tōshōdai-ji, which are a 10-minute walk apart.

Hōryū-ji (法隆寺; ☎ 75-2555; Ikaruga-chō, Hōryūji-sannai 1-1; admission ¥1000; 8am-4.30pm 22 Feb-3 Nov, to 4pm 4 Nov-21 Feb) was founded in 607 by Prince Shōtoku, considered by many to be the patron saint of Japanese Buddhism. Hōryū-ji is a veritable shrine to Shōtoku and is renowned not only as the oldest temple in Japan, but also as a repository for some of the country's rarest treasures. Several of the temple's wooden buildings have survived earthquakes and fires to become the oldest of their kind in the world. The layout of the temple is divided into two parts, Sai-in (West Temple) and Tō-in (East Temple).

The entrance ticket allows admission to Sai-in, Tō-in and the Great Treasure Hall. A detailed map is provided and a guidebook is available in English and several other languages. The JNTO leaflet *Walking Tour Courses in Nara* includes a basic map for the area around Hōryū-ji.

The main approach to the temple proceeds from the south along a tree-lined avenue and continues through Nandai-mon and Chū-mon, the temple's two main gates, before entering the Sai-in precinct. As you enter the Sai-in, you'll see the Hondō (Main Hall) on your right, and a pagoda on your left. On the eastern side of the Sai-in are the two concrete buildings of the Daihōzō-den (Great Treasure Hall), containing numerous treasures from Hōryū-ji's long history. If you leave this hall and continue east through the Tōdai-mon you reach the Tō-in. The Yumedono (Hall of Dreams) in this temple is where Prince Shōtoku is believed to have meditated and been given help with problem sutras by a kindly, golden apparition.

Yakushi-ji (薬師寺; ☎ 33-6001; Nishinokyō-chō 457; admission ¥500; 8.30am-5pm) was established by Emperor Tenmu in 680. With the exception of the east pagoda, which dates to 730, the present

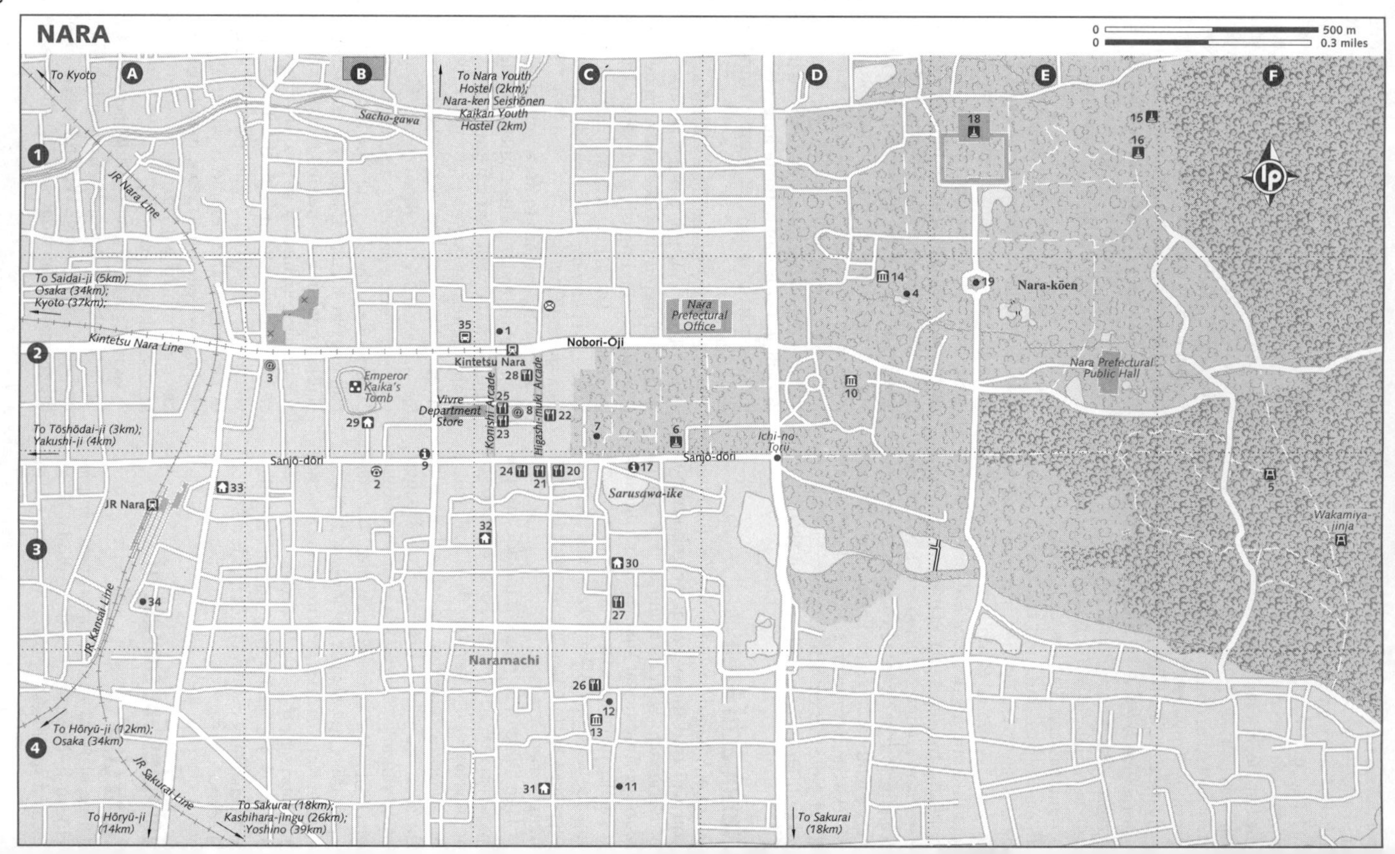
NARA
0 500 m
0 0.3 miles
A
B
C
D
E
F
1
2
3
4
To Kyoto
To Nara Youth Hostel (2km); Nara-ken Seishōnen Kaikan Youth Hostel (2km)
Sacho-gawa
JR Nara Line
To Saidai-ji (5km); Osaka (34km); Kyoto (37km);
Kintetsu Nara Line
Nobori-Ōji
Kintetsu Nara
Nara Prefectural Office
Emperor Kaika's Tomb
Vivre Department Store
Konishi Arcade
Higashi-muki Arcade
To Tōshōdai-ji (3km); Yakushi-ji (4km)
Sanjō-dōri
Ichi-no-Torii
Sarusawa-ike
JR Nara
JR Kansai Line
Naramachi
Nara-kōen
Nara Prefectural Public Hall
Wakamiya-jinja
To Hōryū-ji (12km); Osaka (34km)
JR Sakurai Line
To Hōryū-ji (14km)
To Sakurai (18km); Kashihara-jingu (26km); Yoshino (39km)
To Sakurai (18km)
1
2
3
4
5
6
7
8
9
10
11
12
13
14
15
16
17
18
19
20
21
22
23
24
25
26
27
28
29
30
31
32
33
34
35

NARA

SIGHTS & INFORMATION

Highway Bus Tickets エアポートリムジン切符売り場 ... 1 C2
International ATM 国際 ATM ... (see 1)
International Phone 国際電話 ... 2 B3
Internet Café Suien 水煙 ... 3 B2
Isui-en 依水園 ... 4 D2
Kasuga Taisha 春日大社 ... 5 F3
Kōfuku-ji Five-Storey Pagoda 興福寺五重塔 ... 6 C2
Kōfuku-ji National Treasure Hall 興福寺国宝館 ... 7 C2
Media-Café Cocoon メディアカフェコクーン ... 8 C2
Nara City Tourist Center 奈良市観光センター ... 9 B3
Nara National Museum 奈良国立博物館 ... 10 D2
Naramachi Koushi-no-Ie ならまち資料館 ... 11 C4
Naramachi Monogatari-kan 奈良町物語館 ... 12 C4
Naramachi Shiryō-kan Museum 奈良町資料館 ... 13 C4
Neiraku Art Museum 寧楽美術館 ... 14 D2
Nigatsu-dō 二月堂 ... 15 E1
Sangatsu-dō 三月堂 ... 16 E1
Sarusawa Tourist Information Office 猿沢観光案内所 ... 17 C3
Todai-ji Daibutsu-den 東大寺大仏殿 ... 18 E1
Todai-ji Nandai-mon 東大寺南大門 ... 19 E2

EATING

Ayura Café アユラ カフェ ... 20 C3
Bikkuri Udon Miyoshino びっくりうどん三好野 ... 21 C3
Don ザドン ... 22 C2
Doutor ドトール ... 23 C2
Kyōshō-An 京匠庵 ... 24 C3
Mellow Café メロー カフェ ... 25 C2
Nonohana Ohka ののはな黄花 ... 26 C4
Tempura Asuka 天ぷら飛鳥 ... 27 C3
Tonkatsu Ganko とんかつがんこ ... 28 C2

SLEEPING

Hotel Fujita Nara ホテルフジタ奈良 ... 29 B2
Ryokan Matsumae 旅館松前 ... 30 C3
Ryokan Seikan-so 旅館静観荘 ... 31 C4
Ryokan Tsubakisō 旅館椿荘 ... 32 C3
Super Hotel スーパーホテル ... 33 A3

TRANSPORT

Eki Renta Car 駅レンタカー ... 34 A3
Local Bus Stop 市バス停 ... 35 B2

buildings either date from the 13th century or are very recent reconstructions. The main hall was rebuilt in 1976 and houses several images, including the famous Yakushi Triad (the Buddha Yakushi flanked by the Bodhisattvas of the sun and moon), dating from the 8th century. Behind the east pagoda is the Tōin-do (East Hall), which houses the famous Shō-Kannon image, dating from the 7th century.

Tōshōdai-ji (唐招提寺; ☎ 33-7900; Gojō-chō 13-46; admission ¥600; 8.30am-5pm) was established in 759 by the Chinese priest Ganjin (Jian Zhen), who had been recruited by Emperor Shōmu to reform Buddhism in Japan. Ganjin didn't have much luck with his travel arrangements from China to Japan: five attempts were thwarted by shipwreck, storms and bureaucracy. Despite being blinded by eye disease, he finally made it on the sixth attempt and spread his teachings to Japan. The lacquer sculpture in the Miei-dō hall is a moving tribute to Ganjin: blind and rock steady. It is shown only once a year on 6 June – the anniversary of Ganjin's death.

If you're not lucky enough to be in Nara on that day, it's still well worth visiting this temple to see the fantastic trinity of Buddhas in the Hondō of the temple. The centrepiece is a seated image of Rushana Buddha, which is flanked by two standing Buddha images, Yakushi-Nyorai and Senjū-Kannon.

Tōshōdai-ji is a 10-minute walk north of Yakushi-ji's north gate.

INFORMATION

The best source of information is the Nara City Tourist Center (☎ 22-3900; Sanjō-dōri; 9am-9pm). It's only a short walk from JR Nara or Kintetsu Nara Stations. There are two other information offices in Nara: the JR Nara Station Office (☎ 22-9821; 9am-5pm), and the Sarusawa Tourist Information Office (☎ 26-1991; Sanjō-dōri; 9am-5pm).

While you're at any of the tourist offices, pick up a copy of the useful *Welcome to Nara: Sightseeing Map*.

The tourist centre can put you in touch with volunteer guides who speak English and other languages, but you will have to book in advance. Two such services are the YMCA Goodwill Guides (☎ 45-5920; www.geocities.com/egg_nara) and Nara Student Guides (☎ 26-4753; www.narastudentguide.org). Remember that the guides are volunteers so you should offer to cover the day's expenses (although most temple and museum admissions are waived for registered guides).

There is an ATM that accepts international cards on the ground floor of the building opposite Kintetsu Nara Station. In the same building you can purchase tickets for highway buses (to Tokyo etc), airport buses (to Kansai airport) and tour buses (around Nara and surrounding areas).

You'll find an international telephone located on Sanjō-dōri, in front of the NTT building.

For internet access, try the following places:

Internet Café Suien (☎ 22-2577; 1-58 Aburasaka-chō; per hr ¥200, per 2hr incl 1 drink ¥500; 7.30am-11pm) Inside Hotel Asyl Nara.

Media-Café Cocoon (☎ 27-2039; Konishi-chō 5; per hr incl drink ¥400; 11am-10pm)

FESTIVALS & EVENTS

Nara has plenty of festivals throughout the year. The following is a brief list of the more interesting ones. More extensive information is readily available from Nara tourist offices (see p163) or from the Kyoto Tourist Information Center (TIC; p199).

Yamayaki (Grass Burning Festival) To commemorate a feud many centuries ago between the monks of Tōdai-ji and Kōfuku-ji, Wakakusa-yama is set alight at 6pm on 15 January with an accompanying display of fireworks.

Mantōrō (Lantern Festival) Held at Kasuga Taisha at 6pm from 2 to 4 February, this festival is renowned for its illumination with 3000 stone and bronze lanterns.

Omizutori (Water-Drawing Ceremony) The monks of Tōdai-ji enter a special period of initiation from 1 to 14 March. On the evening of 12 March, they parade enormous flaming torches around the balcony of Nigatsu-dō (in the temple grounds) and embers rain down on the spectators to purify them. The water-drawing ceremony is performed after midnight.

Mantōrō (Lantern Festival) The same as the February festival but takes place on 14 and 15 August.

EATING

Restaurants in this section are open standard hours – from 11am to 2pm and from 5pm to 10pm. Exceptions to this are noted in individual reviews.

Ayura Café (☎ 26-5339; Hashimoto-chō 28; set meals from ¥1000) We highly recommend this tiny café for its wonderful (mostly veggie) set lunch or a quick cuppa.

Kyōshō-An (☎ 27-7715; Hashimoto-chō 26-3; green tea & sweets from ¥420) An upstairs tea shop where you can enjoy green tea and a whole range of Japanese sweets.

Mellow Café (☎ 27-9099; Konishi-chō 1-8; lunch from ¥950) Located down a narrow alley, this open-plan café usually displays their daily lunch special for all to see.

Bikkuri Udon Miyoshino (☎ 22-5239; Hashimoto-chō 27; lunch & dinner from ¥650; closed Wed) A simple place that does good-value sets of typical Japanese fare. Stop by and check the daily lunch specials on display outside.

Tempura Asuka (☎ 26-4308; Shōnami-chō 11; lunch/dinner from ¥1575/3675; closed Mon) Tempura Asuka serves attractive sets of tempura and sashimi in a relatively casual atmosphere. At lunch time try the nicely presented *yumei-dono bentō* (lunch box containing assorted tasty titbits such as sashimi and rice) for ¥1500.

Don (☎ 27-5314; Higashimukiminami-machi 13-2; lunch & dinner from ¥500) The name is short for *donburi* (rice bowl) and this place takes the honours in the cheapest eats category. It's healthy Japanese fast food and there's a picture menu to make ordering easier.

Nonohana Ohka (☎ 22-1139; Nakashinya-chō 13; coffee & tea ¥500) With indoor and outdoor garden seating, this café is one of our favourite places for a drink or a light meal when in Naramachi. It has an English menu.

Tonkatsu Ganko (☎ 25-4129; Higashimukinaka-machi 19; meals from ¥780) This *tonkatsu* (deep-fried breaded pork cutlet) specialist in the Higashimuki arcade is around the corner from Kintetsu Nara and has an English menu.

Lastly, if you just need a quick cuppa or an eat-in or take away sandwich, there is a branch of the coffee shop Doutor close to Kintetsu Nara.

SLEEPING

Hotel Fujita Nara (☎ 23-8111; Shimosanjō-chō 47-1; s/tw from ¥7500/12,600) This is a clean, new hotel with a convenient location.

Nara Youth Hostel (奈良ユースホステル; ☎ 22-1334; fax 22-1335; Hōren-chō 1716; dm ¥3150) This clean and newish YH is easy to get to and well run. The reception here is efficient but brusque. From bus stand 7 at JR Nara Station or bus stand 13 at Kintetsu Nara Station, take bus 108, 109, 111, 113 or 115 and get off at the Shieikyūjō-mae bus stop – the hostel is almost directly next to it. Breakfast costs ¥650 and dinner ¥1050.

Nara-ken Seishōnen Kaikan Youth Hostel (奈良県青少年会館ユースホステル; ☎/fax 22-5540; Handahiraki-chō 72-7; dm/r per person ¥2650/3350) This YH is older and less pristine than the Nara Youth Hostel, but the warm and friendly staff more than makes up for this. From bus stand 9 at JR Nara Station or bus stand 13 at Kintetsu Nara Station, take bus 12, 13, 131 or 140 and get off at the Ikuei-gakuen bus stop, from which the hostel's a five-minute walk. The information offices (p163) have maps and directions.

Ryokan Matsumae (☎ 22-3686; Higashiterabayashi-chō 28-1; per person without bathroom from ¥5250) This compact little ryokan gets excellent reviews from our readers. Some of the rooms are a little dark, but the feeling here is warm and relaxing. The friendly owner speaks English.

Ryokan Seikan-sō (☎/fax 22-2670; Higashikitsuji-chō 29; per person without bathroom from ¥4200) This traditional ryokan has reasonable rates and a good

Naramachi location. The rooms are clean and spacious with shared bathrooms and a large communal bathtub.

Ryokan Tsubakisō (☎ 22-5330; fax 27-3811; tubaki@pc5.so-net.ne.jp; r per person without bath from ¥12,000; 💻) Popular with foreign guests, this excellent ryokan is a homey and wonderful place to stay in Nara. The bedrooms and bathrooms are clean and well maintained, and the owner can prepare vegetarian meals upon request. Highly recommended.

Super Hotel (☎ 20-9000; Sanjō-chō 500-1; s/d from ¥4980/6980) Directly across from JR Nara Station, the Super Hotel is a part of a no-frills hotel chain that offers clean, small business hotel rooms at very reasonable prices.

OSAKA

☎ 06

Kyoto and Osaka are the two poles of the Japanese experience: if you want high culture, old culture and refined culture, you go to Kyoto. If you want popular culture, modern culture and down-to-earth culture, you go to Osaka. As such, Osaka makes the perfect counterpoint to Kyoto and it's a fun day or half-day trip out of the old capital (it's less than an hour from Kyoto by three different train lines).

Osaka's highlights include a fine reconstructed castle, Osaka-jō; an aquarium with a whale shark on display, Osaka Aquarium; and the neon-strewn entertainment district of Dōtombori. But Osaka has more to offer than its specific sights; like Tokyo, Osaka is a city to be experienced in its totality, and casual strolls are likely to be just as rewarding as structured sightseeing tours.

Osaka is usually divided into two areas: Kita and Minami. Kita (north) is the city's main business and administrative centre. Minami (south) is the city's entertainment district and contains the bustling shopping and nightlife zones of Namba and Shinsaibashi.

The dividing line between Kita and Minami is formed by the Dōjima-gawa and the Tosabori-gawa, between which you'll find Nakano-shima, a peaceful green island that is home to the Museum of Oriental Ceramics. Roughly 1km east of Nakano-shima, you will find Osaka-jō and its surrounding park, Osaka-jō-kōen.

To the south of the Minami area you'll find another group of sights clustered around Tennō-ji Station. These include Shitennō-ji, Den-Den Town and the seriously low-rent entertainment district of Shin-Sekai.

For Osaka's local speciality, head over to Den-Den Town, an area of shops that is almost exclusively devoted to electronic goods. To avoid sales tax, check if the store has a 'Tax Free' sign outside and bring your passport. Most stores are closed on Wednesdays. Take the Sakaisuji subway line to Ebisu-chō Station and use either exit 1 or 2. Alternatively,

TRANSPORT: OSAKA

Getting There

Distance from Kyoto 45km

Direction Southwest

Train Other than the *shinkansen*, the fastest way between Kyoto Station and Osaka is a JR *shinkaisoku* (special rapid train; ¥540, 29 minutes). There is also the cheaper private Hankyū line, which runs between Kawaramachi, Karasuma and Ōmiya Stations in Kyoto and Umeda Station in Osaka (Kawaramachi–Umeda limited express; ¥390, 40 minutes). Alternatively, you can take the Keihan line between Demachiyanagi, Marutamachi, Sanjō, Shijō or Shichijō Stations in Kyoto and Yodoyabashi Station in Osaka (Sanjō–Yodoyabashi limited express; ¥400, 45 minutes).

Getting Around

Train Like Tokyo, Osaka has a JR loop line (known in Japanese as the JR *kanjō-sen*) that circles the city area. There are also seven subway lines, the most useful of which is the Midō-suji line, which runs north–south stopping at Shin-Osaka, Umeda (next to Osaka Station), Shinsaibashi, Namba and Tennō-ji Stations.

Tickets If you're going to be using the rail system a lot on any day, it might be worth considering a 'one-day free ticket'. For ¥850 (¥650 on Fridays and the 20th of every month) you get unlimited travel on any subway, the New Tram line and all city buses (but not the JR line). Note that you'd really have to be moving around a lot to save any money with this ticket. They are available at the staffed ticket windows in most subway stations.

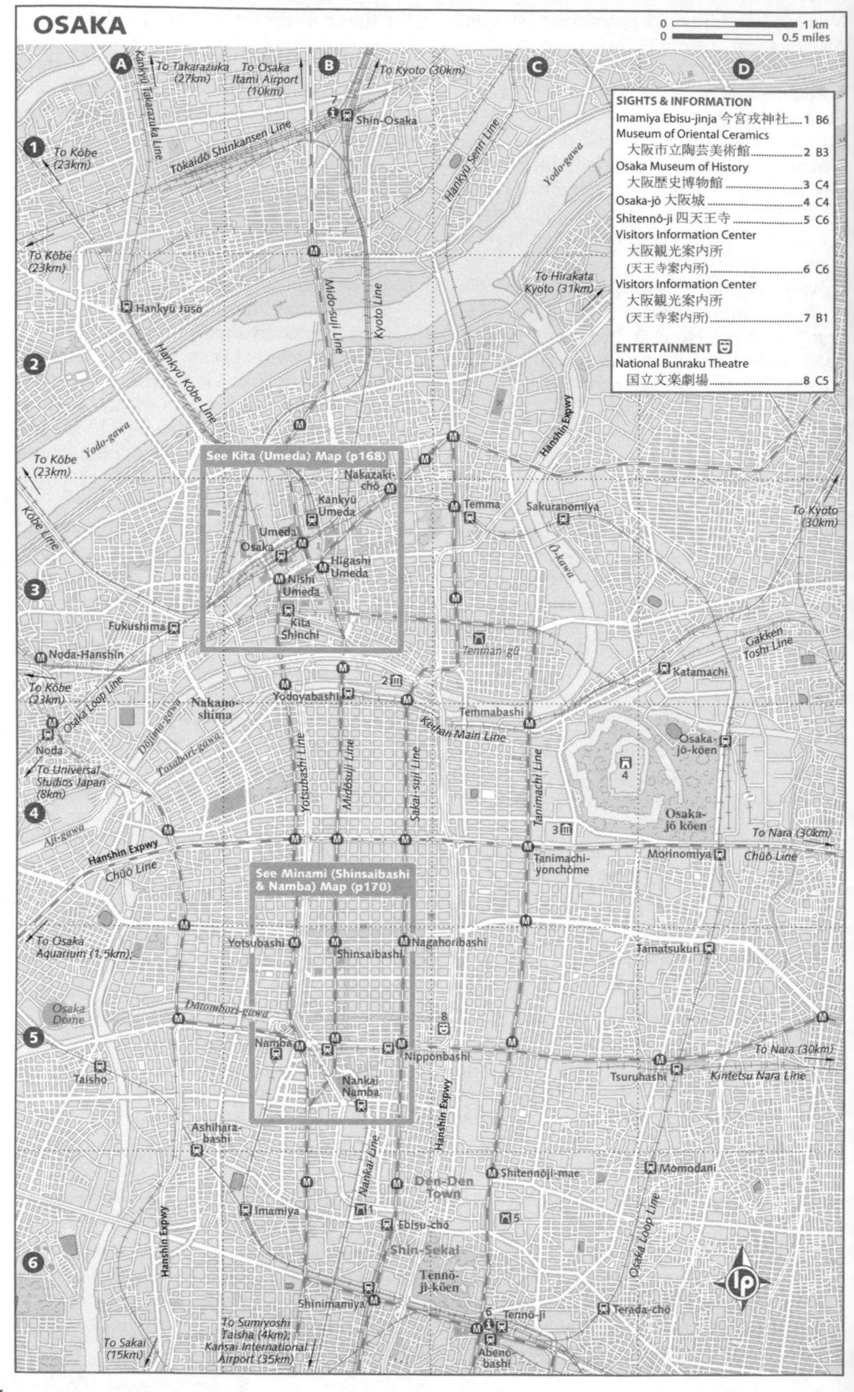
OSAKA
0 1 km
0 0.5 miles
SIGHTS & INFORMATION
Imamiya Ebisu-jinja 今宮戎神社 1 B6
Museum of Oriental Ceramics 大阪市立陶芸美術館 2 B3
Osaka Museum of History 大阪歴史博物館 3 C4
Osaka-jō 大阪城 4 C4
Shitennō-ji 四天王寺 5 C6
Visitors Information Center 大阪観光案内所 (天王寺案内所) 6 C6
Visitors Information Center 大阪観光案内所 (天王寺案内所) 7 B1
ENTERTAINMENT
National Bunraku Theatre 国立文楽劇場 8 C5
See Kita (Umeda) Map (p168)
See Minami (Shinsaibashi & Namba) Map (p170)
To Takarazuka (27km)
To Osaka Itami Airport (10km)
To Kyoto (30km)
To Kōbe (23km)
To Hirakata Kyoto (31km)
To Universal Studios Japan (8km)
To Osaka Aquarium (1.5km)
To Nara (30km)
To Sumiyoshi Taisha (4km); Kansai International Airport (35km)
To Sakai (15km)
Shin-Osaka
Hankyū Jūsō
Nakazaki-chō
Kankyū Umeda
Umeda
Osaka
Higashi Umeda
Nishi Umeda
Kita Shinchi
Fukushima
Noda-Hanshin
Noda
Temma
Sakuranomiya
Tenman-gū
Yodoyabashi
Temmabashi
Katamachi
Nakano-shima
Osaka-jō-kōen
Osaka-jō kōen
Tanimachi-yonchōme
Morinomiya
Yotsubashi
Shinsaibashi
Nagahoribashi
Tamatsukuri
Osaka Dome
Namba
Nankai Namba
Nipponbashi
Tsuruhashi
Taisho
Ashihara-bashi
Shitennōji-mae
Momodani
Den-Den Town
Imamiya
Ebisu-chō
Shin-Sekai
Tennō-ji-kōen
Shinimamiya
Tenno-ji
Abeno-bashi
Terada-chō
Tōkaidō Shinkansen Line
Kankyū Takarazuka Line
Hankyū Kōbe Line
Hankyū Senri Line
Mido-suji Line
Kyoto Line
Kōbe Line
Osaka Loop Line
Yotsubashi Line
Midōsuji Line
Sakai-suji Line
Tanimachi Line
Keihan Main Line
Gakken Toshi Line
Chūō Line
Hanshin Expwy
Nankai Line
Kintetsu Nara Line
Yodo-gawa
Ō-kawa
Dōjima-gawa
Tosabori-gawa
Aji-gawa
Dōtombori-gawa

Den-Den Town's a 15-minute walk south of Nankai Namba Station.

Keep in mind that while Osaka Station (also known as JR Osaka Station) is centrally located in the Kita area, if you're coming from Tokyo by *shinkansen* you will arrive at Shin-Osaka Station, which is three stops (about five minutes) north of Osaka Station on the Midō-suji subway line.

Kita (Umeda)

By day, Osaka's centre of gravity is the Kita area. While Kita doesn't have any great attractions to detain the traveller, it does have a few good department stores, lots of good places to eat and the Umeda Sky Building.

Just northwest of Osaka Station, the **Umeda Sky Building** (Map p168; ☎ 6440-3855; Kita-ku, Ōyodonaka 1-1-88; admission ¥700; 10am-10.30pm) is Osaka's most dramatic piece of architecture. The twin-tower complex looks like a space-age version of Paris' Arc de Triomphe. It has two observation galleries: an open-air one on the roof and an indoor one on the floor below. Getting to the top is half the fun, as you take a glassed-in escalator for the final five storeys (definitely not for sufferers of vertigo). Tickets for the observation decks can be purchased on the 3rd floor of the east tower. In the basement of the towers, you'll find **Takimi-kōji Alley**, a re-creation of a Showa-era market street crammed with restaurants and *izakaya* (Japanese pubs/eateries). The Umeda Sky Building is reached via an underground passage that starts just north of Osaka and Umeda Stations.

Central Osaka

The main attractions of Central Osaka include the Museum of Oriental Ceramics and Osaka-jō.

With more than 1300 exhibits, the **Museum of Oriental Ceramics** (Map p166; ☎ 6223-0055; Kita-ku, Nakanoshima 1-1-26; admission ¥500; 9.30am-5pm, closed Mon) has one of the world's finest collections of Chinese and Korean ceramics. To get to the museum, go to Yodoyabashi Station on either the Midō-suji line or the Keihan line. Walk north to the river and cross to Nakanoshima. Turn right, pass the city hall on your left, bear left with the road and the museum is on the left.

Osaka's most popular attraction, **Osaka-jō** (Map p166; ☎ 6941-3044; Chūō-ku, Osaka-jō 1-1; grounds/castle keep admission free/¥600; 9am-5pm, to 8pm in summer) is a 1931 concrete reconstruction of the original castle, which was completed in 1583 as a display of power on the part of Toyotomi Hideyoshi. Refurbished at great cost in 1997, today's castle has a decidedly modern look. The interior of the castle houses a museum of Toyotomi Hideyoshi memorabilia, as well as displays relating the history of the castle.

Ōte-mon, the gate that serves as the main entrance to the park, is a 10-minute walk northeast of Tanimachi-yonchōme Station on the Chūō and Tanimachi subway lines. You can also take the Osaka loop line; get off at Osaka-jō-kōen Station and enter through the back of the castle.

Just southwest of Osaka-jō, the excellent **Osaka Museum of History** (Map p166; Osaka Rekishi Hakubutsukan; ☎ 6946-5728; Chūō-ku, Ōtemae 4-1-32; admission ¥600; 9.30am-5pm) is housed in a fantastic new building adjoining the Osaka NHK Broadcast Center. The display floors of the museum occupy the 7th to 10th floors of the new sail-shaped building.

The museum's displays are broken into four sections by floor; you start at the top and work your way down, passing in time from the past to the present. The displays are very well done and there are plenty of English explanations; taped tours are available.

The museum is a two-minute walk northeast of Tanimachi-yonchōme Station.

Minami (Shinsaibashi & Namba)

A few stops south of Kita on the Midō-suji subway line (get off at either Shinsaibashi or Namba Stations), the Minami area is the place to spend the evening in Osaka. Its highlights include the Dōtombori arcade, the National Bunraku Theatre, Dōguya-suji arcade and Amerika-Mura.

Meaning 'America Village', **Amerika-Mura** (Map p170) is a compact enclave of trendy shops and restaurants, with a few discreet love hotels thrown in for good measure. The best reason to come here is to view the hordes of colourful Japanese teens living out the myth of *Amerika*. Amerika-Mura is located one or two blocks west of Midō-suji, bounded on the north by Suomachi-suji and the south by Dōtombori-gawa. The heart of Amerika-Mura is a crowded bit of concrete known as **Amerika-Mura Triangle Park**.

Dōtombori (Map p170) is Osaka's liveliest nightlife area. It's centred on **Dōtombori-gawa** and

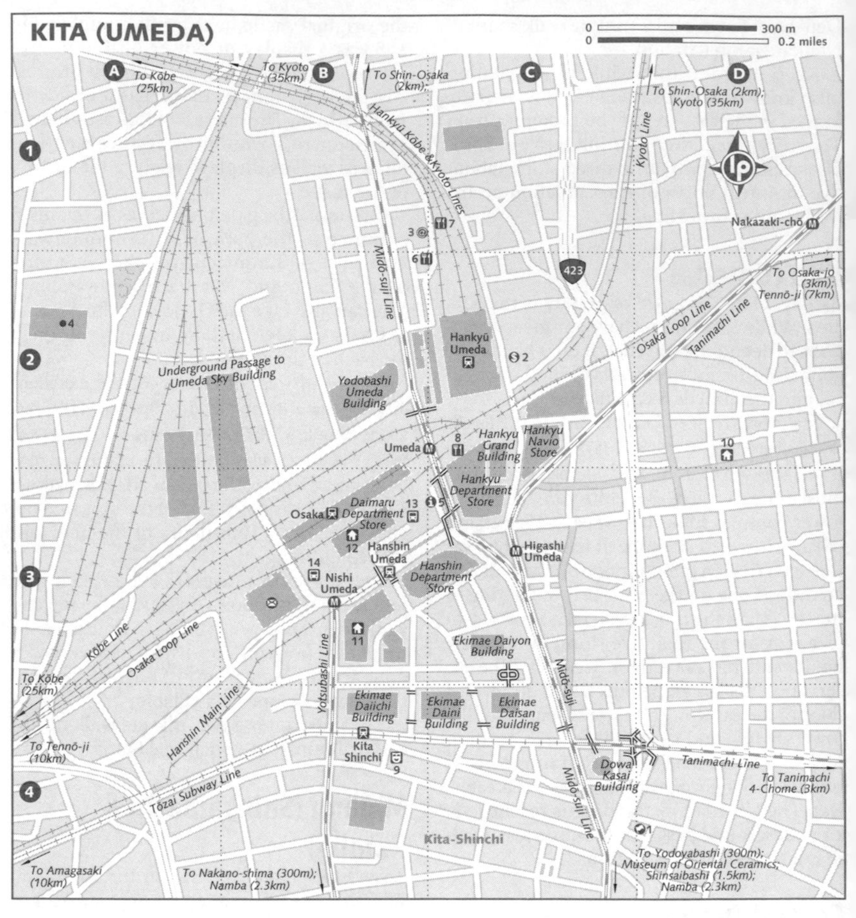

Dōtombori arcade. In the evening, head to **Ebisubashi**, the main footbridge over the canal, to sample the glittering nightscape, which calls to mind a scene from the sci-fi movie *Blade Runner*.

Only a short walk south of Dōtombori arcade, you'll find **Hōzen-ji** (Map p170), a tiny temple hidden down a narrow alley. The temple is built around a moss-covered **Fudō-myōō statue**. This statue is a favourite of people employed in the so-called 'water trade', or *mizu shōbai*. Nearby, you'll find the atmospheric **Hōzen-ji Yokochō**, a tiny alley filled with traditional restaurants and bars.

If you desperately need a *tako-yaki* (octopus ball) fryer, a red lantern to hang outside your shop or plastic food models to lure the customers, the **Dōguya-suji arcade** (Map p170) is the place to go. You'll also find endless knives, pots and almost anything else that's even remotely related to the preparation and consumption of food.

Other Areas

Founded in 593, **Shitennō-ji** (Map p166; ☎ 6771-0066; Tennōji-ku, Shitennō-ji 1-11-18; admission free; 🕑 9am-5pm, closed 28 Dec-1 Jan) has the distinction of being one of the oldest Buddhist temples in Japan. None of the present buildings, however, are originals: most are concrete reproductions, with the exception of the big stone **torii**. The *torii* (shrine gate) dates back to 1294, making it the oldest of its kind in Japan. The temple is most easily reached from Shitennōji-mae Station on the Tanimachi subway line. Take the southern exit, cross to the left side of the road and take the small road that goes off at

KITA (UMEDA)

SIGHTS & INFORMATION

American Consulate アメリカ領事館	1 D4
Citibank (International ATM) シティバンク	2 C2
German Consulate ドイツ総領事館	(see 4)
Media Café Popeye メディアカフェポパイ	3 B1
Umeda Sky Building 梅田スカイビル	4 A2
Visitors Information Center 大阪観光案内所(梅田案内所)	5 C3

EATING

Ganko Umeda Honten がんこ梅田本店	6 B2
Gataro がたろ	(see 7)
Hilton Plaza ヒルトンプラザ	(see 11)
Kappa Yokochō Arcade かっぱ横丁	7 C1
Maru 丸	(see 8)
Pina Khana ピーナカーナ	(see 7)
Shin-Umeda Shokudō-Gai 新梅田食道街	8 C2
Shinkiraku 新善楽	(see 11)

ENTERTAINMENT

Karma カーマ	9 B4
Windows on the World ウィンドーズオンザ ワールド	(see 11)

SLEEPING

Capsule Inn Osaka/Umeda New Japan Sauna 梅田ニュージャパンサウナ·カプセルイン大阪	10 D2
Hilton Osaka 大阪ヒルトンホテル	11 B3
Hotel Granvia Osaka ホテルグランヴィア大阪	12 B3

TRANSPORT

City Bus Terminal 市バスターミナル	13 B3
JR Highway Bus Terminal 高速バスターミナル	14 B3

an angle away from the subway station. The entrance to the temple is on the left.

Osaka's most important shrine, **Sumiyoshi Taisha** (住吉大社; ☎ 6672-0753; Sumiyoshi 2-9-89; admission free; dawn-dusk) is dedicated to Shintō deities associated with the sea and sea travel, in commemoration of a safe passage to Korea by a 3rd-century empress. Having survived the bombing of WWII, Sumiyoshi Taisha actually has a couple of buildings that date to 1810. The shrine was founded in the early 3rd century and the buildings that can be seen today are faithful replicas of the originals. The shrine is next to both Sumiyoshi Taisha and Sumiyoshi-torii-mae Stations on the Nankai tram line. Catch the tram from Tennō-ji Station.

Osaka Aquarium (海遊館; Kaiyūkan; ☎ 6576-5501; Minato-ku, Kaizan-dōri 1-1-10; adult/child ¥2000/900; 10am-8pm) is worth a visit, especially for those who have children in tow. The aquarium is centred on the world's largest aquarium tank, which is home to the star attractions – two enormous whale sharks as well as a variety of smaller sharks, rays and other fish. To get there, take the Chūō subway line to the last stop (Osaka-kō), and from here it's about a five-minute walk to the aquarium. Get there for opening time if you want to beat the crowds – on weekends and public holidays long queues are the norm.

Universal Studios Japan (ユニバーサルスタジオジャパン; ☎ 4790-7000; Universal city; adult/child ¥5800/3900; 9am-7pm Mon-Fri, to 9pm Sat, Sun & public holidays) is Osaka's answer to Tokyo Disneyland. Although it wasn't open while we were researching this guide, word has it that the park is a faithful reproduction of the American park, complete with all manner of movie-themed rides, stores and shops. To get there, take the JR loop line to Nishi-kujō Station, switch to one of the distinctively painted Universal Studio shuttle trains and get off at Universal City Station. From Osaka Station the trip costs ¥170 and takes about 20 minutes. There are also some direct trains from Osaka Station (ask at the tourist office for times; the price is the same).

INFORMATION

Aprecio (Map p170; ☎ 6634-0199; www.aprecio.co.jp/namba/index.php, in Japanese; per 30min from ¥200; 24hr) Internet access.

Citibank Kita (Map p168; ☎ 4802-0277; www.citibank.co.jp/en/branch/br025a.html; 9am-3pm Mon-Fri, ATM 8am-10pm); Minami (Map p170; ☎ 6213-2731; www.citibank.co.jp/en/branch/br024a.html; 9am-3pm Mon-Fri, ATM 24hr) International ATM.

Kinko's (Map p170; ☎ 6245-1887; Minami; per 10min from ¥200; 24hr) Internet access.

Media Café Popeye (Map p168; ☎ 6292-3800; www2.media-café.ne.jp/branch/umedadd/index.html, in Japanese; per 60min from ¥400; 24hr)

Visitors Information Center (8am to 8pm, closed 31 Dec-3 Jan) Namba Station (Map p170; ☎ 6643-2125); Osaka Station (Map p168; ☎ 6345-2189); Shin-Osaka Station (Map p166; ☎ 6305-3311); Tennō-ji Station (Map p166; ☎ 6774-3077)

The Osaka Station office is the main branch of the tourist association. Many travellers have problems finding it. To get there from Osaka Station, take the Midō-suji exit, turn right, and walk about 50m. The office is just outside the station, beneath a pedestrian overpass. From the subway, take exit 9, and look for the office outside the station, beside the bus terminal. Note that the Osaka Station is presently under construction and there is word that this office might move again.

At any of these offices, you can pick up a copy of the excellent *Osaka City Map* and *Meet Osaka*, a pocket-sized reference guide to current events and festivals.

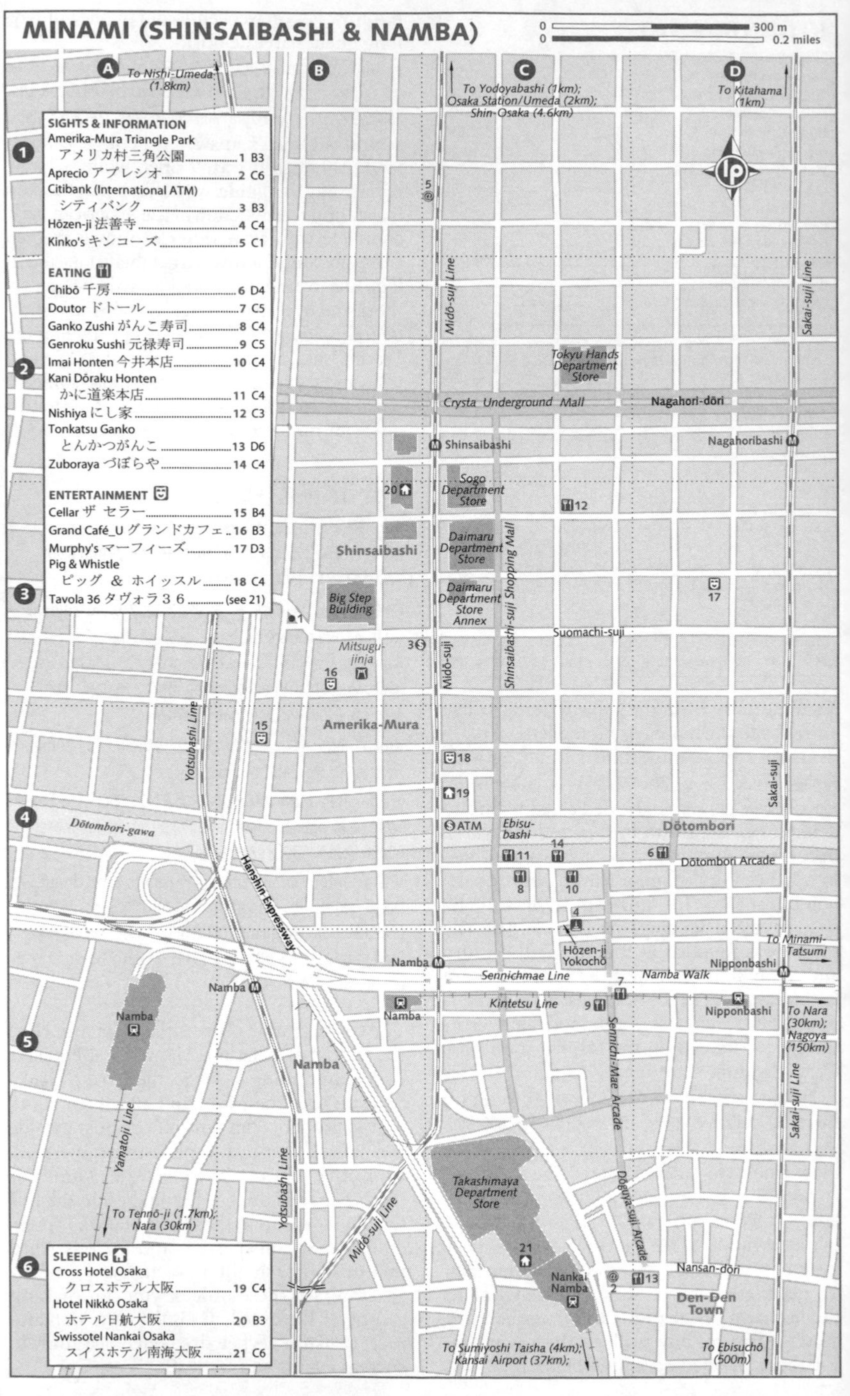
MINAMI (SHINSAIBASHI & NAMBA)
0 300 m
0 0.2 miles
SIGHTS & INFORMATION
Amerika-Mura Triangle Park アメリカ村三角公園 1 B3
Aprecio アプレシオ 2 C6
Citibank (International ATM) シティバンク 3 B3
Hōzen-ji 法善寺 4 C4
Kinko's キンコーズ 5 C1
EATING
Chibō 千房 6 D4
Doutor ドトール 7 C5
Ganko Zushi がんこ寿司 8 C4
Genroku Sushi 元禄寿司 9 C5
Imai Honten 今井本店 10 C4
Kani Dōraku Honten かに道楽本店 11 C4
Nishiya にし家 12 C3
Tonkatsu Ganko とんかつがんこ 13 D6
Zuboraya づぼらや 14 C4
ENTERTAINMENT
Cellar ザ セラー 15 B4
Grand Café_U グランドカフェ 16 B3
Murphy's マーフィーズ 17 D3
Pig & Whistle ピッグ & ホイッスル 18 C4
Tavola 36 タヴォラ３６ (see 21)
SLEEPING
Cross Hotel Osaka クロスホテル大阪 19 C4
Hotel Nikkō Osaka ホテル日航大阪 20 B3
Swissotel Nankai Osaka スイスホテル南海大阪 21 C6
To Nishi-Umeda (1.8km)
To Yodoyabashi (1km); Osaka Station/Umeda (2km); Shin-Osaka (4.6km)
To Kitahama (1km)
Midō-suji Line
Sakai-suji Line
Tokyu Hands Department Store
Crysta Underground Mall
Nagahori-dōri
Shinsaibashi
Nagahoribashi
Sogo Department Store
Daimaru Department Store
Daimaru Department Store Annex
Big Step Building
Shinsaibashi-suji Shopping Mall
Suomachi-suji
Mitsugu-jinja
Midō-suji
Amerika-Mura
Yotsubashi Line
Sakai-suji
Dōtombori-gawa
Ebisu-bashi
Dōtombori
Dōtombori Arcade
Hanshin Expressway
Hōzen-ji Yokochō
Namba
To Minami-Tatsumi
Nipponbashi
Sennichmae Line
Namba Walk
Kintetsu Line
To Nara (30km); Nagoya (150km)
Sennichi-Mae Arcade
Yamatoji Line
Takashimaya Department Store
Dōguya-suji Arcade
To Tennō-ji (1.7km); Nara (30km)
Nankai Namba
Nansan-dōri
Den-Den Town
To Sumiyoshi Taisha (4km); Kansai Airport (37km);
To Ebisuchō (500m)

FESTIVALS & EVENTS

The major festivals held in Osaka include the following:

Tōka Ebisu From 9 to 11 Jan, huge crowds of more than a million people flock to Imamiya Ebisu-jinja (Map p166) to receive bamboo branches hung with auspicious tokens. The shrine is near Imamiya Ebisu Station on the Nankai line.

Doya Doya Billed as a 'huge naked festival', this event on 14 Jan involves a competition between young men, clad in little more than headbands and loincloths, to obtain the 'amulet of the cow god'. This talisman is said to bring a good harvest to farmers. The festival takes place from 2pm at Shitennō-ji (Map p166).

Tenjin Matsuri This is one of Japan's three biggest festivals, taking place on 24 and 25 July. Try to make the second day, when processions of portable shrines and people in traditional attire start at Tenman-gū (Map p166) and end up in the Ō-kawa (in boats). As night falls the festival is marked with a huge fireworks display.

Kishiwada Danjiri Matsuri Osaka's wildest festival is a kind of running of the bulls except with festival *danjiri* (floats), many weighing more than 3 tonnes. The *danjiri* are hauled through the streets on 14 and 15 September by hundreds of people using ropes, and in all the excitement there have been a couple of deaths – take care and stand back. Most of the action takes place on the second day. The best place to see it is west of Kishiwada Station on the Nankai Honsen line (from Nankai Namba Station).

EATING

Restaurants are open during usual business hours (11am to 2pm and 5pm to 10pm) unless otherwise noted.

Kita

The Kita area is chock-a-block with good restaurants. For a wide selection of different cuisines under one roof, try the Kappa Yokochō arcade (Map p168), just north of Hankyū Umeda Station, or the Shin-Umeda Shokudō-gai (Map p168), just east of Osaka Station (beneath the tracks). For something a little more upscale, try the restaurants on the B1 and B2 floors of the Hilton Plaza (Map p168), opposite Osaka Station. There are also several cafés and restaurants in Osaka Station itself.

Ganko Umeda Honten (Map p168; ☎ 6376-2001; Kita-ku, Shibata 1-5-11; meals from ¥800) A giant dining hall serving all the usual Japanese favourites, including sushi. It's a very approachable place where foreign diners can feel comfortable.

Gataro (Map p168; ☎ 6373-1484; Kita-ku, Shibata 1-7-2; dinner around ¥3000) This a cosy little spot that does creative twists on standard *izakaya* themes. Look for the glass front with credit card stickers on the left as you head north in the arcade. Unlike most *izakaya*, this one has an English menu.

Maru (Map p168; ☎ 6361-4552; Kita-ku, Shin-Umeda Shokudō-gai, Kakuda-chō 9-26) Maru serves delicious sashimi sets for lunch and proper fish meals for dinner.

Shinkiraku (Map p168; ☎ 6345-3461; Kita-ku, Umeda 1-8-16; meals from ¥800) This excellent tempura specialist serves a tasty *ebishio-tendon* (shrimp tempura over rice; ¥880) for lunch and an *osusume-gozen* (tempura full set; ¥2079) for dinner. Take the escalator to the Hilton Plaza's B2 floor, go right and look for the small English sign.

Pina Khana (Map p168; ☎ 6375-5828; Kita-ku, Shibata 1-7-2; lunch/dinner from ¥850/3000) This is our favourite Indian restaurant in Kita. The good-value lunch sets usually include a reasonably priced curry, nan or rice, and tandoori chicken. If you go between noon and 1pm, you'll be fighting the salarymen and office ladies for a seat. Look for the Indian flag.

Minami

The place to eat in Minami is the restaurant-packed Dōtombori arcade (Map p170). The restaurants in this area win no points for their refined atmosphere, but the prices are low and the portions large.

Chibō (Map p170; ☎ 6212-2211; Chūō-ku, Dōtombori 1-5-5; okonomiyaki from ¥800) A good spot to sample *okonomiyaki* (literally 'cook what you like'; often called Japanese pancake), one of Osaka's most popular dishes. Chibō's *modan yaki* (a kind of *okonomiyaki*) is a good bet at ¥950.

Ganko Zushi (Map p170; ☎ 6212-1705; Chūō-ku, Dōtombori 1-8-24; set meals from ¥1000) Part of Kansai's most popular sushi chain, this is a good place for ample sushi sets and a variety of other Japanese favourites.

Imai Honten (Map p170; ☎ 6211-0319; Chūō-ku, Dōtombori 1-7-22; udon from ¥550) One of the area's oldest and most revered *udon* (thick white wheat noodle) specialists.

Kani Dōraku Honten (Map p170; ☎ 6211-8975; Chūō-ku, Dōtombori 1-6-18; lunch/dinner from ¥1600/3000) This crab specialist does all kinds of imaginative things with the unfortunate crustaceans. If the main branch is full, there's an annexe just down the road.

Nishiya (Map p170; ☎ 6241-9221; Chūō-ku, Higashi Shinsaibashi 1-18-18; meals from ¥1200) This rustic Osaka landmark serves *udon* noodles and a variety of hearty *nabe* (iron pot) dishes for reasonable prices.

Zuboraya (Map p170; ☎ 6211-0181; Chūō-ku, Dōtombori 1-6-10; fugu sashimi ¥1800, dinner from ¥3000) The place to go when you've worked up the nerve to try *fugu* (Japanese pufferfish). Look for the giant *fugu* hanging out the front.

Genroku Sushi (Map p170; Chūō-ku, Sennichimae 2-11-4; ⏲ 10am-10.40pm) In a busy shopping arcade, this is a bustling automatic sushi place where plates of sushi cost a mere ¥130.

Finally, if you just feel like a Western-style sandwich or a quick cup of (so-so) coffee, drop into the Doutor at the mouth of the Sennichi-Mae arcade.

ENTERTAINMENT

Osaka has a lively nightlife scene, with lots of bars and clubs that see mixed foreign and Japanese clientele. Minami is the place for a wild night out – you simply won't believe the number of bars, clubs and restaurants they've packed into the narrow streets and alleys of Dōtombori, Shinsaibashi, Namba and Amerika-Mura. Go there on a weekend night and you'll be part of a colourful human parade of Osaka characters – this is one of Japan's best spots for people-watching.

There are also plenty of good bars and clubs in the neighbourhoods to the south and east of Osaka Station.

For up-to-date listings of upcoming club and music events, check *Kansai Time Out* (www.japanfile.com), available at bookstores in Osaka and Kyoto.

National Bunraku Theatre (Map p166; ☎ 6212-2531; Chūō-ku, Nipponbashi 1-12-10) Although *bunraku* (puppet theatre) did not originate in Osaka, the art form was popularised at this theatre. Today it is attempting to revive the fortunes of *bunraku*. Performances are only held at certain times of the year: check with the tourist information offices. Tickets normally start at around ¥2300; earphones and programme guides in English are available.

Karma (Map p168; ☎ 6344-6181; Kita-ku, Sonezakishinchi 1-5-18; ⏲ 5pm-2am daily) A long-standing club popular with Japanese and foreigners alike. At weekends Karma usually hosts techno events with cover charges averaging ¥2500.

Windows on the World (Map p168; ☎ 6347-7111; Kita-ku, Umeda 1-8-8; ⏲ 11.30am-12.30am) For drinks with a view, head to this bar on the 35th floor of the Hilton Osaka. Be warned that there's a ¥2500 per person table charge and drinks average ¥1000.

Cellar (Map p170; ☎ 6212-6437; Chūō-ku, Nishishinsaibashi 2-17-13, B1 Shin-sumiya Bldg; ⏲ dusk to late) Live music is often the draw at this popular basement bar on the west side of Nishi-shinsaibashi.

Murphy's (Map p170; ☎ 6282-0677; Chūō-ku, Higashishinsaibashi 1-6-31; per person around ¥1000; ⏲ 5pm-1am Sun-Thu, to 4am Fri & Sat) One of the oldest Irish-style pubs in Japan, this is a good place to rub shoulders with local expats and young Japanese.

Pig & Whistle (Map p170; ☎ 6213-6911; Chūō-ku, Shinsaibashisuji 2-6-14; ⏲ 5pm-midnight Mon-Thu, to 1am Fri & Sat) As is the case with its sister branches in Kita and Kyoto, the Pig is the place to go for a pint and a plate of fish and chips. Drinks cost from ¥720 and food ¥1100.

Tavola 36 (Map p170; ☎ 6646-5125; Chūō-ku, Namba 5-1-60; ⏲ 11am-midnight) This is where we go when we want something a little swanky. It's an Italian restaurant/bar on the 36th floor of the Swissotel Nankai Osaka. The view is fantastic, and so are the prices: there's a ¥1260 per person table charge after 5.30pm and drinks start at ¥1300.

SLEEPING

It makes little sense to stay in Osaka when Kyoto's just over half an hour away. If you do want to stay in Osaka, however, there are lots of business hotels and regular hotels in both the Kita and Minami areas. Considering its wealth of dining and entertainment options, Minami is probably the best place to be based.

Hilton Osaka (Map p168; ☎ 6347-7111; fax 6347-7001; Kita-ku, Umeda 1-8-8; s/d from ¥19,500/23,500) Just south of Osaka Station, this is an excellent hotel that is at home with foreign guests. The rooms are clean and light, with a Japanese touch, and there's a 15m pool in the fitness centre. The views from the Hilton's 35th-floor Windows on the World bar are awesome and there are two basement floors of great restaurants.

Hotel Granvia Osaka (Map p168; ☎ 6344-1235; fax 6344-1130; Kita-ku, Umeda 3-1-1; s/tw/d from ¥16,170/33,495/24,255) You can't beat this hotel for convenience: it's located directly over Osaka Station. Rooms and facilities are of a high standard.

Capsule Inn Osaka/Umeda New Japan Sauna (Map p168; ☎ 6314-2100; Kita-ku, Dōyama-chō 9-5; male-only capsules ¥2500) Located in one of Kita's busiest entertainment districts, this is the place to stay if you miss the last train back to Kyoto. It's fairly clean and well maintained, with sauna (from ¥525), Jacuzzi and optional massage services. Note that it's men-only, and if you're more than 180cm tall you won't be able to lie flat out.

Hotel Nikkō Osaka (Map p170; ☎ 6244-1111; fax 6245-2432; Chūō-ku, Nishishinsaibashi 1-3-3; s/d from ¥21,945/34,650) The Nikkō is one of Osaka's better hotels, with a great selection of restaurants and bars on the premises. All the rooms here are Western style and very clean, including the bathrooms

Cross Hotel Osaka (Map p170; ☎ 6213-8281; fax 6213-8640; Chūō-ku, Shinsaibashisuji 2-5-15; s/d from ¥14,000/18,000) Just a short walk from the Dōtombori area, this is the most reasonably priced hotel (as opposed to business hotel) in Minami. Deluxe rooms, which start at ¥21,000, offer an increase in size and somewhat nicer appointments.

Swissotel Nankai Osaka (Map p170; ☎ 6646-1111; Chūō-ku, Namba 5-1-60; s/d from ¥17,325/23,100) This is Minami's most elegant hotel, with stunning views and clean, well-appointed rooms. You can catch direct connections to Kansai airport via the Nankai line trains that depart from Namba Station below the hotel.

KŌBE

☎ 078

Perched on a hillside overlooking the sea, Kōbe is one of Japan's most cosmopolitan cities, having served as a maritime gateway to Kansai from the earliest days of trade with China. To this day, there are significant populations of other Asian nationalities in Kōbe, as well as plenty of Westerners, many of whom work in nearby Osaka.

Kōbe's relaxed international atmosphere and scenic location make it one of Japan's most pleasant cities. Best of all, it is relatively compact, which means that most of the sights can be reached on foot from the main train stations. Of course, it must be noted that none of these sights are must-sees: Kōbe is likely to appeal more to residents than to travellers. However, it does have some good restaurants, cafés and bars and is a good place for a night out if you just can't face the mayhem of Osaka.

A 20-minute walk north of Sannomiya, the pleasant hillside neighbourhood of Kitano is where local tourists come to enjoy the feeling of foreign travel without leaving Japanese soil. The European/American atmosphere is created by the winding streets and *ijinkan* (foreigners' houses) that once housed some of Kōbe's early Western residents. Admission to some of the *ijinkan* is free, while others cost ¥300 to ¥700; most are open from 9am to 5pm.

Kōbe City Museum (☎ 391-0035; Chūō-ku, Kyōmachi 24; admission varies; 10am-4.30pm, closed Mon) has a collection of Namban (literally 'southern barbarian') art and occasional special exhibits. Namban art is a school of painting that developed under the influence of early Jesuit missionaries in Japan, who taught Western painting techniques to Japanese students. Unless you have a particular interest in Namban art, it's probably best to find out what special exhibit is on before visiting; check at the tourist information offices.

Five minutes' walk southeast of Kōbe Station (on the JR line), Kōbe Harbour Land is awash with new mega-mall shopping and dining developments. This may not appeal to foreign travellers the way it does to local youth, but it's still a nice place for a wander in the afternoon.

Five minutes to the east of Harbour Land, you'll find Meriken Park on a spit of reclaimed land jutting out into the bay. The main attraction here is the Kōbe Maritime Museum (☎ 327-8983; Chūō-ku, Hatoba-chō 2-2; admission ¥500; 10am-4.30pm, closed Mon), which has an extensive collection of high-quality model ships and displays with some English explanations.

Nankinmachi, Kōbe's Chinatown, is not on a par with Chinatowns elsewhere in the world, but it is an atmospheric place to meander and have a bite to eat. It's particularly attractive in the evening. See p174 for details on some of the area's restaurants.

Kōbe's two main entry points are Sannomiya and Shin-Kōbe Stations. Shin-Kōbe, in the northeast of town, is where the *shinkansen* pauses. A subway runs from here to the busier Sannomiya Station, which has frequent rail connections with Osaka and Kyoto. It's possible to walk between the two stations in around 15 minutes. Sannomiya (not Kōbe) Station marks the city centre.

The Luminarie festival, Kōbe's biggest yearly event, is held every evening from 13 to 26 December to celebrate the city's miraculous recovery from the 1995 earthquake. Check dates with the Kōbe tourist office because they change slightly every year. The streets

TRANSPORT: KŌBE

Getting There

Distance from Kyoto 65km

Direction Southwest

Train Sannomiya Station is on the JR Tōkaidō/San-yō line as well as the private Hankyū line, both of which connect it to Kyoto. The fastest way between Kōbe and Kyoto is a JR *shinkaisoku* (special rapid train) from Kyoto Station (¥1050, 48 minutes). The Hankyū line, which leaves from Kyoto's Kawaramachi, Karasuma and Ōmiya Stations, is cheaper (¥600) but less convenient; to/from Kawaramachi Station the limited express takes one hour and requires a change at Osaka's Jūsō or Umeda Stations. Japan Rail Pass holders should also note that Shin-Kōbe Station is on the Tōkaidō/San-yō *shinkansen* (bullet train) line.

Getting Around

Train While Kōbe is small enough to get around on foot, the JR, Hankyū and Hanshin railway lines run east–west across Kōbe, providing access to most of the city's more distant sights. A subway line also connects Shin-Kōbe Station with Sannomiya Station (¥200, three minutes).

Bus A city loop bus service makes a grand circle tour of most of the city's sightseeing spots (¥250 per ride, ¥600 for an all-day pass). The bus stops at both Sannomiya and Shin-Kōbe Stations.

southwest of Kōbe City Hall are decorated with countless illuminated metal archways and people flock from all over Kansai to walk around and enjoy the usual festival food and drink.

INFORMATION

Before starting your exploration of Kōbe, pick up a copy of the *Kōbe City Map* at one of the two information centres.

Outside Sannomiya Station you'll find the city's main tourist information office (☎ 322 0220; 9am-7pm). There's also a smaller counter on the 2nd floor of Shin-Kōbe Station, open from 9am to 5pm.

Behind Kōbe City Hall, there's a Citibank with machines that also accept a variety of cards.

For English-language books, try Random Walk (☎ 332-9200; 10am-8pm), close to Motomachi Station on the JR Kōbe line.

EATING

Kōbe is most famous for its Indian food and has many places to choose from. There are also lots of trendy café-style spots, including a clutch of restaurants just north of Motomachi Station in the fashionable Tor Rd area. For Chinese food, the natural choice is Nankin-machi (Chinatown), just south of Motomachi Station.

Although Kōbe is more famous for its international cuisine, there are, of course, plenty of good Japanese restaurants to be found.

The restaurants in this section are open from 11am to 2pm and 5pm to 10pm, unless otherwise noted.

Kintoki (☎ 331-1037; Chūō-ku, Motomachi-dōri 1-7-2; lunch & dinner from ¥500) For a taste of what Japan was like before it got rich, try this atmospheric old *shokudō* (Japanese-style cafeteria/cheap restaurant) that serves the cheapest food in the city. You can order standard noodle and rice dishes from the menu (plain *soba* – thin brown buckwheat noodles – or *udon* noodles cost ¥250 and a small rice costs ¥160) or choose from a variety of dishes laid out on the counter.

Mikami (☎ 242-5200; Kitano-chō, 2-5-9; lunch & dinner from ¥400; 11.30am-10pm, closed Sun & public holidays) Try this friendly spot for good-value lunch and dinner sets of standard Japanese fare. Noodle dishes are available from ¥400 and *teishoku* (set-course meals) from ¥600. There is also an English menu.

Okagawa (☎ 222-3511; Chūō-ku, Hachiman-dōri 4-1-11; tempura from ¥1100; closed Mon) Not far from Kōbe City Hall, this fine tempura specialist is an oasis of calm, clean lines and good service. Hard to spot, it's at the top of a flight of steps above a place called Daiichi (the stairs are on the left – look for the giant black spoon). There is a small English sign on street level and English menus inside.

Toritetsu (☎ 327-5529; Chūō-ku, Nakayamate-dōri 1-16-12; dinner from ¥3000; 5pm-midnight) Almost

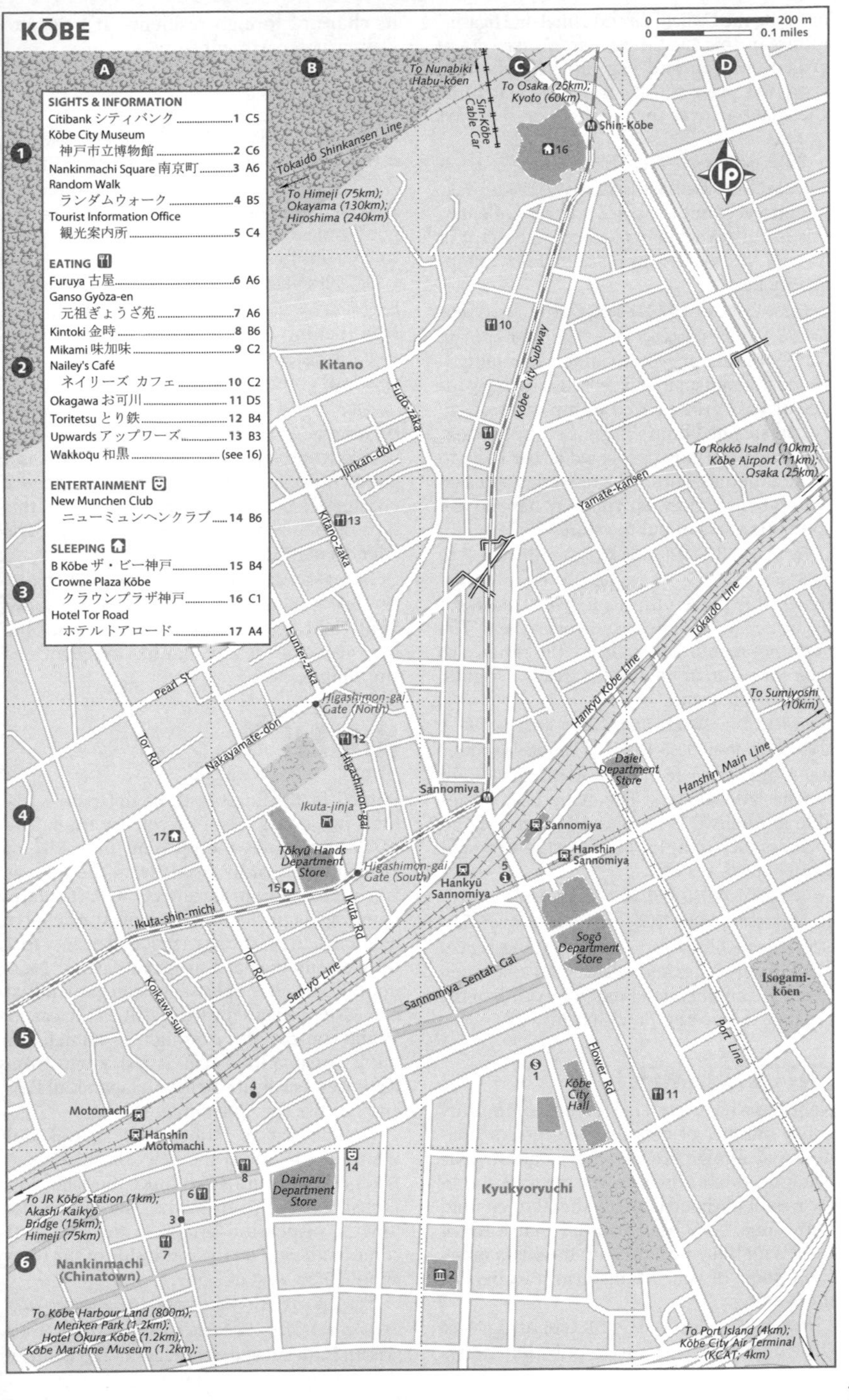
KŌBE
0 200 m
0 0.1 miles
A
B
C
D
1
2
3
4
5
6
SIGHTS & INFORMATION
Citibank シティバンク 1 C5
Kōbe City Museum 神戸市立博物館 2 C6
Nankinmachi Square 南京町 3 A6
Random Walk ランダムウォーク 4 B5
Tourist Information Office 観光案内所 5 C4
EATING
Furuya 古屋 6 A6
Ganso Gyōza-en 元祖ぎょうざ苑 7 A6
Kintoki 金時 8 B6
Mikami 味加味 9 C2
Nailey's Café ネイリーズ カフェ 10 C2
Okagawa お可川 11 D5
Toritetsu とり鉄 12 B4
Upwards アップワーズ 13 B3
Wakkoqu 和黒 (see 16)
ENTERTAINMENT
New Munchen Club ニューミュンヘンクラブ 14 B6
SLEEPING
B Kōbe ザ・ビー神戸 15 B4
Crowne Plaza Kōbe クラウンプラザ神戸 16 C1
Hotel Tor Road ホテルトアロード 17 A4
To Nunabiki Habu-kōen
Sin-Kōbe Cable Car
To Osaka (25km); Kyoto (60km)
Shin-Kōbe
Tōkaidō Shinkansen Line
To Himeji (75km); Okayama (130km); Hiroshima (240km)
Kitano
Kōbe City Subway
Fudō-zaka
Ijinkan-dōri
Kitano-zaka
Yamate-kansen
To Rokkō Isalnd (10km); Kōbe Airport (11km); Osaka (25km)
Tōkaidō Line
Hunter-zaka
Pearl St
Higashimon-gai Gate (North)
Tor Rd
Nakayamate-dōri
Hankyū Kōbe Line
To Sumiyoshi (10km)
Higashimon-gai
Daiei Department Store
Hanshin Main Line
Sannomiya
Ikuta-jinja
Tōkyū Hands Department Store
Higashimon-gai Gate (South)
Hankyū Sannomiya
Hanshin Sannomiya
Ikuta-shin-michi
Ikuta Rd
Sogō Department Store
Tor Rd
San-yō Line
Sannomiya Sentah Gai
Koikawa-suji
Isogami-kōen
Port Line
Flower Rd
Kōbe City Hall
Motomachi
Hanshin Motomachi
Daimaru Department Store
Kyukyoryuchi
To JR Kōbe Station (1km); Akashi Kaikyō Bridge (15km); Himeji (75km)
Nankinmachi (Chinatown)
To Kōbe Harbour Land (800m); Meriken Park (1.2km); Hotel Ōkura Kōbe (1.2km); Kōbe Maritime Museum (1.2km);
To Port Island (4km); Kōbe City Air Terminal (KCAT; 4km)

opposite the Daiichi Grand Hotel on Higashi-mon-gai, this bustling *yakitori* (skewers of grilled chicken and vegetables) restaurant is a good place to eat, drink and watch the chefs labour over their grills. The sign says '*yakitori*'.

Wakkoqu (☎ 262-2838; Chūō-ku, Kitano-chō 1-1, 3F Shin Kōbe Oriental Ave; lunch/dinner from ¥2500/6800) Taking into account the price and ease of entry, this is our favourite Kōbe beef restaurant in the city. It's an elegant place that serves top-quality beef.

Ganso Gyōza-en (☎ 331-4096; Chūō-ku, Sakaemachi-dōri 2-8-11; per 6 dumplings ¥380) The best spot in Nankinmachi for *gyōza* (Chinese dumplings), which is about all that is served. Try the wonderful *yaki gyōza* (fried dumplings) or *sui gyōza* (steamed dumplings). Use the vinegar, soy sauce and miso provided at the table to make a dipping sauce. The red restaurant sign is in Japanese only, so you may have to ask someone to point out the store.

Furuya (☎ 322-1230; Chūō-ku, Motomachi-dōri 1-6-17; per 8 gyōza from ¥320; 🕑 2pm-10pm) We can't quite figure this place out: it's a *gyōza* specialist decorated with skiing, snowboard and *The Sopranos* memorabilia. Above the restaurant look for a sign in English that reads 'Original Gyoza Restaurant'.

Nailey's Café (☎ 231-2008; Chūō-ku, Kanō-chō 2-8-12; lunch/dinner from ¥1050/1200; 🕑 11.30am-late, closed Tue) A hip little café that serves espresso, light lunches and dinners. The menu here (available in English) is European influenced and includes such things as pizza, pasta and salads. Coffee starts at ¥430.

Upwards (☎ 230-8551; Chūō-ku, Yamamoto-dōri 1-7-16; lunch/dinner from ¥1000; 🕑 11.30am-midnight Tue-Sun) This fashionable eatery in Kitano serves pasta, sandwiches and salads in an airy, open space. It's another good spot for a drink in the evening. There's an English sign.

ENTERTAINMENT

Kōbe has a relatively large foreign community and a number of bars that see mixed Japanese and foreign crowds. For Japanese-style drinking establishments, try the *izakaya* in the neighbourhood between the JR tracks and Ikuta-jinja. Also bear in mind that a lot of Kōbe's nightlife is centred on the city's many cafés, most of which transform into bars in the evening.

New Munchen Club (☎ 335-0170; Chūō-ku, Akashi-chō 47) A decent German-style pub that draws its share of foreign residents. It's close to Daimaru department store.

SLEEPING

B Kōbe (☎ 333-4880; fax 333-4876; www.ishinhotels.com/theb-kobe/en/index.html; s/tw/d from ¥8400/15,750/13,650; 💻) The newly renovated and centrally located B Kōbe is a good utilitarian choice if you've got business in Kōbe or just want a clean place to lay your head in the evening.

Hotel Ōkura Kōbe (☎ 333-0111; fax 333-6673; Chūō-ku, Hatoba-chō 2-1; s/d from ¥18,480/28,875) On the waterfront behind Meriken Park, this is the most elegant hotel in town, with fine rooms and spacious common areas.

Hotel Tor Road (☎ 391-6691; fax 391-6570; Chūō-ku, Nakayamate-dōri 3-1-19; s/d from ¥9450/17,850) A step up from the typical business hotel, this is a good choice for those who want a little more comfort. Beds are larger than normal for this type of accommodation and quite clean. The friendly staff is another plus.

Crowne Plaza Kōbe (☎ 291-1121; fax 291-1154; Chūō-ku, Kitano-chō 1; s/d from ¥15,015/26,565) Towering above Shin-Kōbe Station, this hotel commands the best views of the city and has excellent on-site facilities.

HIMEJI

☎ 079

Himeji-jō, the finest castle in all Japan, is less than two hours west of Kyoto by train. The castle dominates the pleasant little city of Himeji and is easily visible from the train as you approach from any direction. Particularly stunning against a backdrop of April cherry blossoms, the castle has a graceful beauty that far exceeds that of European castles. Next door, Kōko-en is a pleasant stroll garden that can easily be paired with a visit to the castle. While you can stay overnight in Himeji, it's quite possible to visit it as a day trip from Kyoto, especially if you have a Japan Rail Pass and can use the *shinkansen*.

On the way to Himeji, take a look out the train window at the new Akashi Kaikyō Bridge. Its 3910m span links the island of Honshū with Awaji-shima, making it the longest suspension bridge in the world. It comes into view on the south side of the train about 15km west of Kōbe.

Himeji-jō (☎ 285-1146; Honmachi 68; admission ¥600, incl Kōko-en ¥720; 🕑 9am-5pm, last admission 4pm, 5pm in summer) is the most magnificent of the handful

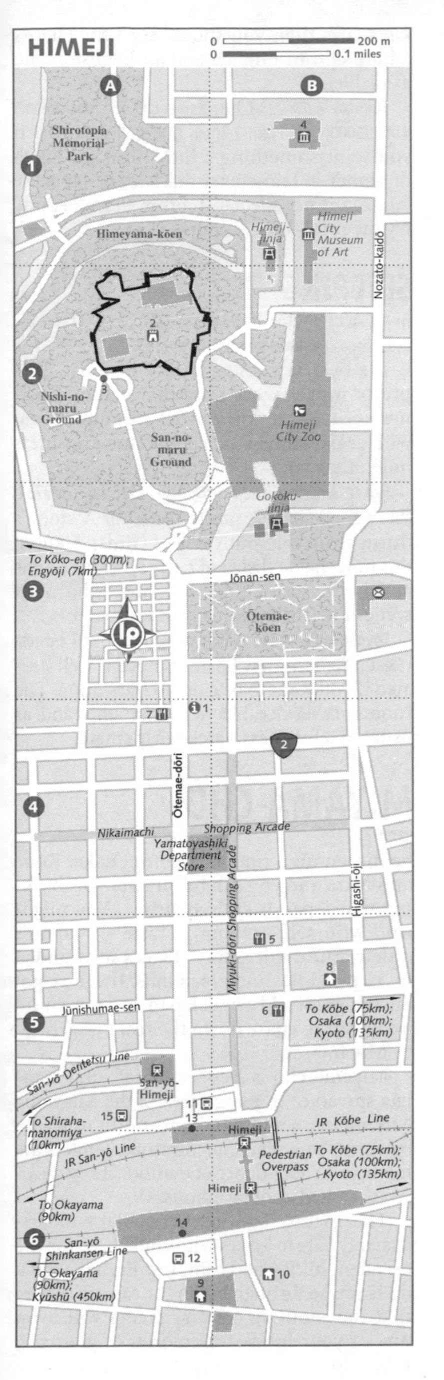

HIMEJI

SIGHTS & INFORMATION

Himeji Tourist Information 姫路観光なびポート 1 A4
Himeji-jō 姫路城 2 A2
Himeji-jō Ticket Office 姫路城切符売り場 3 A2
Hyōgo Prefectural Museum of History 兵庫県立歴史博物館 4 B1

EATING

Fukutei ふく亭 5 B5
Len レン 6 B5
Me-n-me めんめ 7 A4

SLEEPING

Himeji Washington Hotel Plaza 姫路ワシントンホテルプラザ 8 B5
Hotel Nikkō Himeji ホテル日航姫路 9 A6
Tōyoko Inn 東横イン 10 B6

TRANSPORT

City Bus Terminal 市バスターミナル 11 A5
City South Bus Terminal 市バス南ターミナル 12 A6
Himeji North Exit 北口 13 A5
Himeji South Exit 南口 14 A6
Shinki Bus Terminal 神姫バスターミナル 15 A5

of Japanese castles that survive in their original (nonconcrete) form. Although there have been fortifications in Himeji since 1333, this castle was built in 1580 by Toyotomi Hideyoshi and enlarged some 30 years later by Ikeda Terumasa.

The castle has a five-storey main *donjon* (keep) and three smaller *donjons,* and the entire structure is surrounded by moats and defensive walls punctuated by rectangular, circular and triangular openings for firing guns and shooting arrows at attackers.

English-speaking guides are sometimes available and can really add a lot to your tour of the castle. Unfortunately, appointments aren't accepted and it's hit or miss whether one will be available on the day of your visit – ask at the ticket office of the castle and hope for the best. The guide service is free.

The **Hyōgo Prefectural Museum of History** (☎ 288-9011; Honmachi 68; admission ¥200; 🕑 10am-5pm, last admission 4.30pm, closed Mon) is a well-organised museum that has good displays on Himeji-jō and other castles around Japan. The museum also covers the main periods of Japanese history with some English explanations. At 11am, 2pm and 3.30pm you can even try on a suit of samurai armour or a kimono. The museum is a five-minute walk north of the castle.

Just across the moat on the west side of Himeji-jō, you'll find **Kōko-en** (☎ 289-4120; Honmachi 68; admission ¥300, incl Himeji-jō ¥720; 🕑 9am-

TRANSPORT: HIMEJI

Distance from Kyoto 98km

Direction West

Train The best way to get to Himeji from Kyoto is by *shinkaisoku* (special rapid train) on the JR Tōkaidō line (¥2210, one hour and 20 minutes). You can also reach Himeji from Kyoto via the Tōkaidō/San-yō *shinkansen* (bullet train) line and this is a good option for Japan Rail Pass holders.

4.30pm, 9am-5.30pm in summer), a reconstruction of the former samurai quarters of the castle in a garden setting. There are nine separate Edo-style gardens, two ponds, a stream, a tea arbour (*matcha* powdered green tea costs ¥500) and the restaurant, Kassui-ken, where you can enjoy lunch while gazing over the gardens.

Himeji's Nada-no-Kenka Matsuri festival, held on 14 and 15 October, involves a conflict between three *mikoshi* (portable shrines) that are battered against each other until one smashes. The festival is held about five minutes' walk from Shirahamanomiya Station (10 minutes from Himeji Station on the San-yō-Dentetsu line). You should try to go on the second day when the festival reaches its peak – the action starts around noon.

INFORMATION

Himeji Tourist Information (☎ 285-3792) has two outlets, one of which is at the station, on the ground floor to the right as you come off the escalator. Between 10am and 3pm English-speaking staff are on duty and can help with hotel/ryokan reservations.

EATING

The food court in the underground mall at JR Himeji Station has all the usual Western and Japanese dishes. It's just to the right as you exit the north ticket gate of the station.

Me-n-me (☎ 225-0118; Honmachi 68; noodles from ¥480; 11.30am-7pm Thu-Tue) They make their own noodles at this homey little noodle joint a few minutes' walk from the castle. There's usually an English sign on the street and English menus inside.

Len (☎ 225-5505; Eki-mae-chō 324; lunch/dinner ¥1500/3000; 11.30am-midnight Tue-Sun, closed holidays) If you find yourself in Himeji in the evening and feel like a good meal of pan-Asian *izakaya* fare, then you should try Len. There's a blue sign in English and an English menu available.

Fukutei (☎ 223-0981; Kamei-chō 75; lunch/dinner ¥1400/5000; 11am-2.30pm & 4.30-9pm Fri-Wed) If you want something a little nicer for lunch or dinner in Himeji, try this *kaiseki* (Japanese *haute cuisine*) specialist. From 11am to 2pm, try the mini-*kaiseki* course (¥1400).

SLEEPING

Himeji Washington Hotel Plaza (☎ 225-0111; fax 25-0133; Higashiekimae-chō 98; s/d from ¥5800/11,000) This is the best midrange choice in town. It is pretty much everything that a good business hotel should be: well run and clean, with reasonably sized rooms (for a business hotel, that is).

Hotel Nikkō Himeji (☎ 222-2231; fax 24-3731; Minamiekimae-chō 100; s/d ¥10,925/20,700) A stone's throw from the south side of Himeji Station, this hotel has stylish and fairly spacious rooms and is the best choice for those who want something nicer than a business hotel.

Tōyoko Inn (☎ 284-1045; Minamiekimae-chō 97; s/d from ¥5880/7980) This new business hotel is well situated if you want to be close to the station. The rooms are serviceable, well maintained and, as usual in a business hotel, fairly small.

MIYAMA-CHŌ

☎ 0771

Spend enough time in Kyoto, Osaka, Kōbe and Nara and you can be forgiven for thinking that Japan is entirely urban. You might find yourself craving a taste of Japan's quieter rural side – tiny villages surrounded by rice paddies and green hills. If you've got an image of old rural Japan in your mind and want to chase down the real thing, head to Miyama-chō.

Miyama-chō is a collection of rural hamlets spread over a large area of the Kitayama Mountains, about two hours north of Kyoto by car or bus. These picturesque hamlets are home to an abundance of traditional *kayabukiya* (thatched-roof farmhouses).

This picturesque area is popular with artists and nature lovers who come here for the excellent hiking and camping. Even if all you do is cruise through by bus or car, we're sure that the soothing country scenes will form one of your fondest memories of your trip to Kyoto.

It is possible to travel to Miyama-chō as a day trip from Kyoto, but it makes a much nicer overnight trip. The Japanese-language *Map Kyoto*, available at the Kyoto Tourism Federation above Kyoto Station (p199), covers the Miyama-chō area.

The quiet village of Ashiu sits on the far eastern edge of Miyama-chō. The main attraction of Ashiu is the 4200-hectare virgin forest that lies to the east of the village. Safeguarded under the administration of Kyoto University's Department of Agriculture, this is about the only remaining virgin forest in all of Kansai.

The best way to sample the beauty of Ashiu's forest is to hike up into the gorge of the Yuragawa. Lonely Planet's *Hiking in Japan* guide details a four-day hike up the river. Those with less time can do shorter day trips up the gorge. Hikers should get hold of Shōbunsha's Japanese-language *Kyoto Kitayama* map, part of the Yama-to-Kōgen Chizu series (available at bookshops in Kyoto).

Miyama-chō's star attraction is Kitamura (North Village) a hamlet boasting a cluster of some 50 thatched-roof farmhouses. In 1994 the village was designated a national preservation site, and since then the local government has been generously subsidising the exorbitant cost of rethatching the roofs (at an average cost of ¥6 million – more than US$50,000!).

There's not much to do in the village except walk around and admire the old houses.

EATING

Morishige (☎ 75-1086; Miyama-chō, Uchikubo, Taninoshita 15; noodle dishes from ¥630) A thatched-roof place that serves simple but tasty noodle dishes and *nabe* dishes.

Yururi (☎ 76-0741; Miyama-chō, Morisato; sets ¥3000) A wonderfully elegant restaurant occupying a fine thatched-roof house. It's about half an hour north of the centre of Miyama-chō by car. Reservations are required.

SLEEPING

There are a number of interesting places in which to stay in the Miyama-chō area. It's best if you can have a Japanese-speaking person call to make reservations at these places since few lodge-owners speak English. Some owners will pick up guests in Hirogawara, which is the most convenient access point to Miyama-chō.

Matabe (☎ 77-0258; Kita-kuwada-gun, Kita Miyama-chō; per person incl 2 meals ¥8000) This quaint *minshuku* (Japanese-style B&B) in Kitamura is in a traditional thatched-roof house.

Miyama Heimat Youth Hostel (☎ /fax 75-0997; Miyama-chō, Obuchi, Nakasai 57; members/nonmembers ¥3360/3960) One of the cheaper options in the area. This

TRANSPORT: MIYAMA-CHŌ

There are no train lines to Miyama-chō, so you have to rent a car, hitch or take a series of buses from Kyoto.

Distance from Kyoto 50km

Direction North over a series of mountain passes.

Bus To get to Kitamura by bus, take a JR bus from in front of Kyoto Station to Shūzan. At Shimonaka transfer to a Miyama-chō-ei bus to Agake. From Agake, take another Miyama-chō-ei bus bound for Chimiguchi and get off at Kitamura (entire trip ¥2320, 2½ hours).

From Kitamura, you can catch a Miyama-chō-ei bus onward to Chimiguchi, where you can catch another bus to Sasari (for Ashiu get off at Deai and walk the last kilometre into the village). Needless to say, the complexity and cost of this route makes either renting a car or hitching look awfully attractive.

Car & Cycle The best road to Miyama-chō is Rte 162 (Shūzankaidō), though there is a lovely (but time-consuming) alternative route via Kurama in the north of Kyoto and over Hanase-tōgei Pass. Serious cyclists should be able to reach the area via either route by pedalling for about five arduous hours.

Hiking Another option is to take Kyoto bus 32 from Kyoto's Demachiyanagi Station to the last stop, Hirogawara (¥1050, 90 minutes), and hike over Sasari-tōgei Pass. From Hirogawara follow the road to the pass and then take the hiking trail down into Ashiu (you'll probably need a hiking map – see above for details). The hike notwithstanding, this is probably the easiest route into Ashiu since it involves only one bus.

Those intent on seeing a lot of Miyama-chō without renting a car can combine the two bus routes described above to make one grand traverse of the area. Take the buses all the way to Sasari from Kyoto Station, hike over the Sasari-tōgei pass and return to Kyoto by bus from Hirogawara (or vice-versa). Note that the road over the pass is closed in winter, during which season it makes a great cross-country ski or snowshoe route.

simple youth hostel is located in a thatched-roof house and it's on the road to Ōno Dam. Dinner costs ¥1050 and breakfast ¥630.

Yama-no-Ie (☎ 77-0290; Kita-kuwada-gun, Miyama-chō, Ashiu; per person incl 2 meals ¥7350) The only place to stay in Ashiu – other than camping – is in this impressive lodge. There are no meals served but there are simple cooking facilities. It's a few minutes on foot from the forest trailhead.

Hanase Suisen-Kyō (☎ 746-0185; fax 712-7023; www.suisenkyo.com; suisenkyo@mac.com; Hanase Harachi-chō; r per person ¥3200) Located in Hanase, about 15km south of Miyama-chō, this secluded getaway sits alongside a pleasant river. Bookings are by email or fax only. To get here from Kyoto, take Kyoto bus 32 (not Kyoto City bus) from Demachiyanagi (at least four daily, ¥930, 1½ hours) and get off at Naka-no-chō (¥930, 1½ hours).

TRANSPORT

Kyoto is within easy reach of three airports, all of which have air links with North America, Europe, Asia and Oceania, in addition to cities across Japan. Kyoto is also linked to the rest of Japan by a multitude of excellent train and bus lines, including the *shinkansen* (bullet train). Additionally, you can reach Osaka and Kōbe (both close to Kyoto) by ship from China.

Within the city, Kyoto has an excellent public transport system. There is a comprehensive bus network, two subway lines, four train lines (two of which can be used like subways for trips around Kyoto) and a huge fleet of taxis. Furthermore, being largely flat, Kyoto is a great city for cycling – it's perfectly feasible that you could rent or buy a bicycle on your first day in the city and never have to use the public transport system.

Book flights, tours and rail tickets online at www.lonelyplanet.com/travel_services.

AIR

Airlines

Most airlines have offices in Osaka or Tokyo. The ☎ 0120 numbers are toll free.

Air Canada (☎ 0120-048-048; www.aircanada.ca/e-home.html)

Air France (☎ 06-6641-1271; www.airfrance.com)

Air New Zealand (☎ 0120-300-747; www.airnewzealand.co.nz)

Alitalia (☎ 06-6341-3951; www.alitalia.com)

All Nippon Airways (ANA; ☎ international 0120-029-333, domestic 0120-029-222; www.ana.co.jp/eng/)

American Airlines (☎ 0120-000-860; www.aa.com)

Cathay Pacific Airways (☎ 0120-355-747; www.cathaypacific.com)

Delta Air Lines (☎ 0120-333-742; www.delta.com)

Garuda Indonesia (☎ 06-6635-3222; www.garuda-indonesia.com)

Japan Airlines (JAL; ☎ international 0120-255-931, domestic 0120-255-971; www.jal.co.jp/en/)

Jetstar (☎ 800-4008-3900; www.jetstar.com)

KLM Royal Dutch Airlines (☎ 0120-468-215; www.klm.com)

Korean Air (☎ 0088-21-2001; www.koreanair.com)

Lufthansa Airlines (☎ 0120-051-844; www.lufthansa.com)

Northwest Airlines (☎ 0120-120-747; www.nwa.com)

Qantas Airways (☎ 0120-207-020; www.qantas.com)

Scandinavian Airlines (☎ 0120-678-101; www.flysas.com)

Swiss International Air Lines (☎ 0120-667-788; www.swiss.com)

Thai Airways International (☎ 06-6202-5161; www.thaiairways.com)

United Airlines (☎ 0120-114-466; www.united.com)

Things Change...

The information in this chapter is particularly vulnerable to change. Check directly with the airline or a travel agent to make sure you understand how a fare (and ticket you may buy) works and be aware of the security requirements for international travel. Shop carefully. The details given in this chapter should be regarded as pointers and are not a substitute for your own careful, up-to-date research.

Airports

While there is no international or domestic airport in Kyoto, the city is within easy reach of Kansai International Airport (KIX), Central Japan International Airport Centrair (NGO) and Osaka International Itami Airport (ITM; domestic flights only).

The trip between KIX and Kyoto can be quite expensive and time consuming; if you are flying domestically and have a choice of airports, it is cheaper and easier to fly into Osaka International Itami Airport.

It's sometimes cheaper to fly into Tokyo's Narita airport than into KIX. As a rule, it will cost about ¥15,000 and take around five hours to get from Narita to Kyoto by train (taking the N'EX express train and the *shinkansen*). See the boxed text, p183, for more information.

KANSAI INTERNATIONAL AIRPORT

The closest international airport to Kyoto is Osaka's Kansai International Airport (code KIX; www.kansai-airport.or.jp/en), which has direct flights to and from many cities in North America, Asia, Europe and Oceania.

For international departures, there are shower and dayroom facilities, which cost

CLIMATE CHANGE & TRAVEL

Climate change is a serious threat to the ecosystems that humans rely upon, and air travel is the fastest-growing contributor to the problem. Lonely Planet regards travel, overall, as a global benefit, but believes we all have a responsibility to limit our personal impact on global warming.

Flying & Climate Change

Pretty much every form of motor transport generates CO_2 (the main cause of human-induced climate change) but planes are far and away the worst offenders, not just because of the sheer distances they allow us to travel, but because they release greenhouse gases high into the atmosphere. The statistics are frightening: two people taking a return flight between Europe and the US will contribute as much to climate change as an average household's gas and electricity consumption over a whole year.

Carbon Offset Schemes

Climatecare.org and other websites use 'carbon calculators' that allow travellers to offset the greenhouse gases they are responsible for with contributions to energy-saving projects and other climate-friendly initiatives in the developing world – including projects in India, Honduras, Kazakhstan and Uganda.

Lonely Planet, together with Rough Guides and other concerned partners in the travel industry, supports the carbon offset scheme run by climatecare.org. Lonely Planet offsets all of its staff and author travel.

For more information check out our website: www.lonelyplanet.com.

¥1200. These are available only to those who have cleared passport control and to transit passengers.

KIX has information counters throughout the complex with English-speaking staff. The main tourist information counter (☎ 0724-56-6025; 1st fl, International Arrivals Hall; 9am-9pm) is operated by the Osaka prefectural government. It's located roughly in the centre of the international arrivals hall.

If you'd prefer not to lug your bags all the way to Kyoto, there are several luggage delivery services that are located in the arrivals hall.

After clearing customs, it is a short walk to public transport: straight out the doors for buses and up the escalators or elevators for train connections (see the boxed text, opposite). KIX offers short- and long-term baggage storage for ¥350 to ¥1000 per day, depending on the size of the bag. You pay the bill when you pick up your bag.

Note that the area code for KIX is ☎ 0742, which is different from Kyoto's area code of ☎ 075.

CENTRAL JAPAN INTERNATIONAL AIRPORT CENTRAIR

Located in Nagoya is Central Japan International Airport Centrair (code NGO; www.centrair.jp/en), a 45-minute trip east of Kyoto by *shinkansen*. Centrair has flights between Nagoya and Australia, Canada, China, Guam, Hong Kong, Indonesia, Malaysia, New Zealand, the Philippines, Saipan, Singapore, South Korea, Taiwan, Thailand and the USA.

Centrair is one of the two airports in Japan serviced by Jetstar (p181), Australia's new budget airline.

OSAKA INTERNATIONAL ITAMI AIRPORT

Commonly known as Itami, Osaka International Itami Airport (code ITM; www.osaka-airport.co.jp) is Osaka's domestic airport. Itami has connections with dozens of cities in Japan. You may arrive here if you've transferred from an international flight at Narita.

You'll find an information counter with English-speaking staff in the main arrivals hall. There are several luggage delivery services in the arrivals hall if you don't want to carry your bags to Kyoto.

Domestic Air Services

The larger airports in Japan have regular flights to and from Osaka. For most cities in Honshū (the main island of Japan), including Tokyo, Nagoya and Hiroshima, it is usually faster, cheaper and more convenient to travel by *shinkansen* (p187).

Domestic airfares can be rather expensive and tend to vary little between carriers. ANA and JAL offer tickets at up to 50% off if you purchase a month or more in advance, with smaller discounts for purchases made one to three weeks in advance.

GETTING INTO TOWN

To/From KIX

The fastest, most convenient way between KIX and Kyoto is the special JR *haruka* airport express (reserved/unreserved ¥3490/¥2980, 75 minutes). Unreserved seats are almost always available, so you usually don't need to purchase tickets in advance. First and last departures from KIX to Kyoto are at 6.29am and 10.18pm Monday to Friday (6.41am at weekends); first and last departures from Kyoto to KIX are at 5.46am and 8.16pm.

If you have time to spare, you can save some money by taking the *kankū kaisoku* (Kansai airport express) between the airport and Osaka Station and taking a regular *shinkaisoku* (special rapid train) to/from Kyoto (p188). The total journey by this route takes about 90 minutes with good connections, and costs ¥1800.

For those travelling on Japanese airlines (JAL and ANA), there is an advance check-in counter inside the JR ticket office in Kyoto Station (Map p46). This service allows you to check in with your luggage at the station – a real bonus for those with heavy bags.

Osaka Airport Transport (☎ 06-6844-1124; www.okkbus.co.jp/eng) runs direct limousine buses between Kyoto and KIX (adult/child ¥2300/1150, 105 minutes). There are pick-up and drop-off points on the southern side of Kyoto Station (Map p46; in front of Avanti Department Store), and at Kyoto ANA Hotel (Map p74) and Sanjō Keihan Station (Map pp68–9). At KIX the buses leave from the kerb outside the International Arrivals Hall.

Perhaps the most convenient option is the MK Taxi Sky Gate Shuttle limousine van service (☎ 702-5489; www.mk-group.co.jp/english/shuttle/index.html), which will drop you off anywhere in Kyoto for ¥3500 – simply go to the staff counter at the south end of the arrivals hall of KIX and they will do the rest. From Kyoto to the airport it is necessary to make reservations two days in advance and they will pick you up anywhere in Kyoto and take you to the airport. A similar service is offered by Yasaka Taxi (☎ 803-4800).

To/From Central Japan International Airport Centrair

The Meitetsu Tokoname Railroad line connects Centrair with Nagoya Station (¥850, 28 minutes). Nagoya is connected to Kyoto by the Tōkaidō shinkansen line (¥5640, 36 minutes). It is therefore quite convenient to use Centrair as your gateway to Kyoto.

To/From Osaka International Itami Airport

Osaka Airport Transport (☎ 06-6844-1124; www.okkbus.co.jp/eng/) runs frequent airport limousine buses (¥1370, 55 minutes) between Kyoto Station and Itami. There are less frequent pick-ups and drop-offs at some of Kyoto's main hotels. The Kyoto Station stop is in front of Avanti Department Store (Map p46) and the Itami stop is outside the arrivals hall – buy your ticket from the machine near the bus stop. Allow extra time in case of traffic. At Itami the stand for these buses is outside the arrivals hall; buy your ticket from the machines and ask one of the attendants which stand is for Kyoto.

You can also take the MK Taxi Sky Gate Shuttle limousine van service to/from the city for ¥2300. Call at least two days in advance to reserve or ask at the information counter in the arrivals hall in Osaka.

The following are typical one-way prices for flights between Osaka (Itami or KIX) and several major cities in Japan.

Destination	One Way (¥)
Fukuoka	20,100
Kagoshima	24,600
Kōchi	16,100
Kumamoto	21,600
Matsuyama	15,600
Nagasaki	23,600
Naha	31,400
Niigata	26,600
Sapporo	37,900
Sendai	28,300
Tokyo	20,700

BICYCLE

Kyoto is a great city to explore on a bicycle. With the exception of outlying areas, it is mostly flat and there is a bike path running the length of the Kamo-gawa. Many guesthouses rent or lend bicycles to their guests and there are rental shops around Kyoto Station, in Arashiyama and Sagano, and Downtown Kyoto. With a decent bicycle and a good map, you can easily make your way all around the city. Bicycle tours are also available (see p184).

Unfortunately, Kyoto's bike parking facilities must be among the worst in the world – hence the number of bikes you see haphazardly locked up around the city. Many bikes end up stolen or impounded during regular sweeps of the city (particularly those near entrances to train/subway stations). If your bike does disappear, check for a poster (in both Japanese and English) in the vicinity indicating the time of seizure and the inconvenient place you'll have to go to pay the ¥2000 fine and retrieve your bike. The city does not impound bicycles on Sundays or holidays, so you can park pretty much at will on those days.

If you don't want to worry about your bike being stolen or impounded, we recommend using one of the city-operated bicycle and motorcycle parking lots. There is one downtown on Kiyamachi-dōri midway between Sanjō-dōri and Shijō-dōri (Map p50), another near Kyoto Station (Map p46), and another in the north of town near the Eizan Densha station at Demachiyanagi (Map pp68–9). These places charge ¥150 per day (buy a ticket from the machine on your way in or out).

Hire

Budget Inn (Map p46; ☎ 353-6968; www.kyotojp.com) rents large-frame and regular bicycles for ¥800 per day for visitors, ¥690 for staying guests, with a ¥3000 deposit per bike; see p148. Bicycles can be picked up between 8am and 9.30pm.

Another great place to rent a bike is the **Kyoto Cycling Tour Project** (KCTP; Map p46; ☎ 467-5175; www.kctp.net/en). The folks here rent mountain bikes (¥1500 per day) which are perfect for getting around Kyoto. Bicycles can be delivered upon request (¥500) or you can pick them up at their shop. KCTP also conducts a variety of bicycle tours of Kyoto, which are an excellent way to see the city (check the website for details).

Most rental outfits require you to leave ID such as a passport.

Purchase

If you plan on spending more than a week or so exploring Kyoto by bicycle, it might make sense to purchase one second-hand. A simple *mama chari* (shopping bike) can be had for as little as ¥3000. Try the used-cycle shop **Eirin** (Map pp68–9; ☎ 752-0292; Sakyō-ku, Imadegawa-dōri) near Kyoto University. Alternatively, you'll find a good selection of used bikes advertised for sale on the message board at **Kyoto International Community House** (Map pp68–9; ☎ 752-3010; Sakyō-ku, Awataguchi).

BOAT

Domestic Ferries

Osaka and Kōbe are the main ports for ferries between Kansai and Shikoku, and Kyūshū and Okinawa. There is a range of fares available to/from Osaka and Kōbe.

Destination	Cost (¥)	Duration
Imabari (Shikoku)	from ¥5400	7hr
Matsuyama (Shikoku)	from ¥6300	9.5hr
Shinmoji (Kitakyūshū)	from ¥7400	12hr
Beppu (Kyūshū)	from ¥8800	12hr
Ōita (Kyūshū)	from ¥8800	12hr
Miyazaki (Kyūshū)	from ¥10,400	13hr
Shibushi (Kyūshū)	from ¥10,700	14hr
Naha (Okinawa)	from ¥18,800	39hr

From Maizuru, north of Kyoto on the Sea of Japan, you can also catch a ferry as far north as Otaru in Hokkaidō (¥9600, 29 hours).

The Tourist Information Centre (TIC; p199) can provide detailed information on various routes and up-to-date schedules.

International Ferries

There are regular ferries running between Kansai and Korea or China. There is no international departure tax when leaving Japan by boat.

From Naha there are ferries onward to Taiwan (¥16,000, 19 hours).

CHINA

The **Japan China International Ferry Company** (☎ in Japan 06-6536-6541, in China 021-6325-7642; www.fune.co.jp/chinjif, in Japanese) connects Shanghai with Osaka and Kōbe. A 2nd-class ticket costs around US$180. The journey takes around 48 hours. A similar service is provided by the **Shanghai Ferry Company** (☎ in Japan 06-6243-6345, in China 021-6537-5111; www.shanghai-ferry.co.jp, in Japanese).

The **China Express Line** (☎ in Japan 078-321-5791, in China 022-2420-5777; www.celkobe.co.jp, in Japanese) operates a ferry between Kōbe and Tientsin where 1st-/2nd-class tickets cost US$240/210. The journey takes around 48 hours.

SOUTH KOREA

The **Kampu Ferry Service** (☎ in Japan 0832-24-3000, in Korea operating under Pukwan Ferry 051-464-2700; www.kampuferry.co.jp, in Japanese) operates the Shimonoseki–Busan ferry service. One-way fares range from around US$85 to US$180. The journey takes around 12 hours.

An international high-speed hydrofoil service known as the Biitoru (say 'beetle') run by JR Kyūshū (☎ in Japan 092-281-2315, in Korea 051-465-6111; www.jrbeetle.co.jp/english) connects Fukuoka with Busan in Korea (one way US$110, three hours). The Camellia line (☎ in Japan 092-262-2323, in Korea 051-466-7799; www.camellia-line.co.jp, in Japanese & Korean) also has a regular daily ferry service between Fukuoka and Busan (US$80, 16 hours, one way).

BUS

City Buses

Kyoto has an intricate network of bus routes providing an efficient way of getting around at moderate cost. Many of the routes used by visitors have announcements in English. Most buses run between 7am and 9pm, though a few run earlier or later.

The main bus terminals are also train stations: Kyoto Station (Map p46) on the JR and Kintetsu lines, Sanjō Station (Map pp68–9) on the Keihan line/Tōzai subway line, Karasuma-Shijō Station (Map p50) on the Hankyū line/Karasuma subway line, and Kitaōji Station (Map pp54–5) on the Karasuma subway line. The bus terminal at Kyoto Station is on the north side and has three main departure bays (departure points are indicated by the letter of the bay and number of the stop within that bay).

The main bus information centre (Map p46) is located in front of Kyoto Station. Here you can pick up bus maps, purchase bus tickets and passes (on all lines, including highway buses), and get additional information. Nearby, there's an English/Japanese bus information computer terminal; just enter your intended destination and it will tell you the correct bus and bus stop.

Three-digit numbers written against a red background denote loop lines: bus 204 runs around the northern part of the city and buses 205 and 206 circle the city via Kyoto Station. Buses with route numbers on a blue background take other routes.

The TIC stocks the *Bus Navi: Kyoto City Bus Sightseeing Map,* which shows the city's main bus lines. But this map is not exhaustive. If you can read a little Japanese, pick up a copy of the regular (and more detailed) Japanese bus map available at major bus terminals throughout the city, including the main bus information centre.

KYOTO BUS & SUBWAY PASSES

To save time and money you can buy a *kaisū-ken* (book of five tickets) for ¥1000. There's also a *shi-basu senyō ichinichi jōshaken cādo* (one-day card) valid for unlimited travel on city buses that costs ¥500. A similar pass (*Kyoto kankō ichinichi jōsha-ken)* that allows unlimited use of the bus and subway costs ¥1200. A *Kyoto kankō futsuka jōsha-ken* (two-day bus/subway pass) costs ¥2000. *Kaisū-ken* can be purchased directly from bus drivers. The other passes and cards can be purchased at major bus terminals and at the bus information centre. Also, be sure to refer to the Kansai Thru Pass entry (p189).

Bus stops usually have a map of destinations from that stop and a timetable for the buses serving that stop. Unfortunately, all of this information is in Japanese, so nonspeakers will simply have to ask locals for help.

Entry to the bus is usually through the back door and exit is via the front door. Inner-city buses charge a flat fare (¥220), which you drop into the clear plastic receptacle on top of the machine next to the driver on your way out. A separate machine gives change for ¥100 and ¥500 coins or ¥1000 notes.

On buses serving the outer areas, you take a *seiri-ken* (numbered ticket) when entering. When you leave, an electronic board above the driver displays the fare corresponding to your ticket number (drop the *seiri-ken* into the ticket box with your fare).

When heading for locations outside the city centre, be careful which bus you board. Kyoto City buses are green, Kyoto buses are tan and Keihan buses are red and white.

Long-Distance Buses

The overnight bus (JR Dream Kyoto Go) runs between Tokyo Station (Yaesu-guchi long-distance bus stop) and Kyoto Station Bus Terminal. The trip takes about eight hours and there are usually two departures nightly in either direction, at 10pm (Friday, Saturday, Sunday and holidays) and 11pm (daily). The fare is ¥8180/14,480 one way/return. You should be able to grab some sleep in the reclining seats. There is a similar service to/from Shinjuku Station's Shin-minami-guchi in Tokyo.

Other JR bus transport possibilities include Kanazawa (one way/return ¥4060/6600) and Hiroshima (one way/return ¥5500/10,000).

CAR & MOTORCYCLE

The Meishin Expressway runs between Nagoya and Kōbe. The best access to Kyoto is from the Kyoto-Minami off-ramp (it will leave you on Rte 1, a few kilometres south of the city centre). Kyoto is also accessible from Osaka on Rte 1, Nishinomiya (Kōbe area) on Rte 171, from the western hills on Rte 9 or from the north (Sea of Japan) on the Shūzan Kaidō (Rte 162).

Kyoto's heavy traffic and narrow roads make driving in the city difficult and stressful. You will almost always do better riding a bicycle or catching public transport. Unless you have specific needs, do not even entertain the idea of renting a car to tour the city – it's far more cost and headache than any traveller needs (plus parking fines start at ¥15,000).

Driving is on the left-hand side in Japan. A litre of petrol costs between ¥120 and ¥150.

Driving Licence & Permits

Travellers from most nations are able to drive in Japan with an International Driving Permit backed up by their own regular licence. The international permit is issued by your national automobile association and costs around US$5 in most countries. Make sure it's endorsed for cars and motorcycles if you're licensed for both.

Travellers from Switzerland, France and Germany (and others whose countries are not signatories to the Geneva Convention of 1949 concerning international driving licences) are not allowed to drive in Japan on a regular international licence. Rather, travellers from these countries must have their own licence backed by an authorised translation of the same licence. These translations can be made by their country's embassy or consulate in Japan or by the **Japan Automobile Federation** (JAF; ☎ 03-6833-9000, 0570-00-2811; www.jaf.or.jp/e/index_e.htm; 2-2-17 Shiba, Minato-ku, Tokyo 105-0014). If you are unsure which category your country falls into, contact the nearest JNTO office (p199).

Foreign licences and International Driving Permits are valid in Japan only for six months. If you are staying longer, you will have to get a Japanese licence from the local department of motor vehicles. To do this, you will need to provide your own licence, passport photos, Alien Registration Card and the fee, and also take a simple eyesight test.

Hire

It makes sense to rent a car if you plan to explore certain rural areas that aren't serviced by train lines (such as Miyama-chō, p178).

There are several car-rental agencies in Kyoto. Nissan Rent-a-Car (Map p46) has an office directly in front of Kyoto Station. Matsuda Rent-a-Car (Map pp54–5; ☎ 361-0201) is close to the intersection of Kawaramachi-dōri and Gojō-dōri. You will need to produce an International Driving Permit.

Typical hire rates for a small car are ¥6825 to ¥9450 for the first day and ¥5775 to ¥7875 per day thereafter. Move up a bracket and you're looking at ¥11,550 to ¥14,700 for the first day and ¥9450 to ¥11,550 thereafter. On top of the hire charge, there's a ¥1000 per day insurance cost.

It's also worth bearing in mind that car hire costs go up during high seasons (28 April to 6 May, 20 July to 31 August and 28 December to 5 January). A car that costs ¥8800 a day will usually go up to ¥9700 during any of the peak times.

Communication can be a major problem when hiring a car. If you cannot find a local to assist you with the paperwork, speaking a little Japanese will help greatly. Some of the offices will have a rent-a-car phrasebook, with questions you might need to ask in English. Otherwise, just speak as slowly as possible and hope for the best.

TAXI

Taxis are a convenient, but expensive, way of getting from place to place about town. A taxi can usually be flagged down in most parts of the city at any time. There are also a large number of *takushī noriba* (taxi stands) in town, outside most train/subway stations, department stores etc. There is no need to touch the back doors of the cars at all – the opening/closing mechanism is controlled by the driver.

Fares generally start at ¥630 for the first 2km. The exception is **MK Taxi** (☎ 721-2237), where fares start at ¥580. Regardless of which taxi company you use, there's a 20% surcharge for rides between midnight and 6am.

MK Taxi also provides tours of the city with English-speaking drivers. For a group of up to four people, prices start at ¥13,280 for three hours.

Two other companies that offer a similar tour service, English-speaking drivers and

USEFUL PHRASES

Train Types

shinkansen	新幹線	bullet train
tokkyū	特急	limited express
shinkaisoku	新快速	JR special rapid train
kyūkō	急行	express
kaisoku	快速	JR rapid or express
futsū	普通	local
kaku-eki-teisha	各駅停車	local

Other Useful Words

jiyū-seki	自由席	unreserved seat
shitei-seki	指定席	reserved seat
green-sha	グリーン車	1st-class car
ōfuku	往復	round trip
katamichi	片道	one way
kin'en-sha	禁煙車	nonsmoking car
kitsuen-sha	喫煙車	smoking car

competitive prices are Kyōren Taxi Service (☎ 672-5111) and Keihan Taxi Service (☎ 602-8162).

TRAIN

Kyoto is reached from most places in Japan by JR (Japan's main train company), but there are also several private lines connecting Kyoto with Nagoya, Nara, Osaka and Kōbe. Where they exist, private lines are always cheaper than JR.

The main train station in Kyoto is Kyoto Station (Map46), which is actually two stations under one roof: JR Kyoto Station and Kintetsu Kyoto Station. This station is in the south of the city, just below Shichijō-dōri. The easiest way to get downtown from this station is to hop on the Karasuma subway line (see below). There is a bus terminal on the north side of the station from where you can catch buses to all parts of town; for more information, see p185.

In addition to the private Kintetsu line that operates from Kyoto Station, there are two other private train lines in Kyoto: the Hankyū line that operates from Downtown Kyoto along Shijō-dōri and the Keihan line that operates from stops along the Kamo-gawa. For more information on these lines, see p188.

Subway

Kyoto has two efficient subway lines, which operate from 5.30am to 11.30pm. Minimum adult fare is ¥210 (children ¥110).

The quickest way to travel between the north and south of the city is the Karasuma subway line. The line has 15 stops and runs from Takeda in the far south, via Kyoto Station, to the Kyoto International Conference Hall (Kokusaikaikan Station) in the north.

The east–west Tōzai subway line traverses Kyoto from Nijō Station in the west, meeting the Karasuma subway line at Karasuma-Oike Station, and continuing east to Sanjō Keihan, Yamashina and Rokujizō in the east and southeast.

To/From Other Parts of Japan

KŌBE

Kobe's Sannomiya Station is on the JR Tōkaidō/Sanyō line as well as the Hankyū line, both of which connect it to Kyoto. The fastest way between Kōbe and Kyoto Station is a JR *shinkaisoku* (¥1050, 55 minutes).

The Hankyū line, which stops at Kawaramachi, Karasuma and Ōmiya Stations in Kyoto (¥590, one hour limited express), is cheaper but less convenient; change at Osaka's Jūsō or Umeda Stations.

JR Rail Pass holders should also note that Shin-Kōbe Station is on the Tōkaidō/Sanyō *shinkansen* line.

KYŪSHŪ

Kyoto is on the JR Tōkaidō/Sanyō *shinkansen* line, which runs to Hakata Station in Fukuoka, northern Kyūshū (¥15,610, three hours). Other places to pick up the train along this route include Shimonoseki (¥14,570, three hours), Hiroshima (¥11,090, 1¾ hours) and Okayama (¥7630, one hour).

NAGOYA

The *shinkansen* (¥5640, 36 minutes) goes to/from Nagoya. You can save around half the cost by taking regular express trains, but you will need to change trains at least once and can expect the trip to take about three hours. For information on getting to/from Nagoya's Central Japan International Airport Centrair, see p183.

NARA

Unless you have a Japan Rail Pass, the best option is the Kintetsu line (sometimes written in English as the Kinki Nippon railway), which links Kintetsu Nara Station and Kintetsu Kyoto Station. There are direct limited express trains (¥1110, 35 minutes) and ordinary express trains (¥610, 45 minutes), which may require a change at Saidai-ji.

The JR Nara line also connects JR Nara Station with Kyoto Station. Your best bet between the two cities is a *kaisoku* (rapid train; ¥690, 63 minutes), but departures are often few and far between.

NORTH OF KYOTO

Kyoto can be reached from the northern cities of Kanazawa and Fukui by the JR Hokuriku and Kosei lines, which run along the west coast of Biwa-ko. From Sea of Japan cities, such as Obama and Maizuru, you can take the JR Obama line to Ayabe and then change to the San-in line coming from Kinosaki.

OSAKA

Other than the *shinkansen,* the fastest way between Osaka Station and Kyoto Station is a JR *shinkaisoku* (¥540, 29 minutes).

There is also the cheaper, private Hankyū line, which runs between Umeda Station in downtown Osaka and Kawaramachi, Karasuma and Ōmiya Stations in Kyoto (¥390, 40 minutes limited express).

Alternatively, you can take the Keihan line between Yodoyabashi Station in Osaka and Demachiyanagi, Marutamachi, Sanjō, Shijō or Shichijō Stations in Kyoto (¥400, 45 minutes limited express).

If you arrive in Osaka at the Osaka-kō or Nan-kō ferry ports, you will find convenient subway connections to JR Osaka Station, Keihan Yodoyabashi Station or the Hankyū Umeda Station. From these stations there are rail connections onwards to Kyoto.

For information on travelling to/from Osaka International Itami Airport and Kansai International Airport, see p183.

TOKYO

The JR *shinkansen* is the fastest and most frequent rail link; the *hikari* superexpress (one way, ¥13,520, two hours and 20 minutes) goes to/from Tokyo Station.

By regular express train (¥7980, around eight hours), the trip involves at least two – possibly three or four – changes along the way.

Note that if you're flying into Tokyo's Narita Airport, you will have to first take a train from Narita into the city and then catch a *shinkansen* from Tokyo Station to Kyoto. For those making this trip, note that Tokyo Station is 66km from Narita Airport. *Shinkansen* run between Tokyo and Kyoto roughly between 6am and 9pm. There are several departures an hour in each direction. Note that the *hikari* and *nozomi* versions of the *shinkansen* are the fastest and are definitely the way to go. The N'EX special express train is the fastest way to travel from Narita to Tokyo Station (¥2940, 53 minutes); the 'Airport Narita' trains are cheaper and fairly fast (¥1280, 1½ hours).

Buying a Ticket

All stations are equipped with automatic ticket machines, which are simple to operate. Destinations and fares are all posted above the machines in both Japanese and English – once you've figured out the fare to your destination, just insert your money and press the yen amount. Most of these machines accept paper currency in addition to coins (usually just ¥1000 notes). If you've made a mistake, press the red *tori-keshi* (cancel) button. There's also a help button to summon assistance.

Train Passes

JAPAN RAIL PASS

One of Japan's few travel bargains is the Japan Rail Pass, which *must be purchased outside Japan*. It is available to foreign tourists and Japanese residents living overseas, but not foreign residents of Japan. The pass lets you use any JR service for seven days for ¥28,300, 14 days for ¥45,100 or 21 days for ¥57,700. Green Car passes are ¥37,800, ¥61,200 and ¥79,600, respectively. The pass cannot be used for the new superexpress *nozomi shinkansen* service, but is OK for everything else (including other *shinkansen* services such as *hikari*).

The only surcharge levied on the Japan Rail Pass is for overnight sleepers. Since a one-way, reserved seat Tokyo–Kyoto *shinkansen* ticket costs ¥13,220, you only have to travel Tokyo–Kyoto–Tokyo to make a seven-day pass come close to paying off. Note that the pass is valid only on JR services; you will still have to pay for private train services.

In order to get a pass, you must first purchase an 'exchange order' at JAL and ANA offices and major travel agencies outside Japan. Once you arrive in Japan, you must bring this exchange order to a JR Travel Service Centre, which can be found in most major JR stations and at Narita and Kansai airports. When you validate your pass, you'll have to show your passport. The pass can only be used by those with a temporary visitor visa.

The clock starts to tick on the pass as soon as you validate it, so don't do so if you're going into Tokyo or Kyoto and intend to hang around for a few days.

For more details on the pass and overseas purchase locations, visit the Japan Rail Pass website at www.japanrailpass.net.

JR WEST KANSAI PASS

A great deal for those who want to explore only the Kansai area, this pass covers unlimited travel on JR lines between most major Kansai cities, such as Himeji, Kōbe, Osaka, Kyoto and Nara. It also covers JR trains to and from Kansai airport but does not cover any *shinkansen* lines. One-, two-, three- and four-day passes cost ¥2000/4000/5000/6000, respectively (children's passes are half-price). These can be purchased at the same places as the countrywide rail pass (both inside and outside Japan) and also entitle you to discounts at train station rental-car offices. Like the Japan Rail Pass, this can only be used by those with a temporary visitor visa. For more information on this pass, see the JR West website, www.westjr.co.jp/english/travel.

KANSAI THRU PASS

This new pass is a real bonus to travellers who plan to do a fair bit of exploration in the Kansai area. It enables you to ride on city subways, private railways and city buses in Kyoto, Nara, Osaka, Kobe and Wakayama. It also entitles you to discounts at many attractions in the Kansai area. A two-day pass costs ¥3800 and a three-day pass costs ¥5000. It is available at the Kansai airport travel counter on the 1st floor of the International Arrivals Hall and at the main bus information centre in front of Kyoto Station, among others. For more information, visit www.surutto.com/conts/ticket/3dayeng/.

SEISHUN JŪHACHI KIPPU

If you don't have a Japan Rail Pass, one of the best deals is a five-day Seishun Jūhachi Kippu (literally a 'Youth 18 Ticket'). Despite its name, it can be used by anyone of any age. For ¥11,500 you get five one-day tickets valid for travel anywhere in Japan on JR lines. The only catches are that you can't travel on *tokkyū* or *shinkansen* trains and each ticket must be used within 24 hours. However, even if you only have to make a return trip, say, between Tokyo and Kyoto, you'll be saving a lot of money. Seishun Jūhachi Kippu can be purchased at most JR stations in Japan.

The tickets are intended to be used during Japanese university holidays. There are three periods of sales and validity: spring – sold between 20 February and 31 March and valid for use between 1 March and 10 April; summer – sold between 1 July and 31 August and valid for use between 20 July and 10 September; and winter – sold between 1 December and 10 January and valid for use between 10 December and 20 January. Note that these periods are subject to change. For more information, ask at any JR ticket window or visit www.jreast.co.jp/e/pass/seishun18.html.

If you don't want to buy the whole book of five tickets, you can sometimes purchase separate tickets at the discount ticket shops around train stations.

Discount Ticket Shops

Known as *kakuyasu-kippu-uriba*, these stores deal in discounted tickets for trains, buses, domestic flights, ferries, and a host of other things such as cut-rate stamps and phonecards. Typical savings on *shinkansen* tickets are between 5% and 10%, which is good news for long-term residents who are not eligible for Japan Rail Passes. Discount ticket agencies are found around train stations in medium and large cities. The best way to find one is to ask at the *kōban* (police box) outside the station.

Around Kyoto Station, you'll find **Tōkai Discount Ticket Shop** (Map p46; ☎ north side 344-0330, south side 662-6640; ⏰ north side 10am-7.30pm Mon-Fri, to 7pm Sat, Sun & holidays, south side 10am-7.30pm Mon-Fri, to 7pm Sat, Sun & holidays). In the Excursions chapter (p158), discount ticket shops are listed on the maps of Himeji (p176), Osaka (p165) and Kōbe (p173).

Left Luggage

There are coin lockers in train stations in Kyoto. Small/medium/large lockers cost ¥300/400/600 for 24 hours. Alternatively, in Kyoto Station there is an *ichiji-nimotsu-azukari* (luggage-storage office) that charges ¥410 per piece of luggage for up to six days, after which the daily rate increases to ¥820. Luggage can be stored for a total of 15 days and there is a size limit up to 2m wide and up to 30kg. The office is on the B1 floor near the central ticket gate.

DIRECTORY

ADDRESSES IN KYOTO

In Japan, finding a place from its address can be difficult, even for locals. The problem is twofold: first, the address is given by an area rather than a street; and second, the numbers are not necessarily consecutive. To find an address, the usual process is to ask directions. The numerous local police boxes are there largely for this purpose.

In this guide, we use a simplified system for addresses. We either give the area (eg Higashiyama-ku, Nanzen-ji) or we give the street on which the place is located, followed by the nearest cross street (eg Karasuma-dōri-Imadegawa). In some cases, we also give additional information to show where the place lies in relation to the intersection of the two streets mentioned. In Kyoto, the land usually slopes gently to the south; thus, an address might indicate whether a place lies above or north of *(agaru)* or below or south of *(sagaru* or *kudaru)* a particular east–west road. An address might also indicate whether a place lies east *(higashi)* or west *(nishi)* of the north–south road. Thus, Karasuma-dōri-Imadegawa simply means the place is near the intersection of Karasuma-dōri and Imadegawa-dōri; Karasuma-dōri-Imadegawa-sagaru indicates that it's south of that intersection.

BUSINESS HOURS

Shops in town are typically open from 10am to 7pm or 8pm, with larger shops staying open later, and smaller, more traditional ones closing earlier. Kyoto's six major department stores are usually open from 10am to 8pm daily.

Although most companies technically operate on a 9am to 5pm, five-day work week, many stay in business on Saturday mornings as well. Banks are open from Monday to Friday, 9am to 3pm, and are closed on Saturdays, Sundays and national holidays.

For those late-night cravings, note that beer and cigarette vending machines shut down after 11pm; there are 24-hour convenience stores all over town, however, some of which sell alcohol and tobacco.

For post office opening hours, see p197.

CHILDREN

Japan is a great place to travel with children; it's safe, clean and extremely convenient. It's possible to book cots in most hotels (but not in many so-called 'business hotels'), and nappy-changing tables are available in the bathrooms of most hotels and in some train stations. Nappies and baby formula are widely available in supermarkets, department stores and convenience stores.

Breast-feeding in public is generally not done in Japan. Child-care facilities are usually available in department stores – ask at the information counter when you enter. Otherwise, child-care facilities are mainly geared to locals only and are hard to access for visitors.

In general, the cost of public transport is half-price for children under 12. Likewise, many of the city's attractions and hotels also offer discounted rates for children.

For more information on child-centred activities in Kyoto, see the boxed text, p48.

CLIMATE

You can visit Kyoto at any time of year, although the hot and humid months of June, July and August and the cold months of December, January and February might be a little uncomfortable for some. The best times are the climatically stable seasons of spring (March to May) and autumn (late September to November).

The highlight of spring is cherry-blossom season, which usually arrives in Kyoto in early April. Bear in mind, though, that the blossoms are notoriously fickle, blooming any time from late March to mid-April.

Autumn is an equally good time to travel, with pleasant temperatures and soothing autumn colours. The shrines and temples of Kyoto look stunning against a backdrop of blazing leaves, which usually peak in mid- to late November.

Of course, the Japanese are well aware that Kyoto is most beautiful at these times and the main attractions can be packed with local tourists. Likewise, accommodation can be hard to find; if you do come at these times, be sure to book well in advance.

Travelling in either winter or summer is a mixed bag. Mid-winter (December to February) weather can be quite cold (but not

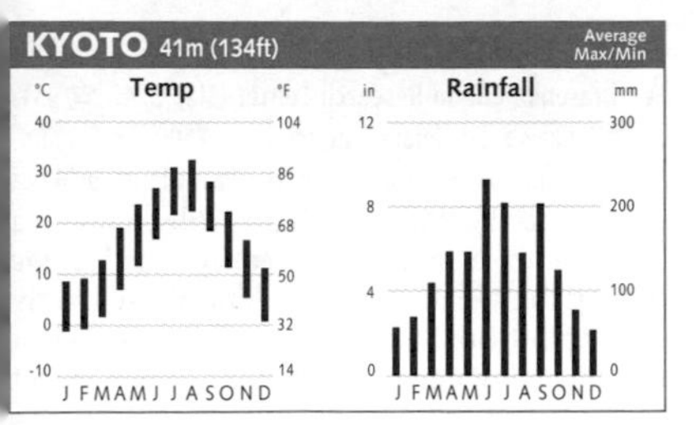

prohibitively so), while the sticky summer months (June to August) can turn even the briefest excursion out of the air-con into a soup bath.

June is the month of Japan's rainy season, which varies in intensity from year to year; some years there's no rainy season to speak of, other years it rains virtually every day.

For more information on the best times to visit Kyoto, see p15.

COURSES & CULTURAL EXPERIENCES

There's more to Kyoto than just temples, shrines and parks: there are several places to get hands-on experience in traditional arts and crafts including tea ceremony, Japanese *washi* paper, textiles, ceramics and calligraphy. This is only a partial list of what's available. The people at the TIC (p199) can help with requests for more specialised activities.

Kyoto International Community House (KICH; Map pp68–9; ☎ 752-3010; Sakyō-ku, Awataguchi, Torii-chō 2-1; 9am-9pm Tue-Sun; 5min walk from Keage Station, Tōzai subway line) Offers an intriguing variety of introductory courses in Japanese culture, open to all for observation (free) and participation. The cost is ¥500 per class, ¥6000 per three-month semester for tea ceremony. It also offers Japanese-language and calligraphy classes. For more on KICH, see p200.

WAK Japan (Map pp54–5; ☎ 212-9993; www.wakjapan.com; Kamigyō-ku, Iseya-chō 412-506; 10min walk from Marutamachi station, Keihan line) offers a wide variety of excellent introductions to Japanese culture: tea ceremony, ikebana (flower arrangement), trying on kimono, home visits, Japanese cooking, calligraphy, origami etc. Presenters/instructors will speak English or else interpreters are provided. Pick-up service is available from your lodgings. This is highly recommended.

Club Ōkitsu Kyoto (Map pp54–5; ☎ 411-8585; www.okitsu-kyoto.com; Kamigyō-ku, Shinmachi, Mototsuchimikado-chō 524-1; 10min walk from Imadegawa Station, Karasuma subway line) Offers an upscale introduction to various aspects of Japanese culture including tea ceremony, incense ceremony and traditional Japanese games. This introduction is performed in an exquisite villa near the Kyoto Gosho and participants get a real sense for the elegance and refinement of traditional Japanese culture. This is also highly recommended.

Ai-Zome Dyeing

Located in the Nishijin area, **Aizen-Kōbō** (Map pp54–5; ☎ 441-0355; Nakasuji-dōri-Ōmiya nishi iru; 10am-5.30pm Mon-Fri, to 4pm Sat & Sun; 5min walk from Imadegawa-Ōmiya bus stop, bus 101 from Kyoto Station) dyes indigo-blue *ai-zome* fabrics in a charming *kyō-machiya* (traditional Japanese town house). You can observe and try your hand at tie-dyeing a scarf (¥5565), which takes about an hour. Reservations should be made a few days in advance.

Braiding

Kyoto's most famous braidmaker, **Adachi Kumihimo-kan** (Map pp54–5; ☎ 432-4113; Demizu-dōri-Karasuma nishi iru; classes ¥2000-5000; 9am-noon & 1-4pm Mon-Fri & 1st Sat of each month; 5min walk from Marutamachi Station, Karasuma subway line) has a gallery of fine items on display. Here you can weave your own braid on wooden hand looms. It takes about two hours, and the cost depends on the length of the class and what you make. Delicately woven *kyō-kumihimo* (Kyoto-style braid work) was developed in the Heian period for fastening kimono, but gradually spread to other ornamental applications. Today the braid is again most commonly used as *obi-jime* (the tie for kimono sashes). Reservations in Japanese are necessary.

Doll Making

Over roughly four hours at **Honke Katsura** (Map p50; ☎ 221-6998; Takakura-dōri-Sanjō kudaru; classes ¥10,500; 10am-6pm Feb-Nov, closed Mon; 10min walk from Sanjō Station, Keihan line) you can learn to paint the face on and assemble a handcrafted *kyō-ningyō* doll. Advance reservations in Japanese are necessary.

Handwoven Textiles

In Nishijin, **Orinasu-kan** (Map p74; ☎ 431-0020; Kamigyō-ku, Daikoku-chō 693; incl museum admission ¥5000; 10am-4pm; 10min walk from Horikawa-Imadegawa bus stop, bus 9 from Kyoto Station) offers traditional weaving workshops. The cost is for a three-hour course and you can take home your handmade fabric. Reservations in Japanese are required one week in advance.

Japanese Language

Kyoto is a great place to study Japanese. **Kawara Juku** (Map p50; ☎ 231-1608; web.kyoto-inet.or.jp/people/wat-sltk/index.html; Nakagyō-ku, Takakura-dōri, Oike sagaru, Kikkōya-chō 609; office 10am-6pm; 10min walk from Karasuma-Oike Station, Karasuma subway line) is a friendly little school that offers three-month part-time courses for ¥85,000. Courses start in April, September and January. It also offers a summer intensive course for the same price. Joining a class here is a great way to meet people when you're new in town.

Metalwork

Kyō-zōgan is a damascene technique of laying fine metals onto figures engraved on brass and can be tried at **Amita-honten** (Map pp68–9; ☎ 761-7000; Okazaki Heian-jingū Kita; 9am, 10am & 2pm Mar-Nov, closes 5.30pm Dec-Feb; 3min walk from Kumanojinja-mae bus stop, bus 206 from Kyoto Station), just beside the Kyoto Handicraft Center on Marutamachi-dōri. The cost of making a small pendant is ¥3500 and it takes about an hour (it will be sent to you one week later).

Paper Fans

You can learn to design your own *kyō-sensu* paper fan in about 90 minutes at **Kyōsen-dō** (Map p46; ☎ 371-4151; www.kyosendo.co.jp/english/index.html; Higashinotōin-dōri-Shōmen agaru, Tsutsugane-chō 46; classes ¥2200; 9am, 10.30am, 1pm & 3pm Mon-Sat, 10am, 1pm & 3pm Sun; 10min walk from Kyoto Station). Reservations in Japanese are necessary a few days in advance. Your fan will be sent to a Japanese address a month later (no overseas deliveries).

Paper Making

Rakushi-kan (Map p50; ☎ 251-0078; rakushikan@kami-kyo.to; Takoyakushi-dōri-Muromachi nishi iru; classes ¥1000-1300; 10am-7pm Tue-Sun; 5min walk from Karasuma-Oike Station, Karasuma subway line) offers paper-making workshops on Thursdays, Fridays and Saturdays, with sessions at 1pm, 2pm, 3pm and 4pm. The one-hour course costs from ¥1000 for making sheets of *washi*, business cards or postcards. Reservations in Japanese should be made a week in advance and courses are held for groups of five or more.

Tea Ceremony

At **Urasenke Chadō Research Center** (Map p74; ☎ 431-6474; Horikawa-dōri-Teranouchi; admission ¥500; 9.30am-4pm Tue-Sun; 5min walk from Horikawa Teranouchi bus stop, bus 9 from Kyoto Station), it's possible to watch a 20-minute tea-making procedure called *temae* during the Urasenke Foundation's quarterly art exhibitions. You can sample a bowl of *matcha* (powdered green tea) and a sweet (included in the cost of visiting the centre's gallery).

Vegetable-Dyeing

In Ōhara, **Ōhara Kōbō** (Map p84; ☎ 744-3138; Ōhara Kusao-chō; 10am-5pm Mon-Sun; 5min walk from Ōhara bus stop, Kyoto bus 17 or 18 from Kyoto Station) offers a chance to dye fabrics using *kusaki-zome*, vivid plant and vegetable dyes. The time and cost depend on the item: choose from a handkerchief (¥500), scarf (¥3000) or plain woollen yarn (enough to knit one sweater; ¥8000); if you bring your own wool to dye, the cost for the latter is ¥5000. The process takes from two to four hours; advance reservations in Japanese are required.

Yūzen Dyeing

At the **Kodai Yūzen-en Gallery** (Map pp54–5; ☎ 823-0500; Takatsuji-dōri-Inokuma; incl museum admission ¥500; 9am-5pm; 5min walk from Horikawa-Matsubara bus stop, bus 9 from Kyoto Station) there are facilities to try Yūzen stencil dyeing, which takes around 40 minutes. You can choose from various items to dye, such as a handkerchief (¥1050) or tie (¥4200).

Offering similar activities is **Yūzen Cultural Hall** (Yūzen Bunka Kaikan; Map pp54–5; ☎ 311-0025; Nishikyogoku-Mameda; incl museum admission ¥400; 9am-5pm Mon-Sat; 6min walk from Nishikyōgoku Station, Hankyū line). In a 20-minute session you can stencil-dye a hankie (¥450 to ¥800) or try hand painting (¥2100). The workshop closes for one hour at lunch (noon to 1pm) and you must arrive before 4pm.

CULTURAL CENTRES

Kyoto is host to German, French and Italian cultural centres. All of these have libraries, sponsor art exhibitions, organise lectures and seminars relating to their respective country, and participate in cross-cultural exchange programmes.

Centres in Kyoto include the following:

Goethe Institute Kyoto (Map pp68–9; ☎ 761-2188; Kawabata-dōri, Imadegawa kudaru; 9am-5pm Mon-Fri, closed Sat & Sun & public holidays; 5min walk from Imadegawa Station, Keihan line)

Institut Franco-Japonais du Kansai (Map pp68–9; ☎ 761-2105; Higashiōji-dōri, Imadegawa kudaru; 9.30am-7pm Tue-Fri, 9.30am-6.30pm Mon & Sat, closed Sun; 10min walk from Imadegawa Station, Keihan line)

Instituto Italiano di Cultura di Kansai (Map pp68–9; ☎ 761-4356; Higashiōji-dōri, Imadegawa kudaru; 11am-7pm Mon-Fri, 11am-6pm Sat, closed Sun & public holidays; 10min walk from Imadegawa Station, Keihan line)

CUSTOMS REGULATIONS

Customs allowances include the usual tobacco products, plus three 760mL bottles of alcohol, 57g of perfume, and gifts and souvenirs up to a value of ¥200,000 or its equivalent. The alcohol and tobacco allowances are available only for those who are aged 20 or older. The penalties for importing drugs are severe. Pornography (magazines, videos etc) in which pubic hair or genitalia are visible is illegal in Japan and will be confiscated by customs officers.

There are no limits on the import of foreign or Japanese currency. The export of foreign currency is also unlimited, but a ¥5 million limit exists for Japanese currency.

DISCOUNT CARDS

An international youth hostel card is useful if you plan to stay in hostels. Japan is also one of the few places left in Asia where a student card can be useful. Officially, you should be carrying an ISIC (International Student Identity Card) to qualify for a discount (usually for entry to places of interest), but in practice you will often find that any youth or student card will do the trick. There are a variety of discounts available in Japan for seniors over the age of 65. In almost all cases a passport will be sufficient proof of age, so seniors' cards are rarely worth bringing.

ELECTRICITY

The Japanese electric current is 100V AC. It's an odd voltage not found elsewhere in the world, although most North American electrical items, designed to run on 117V, will function reasonably well on this current. While Tokyo and eastern Japan are on 50 Hz, Kyoto and the rest of western Japan are on a cycle of 60 Hz.

Identical to North American plugs, Japanese plugs are of the flat, two-pronged variety. Both transformers and plug adaptors are readily available in Kyoto's Teramachi-dōri electronics district, running south of Shijō-dōri (Map p50), or at Bic Camera (p107).

EMBASSIES & CONSULATES

Tokyo

Most countries have embassies in Tokyo (area code ☎ 03), some of which are listed following:

Australia (☎ 5232-4111; www.dfat.gov.au/missions/countries/jp.html; 2-1-14 Mita, Minato-ku)

Canada (☎ 5412-6200; www.dfait-maeci.gc.ca/ni-ka/tokyo-en.asp; 7-3-38 Akasaka, Minato-ku)

China (☎ 3403-3380; 3-4-33 Moto-Azabu, Minato-ku)

France (☎ 5420-8800; www.ambafrance-jp.org in French; 4-11-44 Minami-Azabu, Minato-ku)

Germany (☎ 5791-7700; www.tokyo.diplo.de/Vertretung/tokyo/ja/Startseite.html; 4-5-10 Minami-Azabu, Minato-ku)

Ireland (☎ 3263-0695; www.embassy-avenue.jp/ireland/index_eng.html; 2-10-7 Koji-machi, Chiyoda-ku)

Netherlands (☎ 5401-0411; www.oranda.or.jp/index/english/index.html; 3-6-3 Shiba-kōen, Minato-ku)

New Zealand (☎ 3467-2271; www.nzembassy.com home.cfm; 20-40 Kamiyamachō, Shibuya-ku)

South Korea (☎ 3452-7611; 1-2-5 Minami-Azabu, Minato-ku)

UK (☎ 5211-1100; www.uknow.or.jp/be_e; 1 Ichibanchō, Chiyoda-ku)

USA (☎ 3224-5000; http://tokyo.usembassy.gov/; 1-10-5 Akasaka, Minato-ku)

Osaka

Several countries also have consulates in Osaka (area code ☎ 06):

Australia (☎ 6941-9271; 2-1-61 Shiromi, Chūō-ku)

Canada (☎ 6212-4910; 12F, Dai-san Shoho Bldg, 2-2-3 Nishi-Shinsaibashi, Chūō-ku)

China (☎ 6445-9481; 3-9-2 Utsubo Honmachi, Nishi-ku, Osaka)

France (☎ 4790-1500; 1-2-27 Shiromi, Chūō-ku, Osaka)

Germany (Map p168; ☎ 6440-5070; 35F, Umeda Sky Bldg, Tower East, 1-1-88 Ōyodo-naka, Kita-ku)

Netherlands (☎ 6944-7272; 33F, Tw 21 Mid-Tower, 2-1-61 Shiromi, Chūō-ku)

New Zealand (☎ 6942-9016; 28F, Tw 21 Mid-Tower, 2-1-61 Shiromi, Chūō-ku)

UK (☎ 6120-5600; 19F, Seiko Osaka Bldg, 3-5-1 Bakuro-machi, Chūō-ku)

USA (Map p168; ☎ 6315-5900; 2-11-5 Nishi-Tenma, Kita-ku)

EMERGENCY

Although most emergency operators in Kyoto don't speak English, they will refer you to someone who does. Be sure to have your address handy when calling for assistance.

Ambulance (☎ 119)

Fire (☎ 119)

Police (☎ 110)

Kōban (police boxes) are small police stations typically found at city intersections. Most can be recognised by the small, round red lamp outside. They are a logical place to head in an emergency, but remember that the police may not always speak English.

GAY & LESBIAN TRAVELLERS

With the possible exception of Thailand, Japan is Asia's most enlightened nation with regard to the sexual preferences of foreigners. Some travellers have reported problems when checking into love hotels with a partner of the same sex, and it does pay to be discreet in rural areas. Apart from this, however, same-sex couples are unlikely to encounter too many problems.

While there is a sizable gay community in Kyoto, and a number of establishments where gay men do congregate, they will take a fair amount of digging to discover. There's a more active scene in Osaka, and many of Kyoto's gay residents make the trip there. Lesbian women are poorly served in Kyoto and Osaka and it's difficult to find specifically lesbian-friendly venues.

Utopia (www.utopia-asia.com) is the site most commonly frequented by English-speaking gay and lesbian people.

HEALTH

No immunisations are required for Japan. Despite the very low risk factor, however, you may want to consider vaccinations against Hepatitis A and B. The former is transmitted by contaminated food and drinking water and the latter is spread through contact with infected blood, blood products or body fluids. It is also wise to keep up to date with your tetanus, diphtheria and polio shots (boosters are recommended every 10 years). Tap water is safe to drink, and food is almost uniformly prepared with high standards of hygiene. It is advisable to take out some form of health/travel insurance.

HOLIDAYS

The following public holidays are observed in Kyoto:

Ganjitsu (New Year's Day) 1 January

Seijin-no-hi (Coming-of-Age Day) Second Monday in January

Kenkoku Kinem-bi (National Foundation Day) 11 February

Shumbun-no-hi (Spring Equinox) 20 or 21 March

Showa-no-hi (Shōwa Emperor's Day) 29 April

Kempō Kinem-bi (Constitution Day) 3 May

Midori-no-hi (Green Day) 4 May

Kodomo-no-hi (Children's Day) 5 May

Umi-no-hi (Marine Day) Third Monday in July

Keirō-no-hi (Respect-for-the-Aged Day) Third Monday in September

Shūbun-no-hi (Autumn Equinox) 23 or 24 September

Taiiku-no-hi (Health-Sports Day) Second Monday in October

Bunka-no-hi (Culture Day) 3 November

Kinrō Kansha-no-hi (Labour Thanksgiving Day) 23 November

Tennō Tanjōbi (Emperor's Birthday) 23 December

INTERNET ACCESS

If you plan to bring your laptop with you to Kyoto, first make sure that it is compatible with Japanese current (100V AC; 50Hz in eastern Japan and 60Hz in western Japan, including Kyoto). Most laptops will be fine. Second, check to see if your plug will fit Japanese wall sockets (Japanese plugs have two flat pins, identical to most ungrounded North American plugs). Both transformers and plug adaptors are readily available in the Teramachi-dōri electronics district (Map p50) or at Bic Camera (p107).

Modems and phone jacks are similar to those used in the USA (RJ11 phone jacks). Conveniently, many of the grey IDD pay phones in Japan have a standard phone jack and an infrared port so that you can log on to the internet just about anywhere in the country.

If you're planning on staying in Kyoto or Japan for more than a couple of weeks, ISP options popular with foreigners are Yahoo BB (https://ybb.softbank.jp/) and NTT/Flets (http://flets.com/english/opt/index.html).

Kyoto has no shortage of internet cafés, though rates are much higher than in other countries in the region. If necessary, the TIC (p199) can recommend places to log on in addition to the following:

Kyoto International Community House (KICH; Map pp68–9; ☎ 752-3512; Sakyō-ku, Awataguchi, Torii-chō 2-1; per 30min ¥200; 5min walk from Keage Station, Tōzai subway line) The machines here have Japanese keyboards and you are limited in the sites you can visit, but it's a fairly cheap place to log on.

Kyoto Prefectural International Center (Map p46; ☎ 342-5000; 9th fl, Kyoto Station Bldg; per 15min ¥250; 10am-6pm; Kyoto Station) In addition to using the machines provided, you can also log on with your own laptop here. It's closed on the second and fourth Tuesday of each month.

Kinko's (Map p50; ☎ 213-6802; Nakagyō-ku, Tearaimizu-chō 651-1, Takoyakushi kudaru, Karasuma dōri; per 10min ¥210; 24hr; 5min walk from Karasuma Station, Hankyū line) This copy shop has several terminals where you can log on. It's expensive but conveniently located.

Tops Café (Map p46; ☎ 681-9270; www.topsnet.co.jp, in Japanese; Kyoto-eki, Hachijō-guchi; per 15min ¥120, plus registration fee ¥200; 10am-6pm; Kyoto Station) This is an all-night manga/internet café where you can actually spend the night in the booths if you want. It's just outside the south (Hachijō) exit of Kyoto Station.

MAPS

Available free at the TIC and all JNTO offices (see p199), the *Tourist Map of Kyoto-Nara* fulfils most mapping needs and includes a simplified map of the subway and bus systems. The same offices stock the *Tourist Map of Kyoto*, another decent English-language map of Kyoto, and *Kyoto Walks* details five good walks in and around Kyoto. Also available is the *Bus Navi: Kyoto City Bus Sightseeing Map*, which has detailed information on bus routes in the city and some of the major stops written in both English and Japanese.

There are many other useful maps for sale at local English-language bookshops, some of which are practical for excursions outside Kyoto. Shōbunsha's *Tourist Map of Kyoto, Nara, Osaka and Kōbe* is the best privately produced map of these cities.

MEDICAL SERVICES

Medical care in Japan is relatively expensive. Although the cost of a basic consultation is cheap (around ¥3000), the costs really start to add up with any further examinations, especially with the tendency of Japan's doctors to overprescribe medication. If you do need to visit a hospital in Kyoto, it is not usually necessary to have cash in hand; most hospitals will admit people on a pay-later basis. Credit cards are rarely accepted.

Kyoto University Hospital (Map pp68–9; ☎ 751-3111; 54 Shōgoinkawara-chō, Sakyō-ku; 9am-noon; 5min walk from Konoe-dōri bus stop, bus 206 from Kyoto Station) is the best hospital in Kyoto. There is an information counter near the entrance that can point you in the right direction.

MONEY

The currency in Japan is the yen (¥), and banknotes and coins are easily identifiable. There are ¥1, ¥5, ¥10, ¥50, ¥100 and ¥500 coins, and ¥1000, ¥2000, ¥5000 and ¥10,000 banknotes. The ¥1 coin is of lightweight aluminium, and the ¥5 (said to bring good luck) and ¥50 coins have a hole in the middle. Keep an eye out for the relatively rare ¥2000 notes.

The Japanese postal system has recently linked its ATMs to the international Cirrus and Plus networks, so money is no longer the issue it once was for travellers to Japan. Of course, it always makes sense to carry some foreign cash and some credit cards just to be on the safe side. For those without credit cards, it would be a good idea to bring some travellers cheques as a back up.

For details on costs in Kyoto, see p18, and for current exchange rates, see the inside front cover.

ATMs

Automatic teller machines (ATMs) are almost as common as vending machines in Kyoto. Unfortunately, even if they display Visa and MasterCard logos, most accept only Japan-issued versions of these cards.

Fortunately, Japanese postal ATMs accept cards on the following international networks: VISA, Plus, MasterCard, Maestro, Cirrus American Express and Diners Club cards.

Check the sticker(s) on the back of your card to see what network(s) your card belongs to. Note that the machines work with bank/cash cards, not credit cards. That is, you can make cash withdrawals from cash accounts; you cannot use them to charge money or make cash advances on credit.

You'll find postal ATMs in almost all post offices, and you'll find post offices in even the smallest Japanese village. Most postal ATMs are open 9am to 5pm on weekdays, 9am to noon on Saturdays, and are closed on Sundays and holidays.

Some postal ATMs in very large central post offices are open longer hours. If you need cash outside these hours, try the **Kyoto central post office** (Map p46; ATM 12.05am-11.55pm Mon-Sat, 12.05am-8pm Sun), next to Kyoto Station.

Postal ATMs are relatively easy to use. Here's the drill: press 'English Guide', then select 'Withdrawal'; insert your card and press 'Visitor Withdrawal', then input your pin number and hit the button marked 'Kakunin' (確認 in Japanese); next enter the amount, hit 'Yen' and 'Confirm' and you should soon hear the delightful sound of bills being dispensed.

There's an **international ATM** (Map p46; 10am-9pm) on the B1 floor of the Kyoto Tower Hotel, very close to the TIC and Kyoto Station. In the middle of town, you'll find another **international ATM** (Map p50; 7am-midnight) on the basement floor of the Kyoto Royal Hotel.

Citibank (Map p50) has a 24-hour ATM in its lobby that accepts most foreign-issued cards. Note that only holders of Japan-issued Citibank cards can access the ATM after hours.

Changing Money

You can change cash or travellers cheques at any 'Authorised Foreign Exchange Bank' (signs will always be displayed in English) or at some of Kyoto's larger hotels and department stores. Main post offices will also cash travellers cheques. Rates vary little, if at all, between banks (even the exchange counters at the airport offer rates comparable to those offered by banks downtown).

Most major banks are located near the Shijō-Karasuma intersection, two stops north of Kyoto Station on the Karasuma subway line. Of these, **UFJ Bank** (Map p50; ☎ 211 4583) is the most convenient for changing money and buying travellers cheques. There's also a branch of Citibank (above), which has an international ATM in its lobby.

WARNING: JAPAN IS A CASH SOCIETY!

Be warned that cold hard yen (¥) is the way to pay in Japan. While credit cards are becoming more common, cash is still much more widely used, and travellers cheques are rarely accepted. Do not assume that you can pay for things with a credit card; always carry sufficient cash. The only places where you can count on paying with plastic are department stores and large hotels.

For those without credit cards, it would be a good idea to bring some travellers cheques as a back-up. As in most other countries, the US dollar is still the currency of choice in terms of exchanging cash and cashing travellers cheques.

Credit Cards

You should not rely on credit cards when travelling in Japan. While department stores, top-end hotels and *some* fancy restaurants do accept credit cards, most businesses do not. Cash-and-carry is still very much the rule. Among places that accept credit cards, you will find Visa most useful, followed by MasterCard and Amex.

You can get cash advances on credit cards at the two international ATMs mentioned (left), but not at Citibank or at postal ATMs. For larger amounts, Visa cardholders can also get cash advances at the 1st-floor Hankyū Department Store branch of **Mitsui Sumitomo Bank** (Map p50; ☎ 223-2821).

Currently there is no representation for international cardholders in Kyoto. For inquiries it is often best to try the offices in Tokyo or call the number in your home country on the back of your card:

Amex (☎ 0120-020-120)

MasterCard (☎ 03-5728-5200)

Visa (☎ 03-5275-7604)

Travellers Cheques

Travellers cheques are fairly commonplace in Japan nowadays, though they can only be cashed at banks, major post offices and some hotels. It is not possible to use foreign-currency travellers cheques in stores and restaurants. In most cases the exchange rate for travellers cheques is slightly better than cash. In order to cash travellers cheques or make cash advances at banks, you will need to show your passport or a valid Alien Registration Card.

NEWSPAPERS & MAGAZINES

There are three main English-language daily newspapers in Japan: *Japan Times; Daily Yomiuri;* and *Asahi Shimbun/International Herald Tribune*. All of these can be found at bookshops, at most major hotels and at some newspaper stands in train and subway stations.

Another excellent source of information on Kyoto, and the rest of the Kansai area, is *Kansai Time Out* (www.japanfile.com), a monthly English-language 'what's on' magazine (¥300), available at bookshops.

The monthly *Kyoto Visitor's Guide* is the best source of information on cultural and tourist events. It's available free at the TIC (p199), the KICH (p200), bookshops and most major hotels.

PHARMACIES

Pharmacies can be found in any neighbourhood in the city and are easily spotted by their colourful outdoor displays of shampoo and other pharmaceutical products.

PHOTOGRAPHY

Photo shops offer a wide range of services for digital photographers, such as high-quality prints from digital files. The typical cost for printing digital photos is ¥35 per print.

For amateur and professional photography supplies including slide film, black-and-white film and all the latest gadgets, your best bet is Bic Camera (p107) near Kyoto Station. It also offers reliable processing services.

Another popular place to have film developed is at the Yellow Camera chain, which has several branches in Kyoto; it's easy to spot by its all-yellow façade. One-hour processing tends to be slightly more expensive than overnight, but it is offered at many local shops. Japanese labs usually print on what's called *sābisu saizu* (service size), which is about two-thirds of the standard size in most countries (four by six inches). Unless you're happy with this size, ask to have your photographs printed on *hagaki* (postcard) sized paper.

POST

Most local post offices are open from Monday to Friday, 9am to 5pm, and some are also open on Saturdays from 9am to 12.30pm. The **Kyoto central post office** (Map p46; ☎ 365-2467; 🕑 9am-7pm Mon-Fri, to 5pm Sat, to 12.30pm Sun & holidays) is on the north side of Kyoto Station. Poste restante mail can be collected here. There's a service counter on the south side of the building open 24 hours per day for airmail, small packages, and special express mail services.

Nakagyō post office (Map p50; ☎ 255-1112) at the Nishinotōin-Sanjō crossing is open until 7pm on weekdays but is closed at weekends. There is a 24-hour service window on the west side of the building.

The airmail rate for postcards is ¥70 to any overseas destination; aerograms cost ¥90. Letters weighing less than 25g are ¥90 to other countries within Asia, ¥110 to North America, Europe or Oceania (including Australia and New Zealand) and ¥130 to Africa and South America. One peculiarity of the Japanese postal system is that you will be charged extra if your writing runs over onto the address side (the right side) of a postcard.

All post offices provide a reliable international Express Mail Service (EMS), which is as good or better than private express shipping services.

RADIO

Kyoto's best station with bilingual broadcasts and decent music is Alpha station (89.4 FM), but there are several other Kansai stations worth checking out:

76.5 FM Cocolo Multilingual.

80.2 FM 802 Japanese and English.

85.1 FM Osaka Japanese and English.

89.9 Kiss FM Kōbe Japanese and English.

TAXES & REFUNDS

There is a 5% consumption tax on retail purchases in Japan. Visitors on a short-stay visa can, however, avoid this tax on purchases made at major department stores and duty-free stores such as the Kyoto Handicraft Center (p113). For a refund on purchases, check first that the department store has a service desk for tax refunds. When you make a purchase the tax will be included; take the purchase, receipt and your passport to the service desk for an immediate refund.

If you eat at expensive restaurants and stay at first-class accommodation, you will encounter a service charge, which varies from 10% to 15%. A tax of 5% is added to restaurant bills exceeding ¥5000 or for hotel bills exceeding ¥10,000.

TELEPHONE

The area code for greater Kyoto is ☎075; unless otherwise indicated, all numbers in this book fall into this area. Japanese telephone codes consist of an area code plus a local code and number. You do not dial the area code when making a call in that area. When dialling Japan from abroad, the country code is ☎81, followed by the area code (drop the 0) and the number. The following are the area codes for some of Japan's main cities.

City	Area Code
Fukuoka/Hakata	☎092
Hiroshima	☎082
Kōbe	☎078
Matsuyama	☎0899
Nagasaki	☎0958
Nagoya	☎052
Nara	☎0742
Narita	☎0476
Osaka	☎06
Sapporo	☎011
Sendai	☎022
Tokyo	☎03
Yokohama	☎045

Directory Assistance

For local directory assistance dial ☎104 (the call costs ¥100), or for assistance in English call ☎0120-364-463 from 9am to 5pm weekdays. For international directory assistance dial ☎0057.

International Calls

Due to the lack of pay phones from which you can make international phone calls in Japan, the easiest way to call overseas from Kyoto is to buy a prepaid international phonecard. Common prepaid cards include KDDI Superworld Card, NTT Communications World Card and SoftBank Telecom Comica Card. Most convenience stores carry at least one of these types, which can be used with any regular pay phone in Japan.

Overseas calls can be made from grey international ISDN phones. These are usually found in phone booths marked 'International & Domestic Card/Coin Phone'. Unfortunately, these are very rare; try looking in the lobbies of top-end hotels and at airports. Some new green phones found in phone booths also allow you to make international calls. Calls are charged by the unit, each of which is six seconds, so if you don't have much to say you could phone home for just ¥100. Reverse-charge (collect) overseas calls can be made from any pay phone.

You can save money by dialling late at night. Economy rates are available from 7pm to 8am. Note that it is also cheaper to make domestic calls by dialling outside the standard hours.

To place an international call through the operator, dial ☎0051 (KDDI operator); most international operators speak English. To make the call yourself, dial ☎001 010 (KDDI), ☎0041 010 (SoftBank Telecom) or ☎0033 010 (NTT) – there's very little difference in rates – then the international country code, the local code and the number.

Another option is to dial ☎0038 plus your country code for home country direct, which takes you straight through to a local operator in the country dialled. You can then make a reverse-charge call or a credit-card call with a telephone credit card valid in that country.

Local Calls

The Japanese public telephone system is very well developed. There are a great many public phones and they work almost all of the time. Local calls from pay phones cost ¥10 per minute; unused ¥10 coins are returned after the call is completed but no change is given on ¥100 coins.

In general it's much easier to buy a *terefon kādo* (telephone card) when you arrive rather than worry about always having coins on hand. Phone cards are sold in ¥500 and ¥1000 denominations (the latter earns you an extra ¥50 in calls) and can be used in most green or grey pay phones. They are available from vending machines and convenience stores, come in myriad designs and are also a collectable item.

Renting a Phone

Several companies in Japan specialise in short-term mobile-phone rentals, a good option for travellers whose phones either won't work in Japan or would be prohibitively expensive to use here. Two such companies are recommended:

Mobile Phone Japan (☎075-361-8890; www.mobilephonejp.com) This company offers basic mobile-phone rental for as low as ¥2900 per week. Incoming calls, whether international or domestic, are free, and outgoing domestic calls cost ¥2 per second (outgoing international calls vary according to country and time of day). Free delivery anywhere in Japan and a free prepaid return envelope are included.

Rentafone Japan (☎ 090-9621-7318; www.rentafonejapan.com) This company rents mobile phones for ¥3900 per week and offers free delivery of the phone to your accommodation. Call rates are similar to Mobile Phone Japan.

TIME

Kyoto local time is nine hours ahead of GMT/UTC. There is no daylight-savings time. When it's noon in Kyoto, it's 7pm (the day before) in Los Angeles, 10pm (the day before) in Montreal and New York, 3am (the same day) in London, 4am in Frankfurt, Paris and Rome, 11am in Hong Kong, 1pm in Melbourne, and 3pm in Wellington.

TOURIST INFORMATION

The following local tourist offices are good sources for maps and information:

Kyoto Tourist Information Center (TIC; Map p46; ☎ 344-3300; 10am-6pm, closed 2nd & 4th Tue & 29 Dec-3 Jan; Kyoto Station) Located on the 9th floor of the Kyoto Station building, the TIC is set up especially for foreign visitors. It's your best source on English-language information. To get there from the main concourse of the station, take the west escalator to the 2nd floor, enter Isetan Department Store, take an immediate left, look for the elevator on your left and take it to the 9th floor. It's right outside the elevator, inside the Kyoto Prefectural International Center. There is an International Tourism Center of Japan/Welcome Inn reservation counter at the TIC, which can help with accommodation bookings.

Kyoto City Tourist Information Center (Map p46; ☎ 343-6656; 2nd fl, Kyoto Station Bldg; 8.30am-7pm; Kyoto Station) Located at the top of the west escalator, which leaves from the main concourse, this information centre is geared to Japanese visitors. English speakers are usually on hand, however, and can be of great assistance when the TIC is closed.

Kyoto Tourism Federation (Map p46; ☎ 371-2226; 9.30am-6pm, closed 2nd & 4th Tue & 29 Dec-3 Jan; Kyoto Station) This small office distributes information on outlying destinations in Kyoto Prefecture (it has very little on the city itself). Although most of the literature is only in Japanese, it's worth stopping by to pick up a free map of Kyoto-fu if you plan a trip to outlying areas of the prefecture. Kyoto Tourism Federation is around the corner from the TIC (see above).

Kansai International Airport tourist information counter (☎ 0724-56-6025; 9am-9pm) This counter is on the 1st floor of the international arrivals hall. Staff here can provide information on Kyoto, Kansai and Japan.

Japan National Tourist Organization (JNTO) has several offices overseas:

Australia (☎ 02-9251 3024; Level 18, Australia Square Tower, 264 George St, Sydney, NSW 2000)

Canada (☎ 416-366 7140; 165 University Ave, Toronto, ON M5H 3B8)

France (☎ 01 42 96 20 29; 4 rue de Ventadour, 75001 Paris)

Germany (☎ 069-20353; Kaiserstrasse 11, 60311 Frankfurt am Main)

UK (☎ 020-7734 4290; Heathcoat House, 20 Saville Row, London W1S 3PR)

USA Los Angeles (☎ 213-623 1952; 515 South Figueroa St, Suite 1470, Los Angeles, CA 90071); New York (☎ 212-757 5640; One Rockefeller Plaza, Suite 1250, New York, NY 10020)

TRAVEL AGENCIES

Kyoto has several good central travel agencies that can arrange discount air tickets, car rental and accommodation, as well as other services. These agencies include **IACE Travel** (Map p50; ☎ 212-8944; Sanjō-Kawaramachi, 7F Hayakawa Bldg; office 10am-7pm Mon-Fri, to 5pm Sat, phone consult 10am-5pm Sun & holidays; 5min walk from Sanjō Station, Keihan line)

TRAVELLERS WITH DISABILITIES

Although Kyoto has made some attempts at making public facilities more accessible, its narrow streets and the terrain of sights such as temples and shrines make it a challenging city for people with disabilities, especially for those in wheelchairs.

If you are going to travel by train and need assistance, ask one of the station workers as you enter the station. Try asking: '*Karada no fujiyuū no kata no tame no sharyō wa arimasu ka?*' ('Are there any train carriages for disabled travellers?').

There are carriages on most lines that have areas set aside for those in wheelchairs. Those with other physical disabilities can use one of the seats set aside near the train exits; these are called *yūsen-zaseki* and are usually a different colour from the other seats in the carriage, making them easy to spot. You'll also find these seats near the front of buses; usually they're a different colour from the regular seats.

MK Taxi (☎ 721-2237) can accommodate wheelchairs in many of its cars and is an attractive possibility for anyone interested in touring the city by cab.

Facilities for the visually impaired include musical pedestrian lights at many city intersections and raised bumps on railway platforms for guidance.

AD-Brain (the same outfit that publishes the monthly *Kyoto Visitor's Guide*) has produced a basic city map for people with disabilities and senior citizens. It shows wheelchair-access points in town and gives information on public transport access etc. The map is available at the TIC. You might also try contacting the Kyoto City Association for Disabled Persons (☎ 822-0770, in Japanese), which publishes the very detailed *Handy Map* guidebook on local facility accessibility, presently available in Japanese only.

The most useful information for disabled visitors to Japan is provided by the Japanese Red Cross Language Service Volunteers (☎ 3438-1311; http://accessible.jp.org; c/o Volunteers Division, Japanese Red Cross Society, 1-1-3 Shiba Daimon, Minato-ku, Tokyo 105-8521).

USEFUL ORGANISATIONS

An essential stop for those planning a long-term stay in Kyoto is the Kyoto International Community House (KICH; Map pp68–9; ☎ 752-3010; Sakyō-ku, Awataguchi, Torii-chō 2-1; 9am-9pm Tue-Sun; 5min walk from Keage Station, Tōzai subway line). It can also be quite useful for short-term visitors. It's closed Tuesdays following a Monday national holiday.

The KICH has a library with maps, books, newspapers and magazines from around the world, and a notice board displaying messages regarding work, accommodation, rummage sales etc.

Here you can rent typewriters, send and receive faxes, and use the internet (¥200 per 30 minutes). You can also pick up a copy of its excellent *Guide to Kyoto* map and its *Easy Living in Kyoto* book (but note that both of these are intended for residents). You can also chill out in the lobby and watch CNN news.

VISAS

Most visitors who are not planning to engage in any remunerative activities while in Japan are exempt from obtaining visas and will be issued a *tanki-taizai* (short-stay visa) on arrival.

Stays of up to six months are permitted for citizens of Austria, Germany, Ireland, Mexico, Switzerland and the UK. Citizens of these countries will almost always be given a 90-day short-stay visa on arrival, which can usually be extended for another 90 days at immigration bureaus in Japan (see below).

Citizens of the USA, Australia and New Zealand are granted 90-day short-stay visas, while stays of up to three months are permitted for citizens of Argentina, Belgium, Canada, Denmark, Finland, France, Iceland, Israel, Italy, the Netherlands, Norway, Singapore, Spain, Sweden and a number of other countries.

As well as the information we give on visas and regulations in this chapter, you should check with your nearest Japanese embassy or go to the website of the Japanese Ministry of Foreign Affairs (www.mofa.go.jp/).

Alien Registration Card

Anyone – and this includes tourists – who stays for more than 90 days is required to obtain an Alien Registration Card (Gaikokujin Torokushō). This card can be obtained at the municipal office of the city, town or ward in which you're living; moving to another area requires that you re-register within 14 days.

You must carry your Alien Registration Card at all times as the police can stop you and ask to see it. If you don't have the card, you may be taken back to the station and will have to wait there until someone fetches it for you.

Visa Extensions

With the exception of those nationals whose countries have reciprocal visa exemptions and who can stay for six months, 90 days or three months is the limit for most nationalities. To extend a short-stay visa beyond the standard 90 days or three months, apply at the Osaka Immigration Bureau Kyoto Branch (Map pp68–9; ☎ 752-5997; Sakyō-ku, Kawabata Higashi-iru, Higashi Marutamachi 34-12, 4F Dai Ni Chihō Gōdōchōsha Bldg; 9am-noon & 1-4pm Mon-Fri; 5min walk from Marutamachi Station, Keihan line). You must provide two copies of an Application for Extension of Stay (available at the bureau), a letter stating the reasons for the extension and supporting documentation, as well as your passport. There is a processing fee of ¥4000; be prepared to spend well over an hour completing the process.

The Kyoto branch is best reached from Marutamachi Station on the Keihan line. Take exit 4, turn left and continue east past a church to the second traffic light. The bureau is in the five-storey building on your left.

The Osaka Immigration Bureau (☎ 06-6774-3409; 9am-noon & 1-4pm Mon-Fri) offers an English-language visa information line at its Osaka headquarters, though you can usually have most questions about visas answered in English by calling the Kyoto branch.

Working-Holiday Visas

Australians, Britons, Canadians, Germans, New Zealanders and South Koreans between the ages of 18 and 25 (the age limit can be pushed up to 30 in some cases) can apply for a working-holiday visa. This visa allows a six-month stay and two six-month extensions. It is designed to enable young people to travel extensively during their stay; although employment is supposed to be part-time or temporary, in practice many people work full time.

A working-holiday visa is much easier to obtain than a work visa and is popular with Japanese employers. Single applicants must have the equivalent of US$2000 of funds, a married couple must have US$3000, and all applicants must have an onward ticket from Japan. For details, inquire at the nearest Japanese embassy or consulate (see p193).

Working Visas

Unless you are on a cultural visa and have been granted permission to work, or hold a working-holiday visa, you are not permitted to work in Japan without a proper work visa. As long as you have the proper paperwork and an employer who is willing to sponsor you, the application process is straightforward, although it can be time consuming.

Once you find an employer in Japan who is willing to sponsor you, it is necessary to obtain a Certificate of Eligibility from the nearest immigration office. The same office can then issue your work visa, which is valid for either one or three years. The whole procedure usually takes two to three months.

WOMEN TRAVELLERS

Japan is a relatively safe country for women travellers, though perhaps not as safe as some might think. Women travellers are occasionally subjected to some form of verbal harassment or prying questions. Physical attacks are very rare, but have occurred.

The best advice is to avoid being lulled into a false sense of security by Japan's image as one of the world's safest countries and to take the normal precautions you would in your home country. If a neighbourhood or establishment looks unsafe, then treat it that way. As long as you use your common sense, you will most likely find that Japan is a pleasant and rewarding place to travel as a woman.

Several train companies in Japan have recently introduced women-only cars to protect female passengers from *chikan* (men who feel up women and girls on packed trains). These cars are usually available during rush-hour periods on weekdays on busy urban lines. There are signs (usually pink in colour) on the platform indicating where to board these cars, and the cars themselves are usually labelled in both Japanese and English (again, these are often marked in pink).

If you have a problem and find the local police unhelpful, you can call the Japan Helpline (☎ 0570-000-911), an emergency number that operates 24 hours a day, seven days a week.

Finally, an excellent resource available for any woman setting up in Japan is Caroline Pover's book *Being A Broad in Japan*, which can be found in bookstores and can also be ordered from her website at www.being-a-broad.com.

WORK

Kyoto's popularity makes it one of Japan's most difficult cities in which to find work. Despite both this fact and the increasingly strict immigration policies, there is a relatively quick turnaround of many resident foreigners, so it is often just a case of being patient until something comes up. If you are planning to make a go of it in Kyoto, you'll need to have enough money to survive for three months or so (around US$6000).

Many who would prefer to live in Kyoto end up commuting to jobs in Osaka or other neighbouring cities, at least until they find something closer to home. Apart from teaching English, other popular jobs include bar hostessing (mainly for women), working in restaurants and bars, and carpentry.

The best place to look for work is in *Kansai Time Out*, followed by the *Kansai Flea Market*, and the jobs listing at the KICH (opposite); you can also post messages and offer your services as a private tutor at the KICH. The Monday edition of the *Japan Times* also has a small Kansai employment section. Word of mouth is also a great way to find work in Kyoto – you could try dropping by any of the *gaijin*-friendly bars listed in the Entertainment chapter (p140).

LANGUAGE

It's true – anyone can speak another language. Don't worry if you haven't studied languages before or that you studied a language at school for years and can't remember any of it. It doesn't even matter if you failed English grammar. After all, that's never affected your ability to speak English! And this is the key to picking up a language in another country. You just need to start speaking.

Learn a few key phrases before you go. Write them on pieces of paper and stick them on the fridge, by the bed or even on the computer – anywhere that you'll see them often.

You'll find that locals appreciate travellers trying their language, no matter how muddled you may think you sound. So don't just stand there, say something! If you want to learn more Japanese than we've included here, pick up a copy of Lonely Planet's comprehensive but user-friendly *Japanese Phrasebook*.

PRONUNCIATION

Pronounce double consonants with a slight pause between them, so that each is clearly audible. Vowel length affects meaning, so make sure you distinguish your short and long vowels clearly. Certain vowel sounds (like **u** and **i**) aren't pronounced in some words, but are included as part of the official Romanisation system (which employs a literal system to represent Japanese characters). In the following words and phrases these 'silent' letters are shown in square brackets to indicate that they aren't pronounced.

a	short, as the 'u' in 'run'
ā	long, as the 'a' in 'father'
e	short, as in 'red'
ē	long, as the 'ei' in 'rein'
i	short, as in 'bit'
ii	long **i**, as in 'marine'
o	short, as in 'pot'
ō	long, as the 'aw' in 'paw'
u	short, as in 'put'
ū	long, as in 'rude'

SOCIAL

Meeting People

Hello/Hi.
こんにちは。 konnichi wa

Goodbye.
さようなら。 sayōnara

Yes.
はい。 hai

No.
いえ。 iie

Please.
(when offering something)
どうぞ。 dōzo
(when asking a favour or making a request)
お願いします。 onegai shimas[u]

Thank you (very much).
(どうも)ありがとう（ございます)。 (dōmo) arigatō (gozaimas[u])

You're welcome.
どういたしまして。 dō itashimash[i]te

Excuse me.
(to get attention or to get past)
すみません。 sumimasen

Sorry.
ごめんなさい。 gomen nasai

Could you please ...?
…くれませんか?
... kuremasen ka?
  repeat that
  繰り返して
  kurikaeshite
  speak more slowly
  もっとゆっくり話して
  motto yukkuri hanash[i]te
  write it down
  書いて
  kaite

What's your name?
お名前は何ですか?
o-namae wa nan des[u] ka?

My name is ...
私の名前は…です。
watashi no namae wa ... des[u]

Do you speak English?
英語が話せますか?
eigo ga hanasemas[u] ka?
Do you understand?
わかりましたか?
wakarimash[i]ta ka?
Yes, I do understand.
はい、わかりました。
hai, wakarimash[i]ta
No, I don't understand.
いいえ、わかりません。
iie, wakarimasen

Going Out

What's on ...?
…は何がありますか?
... wa nani ga arimas[u] ka?

locally	
近所に	kinjo ni
this weekend	
今週の週末	konshū no shūmatsu
today	
今日	kyō
tonight	
今夜	konya

Where can I find ...?
どこに行けば…がありますか?
doko ni ikeba ... ga arimas[u] ka?

clubs	
クラブ	kurabu
gay venues	
ゲイの場所	gei no basho
Japanese-style pubs	
居酒屋	izakaya
places to eat	
食事ができる所	shokuji ga dekiru tokoro
pubs	
パブ	pabu

Is there a local entertainment guide?
地元のエンターテイメントガイドはありますか?
jimoto no entāteimento gaido wa arimas[u] ka?

PRACTICAL

Question Words

Who?	
だれ?/どなた?	dare?/donata? (polite)
What?/What is this?	
何?/なに?	nan?/nani?
Which?	
どちら?	dochira?
When?	
いつ?	itsu?
Where?	
どこ?	doko?
How?	
どのように?	dono yō ni?
How much does it cost?	
いくらですか?	ikura des[u] ka?

Numbers

0	ゼロ/零	zero/rei
1	一	ichi
2	二	ni
3	三	san
4	四	shi/yon
5	五	go
6	六	roku
7	七	shichi/nana
8	八	hachi
9	九	ku/kyū
10	十	jū
11	十一	juichi
12	十二	jūni
13	十三	jūsan
14	十四	jūshi/jūyon
15	十五	jūgo
16	十六	jūroku
17	十七	jūshichi/jūnana
18	十八	jūhachi
19	十九	jūku/jūkyū
20	二十	nijū
21	二十一	nijūichi
22	二十二	nijūni
30	三十	sanjū
40	四十	yonjū
50	五十	gojū
60	六十	rokujū
70	七十	nanajū
80	八十	hachijū
90	九十	kyūjū
100	百	hyaku
200	二百	nihyaku
1000	千	sen

Days

Monday	月曜日	getsuyōbi
Tuesday	火曜日	kayōbi
Wednesday	水曜日	suiyōbi
Thursday	木曜日	mokuyōbi
Friday	金曜日	kinyōbi
Saturday	土曜日	doyōbi
Sunday	日曜日	nichiyōbi

Banking

I'd like to …
…をお願いします。
… o onegai shimas[u]
cash a cheque
小切手の現金化
kogitte no genkinka
change a travellers cheque
トラベラーズチェックの現金化
toraberāz[u] chekku no genkinka
change money
両替
ryōgae

Where's …?
…はどこですか?
… wa doko des[u] ka?
an ATM
ATM
ētiiemu
a foreign exchange office
外国為替セクション
gaikoku kawase sekushon

Post

Where is the post office?
郵便局はどこですか?
yūbin kyoku wa doko des[u] ka?

I want to send a/an …
…を送りたいのですが。
… o okuritai no des[u] ga

letter	
手紙	tegami
parcel	
小包	kozutsumi
postcard	
はがき	hagaki

I want to buy a/an …
…をください。
… o kudasai

aerogram	
エアログラム	earoguramu
envelope	
封筒	fūtō
stamp	
切手	kitte

Phones & Mobiles

I want to …
…たいのですが。
…tai no des[u] ga
buy a phonecard
テレフォンカードを買い
terefon kādo o kai
call (Singapore)
(シンガポール)に電話し
(shingapōru) ni denwa shi
make a (local) call
(市内)に電話し
(shinai) ni denwa shi
reverse the charges
コレクトコールで電話し
korekuto-kōru de denwa shi

I'd like a …
…をお願いします。
… o onegai shimas[u]
charger for my phone
携帯電話の充電器
keitaidenwa no jūdenki
mobile/cell phone for hire
携帯電話のレンタル
keitaidenwa no rentaru
prepaid mobile/cell phone
プリペイドの携帯電話
puripeido no keitaidenwa
SIM card for your network
SIMカード
shimukādo

Internet

Where's the local internet café?
インターネットカフェはどこですか?
intānetto-kafe wa doko des[u] ka?

I'd like to …
…したいのですが。
… shitai no des[u] ga
check my email
Eメールをチェック
iimēru o chekku
get internet access
インターネットにアクセス
intānetto ni akuses[u]

Transport

When's the … (bus)?
…(バス)は何時ですか?
… (bas[u]) wa nan-ji des[u] ka?

first	
始発の	shihatsu no
last	
最終の	saishū no
next	
次の	tsugi no

What time does it leave?
これは何時に出ますか?
kore wa nan-ji ni demas[u] ka?

What time does it get to ...?
これは…に何時に着きますか?
kore wa ... ni nan-ji ni tsukimas[u] ka?
Is this taxi available?
このタクシーは空車ですか?
kono tak[u]shii wa kūsha des[u] ka?
Please put the meter on.
メーターを入れてください。
mētā o irete kudasai
How much is it to …?
…までいくらですか?
… made ikura des[u] ka?
Please take me to (this address).
(この住所)までお願いします。
(kono jūsho) made onegai shimas[u]

EMERGENCIES

Help!
たすけて!
tas[u]kete!
It's an emergency!
緊急です!
kinkyū des[u]!
Call the police!
警察を呼んで!
keisatsu o yonde!
Call a doctor!
医者を呼んで!
isha o yonde!
Call an ambulance!
救急車を呼んで!
kyūkyūsha o yonde!
Could you please help?
たすけてください?
tas[u]kete kudasai?
Where's the police station?
警察署はどこですか?
keisatsusho wa doko des[u] ka?

HEALTH

Where's the nearest …?
この近くの…はどこですか?
kono chikaku no ... wa doko des[u] ka?
(night) chemist
(24時間営業の)薬局
(nijūyojikan eigyō no) yakkyoku
doctor
医者
isha
hospital
病院
byōin

I need a doctor (who speaks English).
(英語ができる)お医者さんが必要です。
(eigo ga dekiru) o-isha-san ga hitsuyō des[u]

I'm allergic to …
私は…アレルギーです。
watashi wa … arerugii des[u]

antibiotics	
抗生物質	kōsei busshitsu
aspirin	
アスピリン	as[u]pirin
bees	
蜂	hachi
nuts	
ナッツ類	nattsurui
penicillin	
ペニシリン	penishirin

Symptoms

I have …
私は…があります。
watashi wa … ga arimas[u]

diarrhoea	
下痢	geri
a headache	
頭痛	zutsū
nausea	
吐き気	hakike
a pain	
痛み	itami

FOOD & DRINK

For more detailed information on food and dining out, see p115.

breakfast	朝食	chōshoku
lunch	昼食	chūshoku
dinner	夕食	yūshoku
snack	間食	kanshoku
to eat	食べます	tabemas[u]
to drink	飲みます	nomimas[u]

Can you recommend a ...?
どこかいい…を知っていますか?
doko ka ii ... o shitte imas[u] ka?

bar	
バー	bā
café	
カフェ	kafe
restaurant	
レストラン	restoran

Is service included in the bill?
サービス料込みですか?
sābis[u] ryō komi des[u] ka?
A table for two/five people, please.
(二人/五人)お願いします。
(futari/go-nin) onegai shimas[u]

Do you have an English menu?
英語のメニューがありますか?
eigo no menyū ga arimas[u] ka?
Can you recommend any dishes?
おすすめの料理がありますか?
osusume no ryōri ga arimas[u] ka?
Is this self-service?
ここはセルフサービスですか?
koko wa serufu sābis[u] des[u] ka?
Is service included in the bill?
サービス料は込みですか?
sābis[u] ryō wa komi des[u] ka?
Cheers!
乾杯!
kampai!
Bon appetit!
いただきます!
itadakimas[u]!
Delicious!
おいしい!
oishii!
Thank you. (after a meal)
ごちそうさまでした。
gochisō sama deshita

Please bring ...
…をお願いします。
... o onegai shimas[u]

the bill	
お勘定	o-kanjō
chopsticks	
はし	hashi
a fork	
フォーク	fōku
a glass (of water)	
コップ(一杯の水)	koppu (ippai no mizu)
a knife	
ナイフ	naifu
a spoon	
スプーン	supūn

I can't eat meat.
肉は食べられません。
niku wa taberaremasen
I can't eat chicken.
鶏肉は食べられません。
toriniku wa taberaremasen
I can't eat pork.
豚肉は食べられません。
butaniku wa taberaremasen
I can't eat seafood.
シーフードは食べられません。
shiifūdo wa taberaremasen
I'm a vegetarian.
私はベジタリアンです。
watashi wa bejitarian des[u]

I'm allergic to (peanuts).
私は(ピーナッツ)アレルギーです。
watashi wa (piinattsu) arerugii des[u]

Food Glossary

RICE DISHES

katsu-don かつ丼
rice topped with a fried pork cutlet
niku-don 牛丼
rice topped with thin slices of cooked beef
oyako-don 親子丼
rice topped with egg and chicken
ten-don 天丼
rice topped with tempura shrimp and vegetables

IZAKAYA FARE

agedashi-dōfu 揚げだし豆腐
deep-fried tofu in a dashi broth
jaga-batā ジャガバター
baked potatoes with butter
niku-jaga 肉ジャガ
beef and potato stew
shio-yaki-zakana 塩焼魚
a whole fish grilled with salt
poteto furai ポテトフライ
French fries
chiizu-age チーズ揚げ
deep-fried cheese
hiya-yakko 冷奴
a cold block of tofu with soy sauce and spring onions
tsuna sarada ツナサラダ
tuna salad over cabbage

KAISEKI

bentō 弁当
boxed lunch
ume 梅
regular course
take 竹
special course
matsu 松
extra-special course

YAKITORI

yakitori 焼き鳥
plain, grilled white meat
hasami/negima はさみ/ねぎま
pieces of white meat alternating with leek
sasami ささみ
skinless chicken-breast pieces
kawa 皮
chicken skin
tsukune つくね
chicken meat balls
gyū-niku 牛肉
pieces of beef

rebā レバー
chicken livers
tebasaki 手羽先
chicken wings
shiitake しいたけ
Japanese mushrooms
piiman ピーマン
small green peppers
tama-negi 玉ねぎ
round white onions
yaki-onigiri 焼きおにぎり
a triangle of rice grilled with *yakitori* sauce

SUSHI & SASHIMI

ama-ebi 甘海老
sweet shrimp
awabi あわび
abalone
ebi 海老
prawn or shrimp
hamachi はまち
yellowtail
ika いか
squid
ikura イクラ
salmon roe
kai-bashira 貝柱
scallop
kani かに
crab
katsuo かつお
bonito
maguro まぐろ
tuna
sashimi mori-awase 刺身盛り合わせ
a selection of sliced sashimi
tai 鯛
sea bream
tamago たまご
sweetened egg
toro とろ
the choicest cut of fatty tuna belly
unagi うなぎ
eel with a sweet sauce
uni うに
sea urchin roe

TEMPURA

tempura mori-awase 天ぷら盛り合わせ
a selection of tempura
shōjin age 精進揚げ
vegetarian tempura
kaki age かき揚げ
tempura with shredded vegetables or fish

RĀMEN

rāmen ラーメン
soup and noodles with a sprinkling of meat and vegetables
chāshū-men チャーシュー麺
rāmen topped with slices of roasted pork
wantan-men ワンタン麺
rāmen with meat dumplings
miso-rāmen みそラーメン
rāmen with miso-flavoured broth
chānpon-men ちゃんぽん麺
Nagasaki-style *rāmen*

SOBA & UDON

soba そば
thin brown buckwheat noodles
udon うどん
thick white wheat noodles
kake soba/udon かけそば/うどん
soba/udon noodles in broth
kata yaki-soba 固焼きそば
crispy fried noodles with meat and vegetables
kitsune soba/udon きつねそば/うどん
soba/udon noodles with fried tofu
tempura soba/udon 天ぷらそば/うどん
soba/udon noodles with tempura shrimp
tsukimi soba/udon 月見そば/うどん
soba/udon noodles with raw egg on top
yaki-soba 焼きそば
fried noodles with meat and vegetables
zaru soba ざるそば
cold noodles with seaweed strips served on a bamboo tray

UNAGI

kabayaki 蒲焼き
skewers of grilled eel without rice
unagi teishoku うなぎ定食
full-set *unagi* meal with rice, grilled eel, eel-liver soup and pickles
una-don うな丼
grilled eel over a bowl of rice
unajū うな重
grilled eel over a flat tray of rice

KUSHIAGE & KUSHIKATSU

ebi 海老
prawn or shrimp
ika いか
squid
renkon れんこん
lotus root
tama-negi 玉ねぎ
round white onions
gyū-niku 牛肉
beef pieces
shiitake しいたけ
ginkgo nuts
imo いも
potato

OKONOMIYAKI

mikkusu ミックスお好み焼き
mixed fillings of seafood, *okonomiyaki* meat and vegetables

modan-yaki モダン焼き
okonomiyaki with *yaki-soba* and a fried egg

ika okonomiyaki いかお好み焼き
squid *okonomiyaki*

gyū okonomiyaki 牛お好み焼き
beef *okonomiyaki*

negi okonomiyaki ネギお好み焼き
thin *okonomiyaki* with spring onions

ALCOHOLIC DRINKS

biiru ビール
beer

nama biiru 生ビール
draught beer

shōchū 焼酎
distilled grain liquor

oyu-wari お湯割り
shōchū with hot water

chūhai チューハイ
shōchū with soda and lemon

whisky ウィスキー
whisky

mizu-wari 水割り
whisky, ice and water

onzarokku オンザロック
whisky with ice

NONALCOHOLIC DRINKS

kōhii コーヒー
regular coffee

burendo kōhii ブレンドコーヒー
blended coffee, fairly strong

american kōhii アメリカンコーヒー
weak coffee

kōcha 紅茶
black, British-style tea

kafe ōre カフェオレ
café au lait, hot or cold

orenji jūsu オレンジジュース
orange juice

mizu 水
water

oyu お湯
hot water

JAPANESE TEA

o-cha お茶
green tea

sencha 煎茶
medium-grade green tea

matcha 抹茶
powdered green tea used in the tea ceremony

bancha 番茶
ordinary-grade green tea, brownish in colour

mugicha 麦茶
roasted barley tea

GLOSSARY

agaru – north of
ageya – traditional banquet hall used for entertainment, which flourished during the Edo period
Amida Nyorai – Buddha of the Western Paradise
ANA – All Nippon Airways

bashi – bridge (also *hashi*)
ben – dialect, as in *Kyoto-ben*
bentō – boxed lunch or dinner, usually containing rice, vegetables and fish or meat
bosatsu – a bodhisattva, or Buddha attendant, who assists others to attain enlightenment
bugaku – dance pieces played by court orchestras in ancient Japan
bunraku – classical puppet theatre that uses life-size puppets to enact dramas similar to those of *kabuki*

chadō – tea ceremony, or 'The Way of Tea'
chanoyu – tea ceremony; see also *chadō*
chō – city area (for large cities) sized between a *ku* and a *chōme*
chōme – city area of a few blocks

dai – great; large
Daibutsu – Great Buddha
daimyō – domain lords under the *shōgun*
dera – temple (also *ji* or *tera*)
dōri – street

fugu – poisonous pufferfish, elevated to *haute cuisine*
futon – cushionlike mattress that is rolled up and stored away during the day

gagaku – music of the imperial court
gaijin – foreigner; the contracted form of gaikokujin (literally, 'outside country person')
gawa – river (also *kawa*)
geiko – Kyoto dialect for *geisha*
geisha – a woman versed in the arts and other cultivated pursuits who entertains guests
gū – shrine

haiden – hall of worship in a shrine
haiku – 17-syllable poem
hakubutsukan – museum
hanami – cherry-blossom viewing
hashi – bridge (also *bashi*); chopsticks
higashi – east
hiragana – phonetic syllabary used to write Japanese words
honden – main building of a shrine
hondō – main building of a temple (also *kondō*)

ikebana – art of flower arrangement
irori – open hearth found in traditional Japanese homes
ITJ – International Telecom Japan
izakaya – Japanese pub/eatery

ji – temple (also *tera* or *dera*)
jingū – shrine (also *jinja* or *gū*)
Jizō – bodhisattva who watches over children
JNTO – Japan National Tourist Organization
jō – castle (also *shiro*)
JR – Japan Railways

kabuki – form of Japanese theatre that draws on popular tales and is characterised by elaborate costumes, stylised acting and the use of male actors for all roles
kaiseki – Buddhist-inspired, Japanese *haute cuisine*; called *cha-kaiseki* when served as part of a tea ceremony
kaisoku – rapid train
kaiten-zushi – automatic, conveyor-belt sushi
kamikaze – literally, 'wind of the gods'; originally the typhoon that sank Kublai Khan's 13th-century invasion fleet and the name adopted by Japanese suicide bombers in the waning days of WWII
kampai – cheers, as in a drinking toast
kanji – literally, 'Chinese writing'; Chinese ideographic script used for writing Japanese
Kannon – Buddhist goddess of mercy
karaoke – a now famous export where revellers sing along to recorded music, minus the vocals
karesansui – dry-landscaped rock garden
kawa – river
kayabuki-yane – traditional Japanese thatched-roof farmhouse
KDD – Kokusai Denshin Denwa
ken – prefecture, eg Shiga-ken
kimono – traditional outer garment that is similar to a robe
kita – north
KIX – Kansai International Airport
Kiyomizu-yaki – a distinctive type of local pottery
ko – lake
kōban – local police box
kōen – park
koma-inu – dog-like guardian stone statues found in pairs at the entrance to *Shintō* shrines
kondō – main building of a temple
koto – 13-stringed zitherlike instrument
ku – ward
kudaru – south of (also *sagaru*)
kura – traditional Japanese warehouse
kyōgen – drama performed as comic relief between *nō* plays, or as separate events
kyō-machiya – see *machiya*
kyō-ningyō – Kyoto dolls
kyō-obanzai – see *obanzai*
kyō-ryōri – Kyoto cuisine
Kyoto-ben – distinctive Japanese dialect spoken in Kyoto

LDP – Liberal Democratic Party
live house – a small concert hall where live music is performed

machi – city area (for large cities) sized between a *ku* and a *chōme*
machiya – traditional wooden town house, called *kyō-machiya* in Kyoto
maiko – apprentice geisha
maki-e – decorative lacquer technique using silver and gold powders
mama-san – older women who run drinking, dining and entertainment venues
matcha – powdered green tea served in tea ceremonies
matsuri – festival
mikoshi – portable shrine carried during festivals
minami – south
minshuku – Japanese equivalent of a B&B
minyō – traditional Japanese folk music
Miroku – Buddha of the Future
mizu shōbai – the world of bars, entertainment and prostitution (also known as *water trade*)
momiji – Japanese maple trees
momiji-gari – viewing of the changing autumn colours of trees
mon – temple gate
mōningu setto – morning set of toast and coffee served at cafés
mura – village

Nihon – Japanese word for Japan; literally, 'source of the sun' (also known as *Nippon*)
ningyō – doll (see also *kyō-ningyō*)
niō – temple guardians
Nippon – see *Nihon*
nishi – west
nō – classical Japanese mask drama performed on a bare stage
noren – door curtain for restaurants, usually labelled with the name of the establishment
NTT – Nippon Telegraph & Telephone Corporation

o- – prefix used as a sign of respect (usually applied to objects)
obanzai – Japanese home-style cooking (the Kyoto variant of this is sometimes called *kyō-obanzai*)
obi – sash or belt worn with *kimono*
Obon – mid-August festivals and ceremonies for deceased ancestors
okiya – old-style *geisha* living quarters
onsen – mineral hot spring with bathing areas and accommodation
o-shibori – hot towels given in restaurants

pachinko – vertical pinball game that is a Japanese craze

Raijin – god of thunder
ryokan – traditional Japanese inn
ryōri – cooking; cuisine (see also *kyō-ryōri*)
ryōtei – traditional-style, high-class restaurant; *kaiseki* is typical fare

sabi – a poetic ideal of finding beauty and pleasure in imperfection; often used in conjunction with *wabi*
sagaru – south of (also *kudaru*)
sakura – cherry trees
salaryman – male employee of a large firm
sama – a suffix even more respectful than *san*
samurai – Japan's traditional warrior class
san – a respectful suffix applied to personal names, similar to Mr, Mrs or Ms but more widely used
sen – line, usually railway line
sencha – medium-grade green tea
sensu – folding paper fan
sentō – public bath
setto – set meal; see also *teishoku*
Shaka Nyorai – Historical Buddha
shakkei – borrowed scenery; technique where features outside a garden are incorporated into its design
shakuhachi – traditional Japanese bamboo flute
shamisen – three-stringed, banjolike instrument
shi – city (to distinguish cities with prefectures of the same name)
shidare-zakura – weeping cherry tree
shinkaisoku – special rapid train
shinkansen – bullet train (literally, 'new trunk line')
Shintō – indigenous Japanese religion
shiro – castle
shodō – Japanese calligraphy; literally, 'the way of writing'
shōgun – military ruler of pre-Meiji Japan
shōjin-ryōri – Buddhist vegetarian cuisine
shokudō – Japanese-style cafeteria/cheap restaurant
shukubō – temple lodging
soba – thin brown buckwheat noodles

tatami – tightly woven floor matting on which shoes should not be worn
teishoku – set meal in a restaurant
tera – temple (also *dera* or *ji*)
TIC – Tourist Information Center (usually refers to Kyoto Tourist Information Center)
tokkyū – limited express train
torii – entrance gate to a *Shintō* shrine
tsukemono – Japanese pickles

udon – thick white wheat noodles
ukiyo-e – woodblock prints; literally, 'pictures of the floating world'

wabi – a Zen-inspired aesthetic of rustic simplicity
wagashi – traditional Japanese sweets that are served with tea
wasabi – spicy Japanese horseradish
washi – Japanese paper
water trade – see *mizu shōbai*

yakuza – Japanese mafia
yudōfu – bean curd cooked in an iron pot; common temple fare

Zen – a form of Buddhism

THIS BOOK

This 4th edition of *Kyoto* was written by Chris Rowthorn. He also wrote the 2nd and 3rd editions. Morgan Pitelka wrote the boxed text 'Japanese Tea Culture' and Alex Kerr wrote 'Machiya Town Houses: Life in the Old City', both of which appear in the Background chapter. Marc Peter Keane wrote the boxed text 'Gardens by Design', which appears in the Neighbourhoods chapter. This guidebook was commissioned in Lonely Planet's Melbourne office and produced by the following:

Commissioning Editors Rebecca Chau, George Dunford

Coordinating Editor Susan Paterson

Coordinating Cartographer Ross Butler

Coordinating Layout Designer Yvonne Bischofberger

Managing Editor Imogen Bannister

Managing Cartographer David Connolly

Managing Layout Designer Celia Wood

Assisting Editors Sarah Bailey, Katie O'Connell, Alison Ridgway

Assisting Layout Designers Jacqui Saunders, Cara Smith

Cover Designer Karina Dea

Project Managers Craig Kilburn, Glenn van der Knijff

Language Content Coordinator Quentin Frayne

Thanks to David Burnett, Laura Crawford, Hunor Csutoros, Ryan Evans, Mark Germanchis, Lauren Hunt, Rebecca Kimoto, Yvonne Kirk, Lisa Knights, Rebecca Lalor, John Mazzocchi, Naomi Parker, Mik Ruff, Adam Stanford, Gerard Walker

Cover photographs Rock garden in Daitoku-ji, Kita-ku, Kyoto, Japan, Corbis (top); Path through the bamboo forest, Arashiyama, Ukyō-ku, Kyoto, Japan, Akira Kaede/Getty Images (bottom)

Internal photographs p5 (#1) Christian Kober/Alamy; p10 (#1) DAJ/Alamy; p11 (#3) Kogeiso/Sebun Photo/Getty Images. All other photographs by Lonely Planet Images: p11 (#1), p12 (#2), p100 Brent Winebrenner; p6 (#2), p8, p12 (#1), p12 (#3), p93, p96 (left) Frank Carter; p3, p2, p4 (#2), p5 (#3), p5 (#2), p4 (#1), p7 (#2), p7 (#1), p9 (#3), p10 (#2), p10 (#3), p11 (#2), p95 (left), p95 (right), p94, p96 (right), p97, p99 (left), p99 (right) p98 Greg Elms; p7 (#3), p6 (#3), p6 (#1), p9 (#2) Phil Weymouth; p4 (#3) Tony Wheeler

THANKS

CHRIS ROWTHORN

Chris would like to thank the following people: Hiroe Kamine, Keiko Hagiwara, Anthony Weersing, Paul Carty, KS and HS, Ian Ropke, Rebecca Chau, David Connolly, Ross Butler, Susan Paterson and Perrin Lindelauf. Chris would also like to thank all the readers of Lonely Planet Japan books who sent in letters and emails with information about Japan/Kyoto – your input really helps and I've tried

THE LONELY PLANET STORY

Fresh from an epic journey across Europe, Asia and Australia in 1972, Tony and Maureen Wheeler sat at their kitchen table stapling together notes. The first Lonely Planet guidebook, *Across Asia on the Cheap*, was born.

Travellers snapped up the guides. Inspired by their success, the Wheelers began publishing books to Southeast Asia, India and beyond. Demand was prodigious, and the Wheelers expanded the business rapidly to keep up. Over the years, Lonely Planet extended its coverage to every country and into the virtual world via lonelyplanet.com and the Thorn Tree message board.

As Lonely Planet became a globally loved brand, Tony and Maureen received several offers for the company. But it wasn't until 2007 that they found a partner whom they trusted to remain true to the company's principles of travelling widely, treading lightly and giving sustainably. In October of that year, BBC Worldwide acquired a 75% share in the company, pledging to uphold Lonely Planet's commitment to independent travel, trustworthy advice and editorial independence.

Today, Lonely Planet has offices in Melbourne, London and Oakland, with over 500 staff members and 300 authors. Tony and Maureen are still actively involved with Lonely Planet. They're travelling more often than ever, and they're devoting their spare time to charitable projects. And the company is still driven by the philosophy of *Across Asia on the Cheap*: 'All you've got to do is decide to go and the hardest part is over. So go!'

to use as much of it as possible. Finally, I would like to thank the people of Kyoto!

OUR READERS

Many thanks to the travellers who used the last edition and wrote to us with helpful hints, useful advice and interesting anecdotes:

Mark Adler, Mike Barker, David Barrier, Alex Bates, Valentino Boccato, Jan Brown, Lynette Byrnes, Frank Carter, Henry Coggill, Erin Corry, Daniel Dourneau, Karen Hastings, Derek Ho, Juerg Jenny, Nobutaka Kanaya, Marcus Karia, Deborah Lewis, D Mcnulty, Ming Ming, Jeroen Neleman, Michael O'Brien, Matthew O'Leary, Sarah Park, Dominic Powell, Ed Schlenk, Tobias Schoep, Roger Sinsheimer, Hajime Tanaka, Alaina Taylor, Stephen Taylor, Eleonore van der Horst, Kevin Walsh

SEND US YOUR FEEDBACK

We love to hear from travellers – your comments keep us on our toes and help make our books better. Our well-travelled team reads every word on what you loved or loathed about this book. Although we cannot reply individually to postal submissions, we always guarantee that your feedback goes straight to the appropriate authors, in time for the next edition. Each person who sends us information is thanked in the next edition – and the most useful submissions are rewarded with a free book.

To send us your updates – and find out about Lonely Planet events, newsletters and travel news – visit our award-winning website: www.lonelyplanet.com/contact.

Note: We may edit, reproduce and incorporate your comments in Lonely Planet products such as guidebooks, websites and digital products, so let us know if you don't want your comments reproduced or your name acknowledged. For a copy of our privacy policy visit www.lonelyplanet.com/privacy.

INDEX

See also separate subindexes for:

Eating	p216
Entertainment	p217
Shopping	p217
Sights	p217
Sleeping	p218
Top Picks	p219

000 map pages
000 photographs

000 map pages
000 photographs

EATING

CAFÉS

FOOD COURTS

INTERNATIONAL

IZAKAYA

JAPANESE

KAISEKI

NOODLES

GREENDEX

GOING GREEN GREENDEX

With one of the world's best public transport systems, a relatively enlightened recycling programme and a population that has always made do without clothes dryers, large cars and central heating, Kyoto is a relatively green city. You can do your part by patronising some of the earth-friendly businesses listed here. For more hints on how to minimise your environmental impact, see Sustainable Kyoto (p18) and the Climate Change & Travel boxed text (p182).

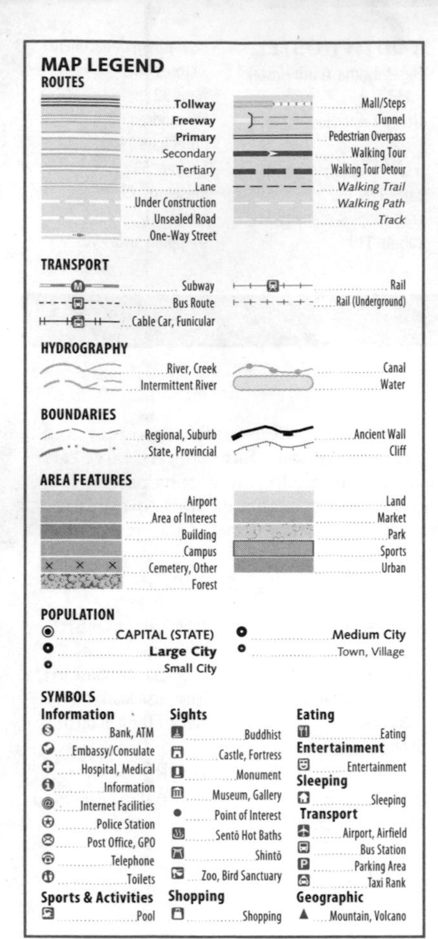

Published by Lonely Planet Publications Pty Ltd
ABN 36 005 607 983

Australia Head Office, Locked Bag 1, Footscray, Victoria 3011, ☎03 8379 8000, fax 03 8379 8111, talk2us@lonelyplanet.com.au

USA 150 Linden St, Oakland, CA 94607, ☎510 250 6400, toll free 800 275 8555, fax 510 893 8572, info@lonelyplanet.com

UK 2nd fl, 186 City Rd, London, EC1V 2NT, ☎020 7106 2100, fax 020 7106 2101, go@lonelyplanet.co.uk

Printed through Colorcraft Ltd, Hong Kong.
Printed in China.

710-94
Nara period - Buddhist inc power [Nagaoka]
784- Emperor Kammu moves capitol Nagaoka